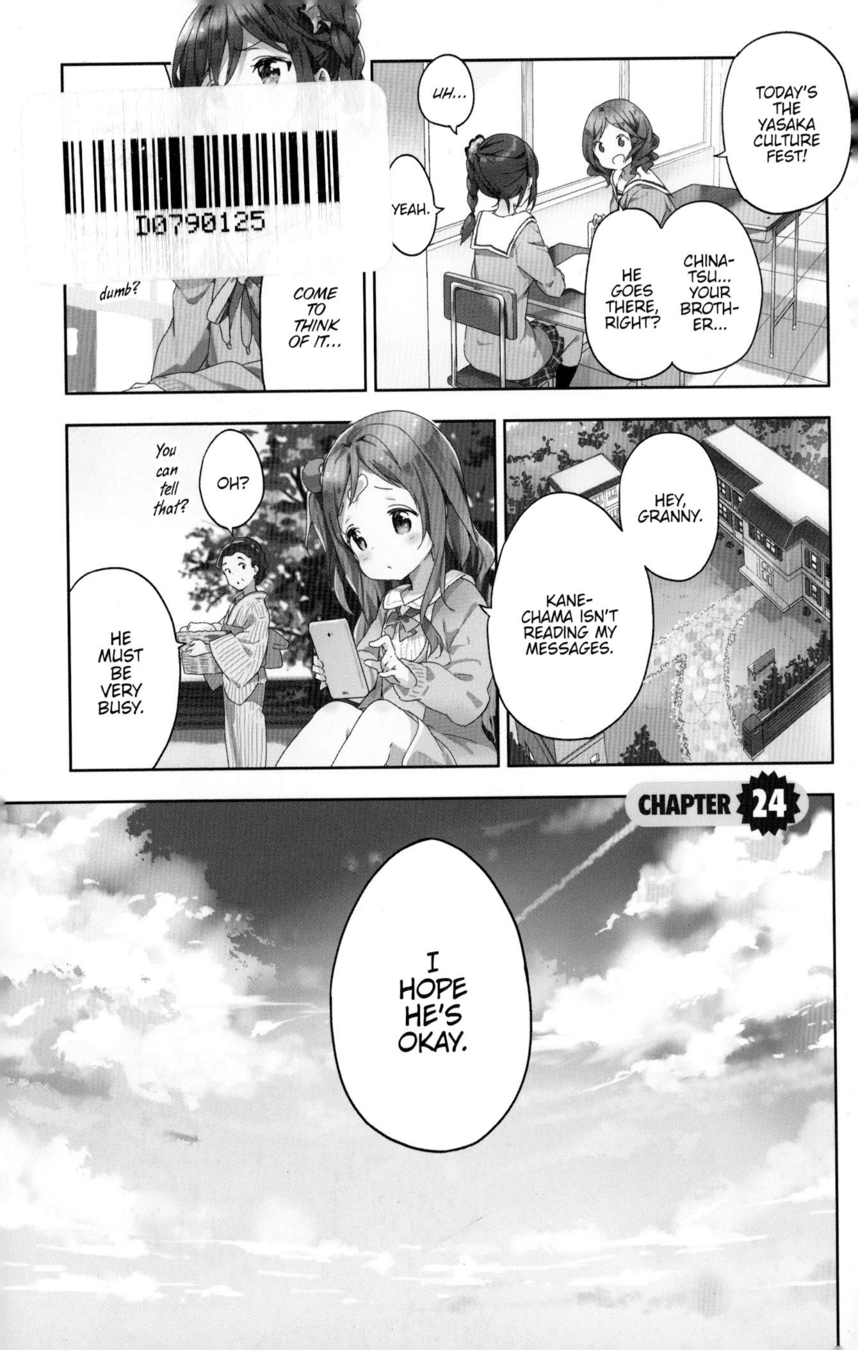
TODAY'S THE YASAKA CULTURE FEST!
UH...
YEAH.
CHINA-TSU... YOUR BROTH-ER...
HE GOES THERE, RIGHT?
COME TO THINK OF IT...
dumb?
HEY, GRANNY.
KANE-CHAMA ISN'T READING MY MESSAGES.
OH?
You can tell that?
HE MUST BE VERY BUSY.
CHAPTER 24
I HOPE HE'S OKAY.

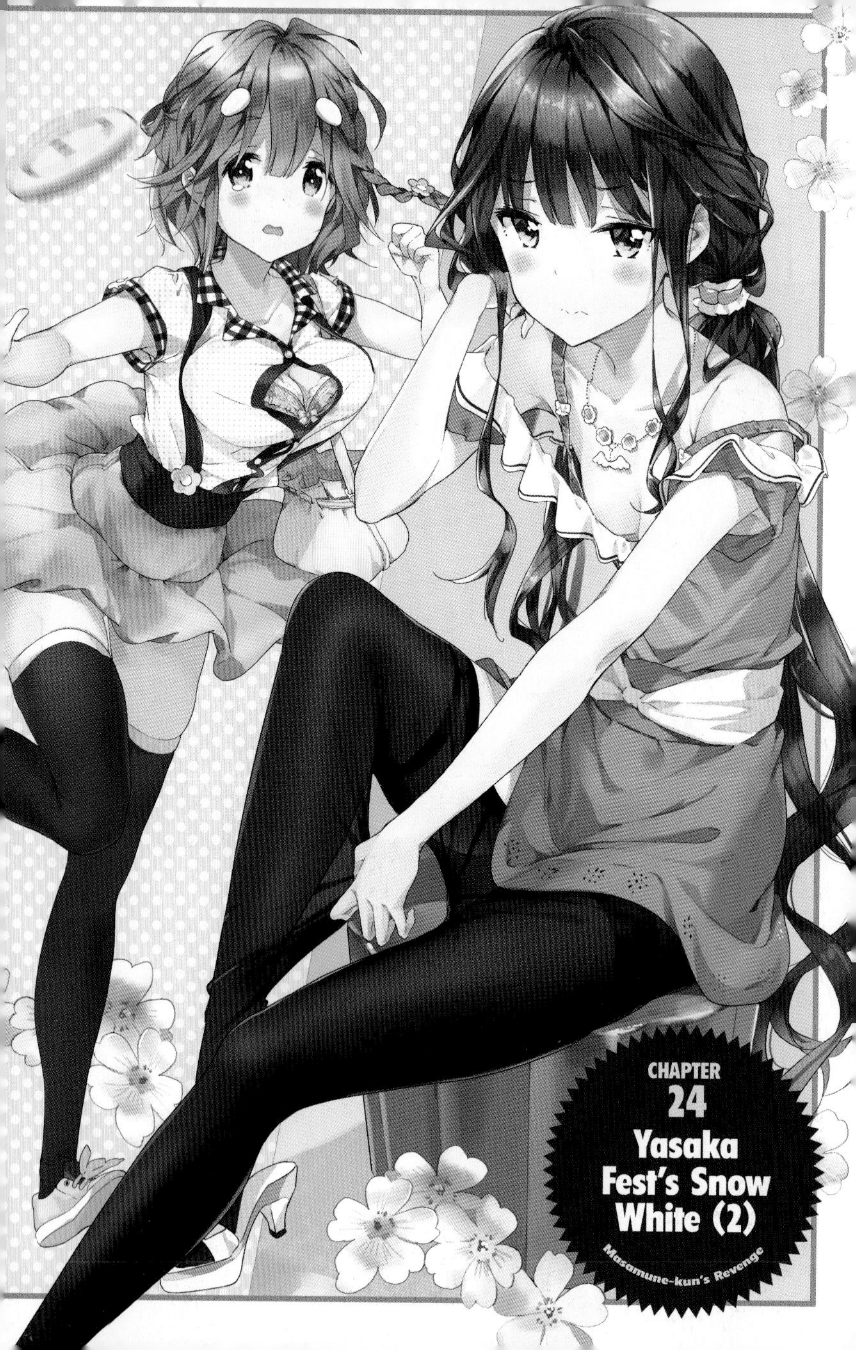
CHAPTER
24
Yasaka Fest's Snow White (2)
Masamune-kun's Revenge

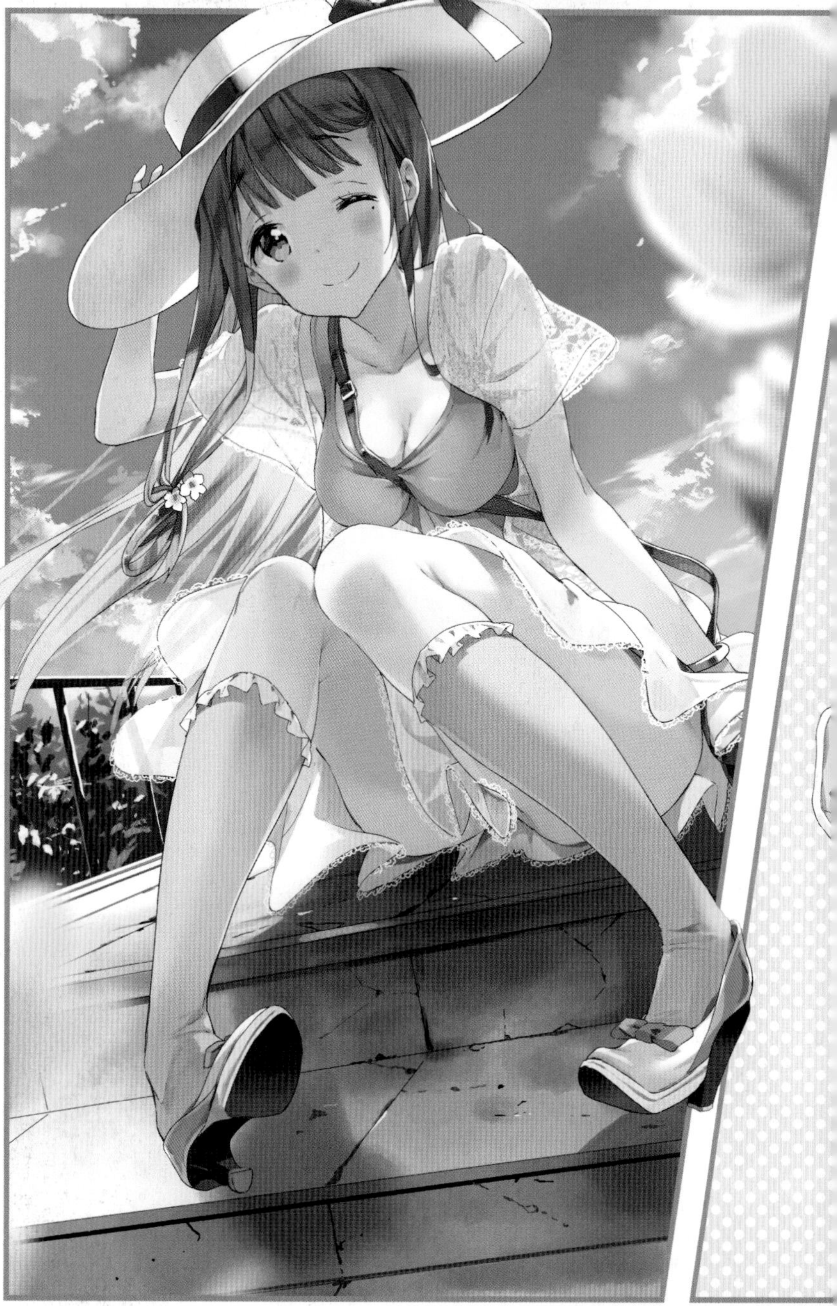

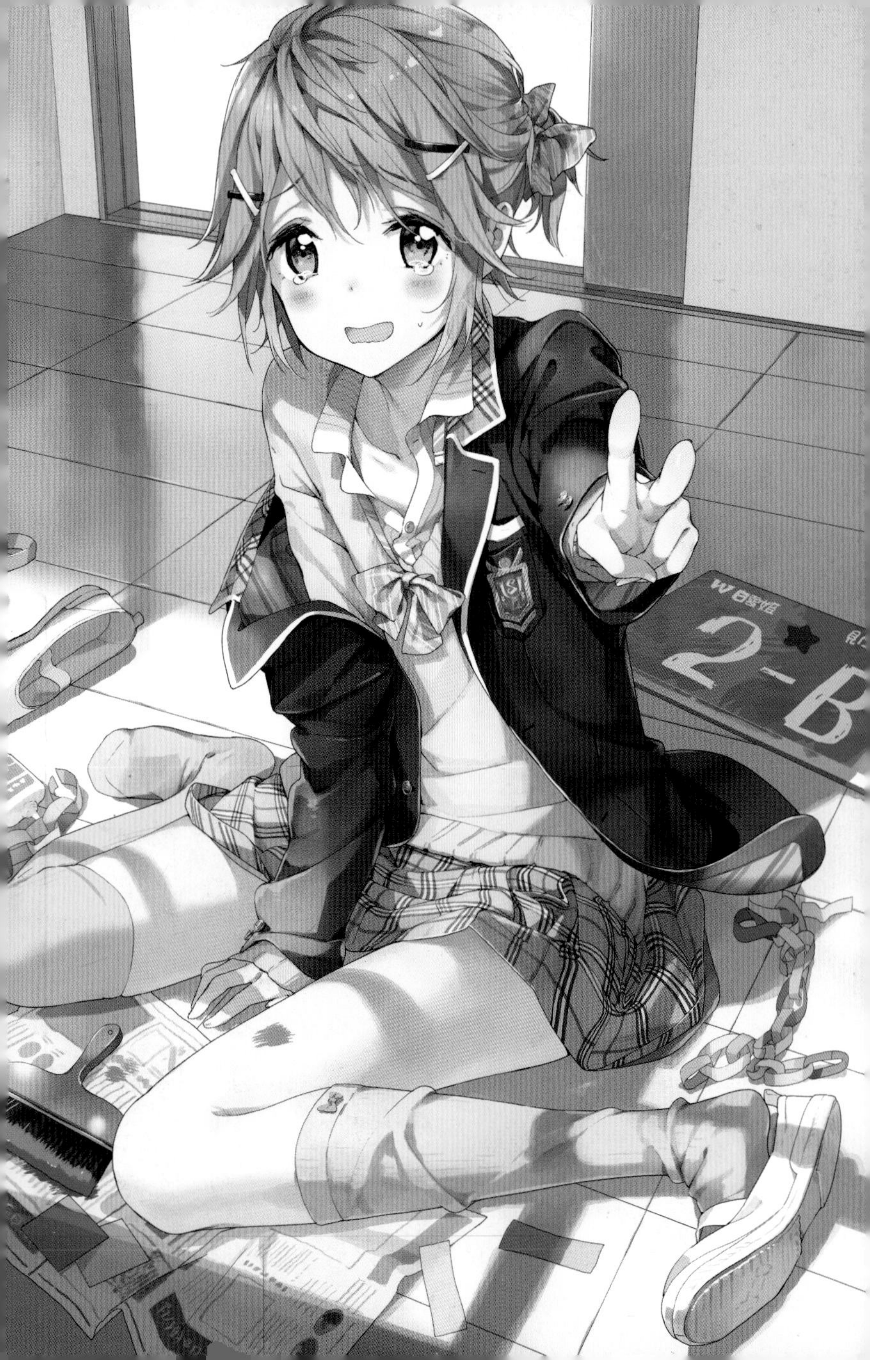
2-B

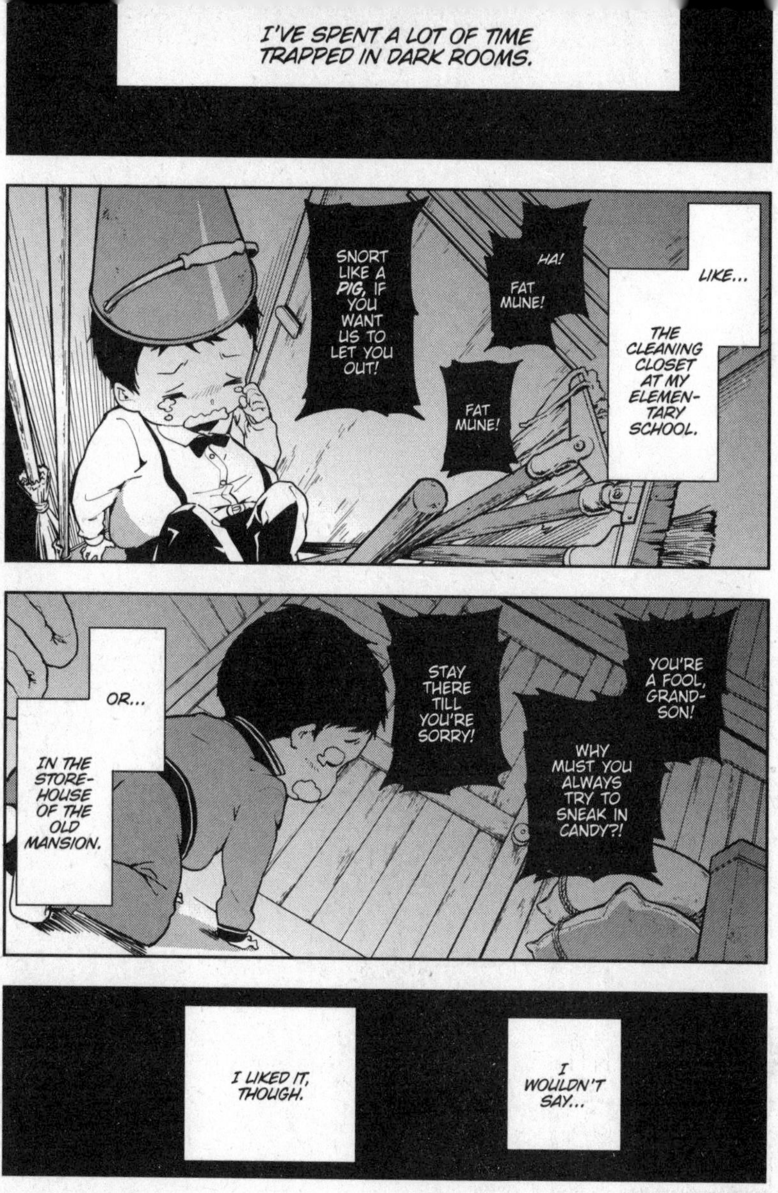
I'VE SPENT A LOT OF TIME TRAPPED IN DARK ROOMS.
LIKE...
THE CLEANING CLOSET AT MY ELEMENTARY SCHOOL.
HA! FAT MUNE!
FAT MUNE!
SNORT LIKE A PIG, IF YOU WANT US TO LET YOU OUT!
YOU'RE A FOOL, GRANDSON!
WHY MUST YOU ALWAYS TRY TO SNEAK IN CANDY?!
STAY THERE TILL YOU'RE SORRY!
OR...
IN THE STOREHOUSE OF THE OLD MANSION.
I WOULDN'T SAY...
I LIKED IT, THOUGH.

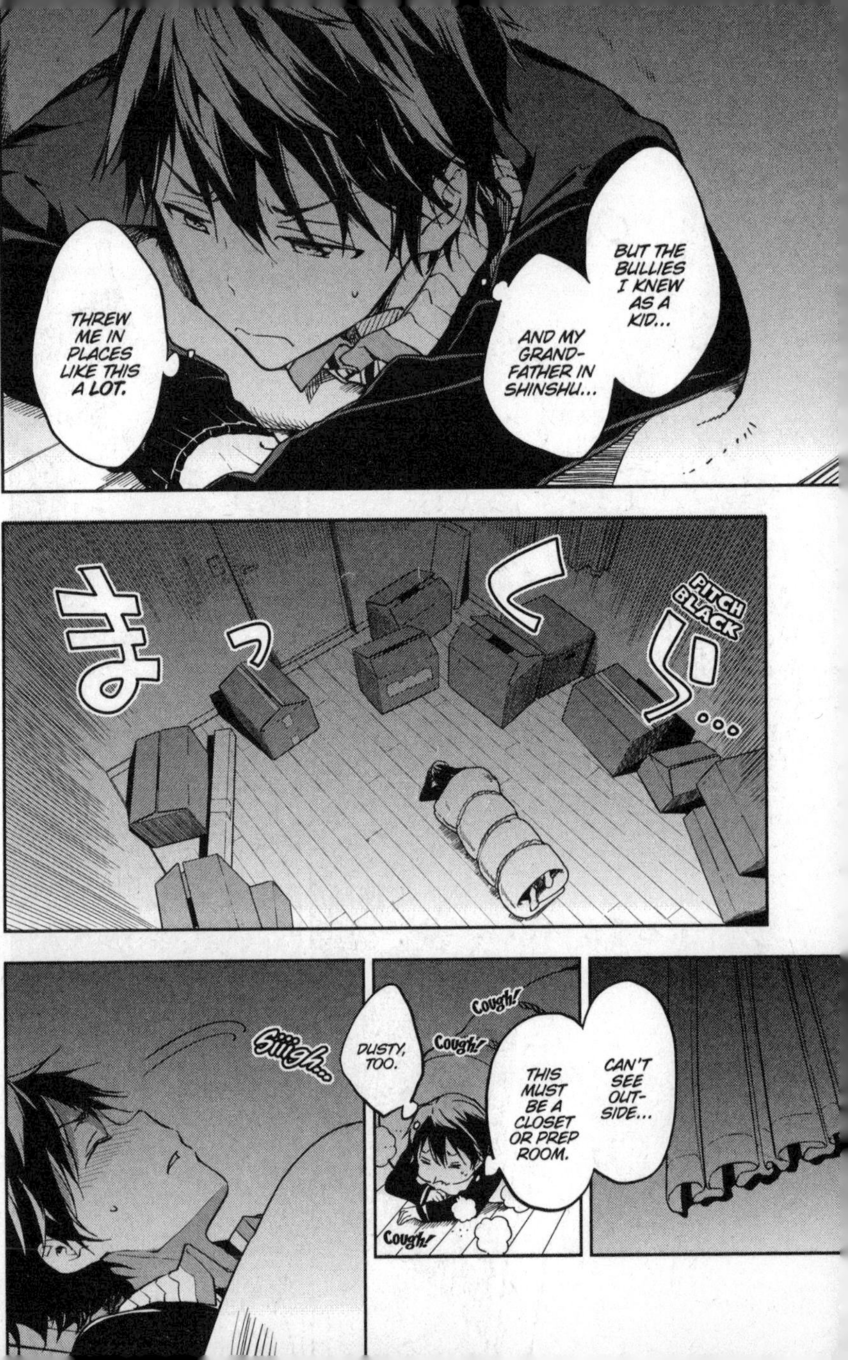
BUT THE BULLIES I KNEW AS A KID...
AND MY GRANDFATHER IN SHINSHU...
THREW ME IN PLACES LIKE THIS A LOT.
PITCH BLACK
まっくら…
CAN'T SEE OUT-SIDE...
THIS MUST BE A CLOSET OR PREP ROOM.
Cough!
Cough!
DUSTY, TOO.
Cough!
Siiigh...

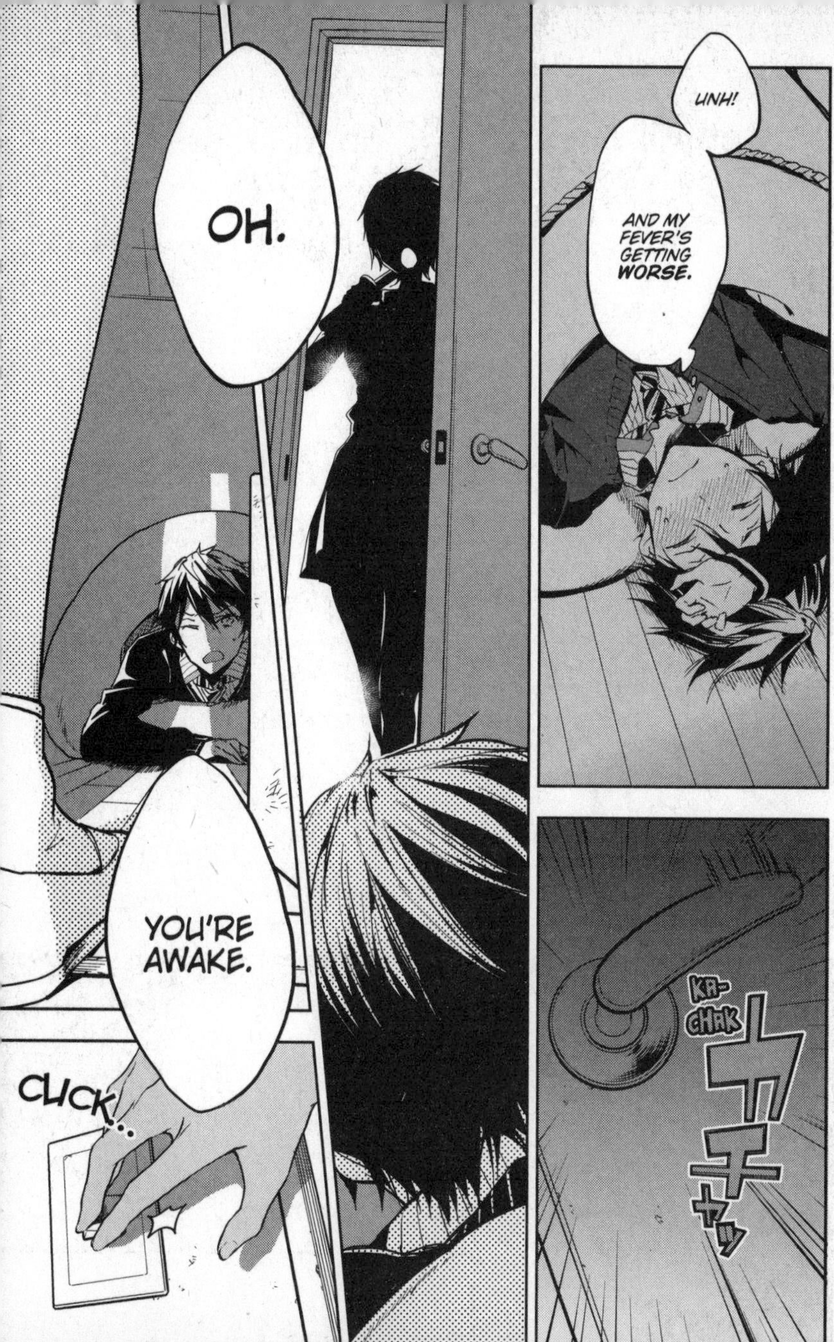
UNH!
AND MY FEVER'S GETTING WORSE.
KA-CHAK
カチャッ
OH.
YOU'RE AWAKE.
CLICK...

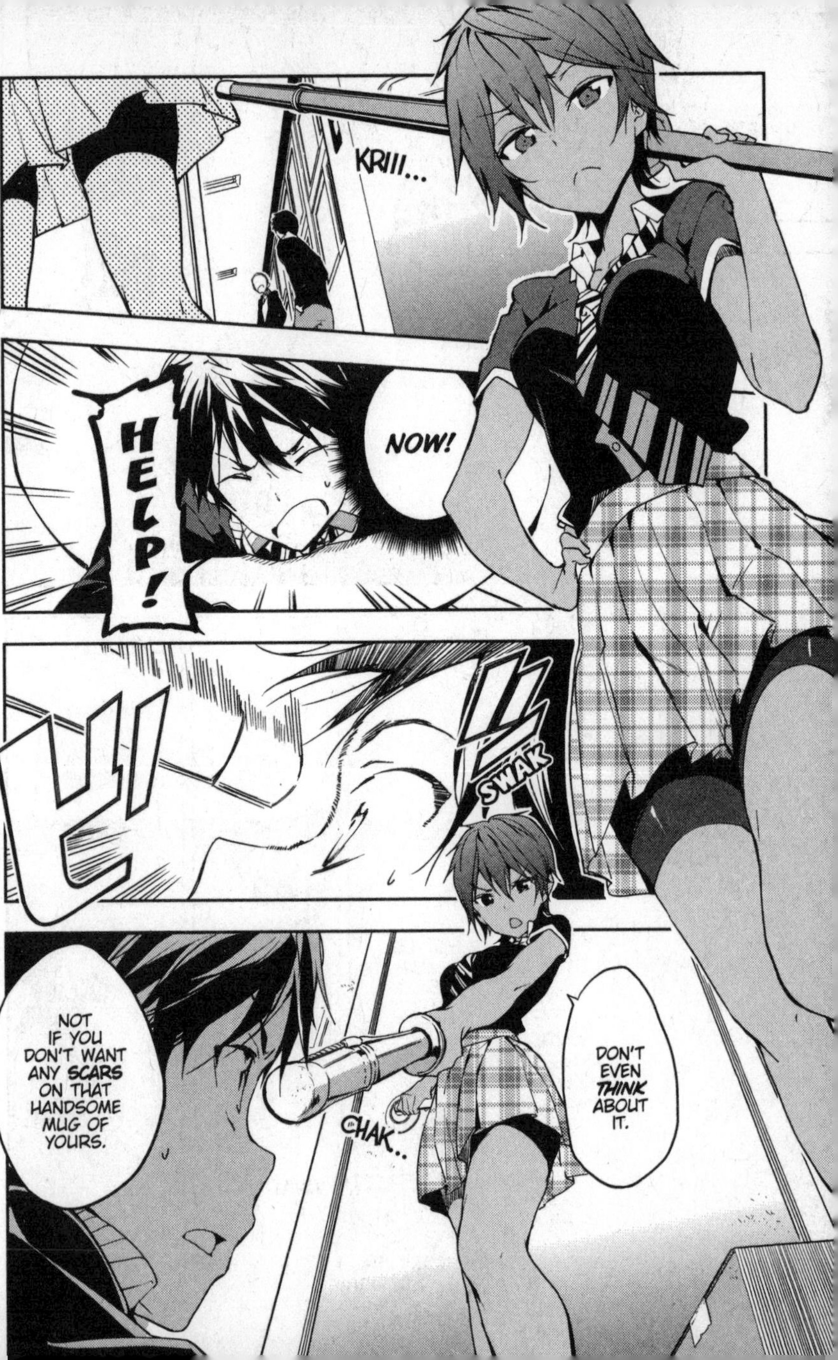

KRIII...
NOW!
HELP!
SWAK
DON'T EVEN THINK ABOUT IT.
CHAK...
NOT IF YOU DON'T WANT ANY SCARS ON THAT HANDSOME MUG OF YOURS.

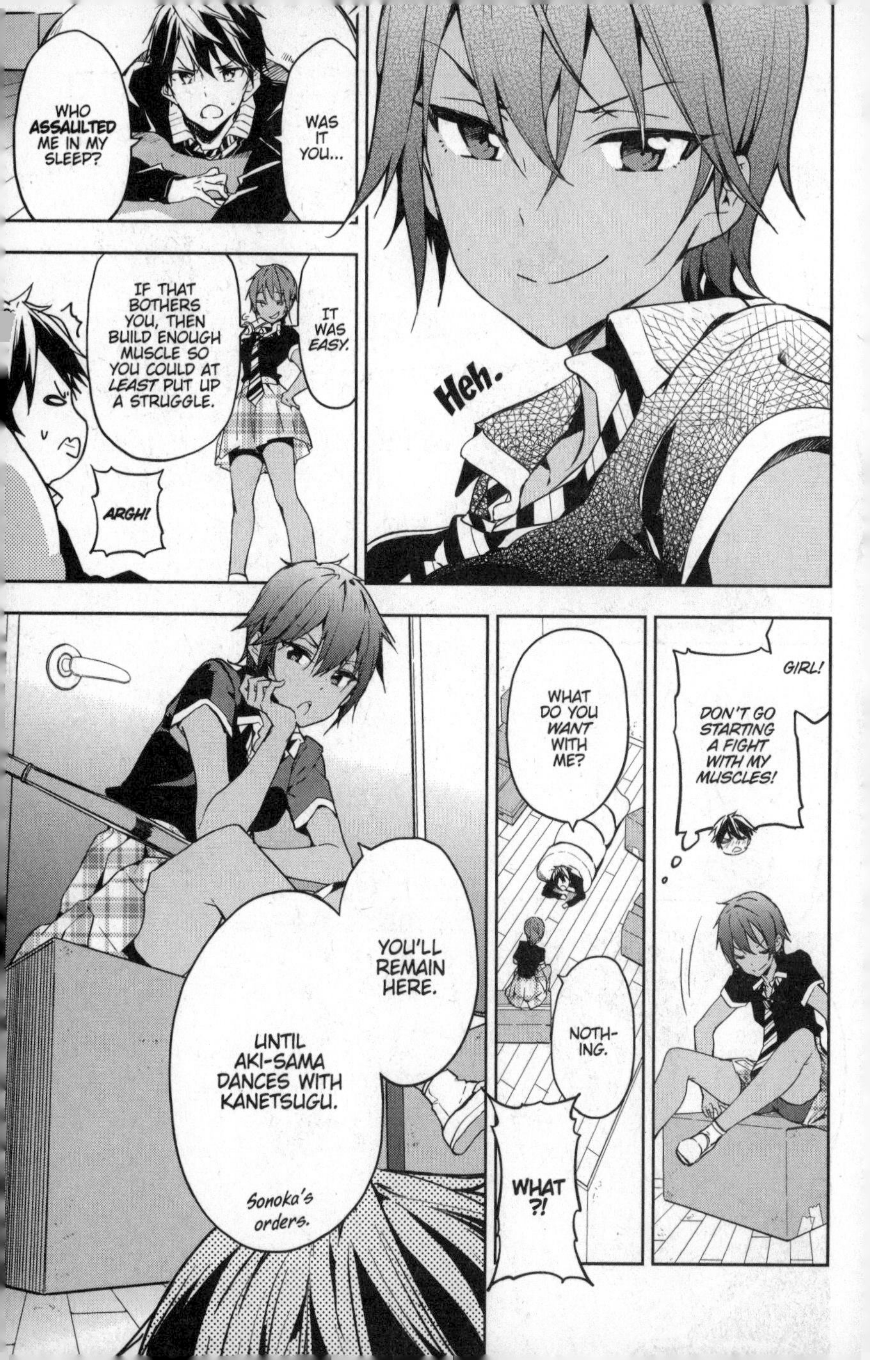
Heh.
WAS IT YOU...
WHO ASSAULTED ME IN MY SLEEP?
IT WAS EASY.
IF THAT BOTHERS YOU, THEN BUILD ENOUGH MUSCLE SO YOU COULD AT LEAST PUT UP A STRUGGLE.
ARGH!
GIRL!
DON'T GO STARTING A FIGHT WITH MY MUSCLES!
WHAT DO YOU WANT WITH ME?
NOTH-ING.
YOU'LL REMAIN HERE.
UNTIL AKI-SAMA DANCES WITH KANETSUGU.
Sonoka's orders.
WHAT?!

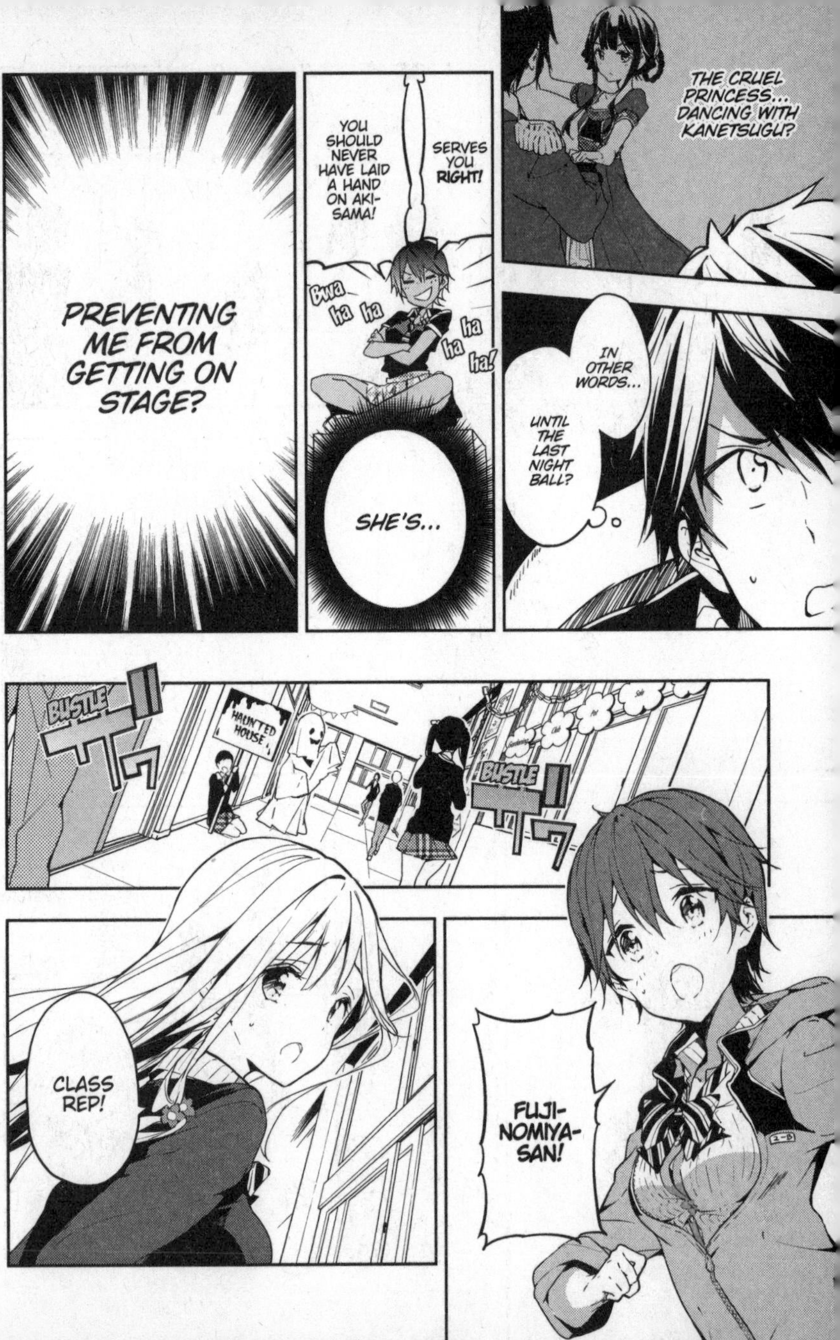
THE CRUEL PRINCESS... DANCING WITH KANETSUGU?
IN OTHER WORDS...
UNTIL THE LAST NIGHT BALL?
SERVES YOU RIGHT!
YOU SHOULD NEVER HAVE LAID A HAND ON AKI-SAMA!
Bwa ha ha ha ha ha!
SHE'S...
PREVENTING ME FROM GETTING ON STAGE?
BUSTLE
BUSTLE
HAUNTED HOUSE
FUJI-NOMIYA-SAN!
CLASS REP!

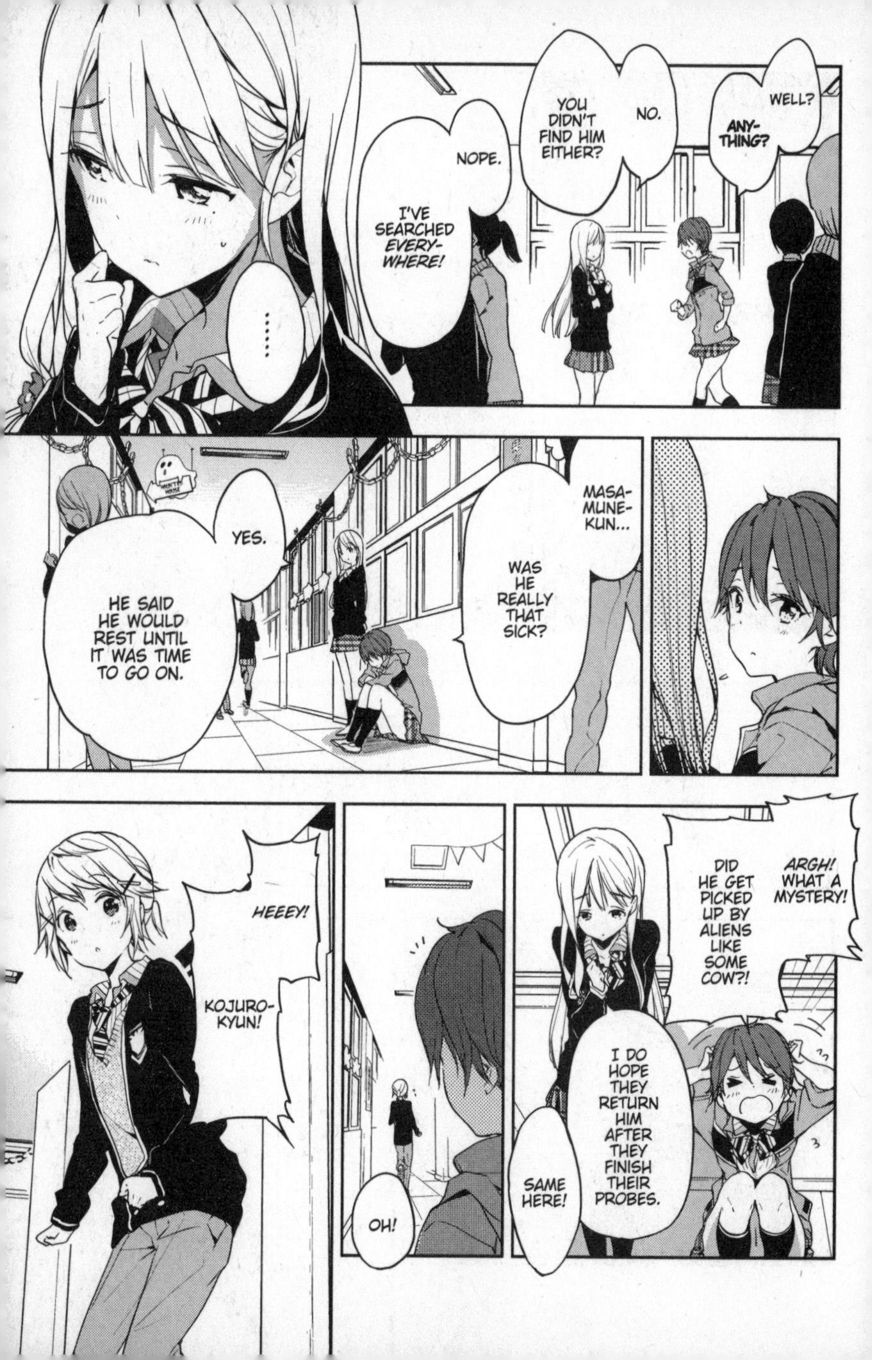
WELL?
ANY-THING?
NO.
YOU DIDN'T FIND HIM EITHER?
NOPE.
I'VE SEARCHED *EVERY-WHERE!*
......
MASA-MUNE-KUN...
WAS HE REALLY THAT SICK?
YES.
HE SAID HE WOULD REST UNTIL IT WAS TIME TO GO ON.
ARGH! WHAT A MYSTERY!
DID HE GET PICKED UP BY ALIENS LIKE SOME COW?!
I DO HOPE THEY RETURN HIM AFTER THEY FINISH THEIR PROBES.
SAME HERE!
OH!
HEEEY!
KOJURO-KYUN!

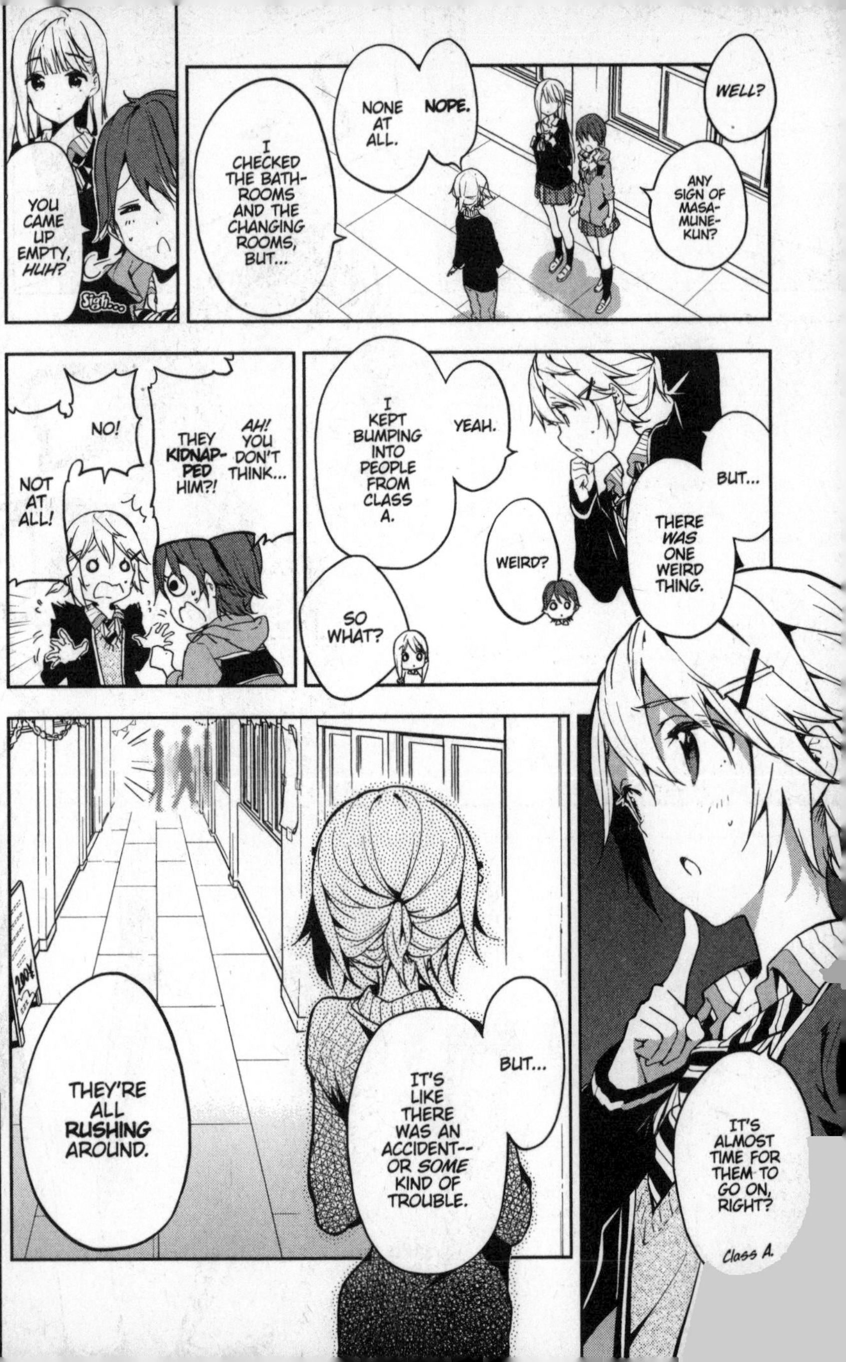
WELL?
ANY SIGN OF MASA-MUNE-KUN?
NOPE.
NONE AT ALL.
I CHECKED THE BATH-ROOMS AND THE CHANGING ROOMS, BUT...
YOU CAME UP EMPTY, HUH?
Sigh...
YEAH.
I KEPT BUMPING INTO PEOPLE FROM CLASS A.
BUT...
THERE WAS ONE WEIRD THING.
WEIRD?
SO WHAT?
AH! YOU DON'T THINK...
THEY KIDNAP-PED HIM?!
NO!
NOT AT ALL!
IT'S ALMOST TIME FOR THEM TO GO ON, RIGHT?
Class A.
BUT...
IT'S LIKE THERE WAS AN ACCIDENT-- OR SOME KIND OF TROUBLE.
THEY'RE ALL RUSHING AROUND.

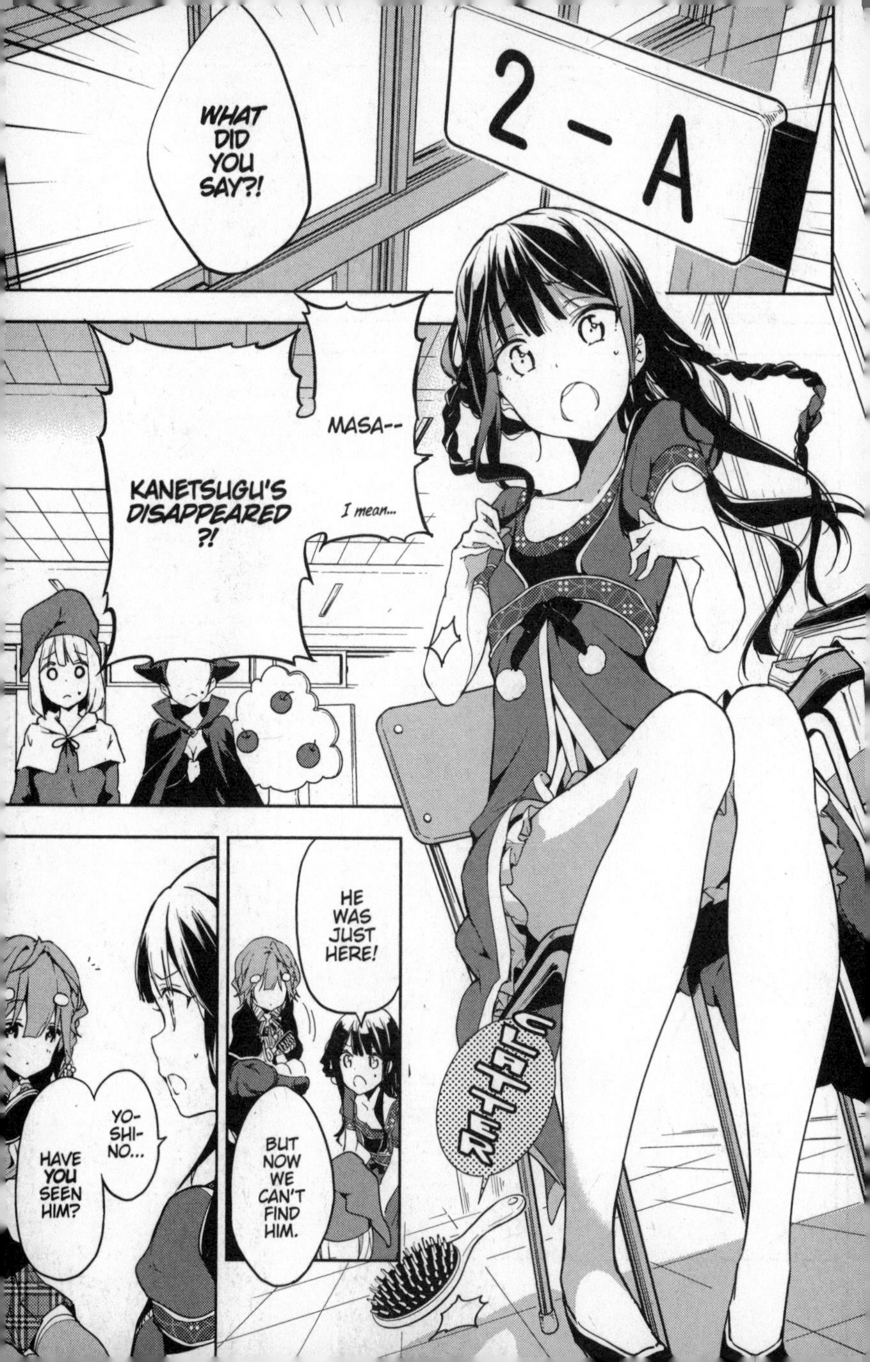
WHAT DID YOU SAY?!
CLATTER
MASA--
I mean...
KANETSUGU'S DISAPPEARED ?!
HE WAS JUST HERE!
BUT NOW WE CAN'T FIND HIM.
YO-SHI-NO...
HAVE YOU SEEN HIM?

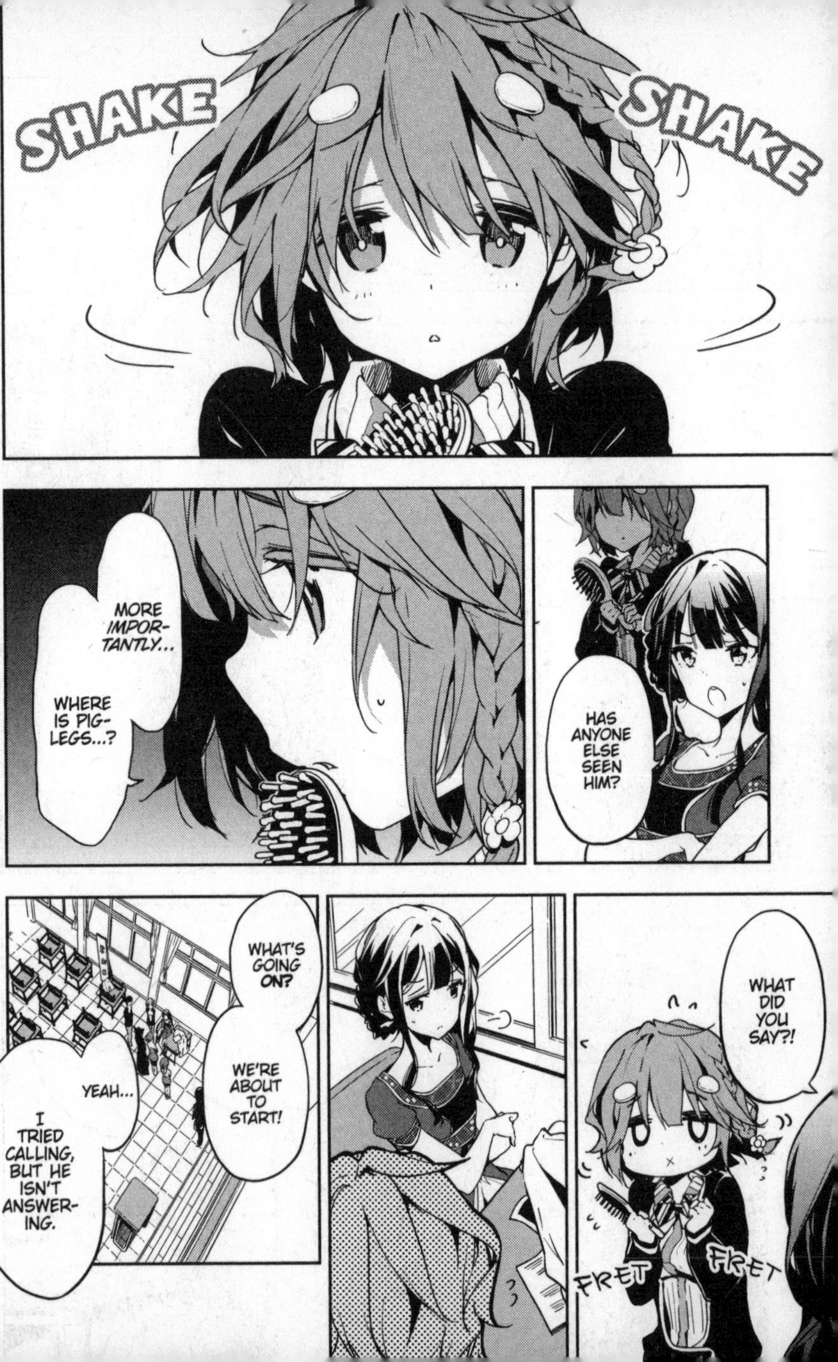
SHAKE
SHAKE
HAS ANYONE ELSE SEEN HIM?
MORE IMPORTANTLY...
WHERE IS PIG-LEGS...?
WHAT DID YOU SAY?!
FRET
FRET
WHAT'S GOING ON?
WE'RE ABOUT TO START!
YEAH...
I TRIED CALLING, BUT HE ISN'T ANSWERING.

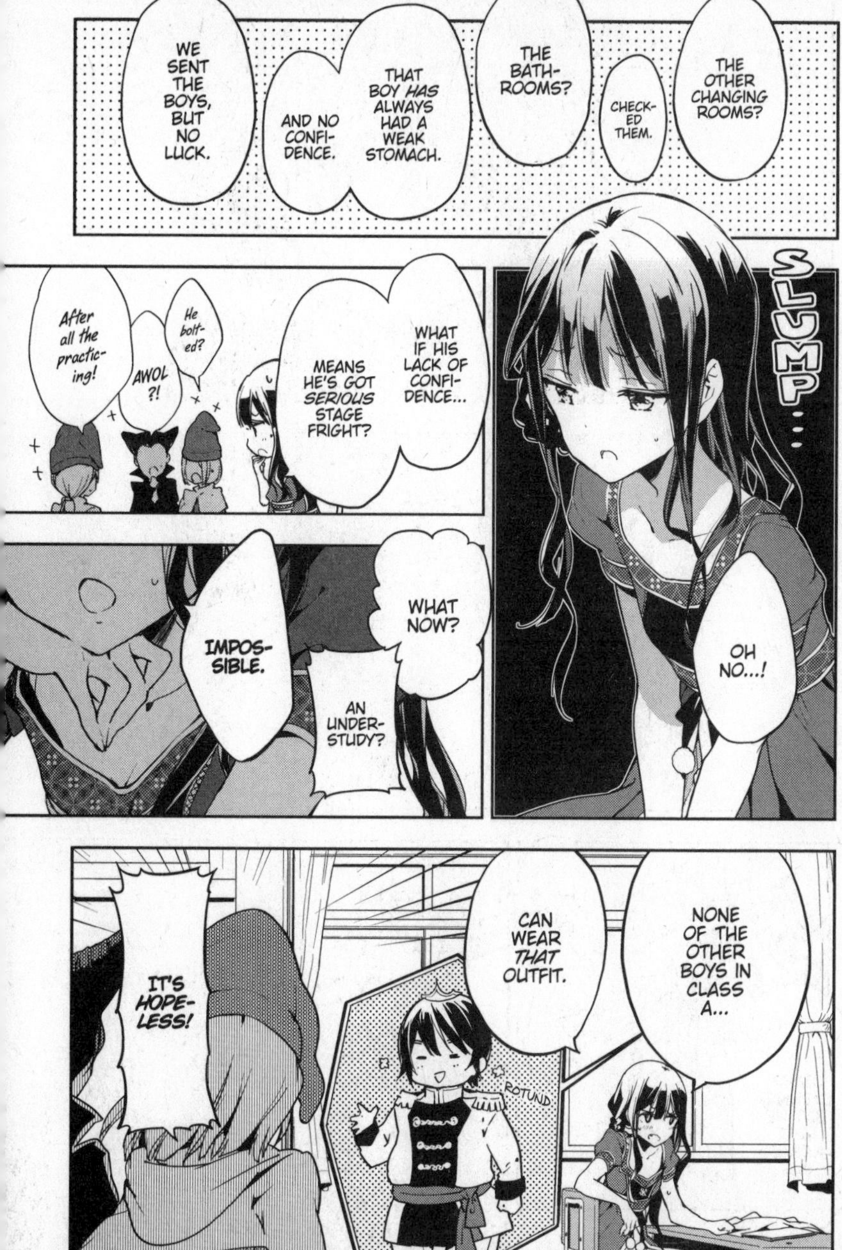

THE OTHER CHANGING ROOMS?
CHECKED THEM.
THE BATHROOMS?
THAT BOY *HAS* ALWAYS HAD A WEAK STOMACH.
AND NO CONFIDENCE.
WE SENT THE BOYS, BUT NO LUCK.
SLUMP...
OH NO...!
WHAT IF HIS LACK OF CONFIDENCE...
MEANS HE'S GOT *SERIOUS* STAGE FRIGHT?
He bolted?
AWOL?!
After all the practicing!
WHAT NOW?
AN UNDERSTUDY?
IMPOSSIBLE.
NONE OF THE OTHER BOYS IN CLASS A...
CAN WEAR *THAT* OUTFIT.
ROTUND
IT'S *HOPELESS!*

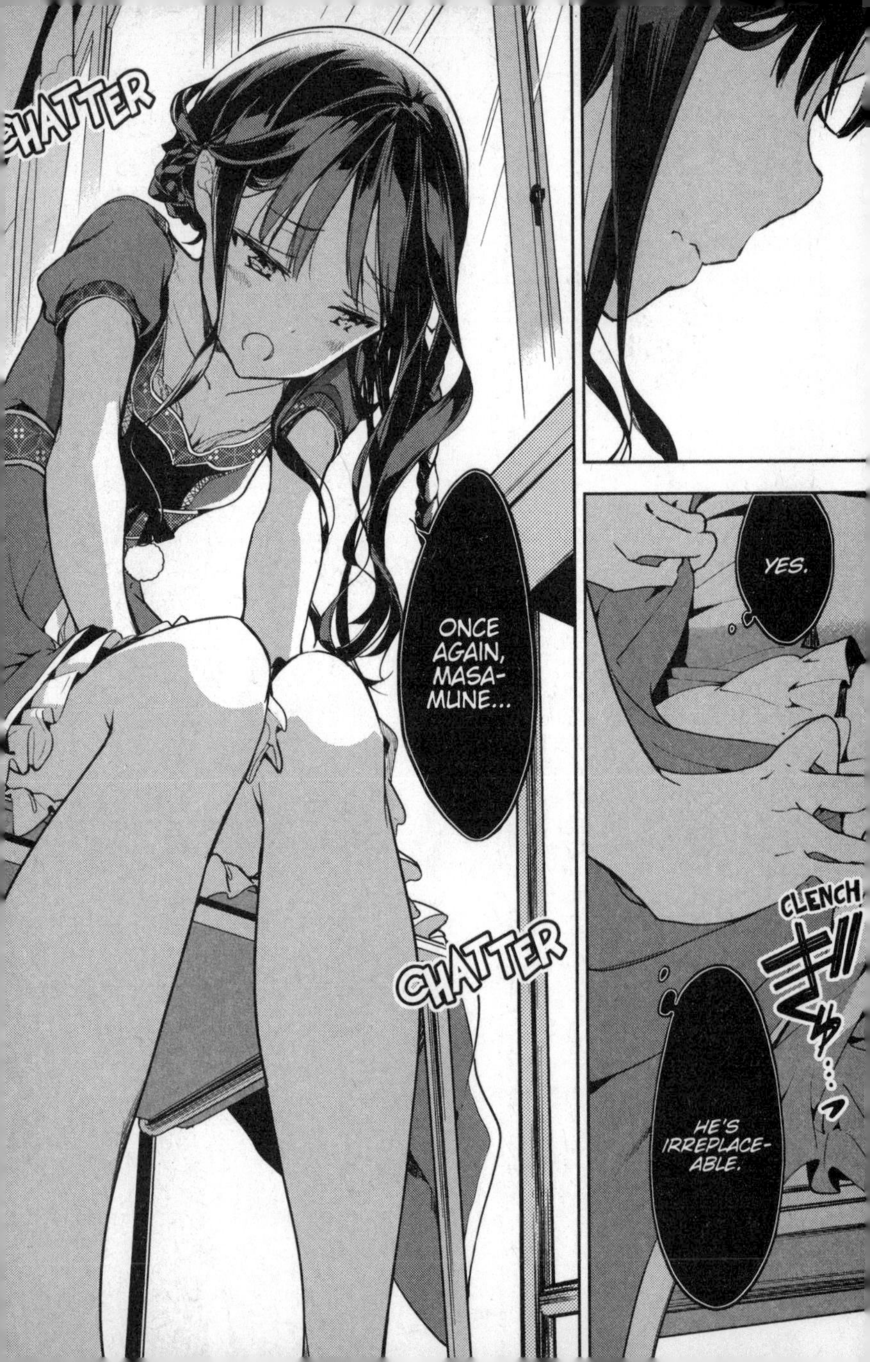
YES.
CLENCH
HE'S IRREPLACE-ABLE.
CHATTER
ONCE AGAIN, MASA-MUNE...
CHATTER

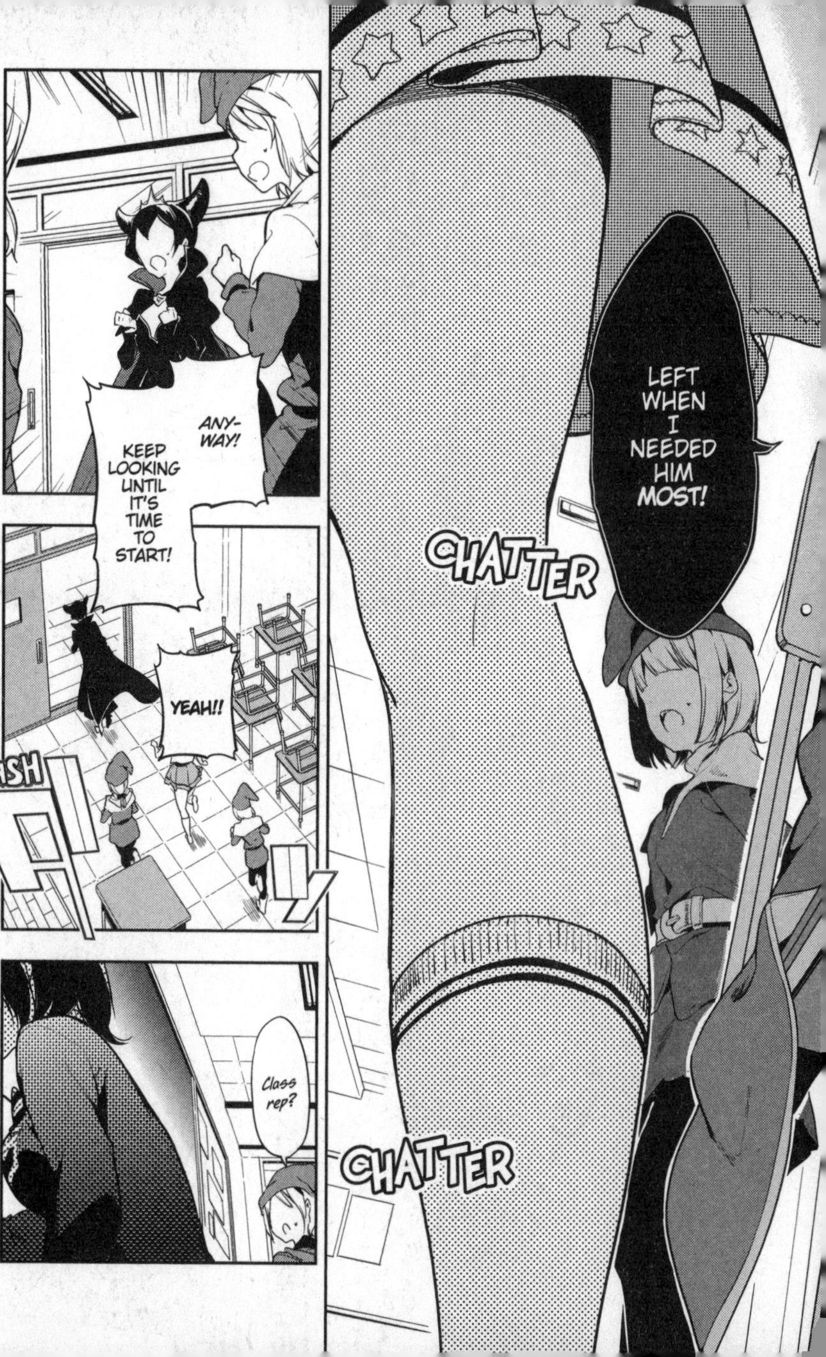
LEFT WHEN I NEEDED HIM MOST!
CHATTER
CHATTER
ANY-WAY!
KEEP LOOKING UNTIL IT'S TIME TO START!
YEAH!!
DASH
Class rep?

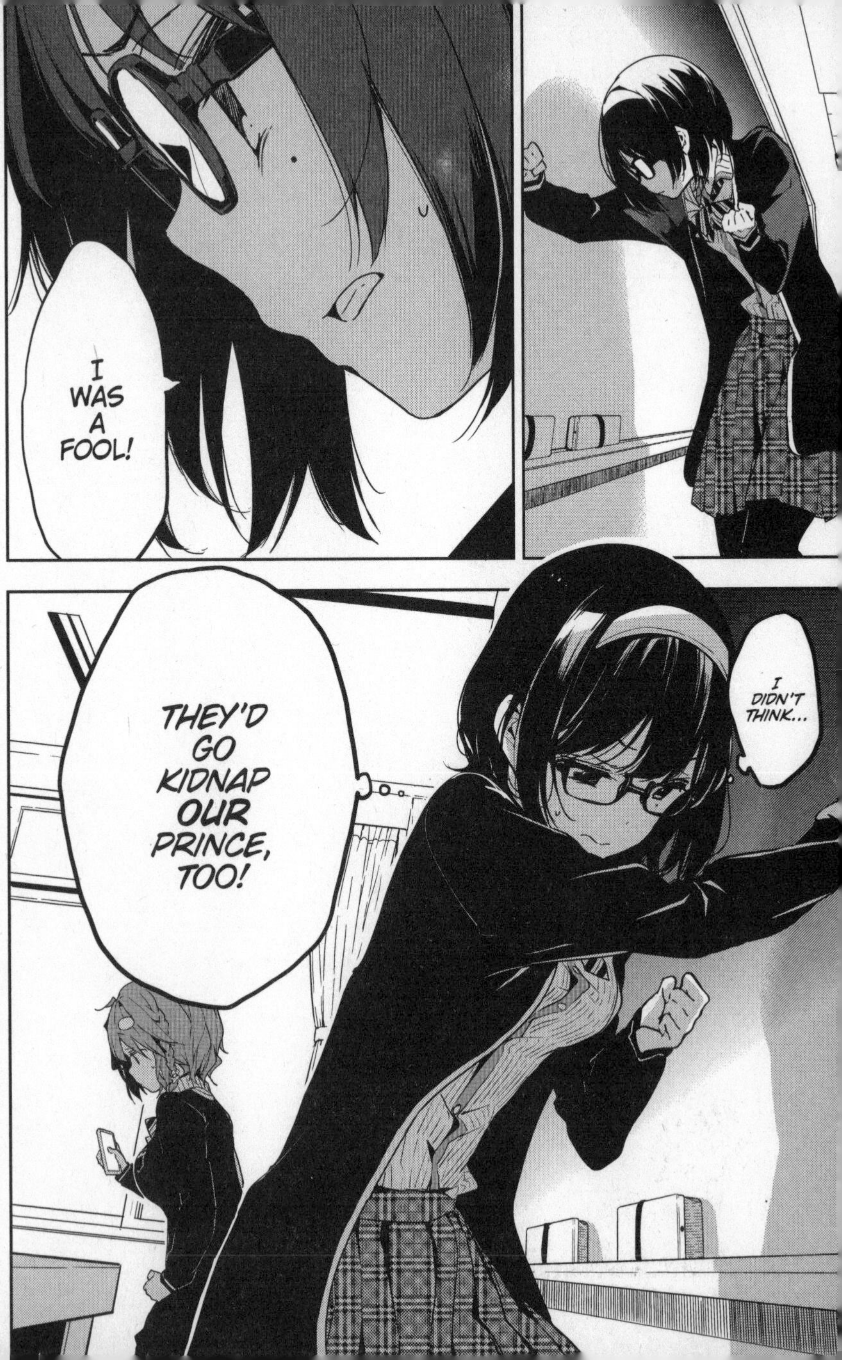
I WAS A FOOL!
I DIDN'T THINK...
THEY'D GO KIDNAP OUR PRINCE, TOO!

Masamune-kun's
REVENGE
Presented by Hazuki Takeoka & TIV

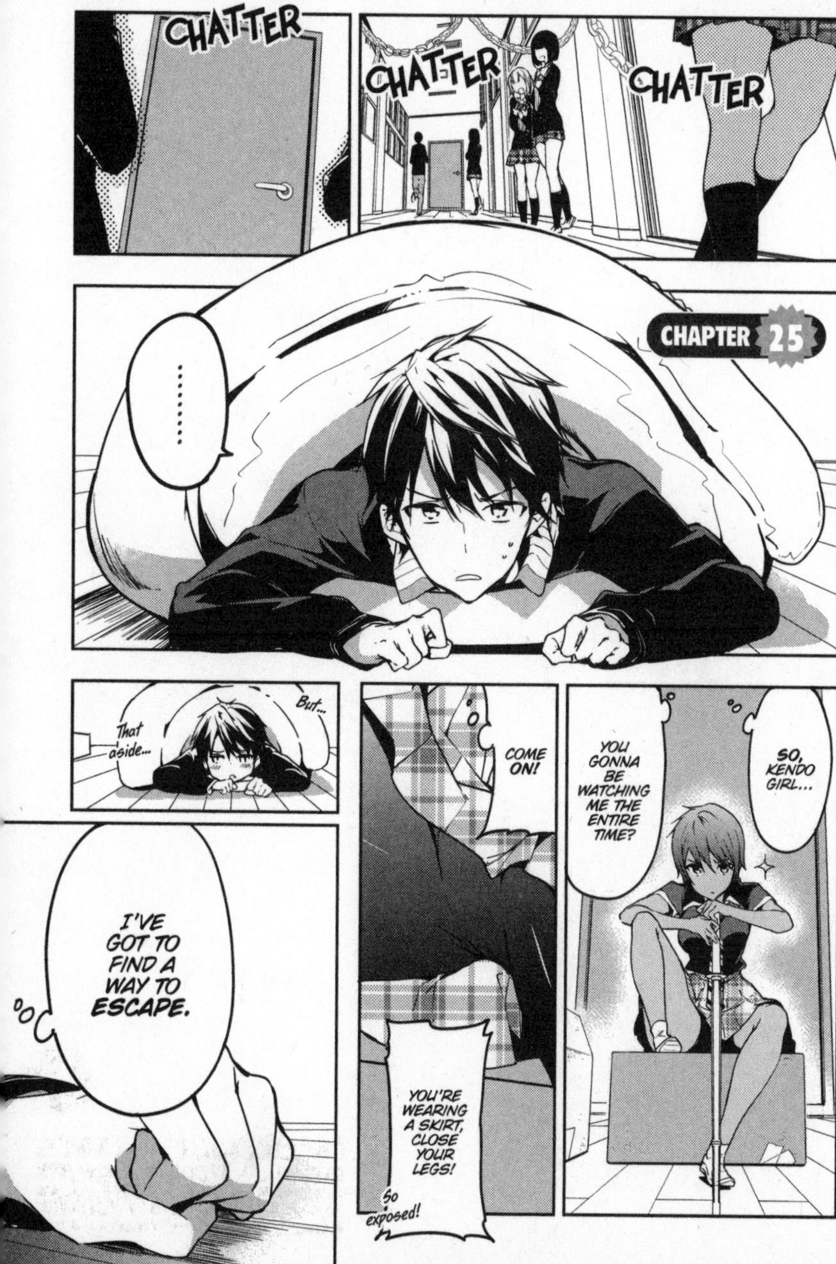
CHATTER
CHATTER
CHATTER
CHAPTER 25
......
SO, KENDO GIRL...
YOU GONNA BE WATCHING ME THE ENTIRE TIME?
COME ON!
YOU'RE WEARING A SKIRT, CLOSE YOUR LEGS!
So exposed!
But...
That aside...
I'VE GOT TO FIND A WAY TO ESCAPE.

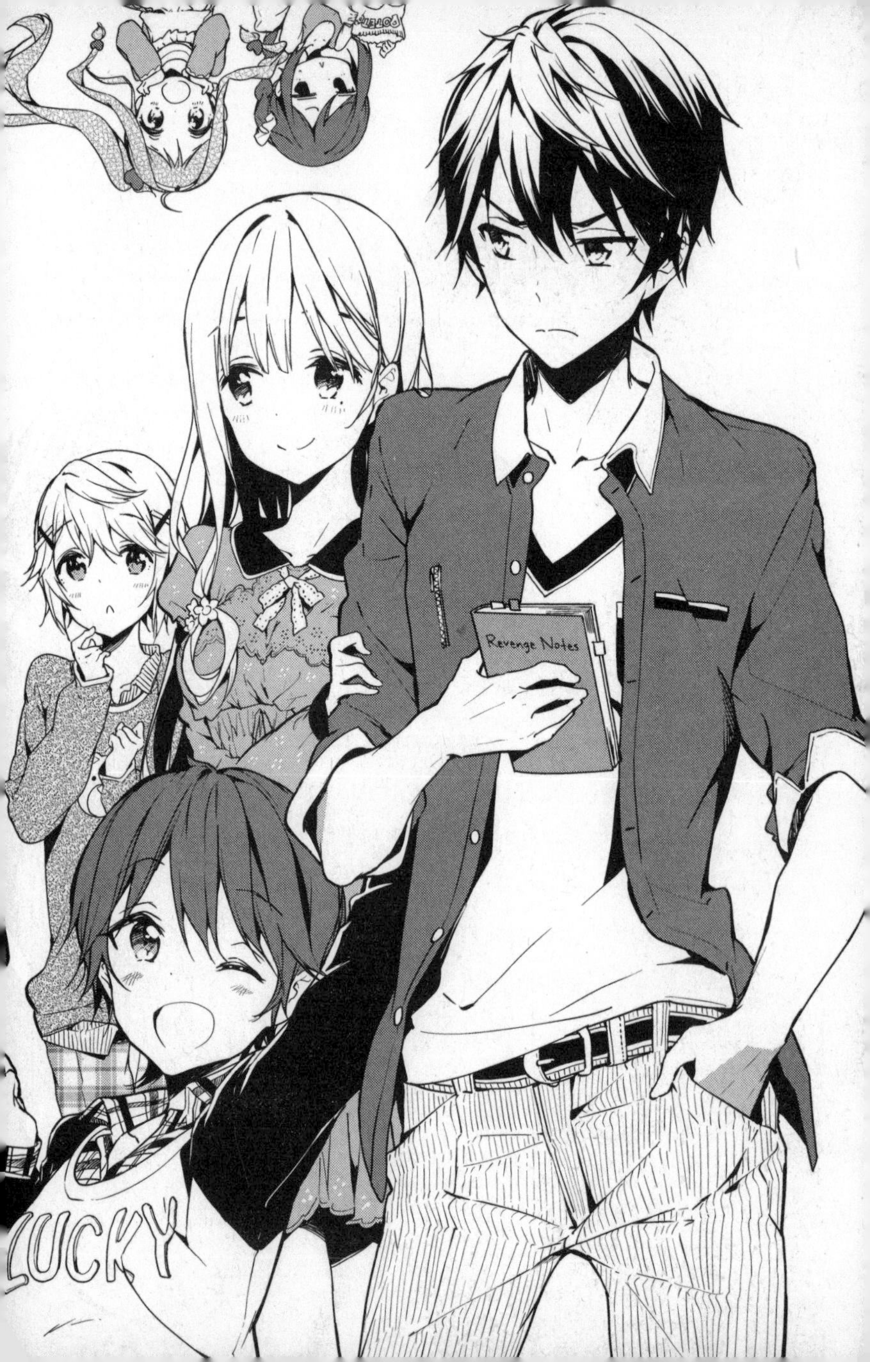
Revenge Notes
LUCKY

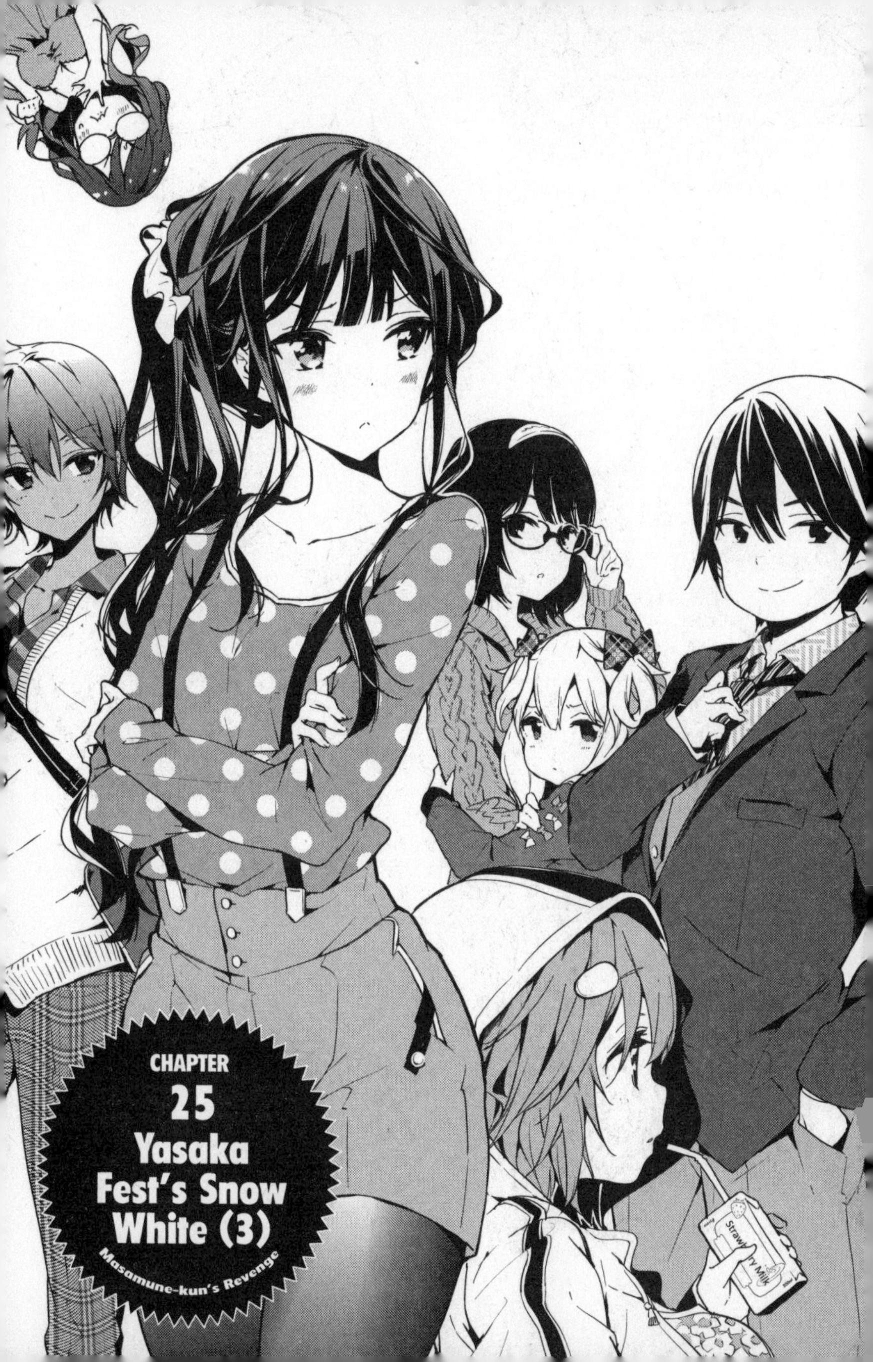
CHAPTER
25
Yasaka Fest's Snow White (3)
Masamune-kun's Revenge

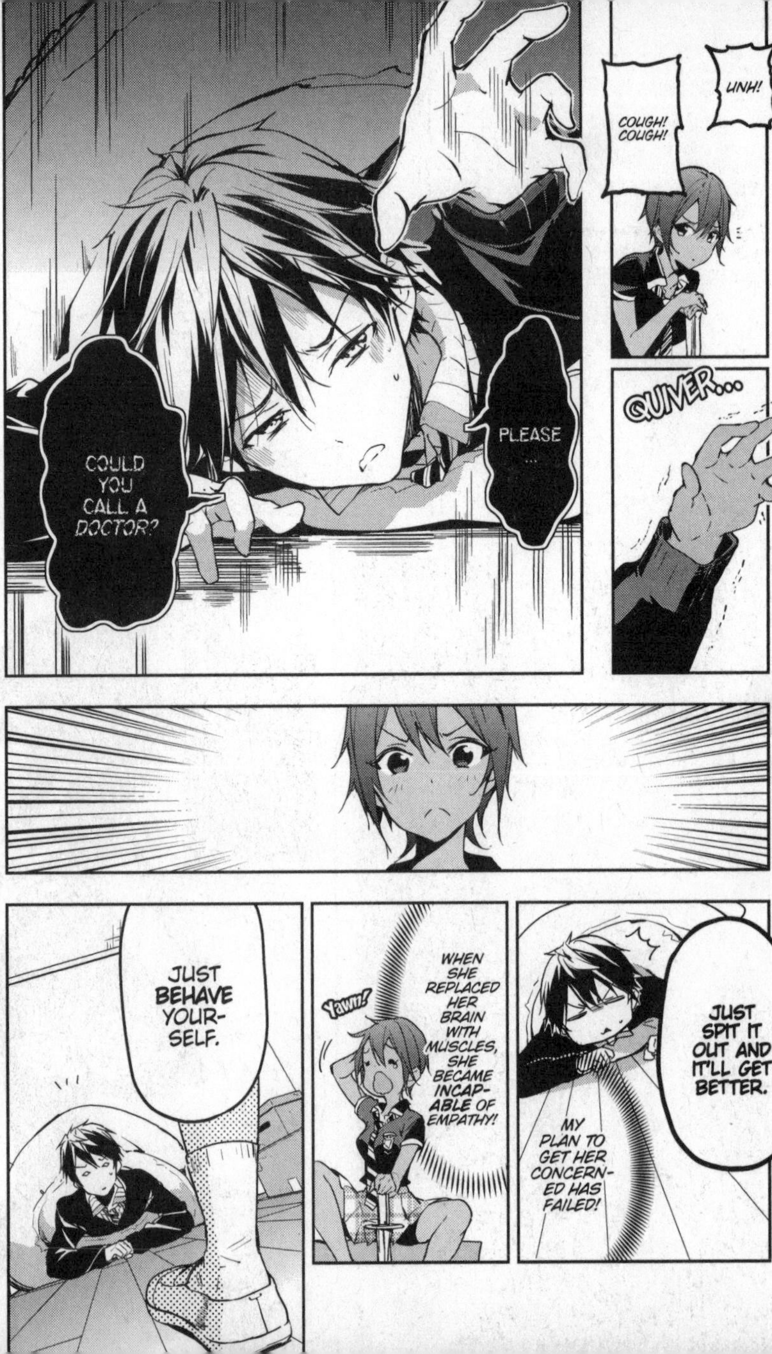
UNH!
COUGH! COUGH!
QUIVER...
PLEASE ...
COULD YOU CALL A DOCTOR?
JUST SPIT IT OUT AND IT'LL GET BETTER.
MY PLAN TO GET HER CONCERNED HAS FAILED!
WHEN SHE REPLACED HER BRAIN WITH MUSCLES, SHE BECAME INCAPABLE OF EMPATHY!
Yawn!
JUST BEHAVE YOURSELF.

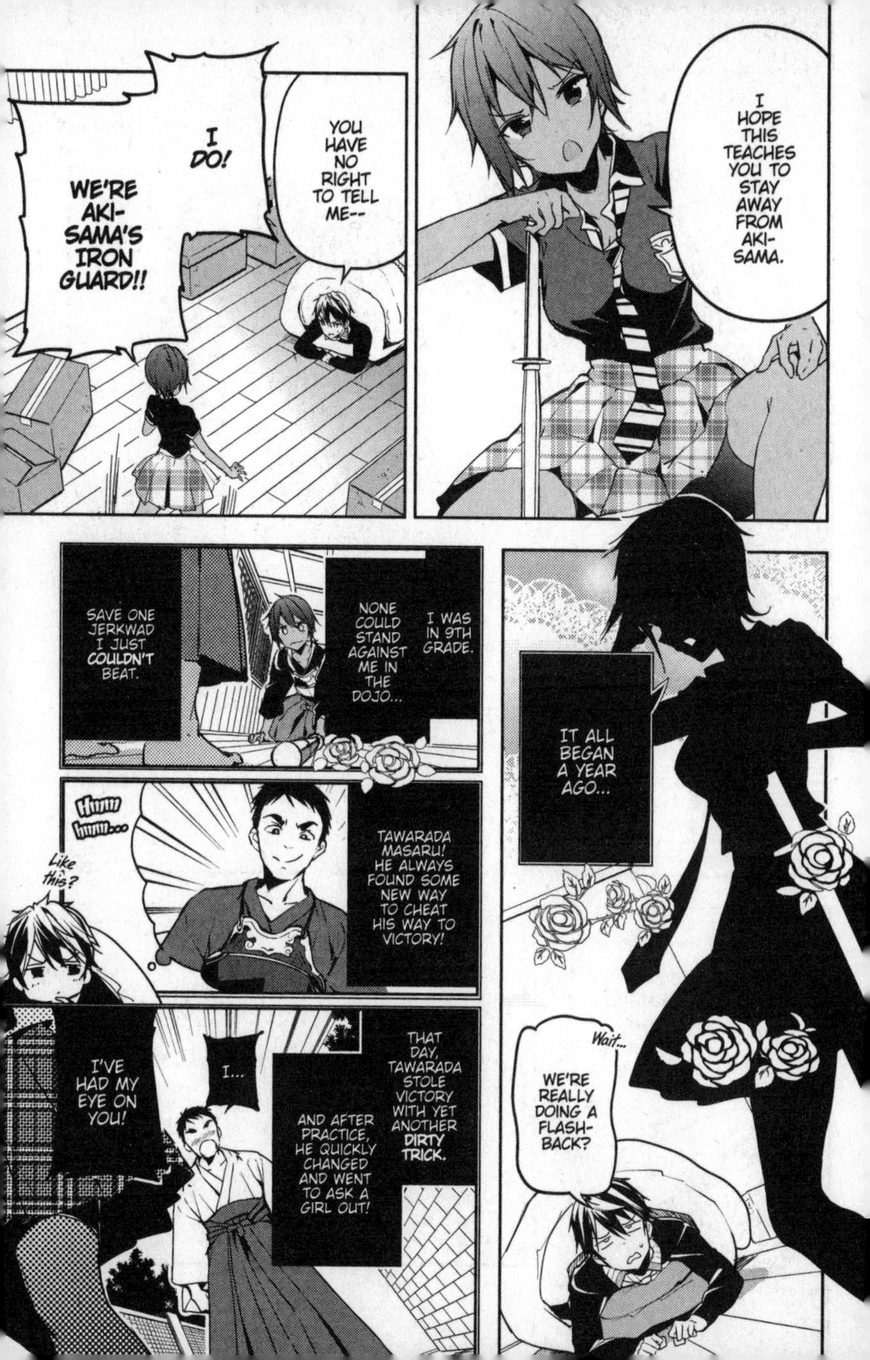
I HOPE THIS TEACHES YOU TO STAY AWAY FROM AKI-SAMA.
YOU HAVE NO RIGHT TO TELL ME--
I DO!
WE'RE AKI-SAMA'S IRON GUARD!!
IT ALL BEGAN A YEAR AGO...
Wait...
WE'RE REALLY DOING A FLASH-BACK?
I WAS IN 9TH GRADE.
NONE COULD STAND AGAINST ME IN THE DOJO...
SAVE ONE JERKWAD I JUST COULDN'T BEAT.
TAWARADA MASARU! HE ALWAYS FOUND SOME NEW WAY TO CHEAT HIS WAY TO VICTORY!
Hmm hmm...
Like this?
THAT DAY, TAWARADA STOLE VICTORY WITH YET ANOTHER DIRTY TRICK.
AND AFTER PRACTICE, HE QUICKLY CHANGED AND WENT TO ASK A GIRL OUT!
I...
I'VE HAD MY EYE ON YOU!

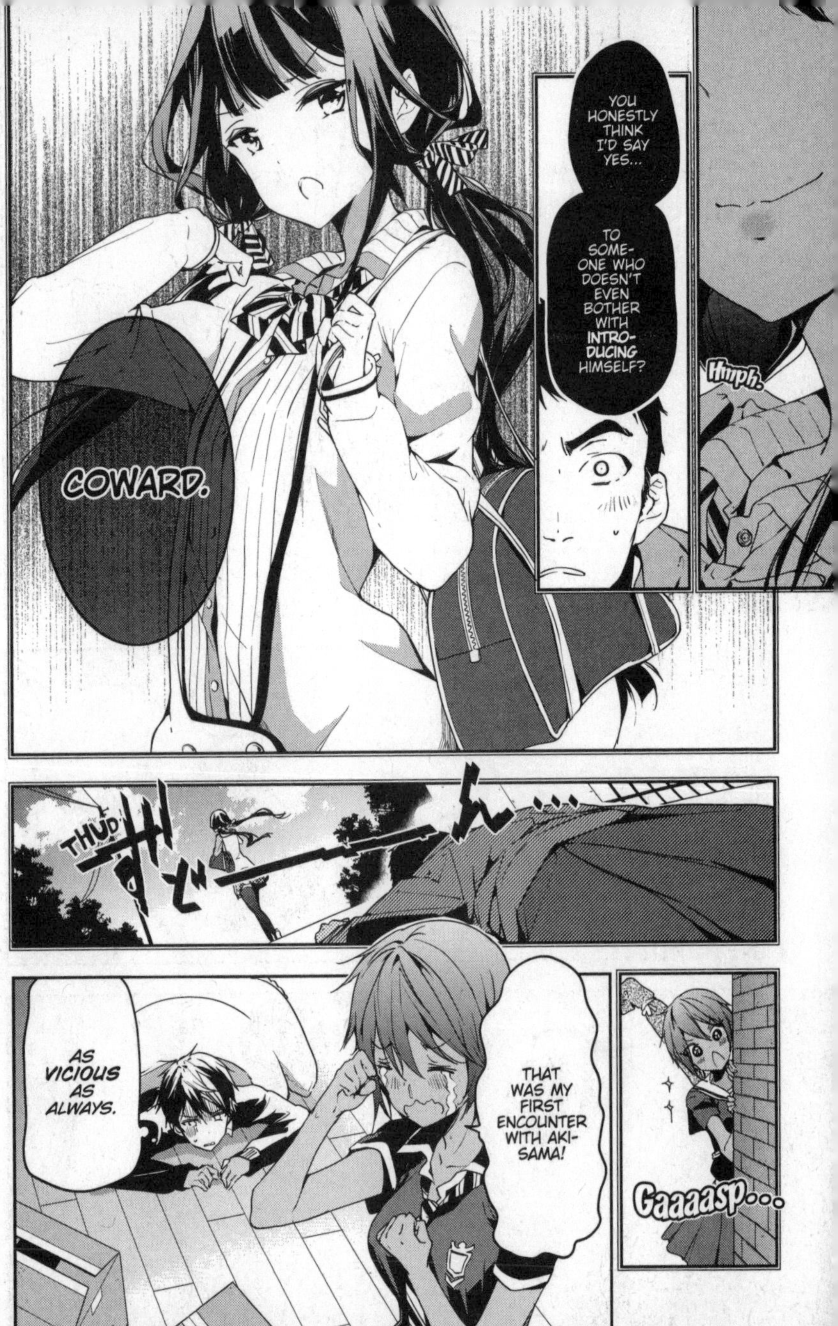
Hmph.
YOU HONESTLY THINK I'D SAY YES...
TO SOMEONE WHO DOESN'T EVEN BOTHER WITH INTRODUCING HIMSELF?
COWARD.
THUD
Gaaaasp...
THAT WAS MY FIRST ENCOUNTER WITH AKI-SAMA!
AS VICIOUS AS ALWAYS.

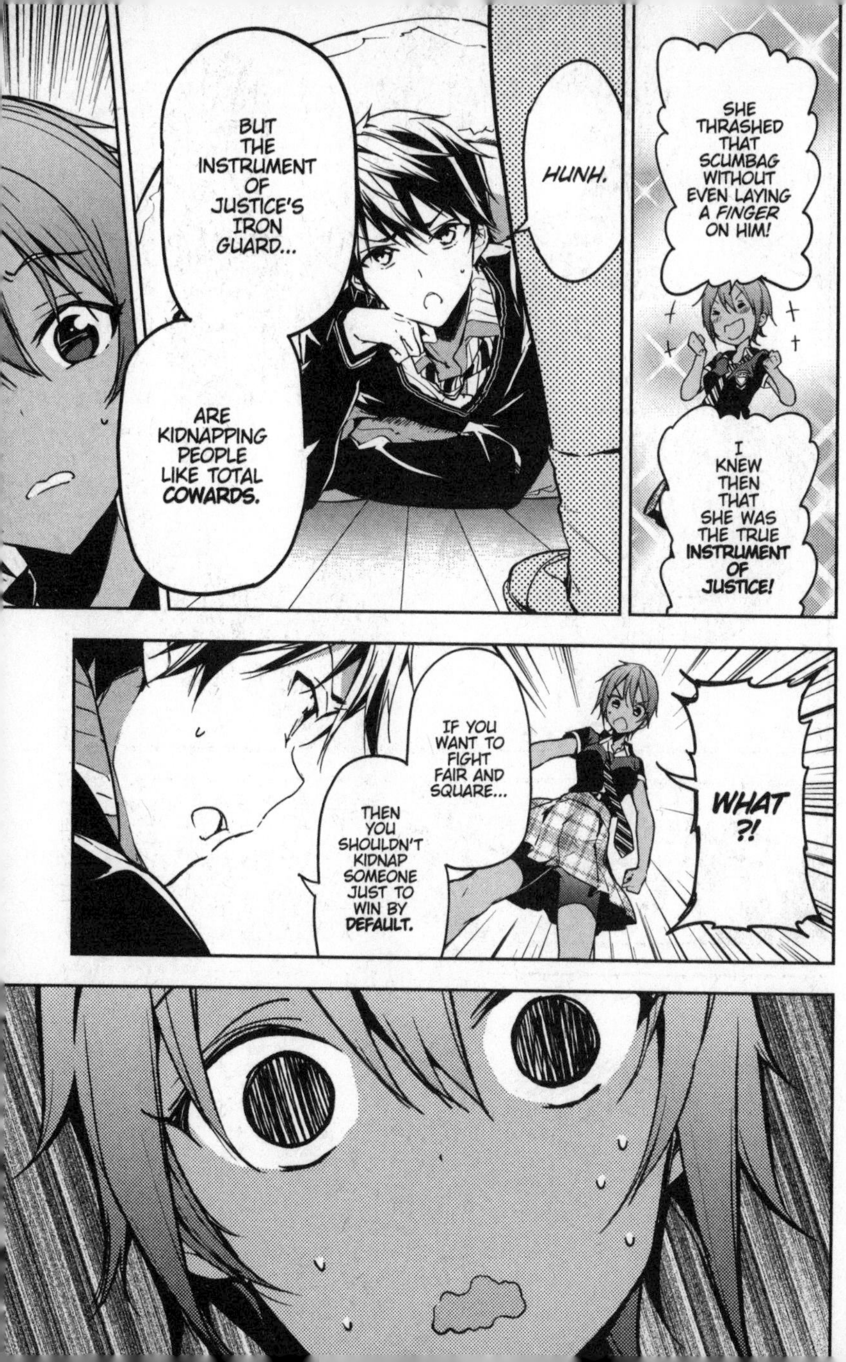
SHE THRASHED THAT SCUMBAG WITHOUT EVEN LAYING A *FINGER* ON HIM!
I KNEW THEN THAT SHE WAS THE TRUE **INSTRUMENT OF JUSTICE!**
HUNH.
BUT THE INSTRUMENT OF JUSTICE'S IRON GUARD...
ARE KIDNAPPING PEOPLE LIKE TOTAL **COWARDS.**
WHAT ?!
IF YOU WANT TO FIGHT FAIR AND SQUARE...
THEN YOU SHOULDN'T KIDNAP SOMEONE JUST TO WIN BY **DEFAULT.**

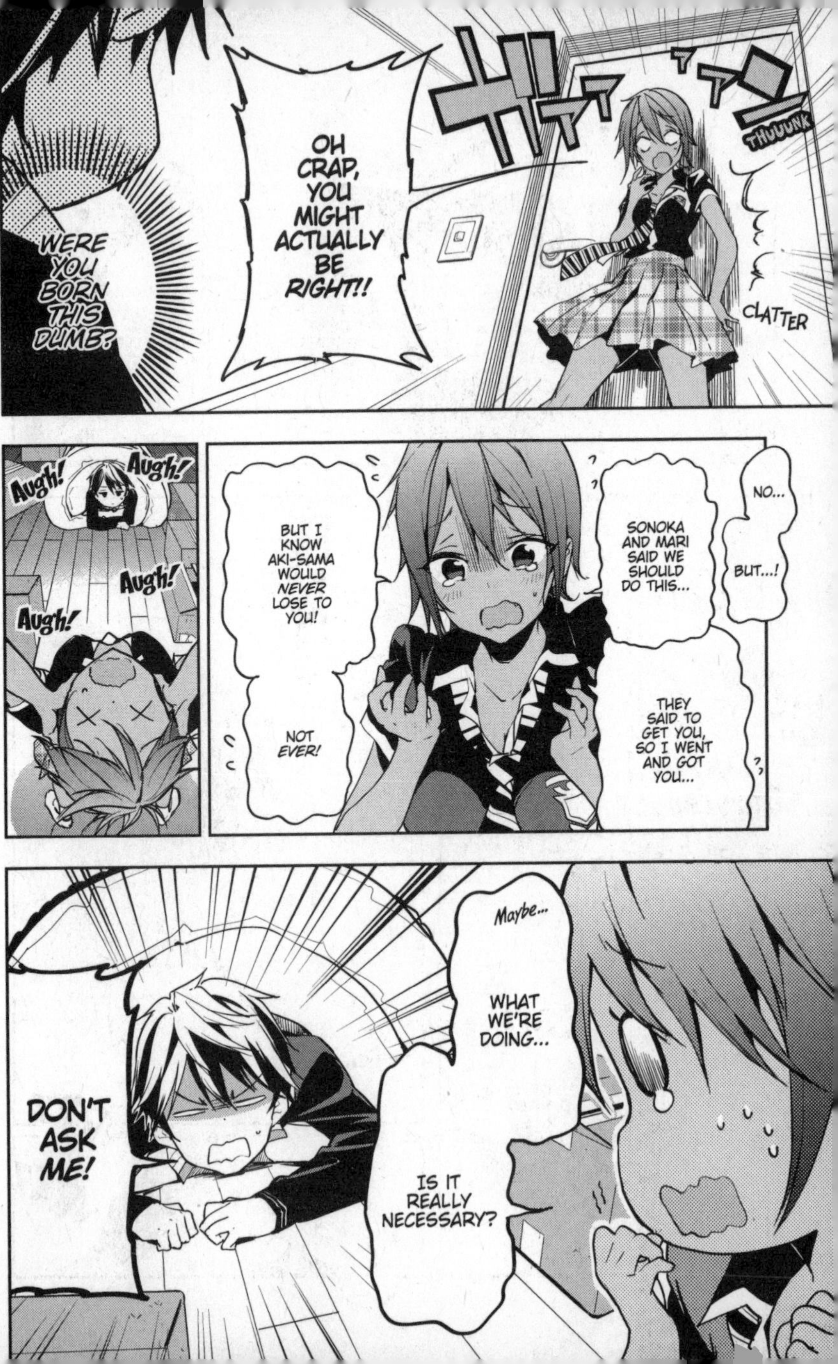
THUUUNK
CLATTER
OH CRAP, YOU MIGHT ACTUALLY BE RIGHT!!
WERE YOU BORN THIS DUMB?
NO...
BUT...!
SONOKA AND MARI SAID WE SHOULD DO THIS...
THEY SAID TO GET YOU, SO I WENT AND GOT YOU...
BUT I KNOW AKI-SAMA WOULD *NEVER* LOSE TO YOU!
NOT *EVER!*
Augh!
Augh!
Augh!
Augh!
Maybe...
WHAT WE'RE DOING...
IS IT REALLY NECESSARY?
DON'T ASK ME!

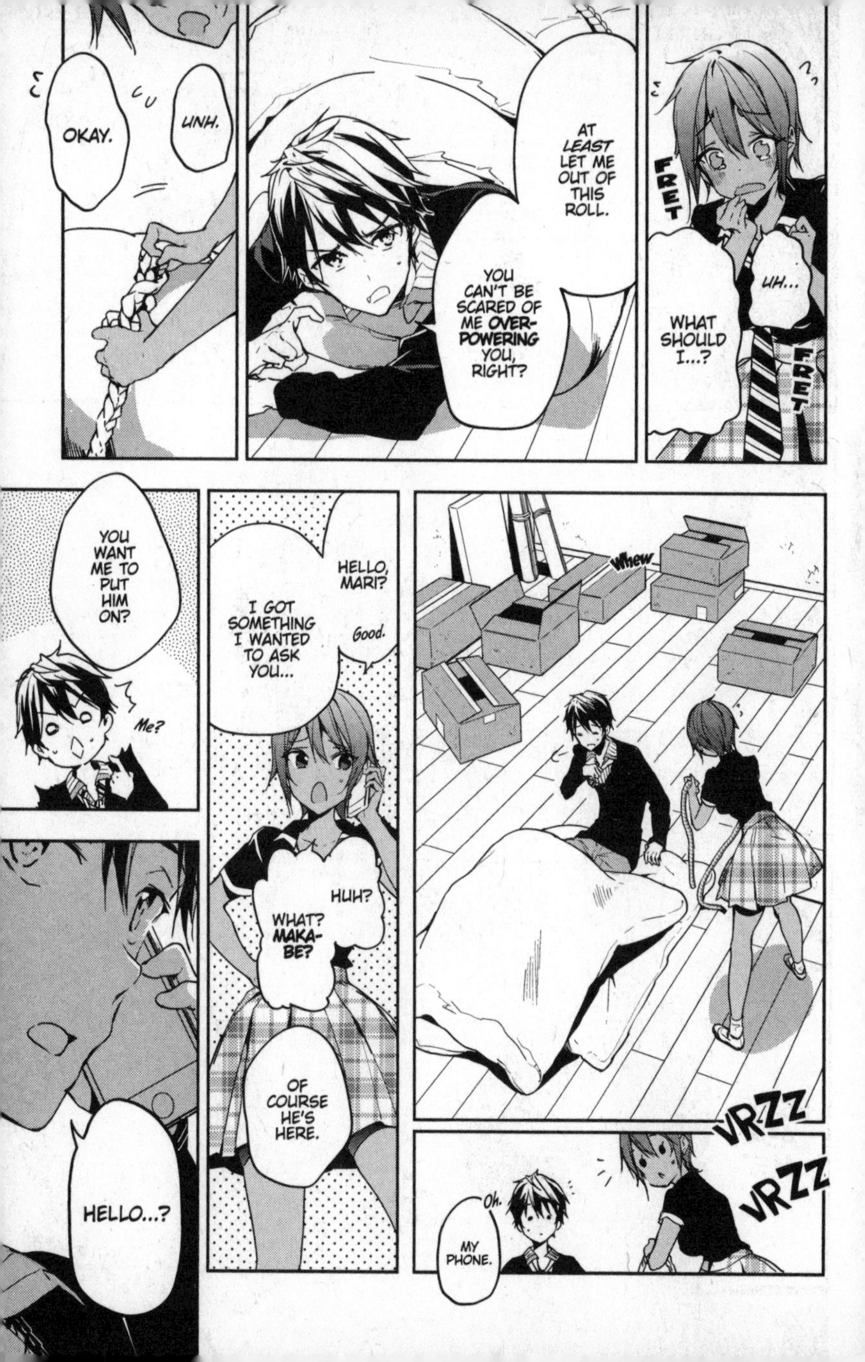
FRET
UH...
WHAT SHOULD I...?
FRET
AT LEAST LET ME OUT OF THIS ROLL.
YOU CAN'T BE SCARED OF ME OVER-POWERING YOU, RIGHT?
UNH.
OKAY.
Whew
VRZZ
VRZZ
Oh.
MY PHONE.
HELLO, MARI?
I GOT SOMETHING I WANTED TO ASK YOU...
Good.
HUH?
WHAT? MAKA-BE?
OF COURSE HE'S HERE.
YOU WANT ME TO PUT HIM ON?
Me?
HELLO...?

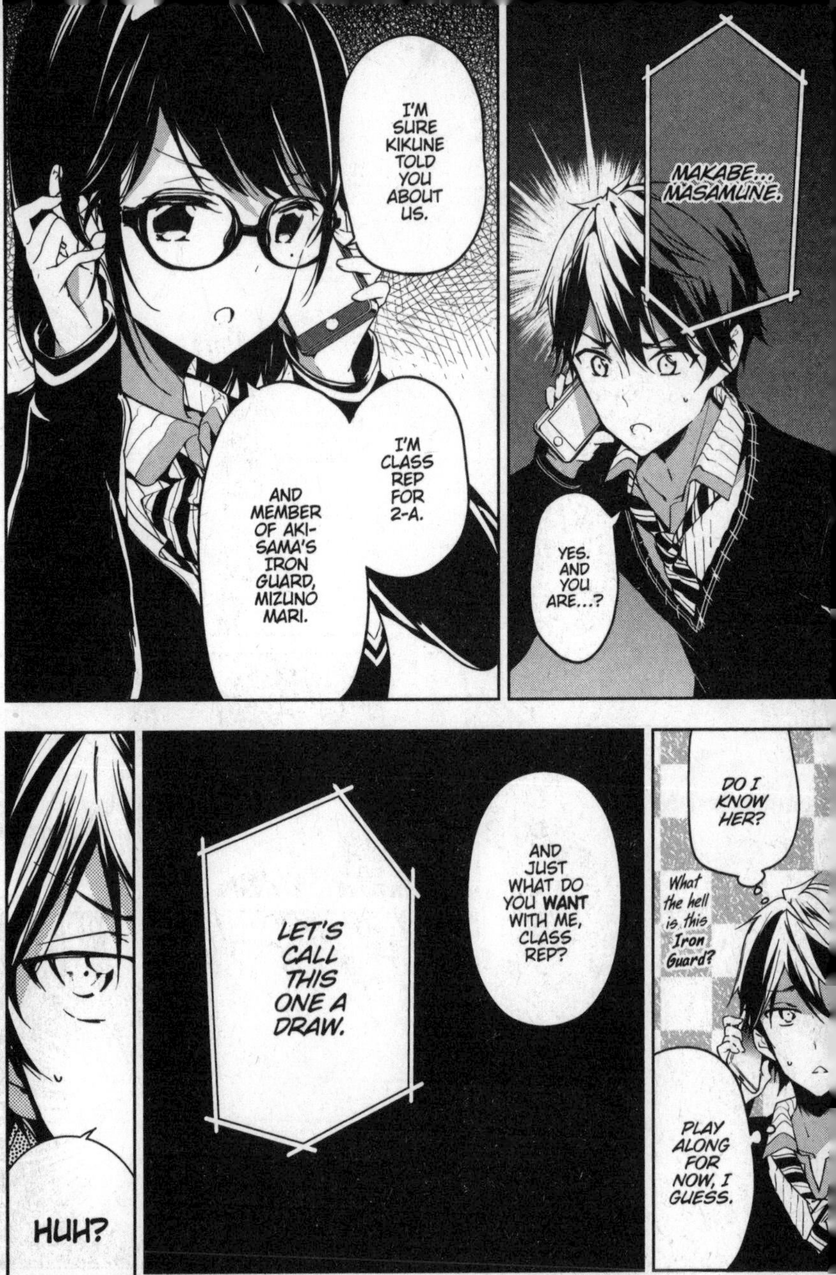
MAKABE... MASAMUNE.
YES. AND YOU ARE...?
I'M SURE KIKUNE TOLD YOU ABOUT US.
I'M CLASS REP FOR 2-A.
AND MEMBER OF AKI-SAMA'S IRON GUARD, MIZUNO MARI.
DO I KNOW HER?
What the hell is this Iron Guard?
PLAY ALONG FOR NOW, I GUESS.
AND JUST WHAT DO YOU WANT WITH ME, CLASS REP?
LET'S CALL THIS ONE A DRAW.
HUH?

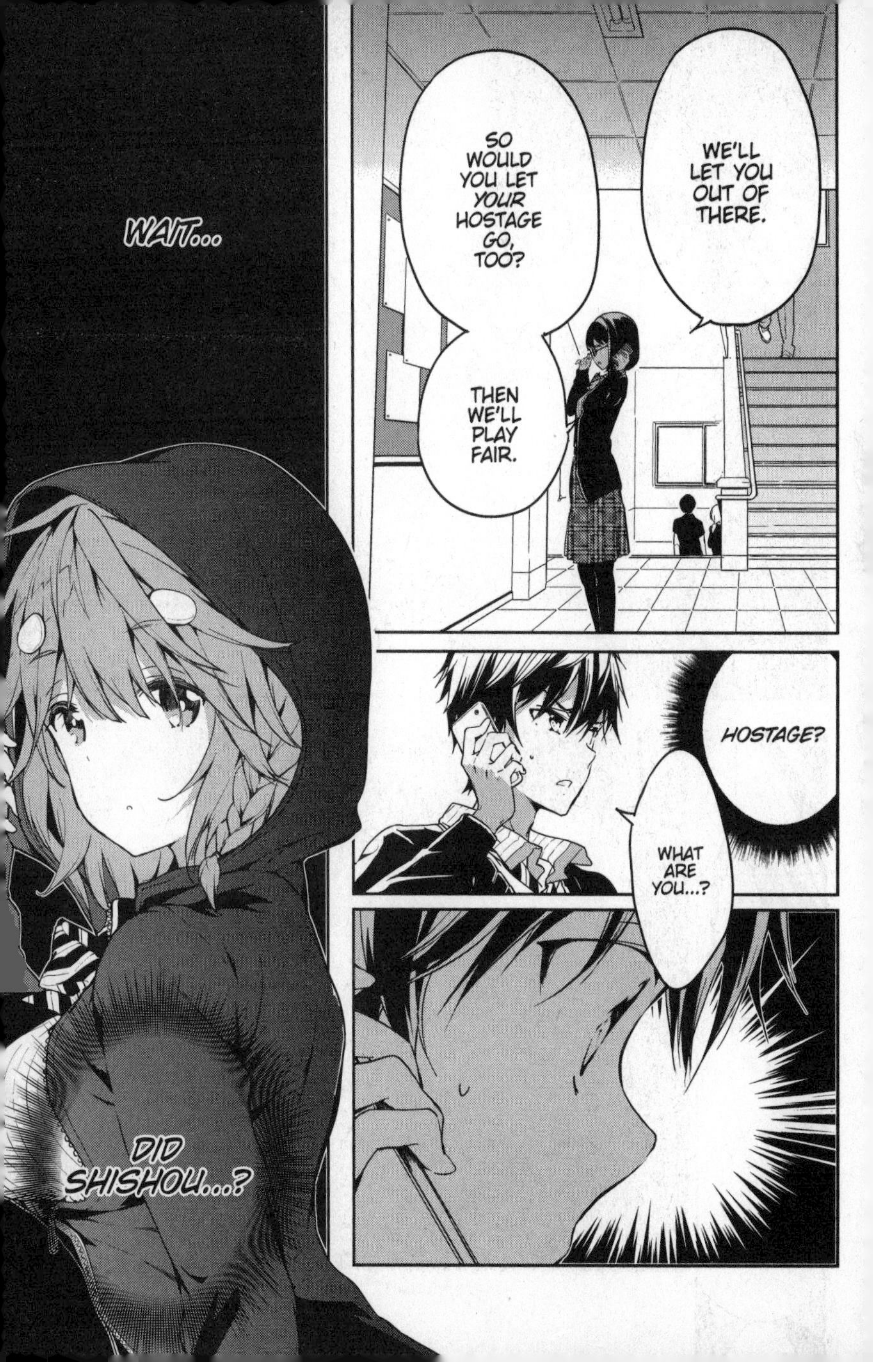
WE'LL LET YOU OUT OF THERE.
SO WOULD YOU LET *YOUR* HOSTAGE GO, TOO?
THEN WE'LL PLAY FAIR.
HOSTAGE?
WHAT ARE YOU...?
WAIT...
DID SHISHOU...?

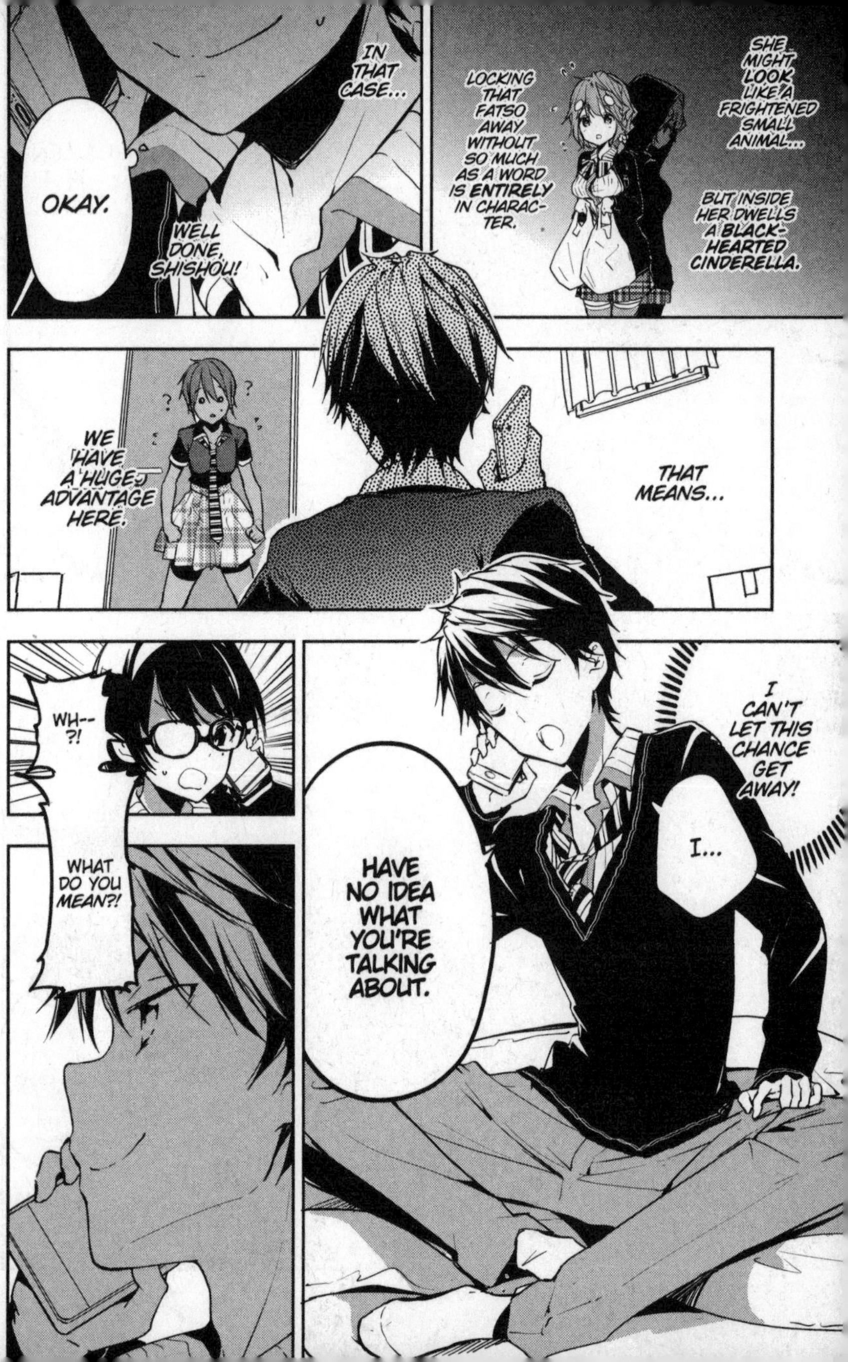
SHE MIGHT LOOK LIKE A FRIGHTENED SMALL ANIMAL...
BUT INSIDE HER DWELLS A BLACK-HEARTED CINDERELLA.
LOCKING THAT FATSO AWAY WITHOUT SO MUCH AS A WORD IS ENTIRELY IN CHARACTER.
IN THAT CASE...
OKAY.
WELL DONE, SHISHOU!
THAT MEANS...
WE HAVE A HUGE ADVANTAGE HERE.
I CAN'T LET THIS CHANCE GET AWAY!
I...
HAVE NO IDEA WHAT YOU'RE TALKING ABOUT.
WH--?!
WHAT DO YOU MEAN?!

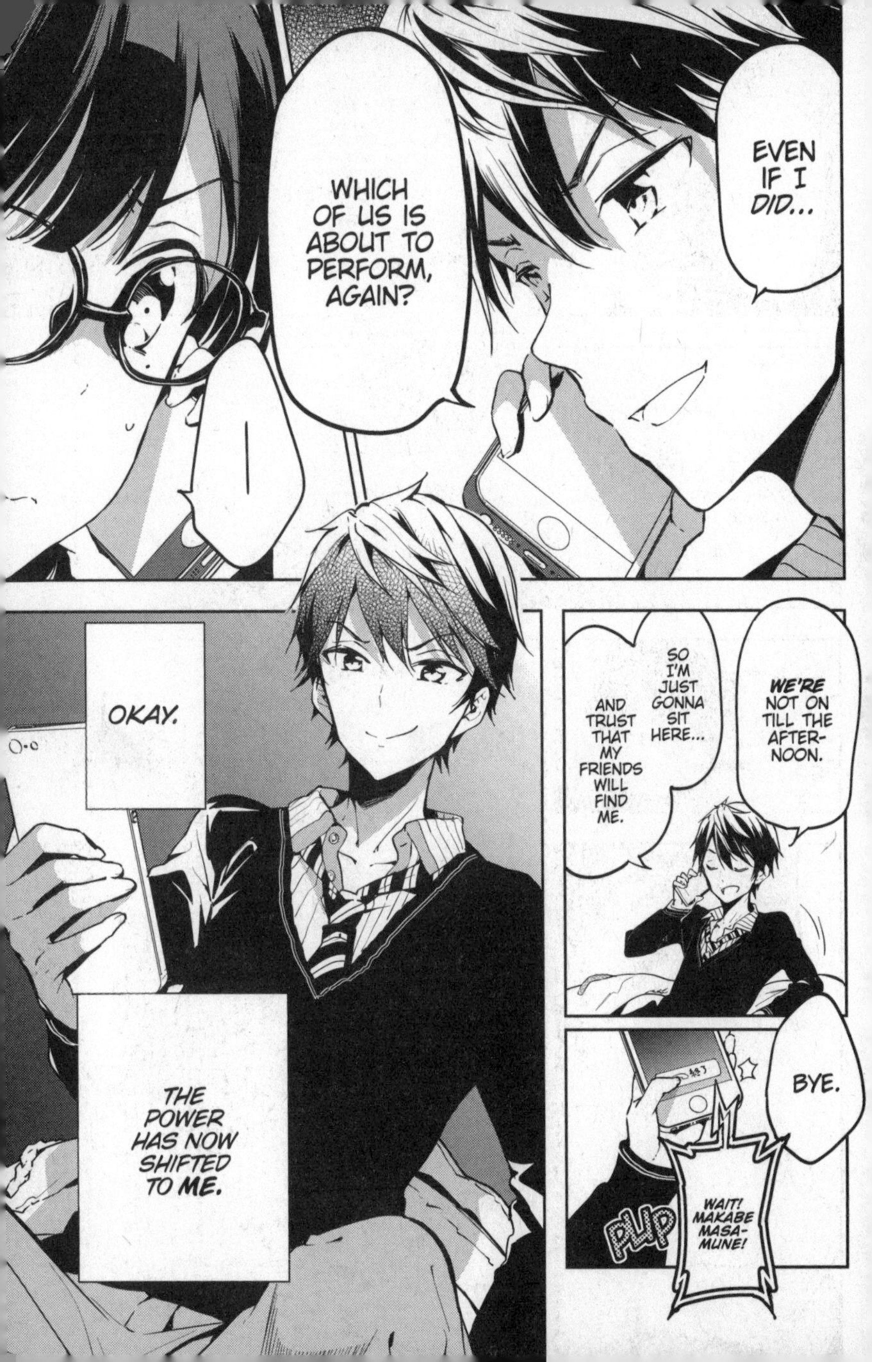
EVEN IF I DID...
WHICH OF US IS ABOUT TO PERFORM, AGAIN?
WE'RE NOT ON TILL THE AFTER-NOON.
SO I'M JUST GONNA SIT HERE...
AND TRUST THAT MY FRIENDS WILL FIND ME.
BYE.
WAIT! MAKABE MASA-MUNE!
PLIP
OKAY.
THE POWER HAS NOW SHIFTED TO ME.

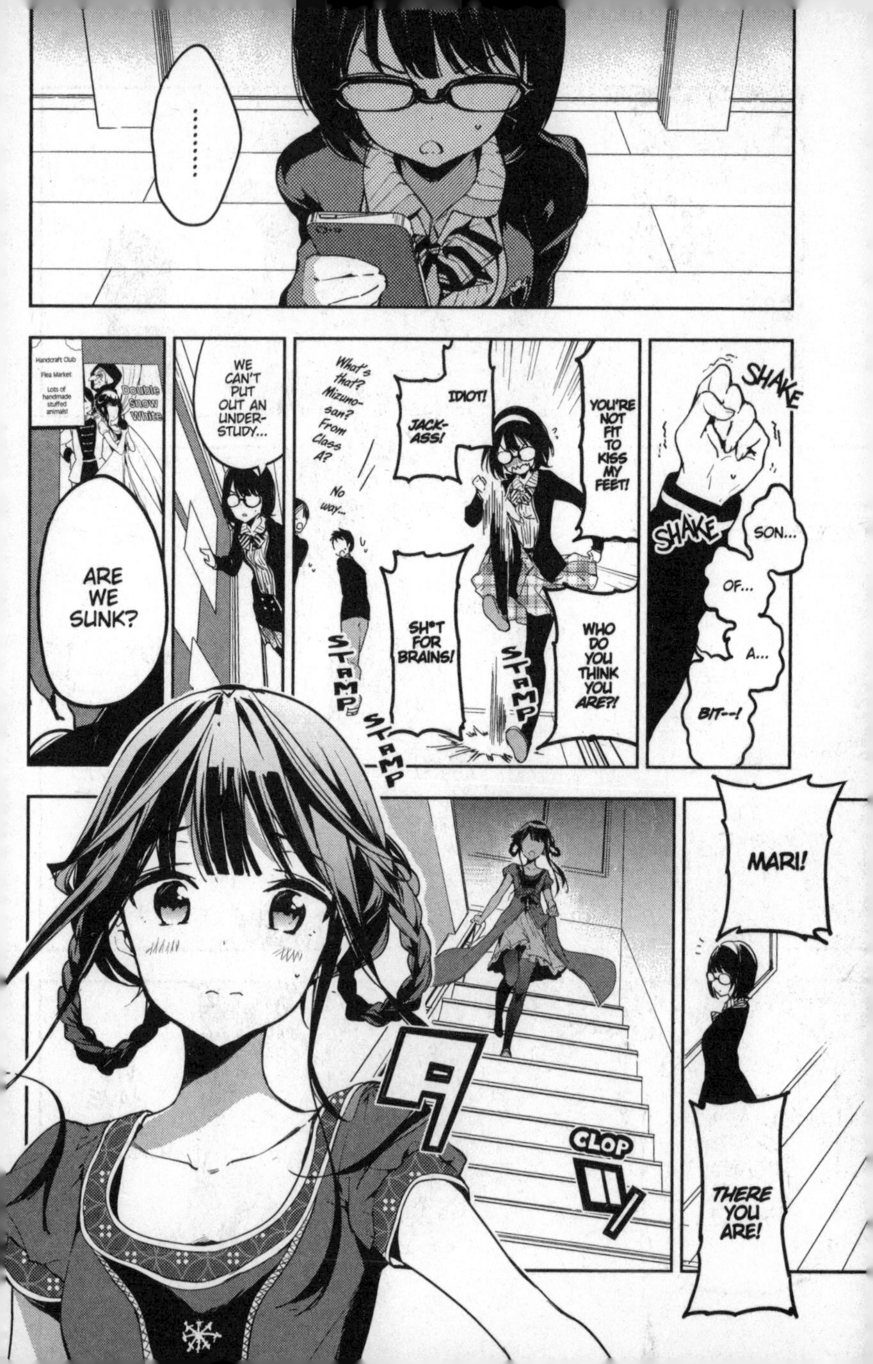
......
SHAKE
SHAKE
SON...
OF...
A...
BIT--!
YOU'RE NOT FIT TO KISS MY FEET!
IDIOT!
JACK-ASS!
What's that? Mizuno-san? From Class A?
No way...
WHO DO YOU THINK YOU ARE?!
SH*T FOR BRAINS!
STAMP
STAMP
STAMP
WE CAN'T PUT OUT AN UNDER-STUDY...
Handcraft Club
Flea Market
Lots of handmade stuffed animals!
Double Snow White
ARE WE SUNK?
MARI!
THERE YOU ARE!
CLOP

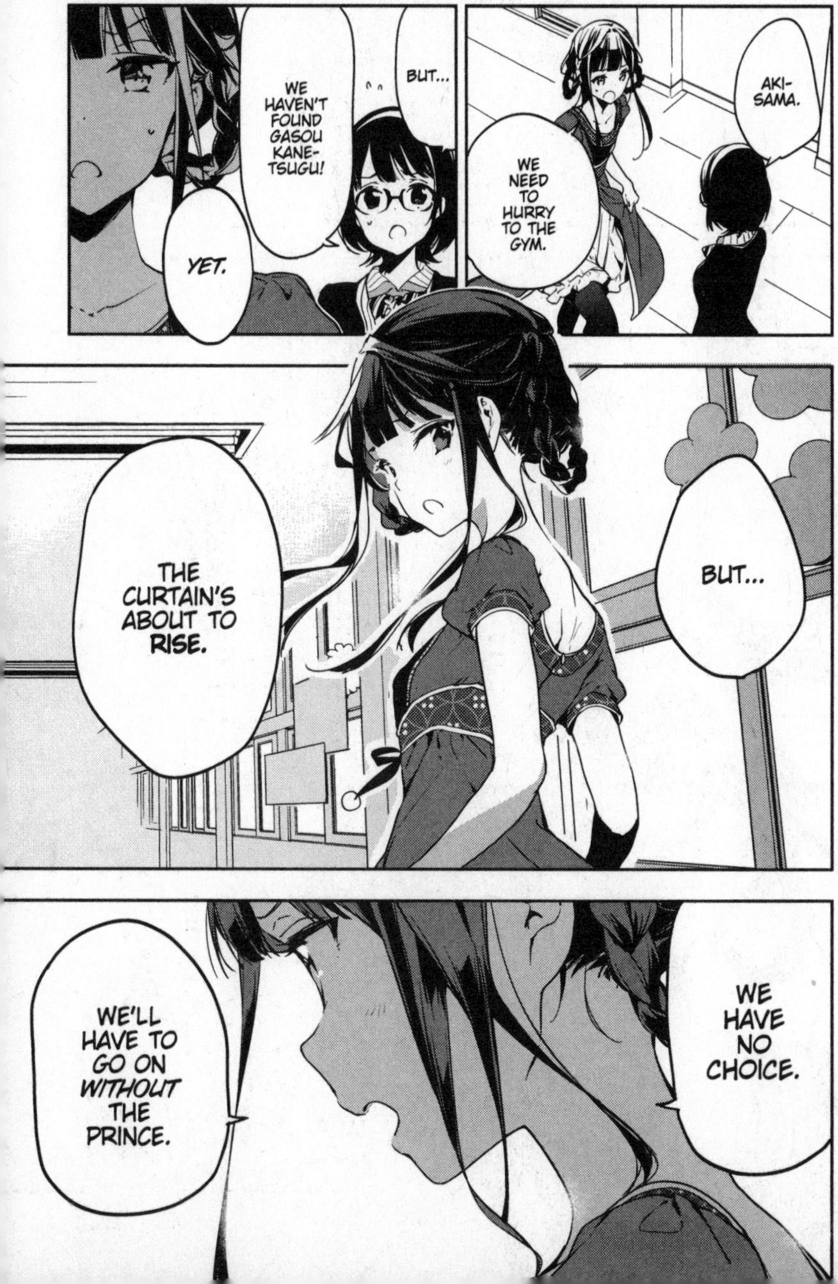
AKI-SAMA.
WE NEED TO HURRY TO THE GYM.
BUT...
WE HAVEN'T FOUND GASOU KANE-TSUGU!
YET.
BUT...
THE CURTAIN'S ABOUT TO RISE.
WE HAVE NO CHOICE.
WE'LL HAVE TO GO ON *WITHOUT* THE PRINCE.

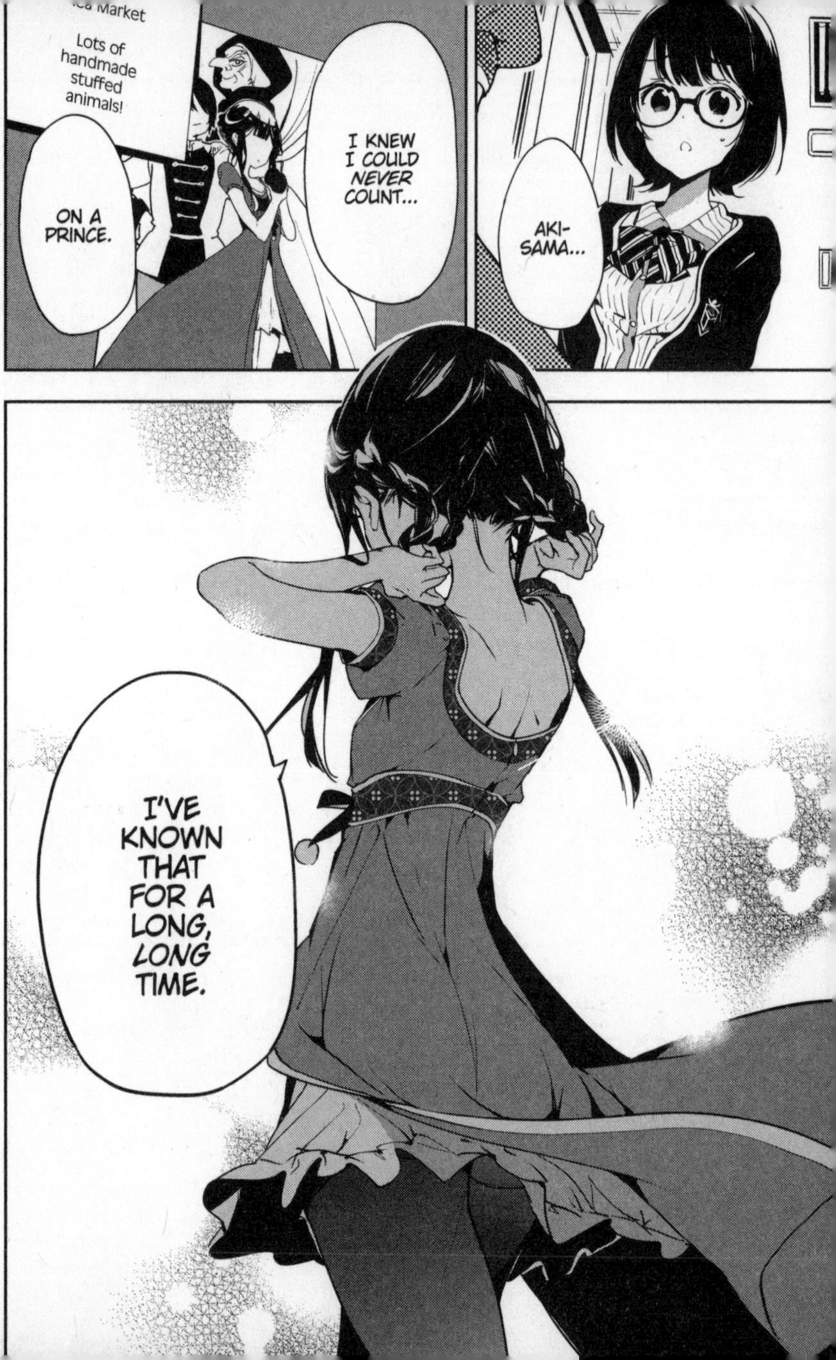
AKI-SAMA...
I KNEW I COULD *NEVER* COUNT...
Market
Lots of handmade stuffed animals!
ON A PRINCE.
I'VE KNOWN THAT FOR A LONG, *LONG* TIME.

Did you see that?

I did...

6

Masamune-kun's
REVENGE
Presented by Hazuki Takeoka & TIV

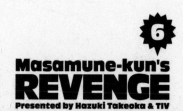

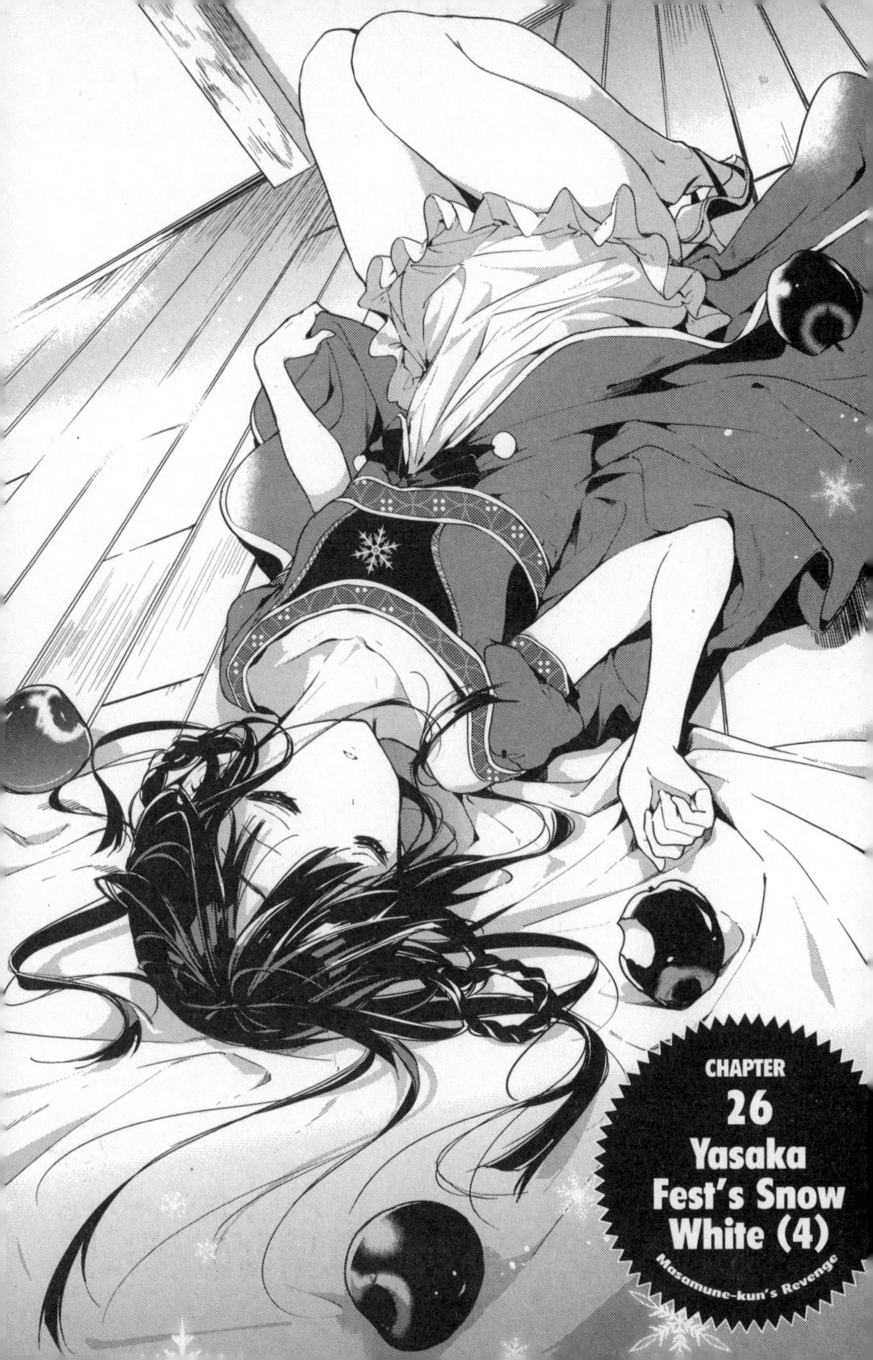
CHAPTER
26
Yasaka Fest's Snow White (4)
Masamune-kun's Revenge

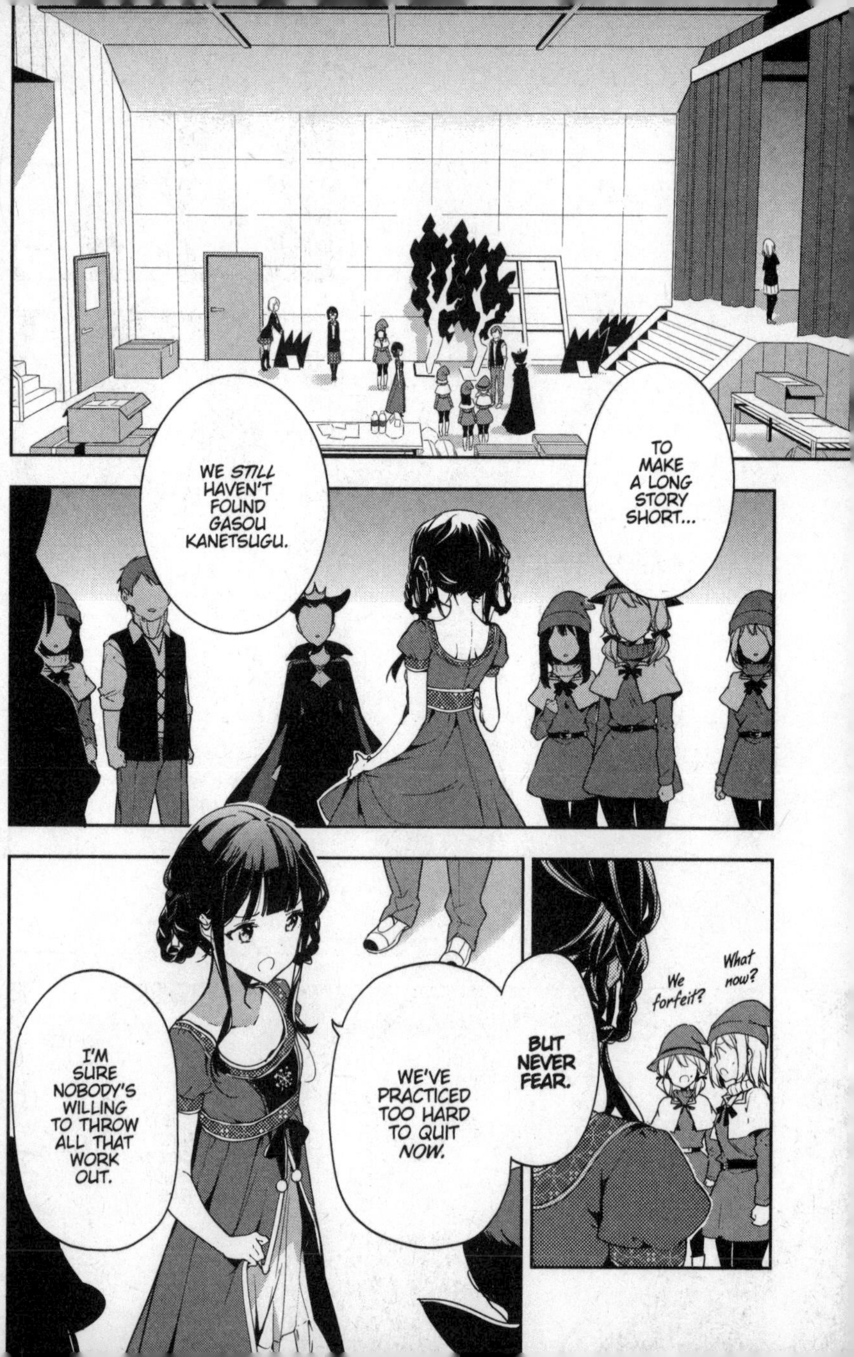
TO MAKE A LONG STORY SHORT...
WE *STILL* HAVEN'T FOUND GASOU KANETSUGU.
What now?
We forfeit?
BUT NEVER FEAR.
WE'VE PRACTICED TOO HARD TO QUIT *NOW*.
I'M SURE NOBODY'S WILLING TO THROW ALL THAT WORK OUT.

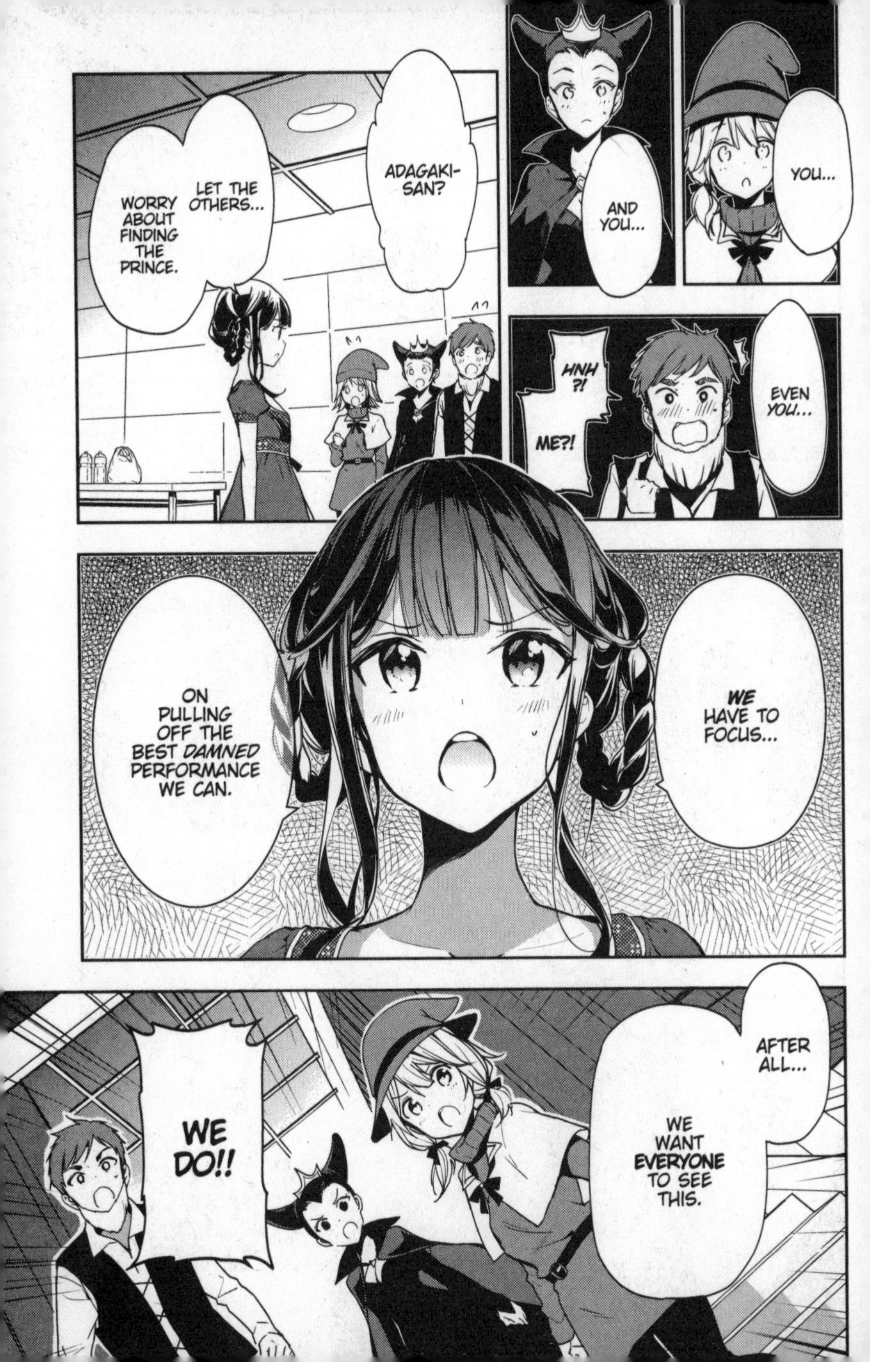
YOU...
AND YOU...
EVEN YOU...
HNH ?! ME?!
ADAGAKI-SAN?
LET THE OTHERS... WORRY ABOUT FINDING THE PRINCE.
WE HAVE TO FOCUS...
ON PULLING OFF THE BEST DAMNED PERFORMANCE WE CAN.
AFTER ALL...
WE WANT EVERYONE TO SEE THIS.
WE DO!!

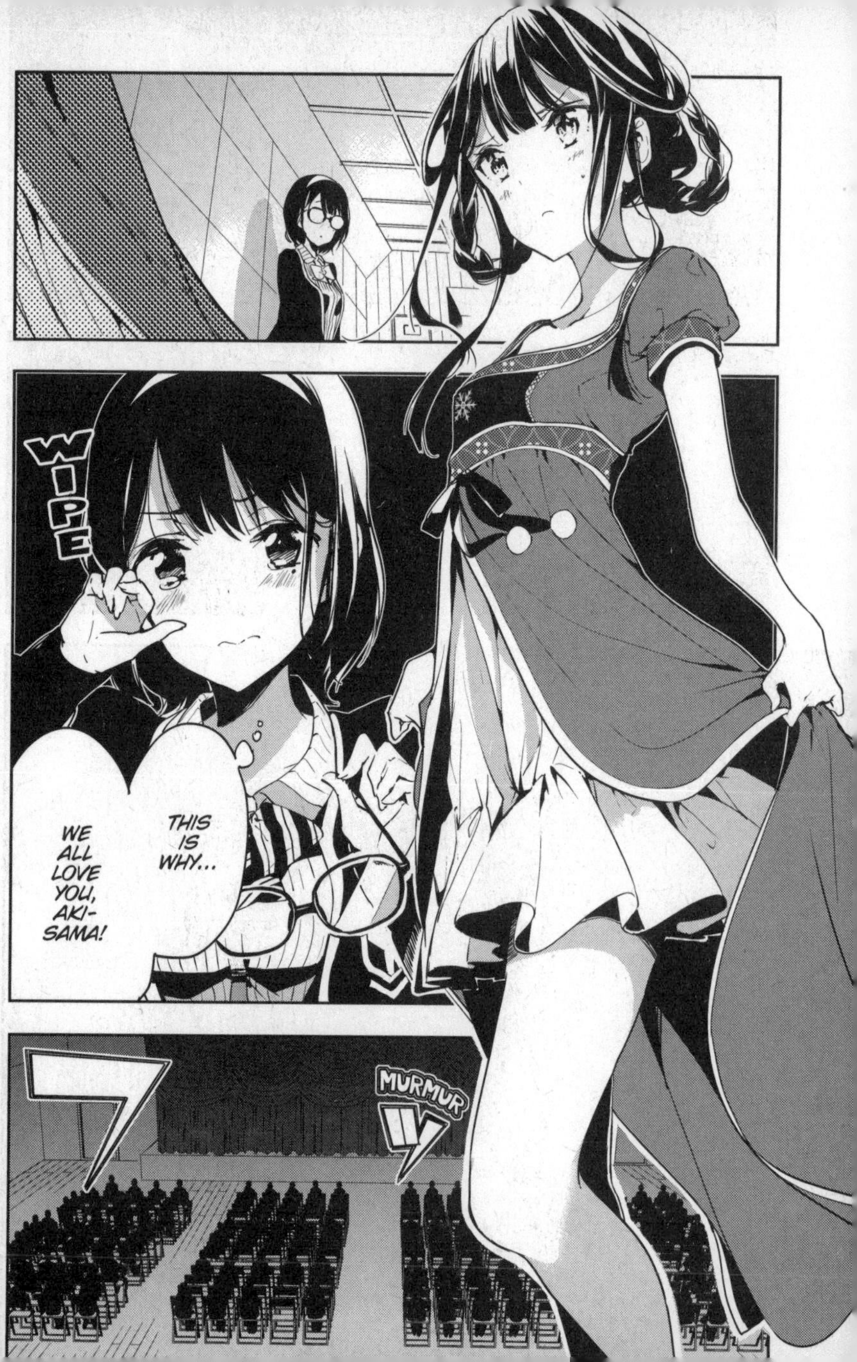
WIPE
THIS IS WHY...
WE ALL LOVE YOU, AKI-SAMA!
MURMUR

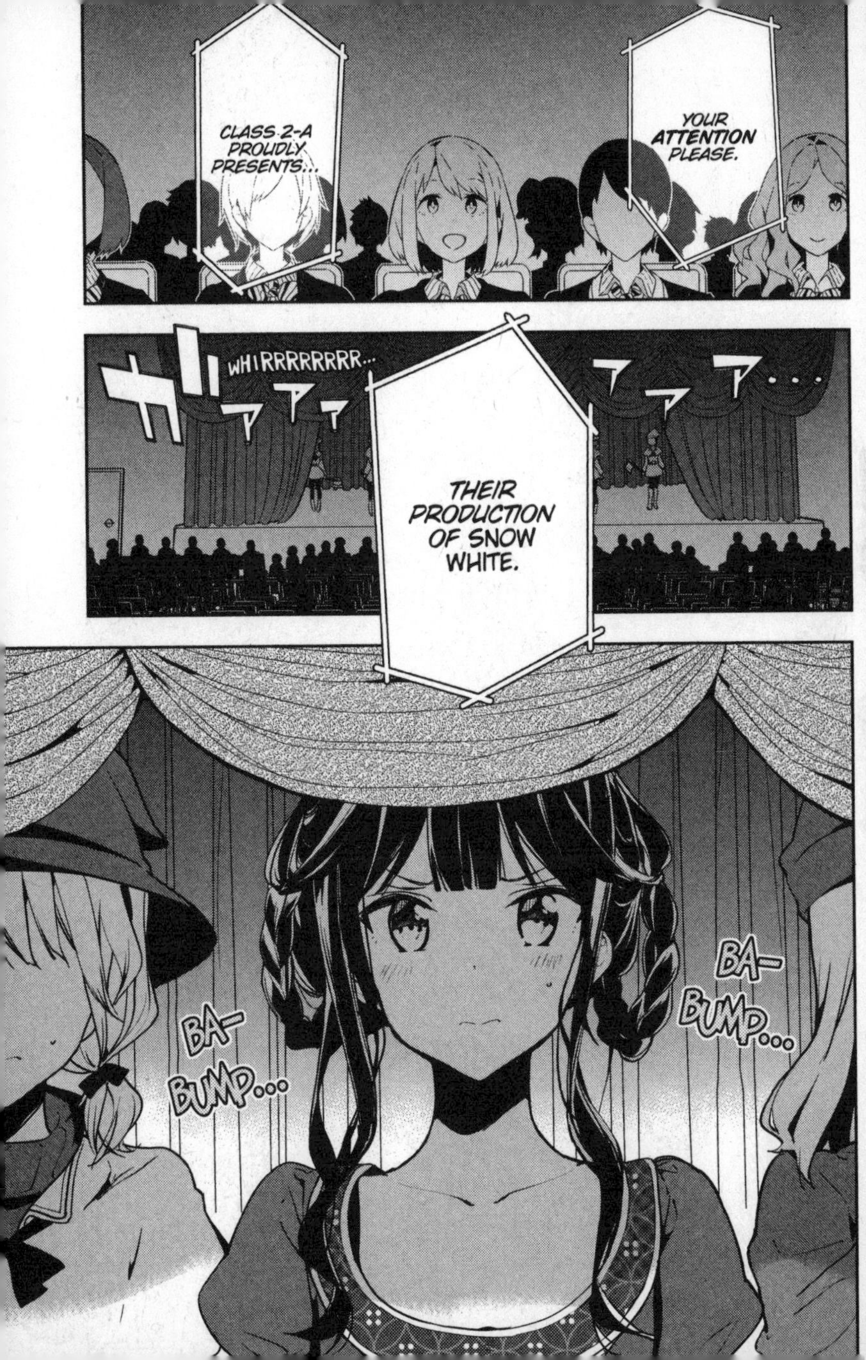
YOUR ATTENTION PLEASE.
CLASS 2-A PROUDLY PRESENTS...
WHIRRRRRRRR...
THEIR PRODUCTION OF SNOW WHITE.
BA-BUMP...
BA-BUMP...

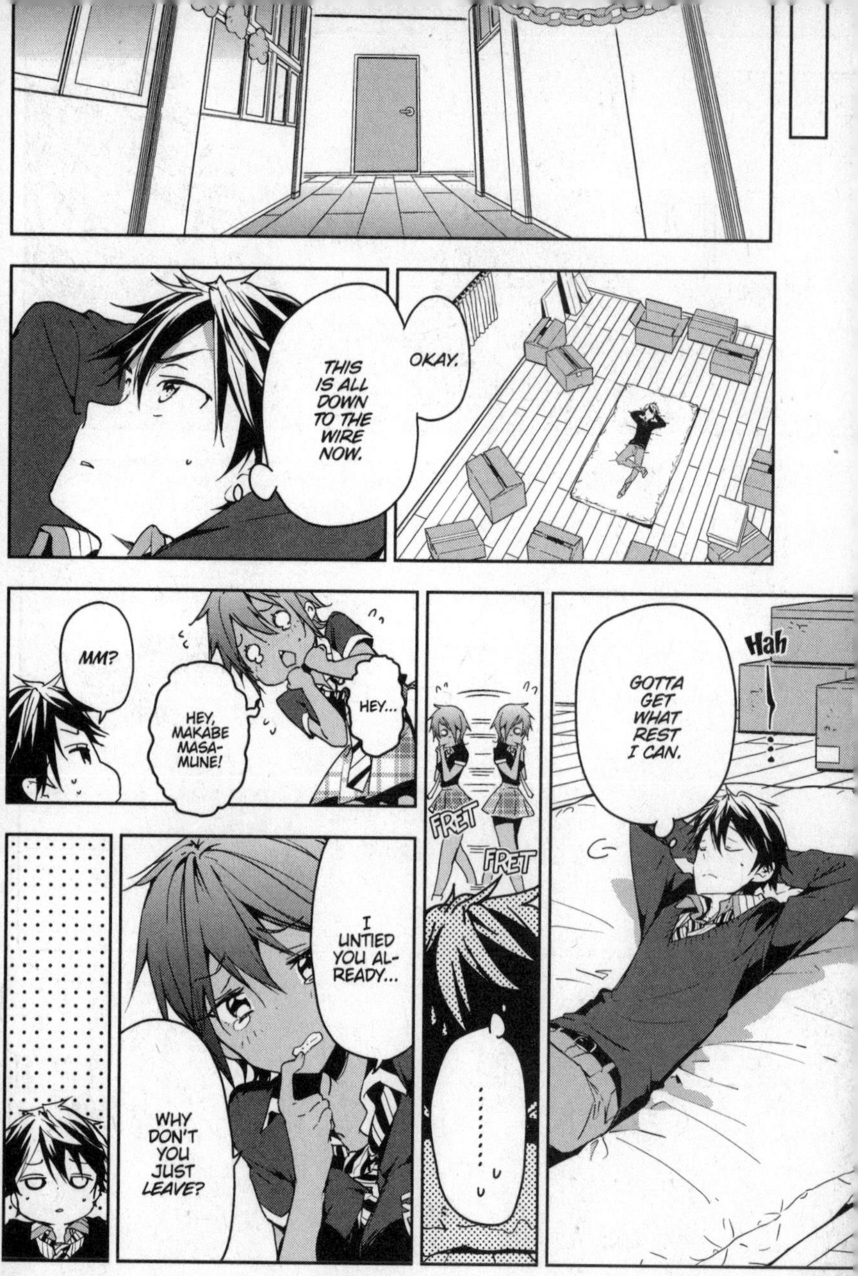
OKAY.
THIS IS ALL DOWN TO THE WIRE NOW.
Hah
GOTTA GET WHAT REST I CAN.
FRET
FRET
......
HEY...
HEY, MAKABE MASA-MUNE!
MM?
I UNTIED YOU AL-READY...
WHY DON'T YOU JUST LEAVE?

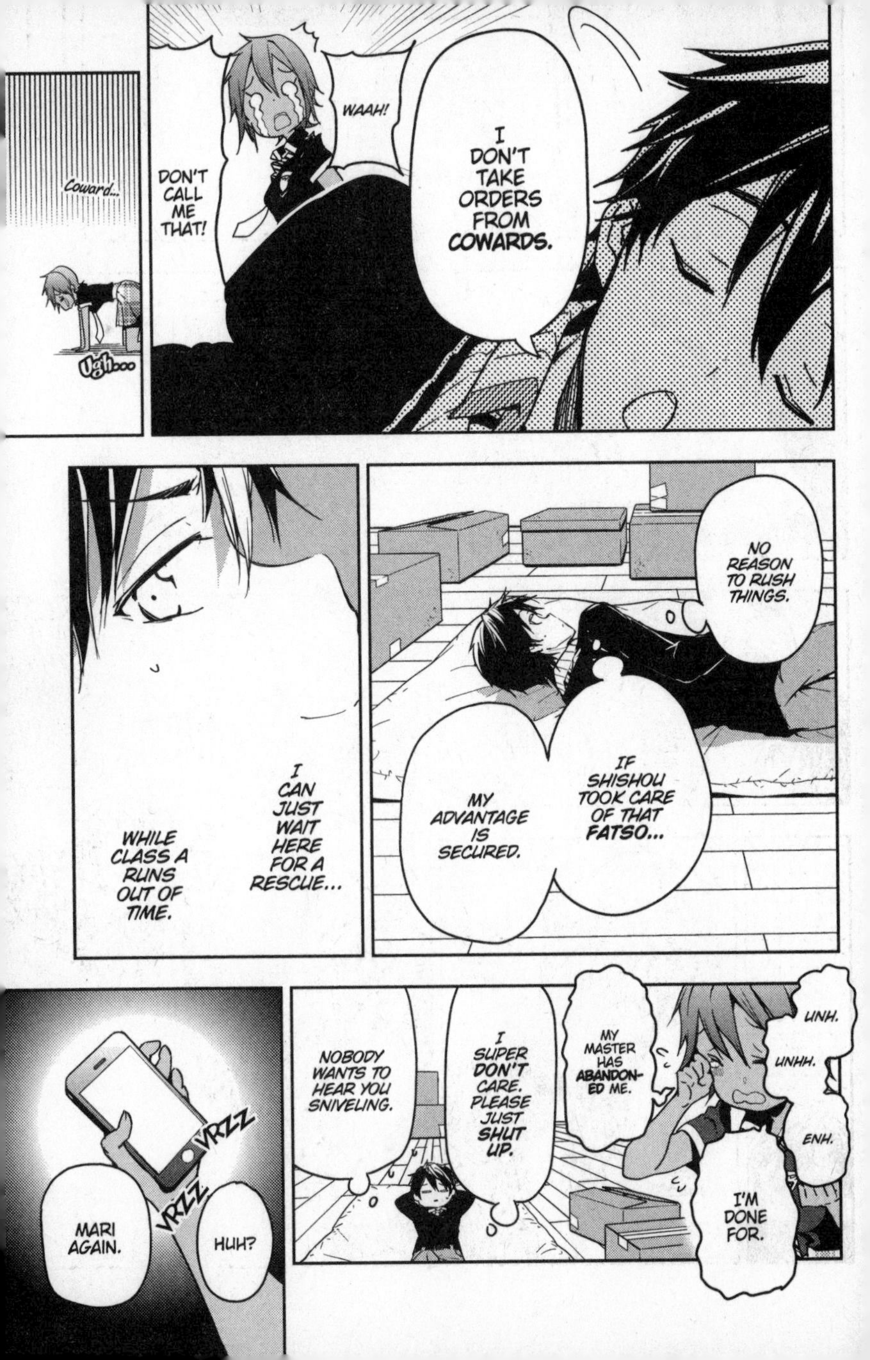
I DON'T TAKE ORDERS FROM COWARDS.
WAAH!
DON'T CALL ME THAT!
Coward...
Ugh...
NO REASON TO RUSH THINGS.
IF SHISHOU TOOK CARE OF THAT FATSO...
MY ADVANTAGE IS SECURED.
I CAN JUST WAIT HERE FOR A RESCUE...
WHILE CLASS A RUNS OUT OF TIME.
UNH.
UNHH.
ENH.
MY MASTER HAS ABANDONED ME.
I'M DONE FOR.
I SUPER DON'T CARE. PLEASE JUST SHUT UP.
NOBODY WANTS TO HEAR YOU SNIVELING.
VRZZZ
VRZZZ
HUH?
MARI AGAIN.

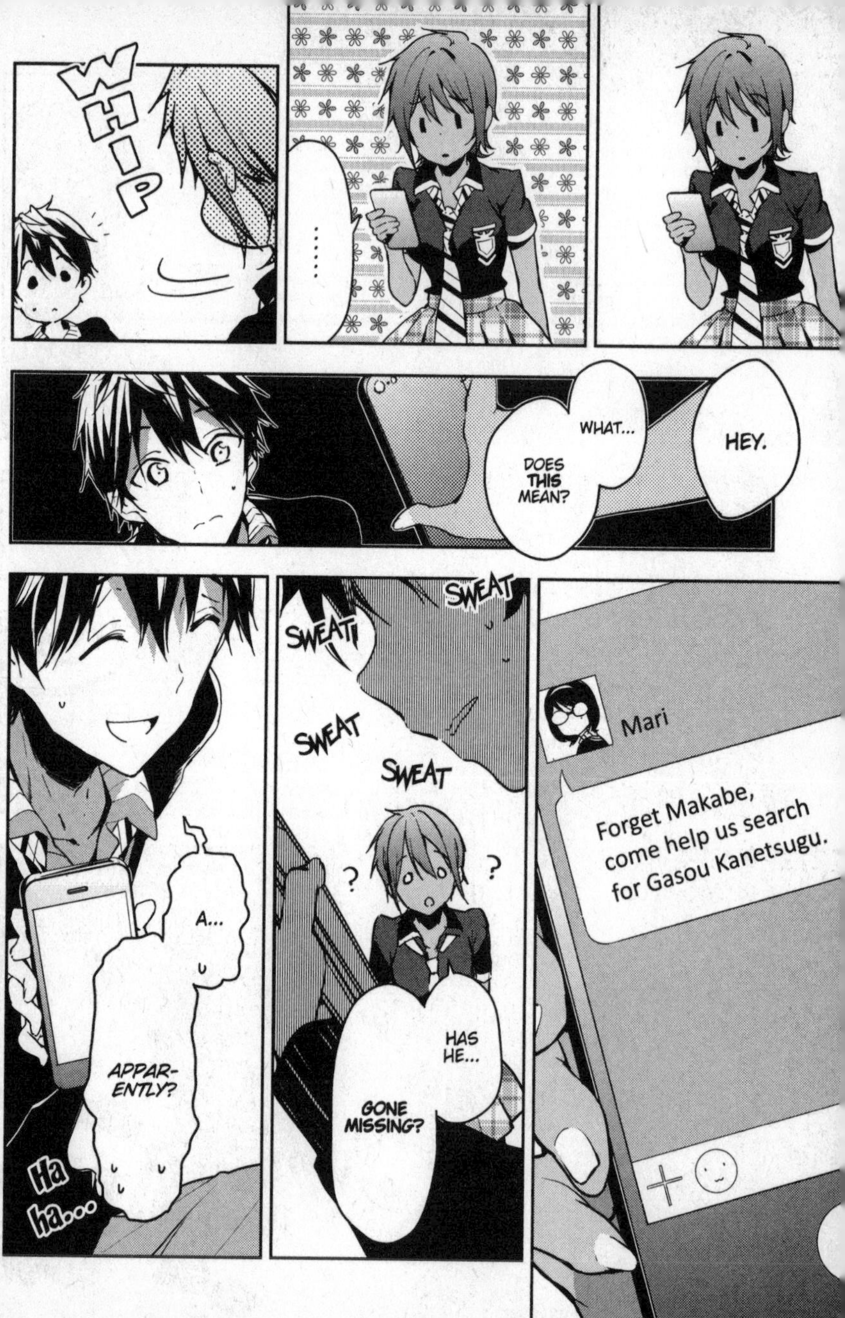
......
WHIP
HEY.
WHAT... DOES THIS MEAN?
Mari
Forget Makabe, come help us search for Gasou Kanetsugu.
SWEAT
SWEAT
SWEAT
SWEAT
? ?
HAS HE... GONE MISSING?
A... U
APPARENTLY?
Ha ha...

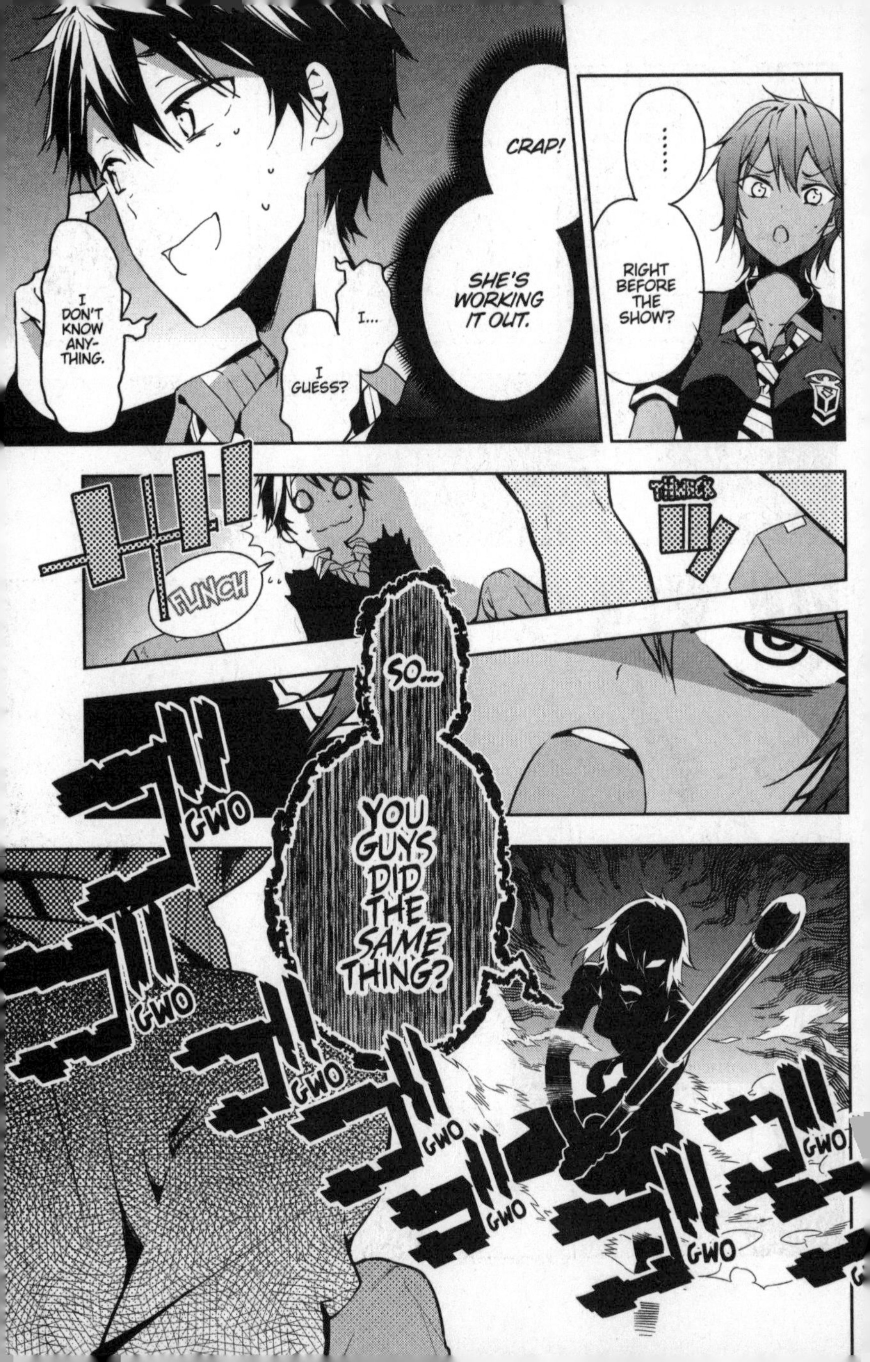
......
RIGHT BEFORE THE SHOW?
CRAP!
SHE'S WORKING IT OUT.
I...
I GUESS?
I DON'T KNOW ANY-THING.
FLINCH
SO...
YOU GUYS DID THE SAME THING?
GWO
GWO
GWO
GWO
GWO
GWO
GWO

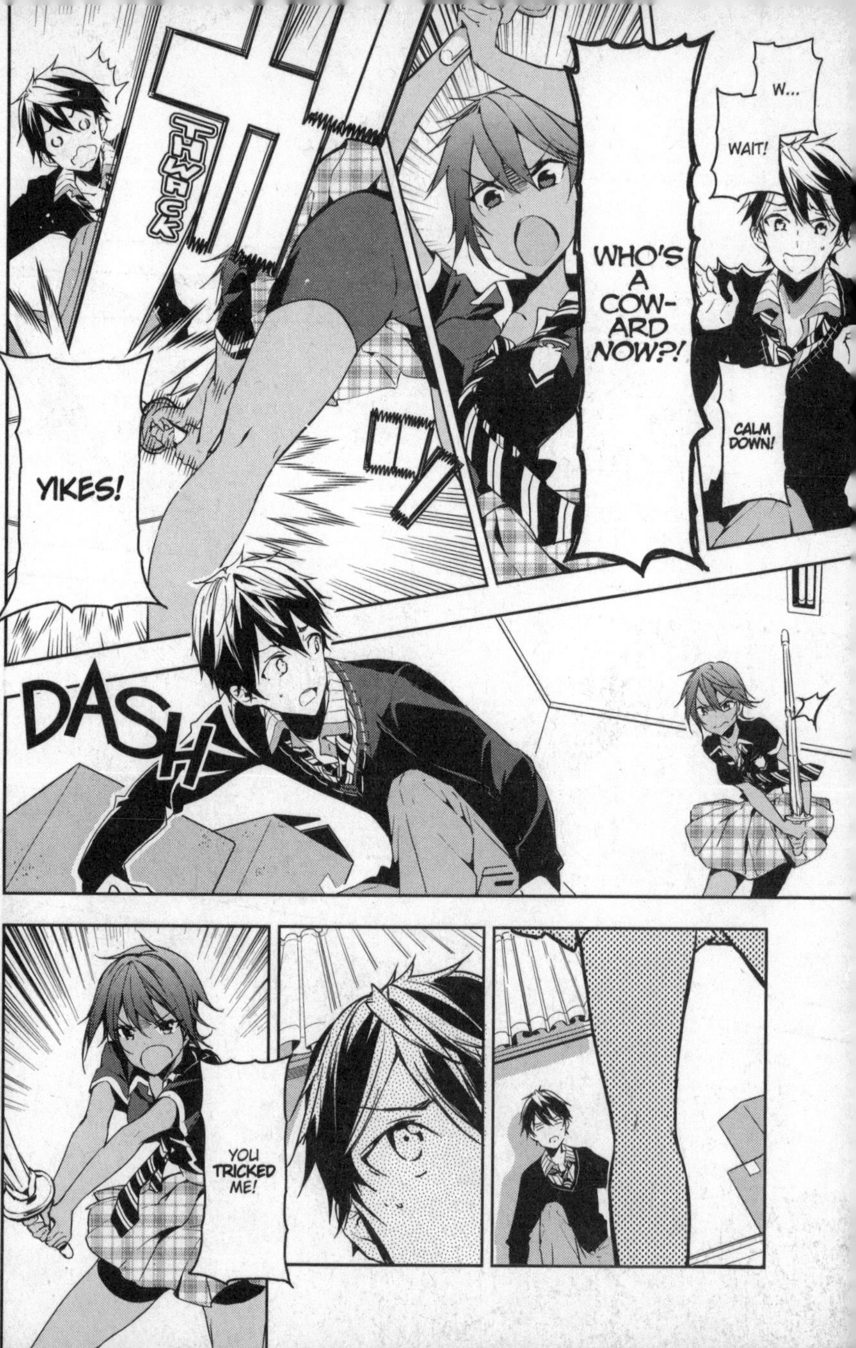
W...
WAIT!
CALM DOWN!
WHO'S A COW- ARD NOW?!
THWACK
YIKES!
DASH
YOU TRICKED ME!

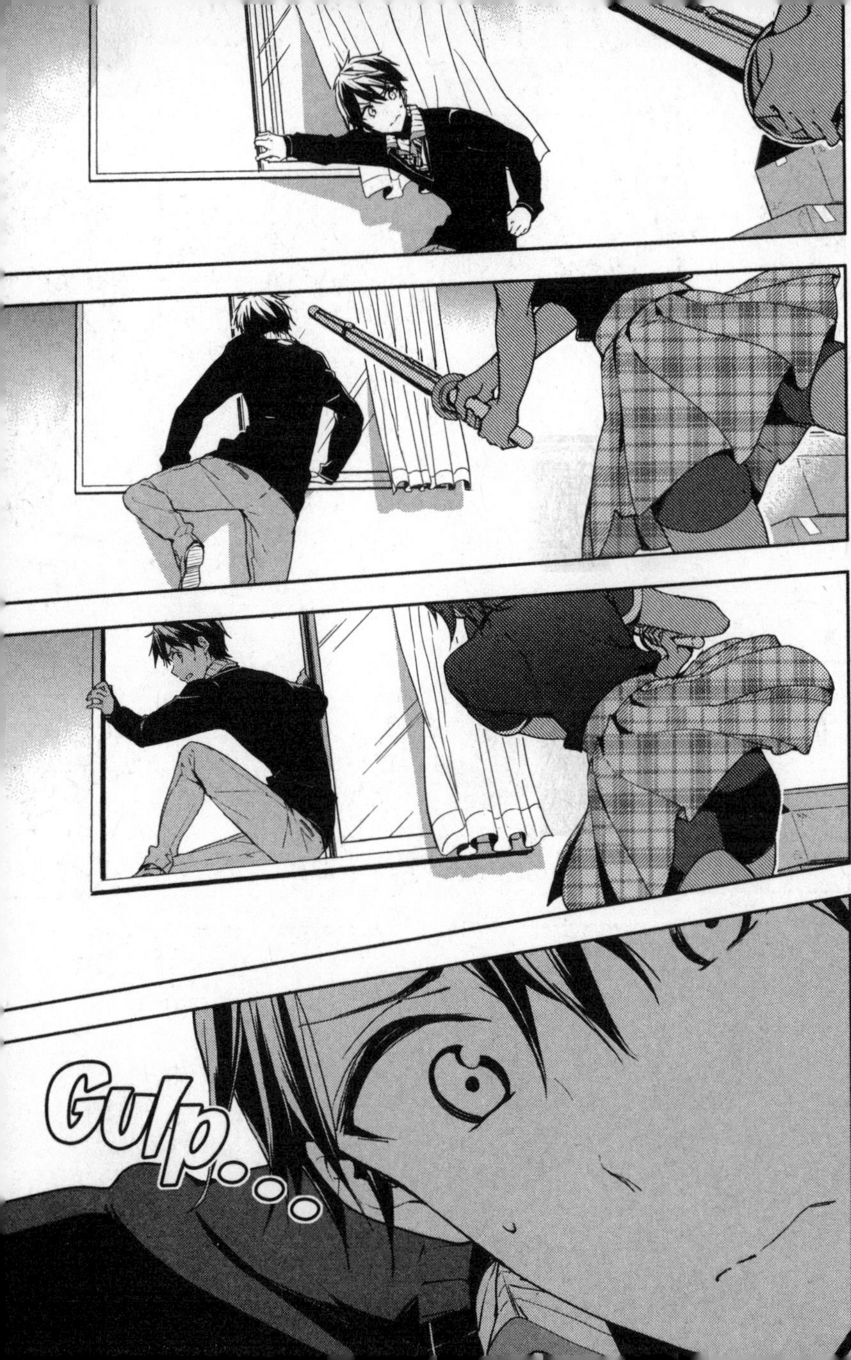
Gulp...

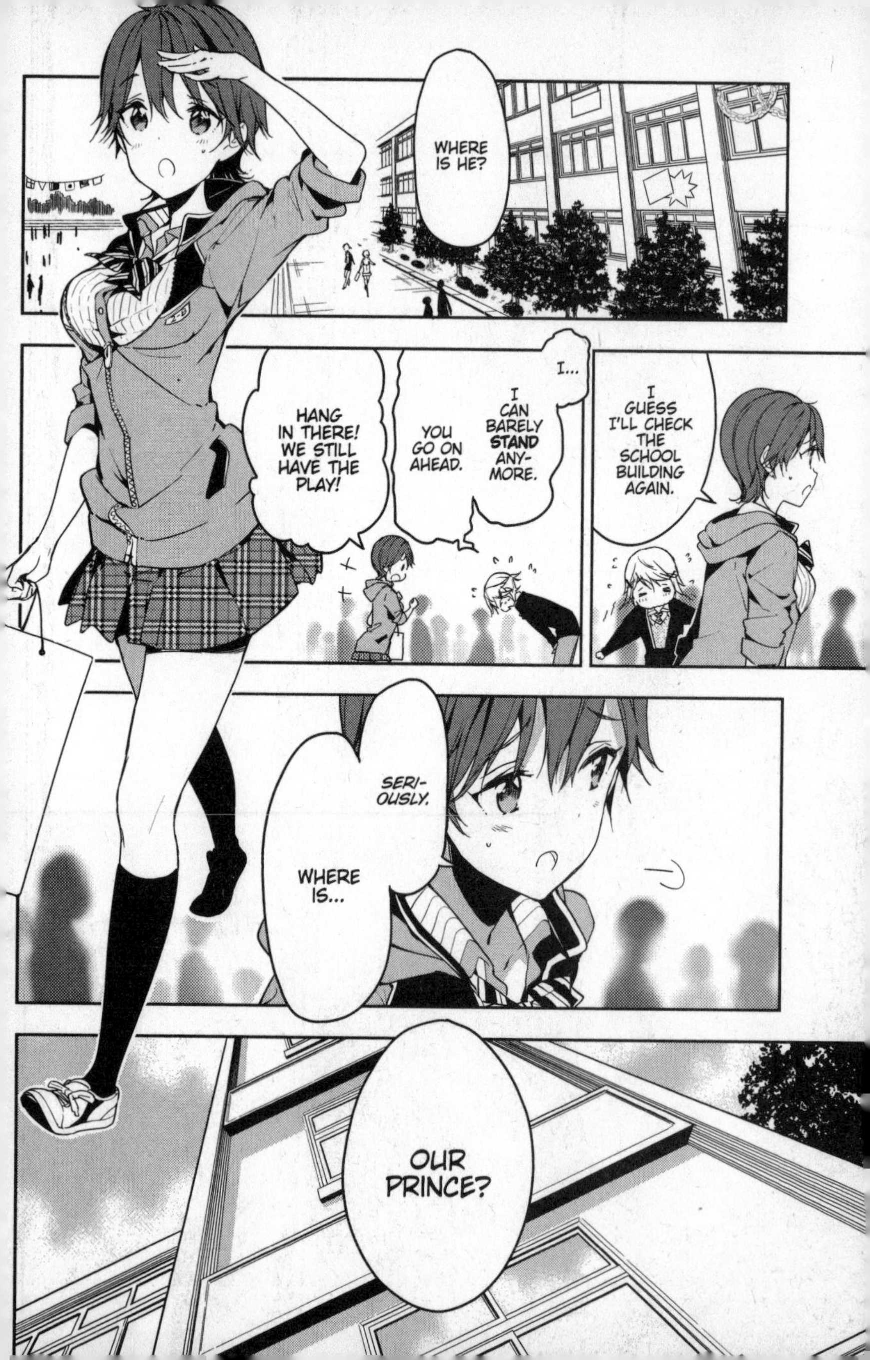
WHERE IS HE?
I GUESS I'LL CHECK THE SCHOOL BUILDING AGAIN.
I...
I CAN BARELY STAND ANYMORE.
YOU GO ON AHEAD.
HANG IN THERE! WE STILL HAVE THE PLAY!
SERI-OUSLY.
WHERE IS...
OUR PRINCE?

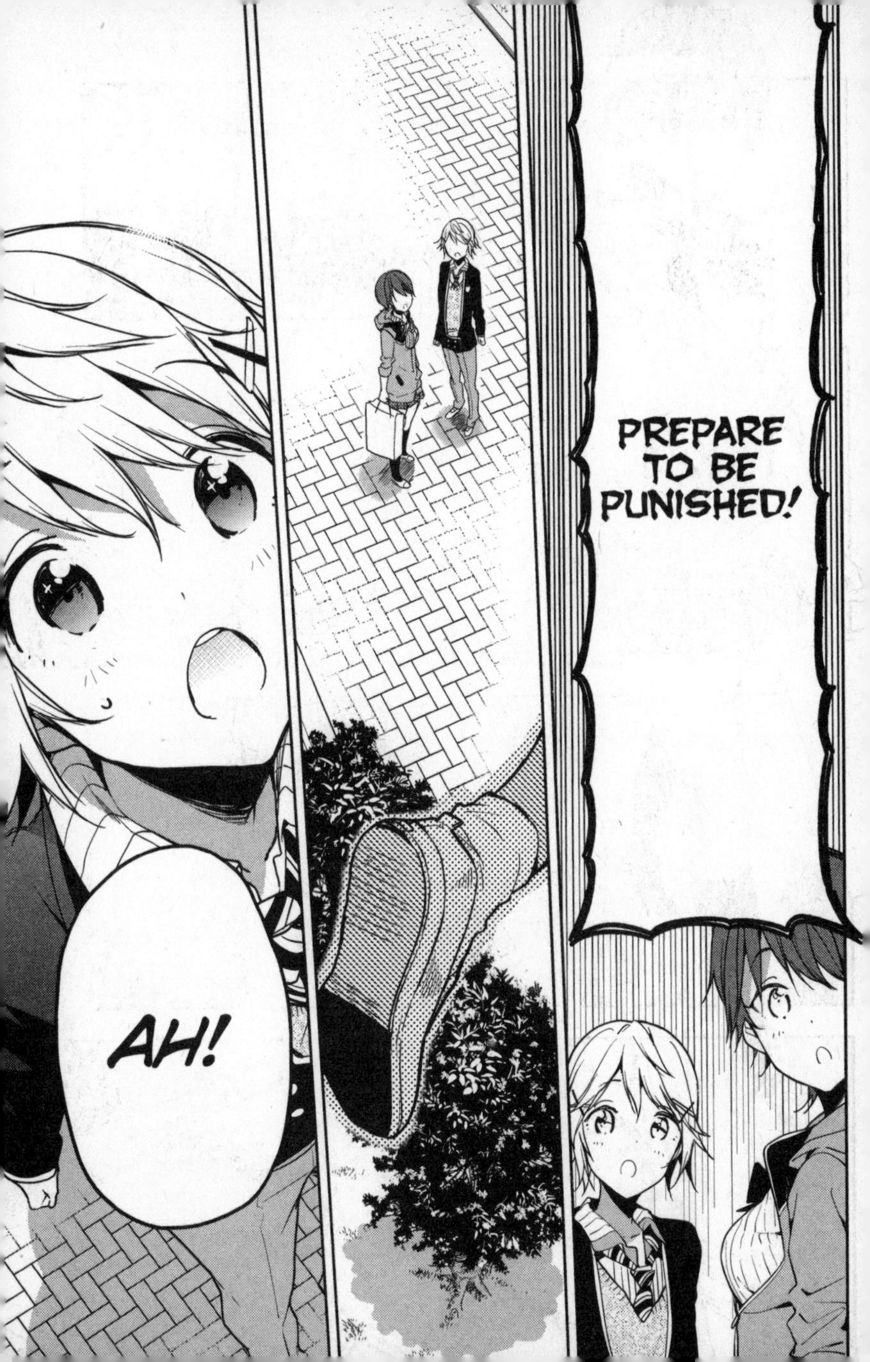
PREPARE TO BE PUNISHED!
AH!

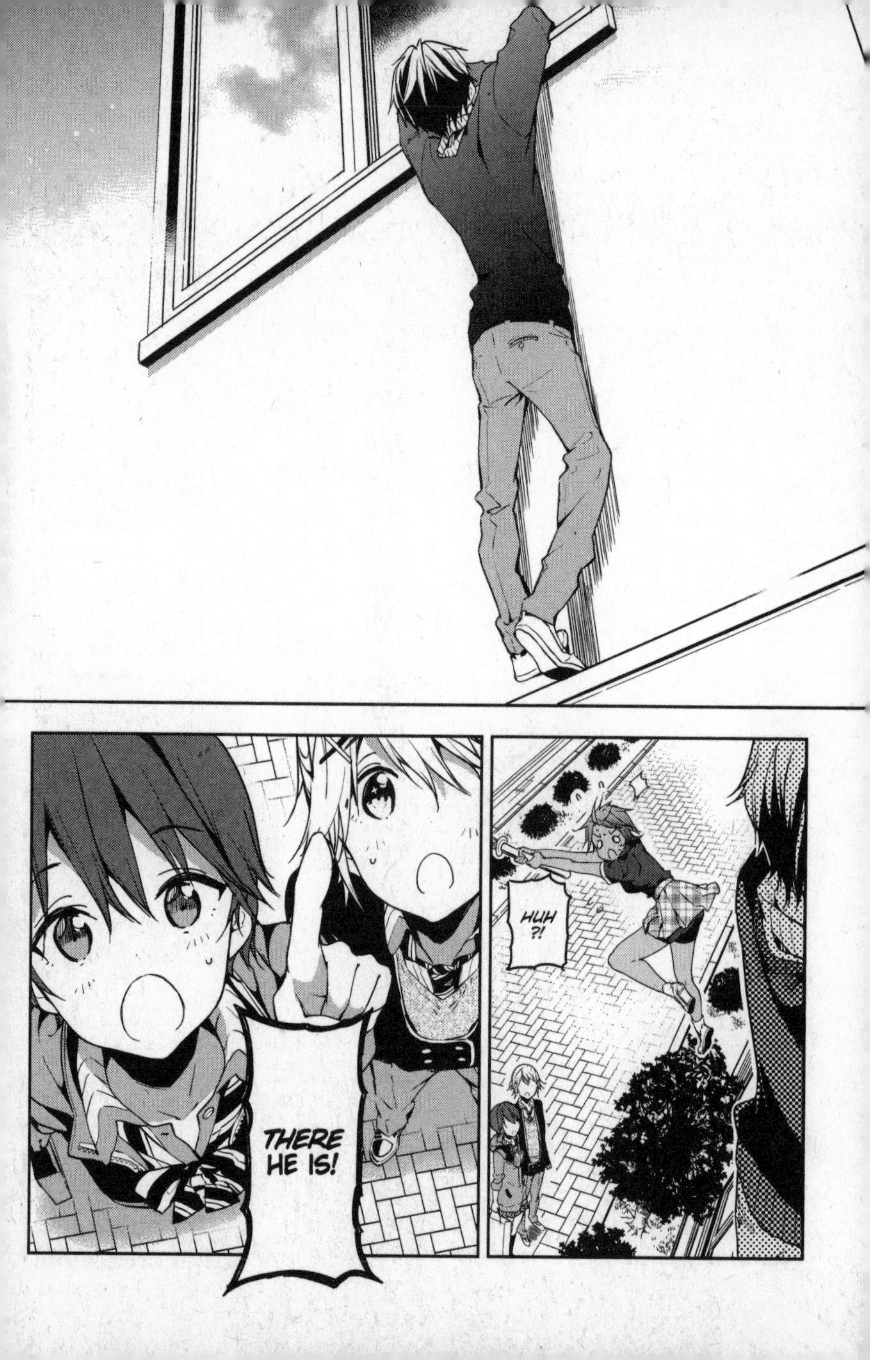
HUH ?!
THERE HE IS!

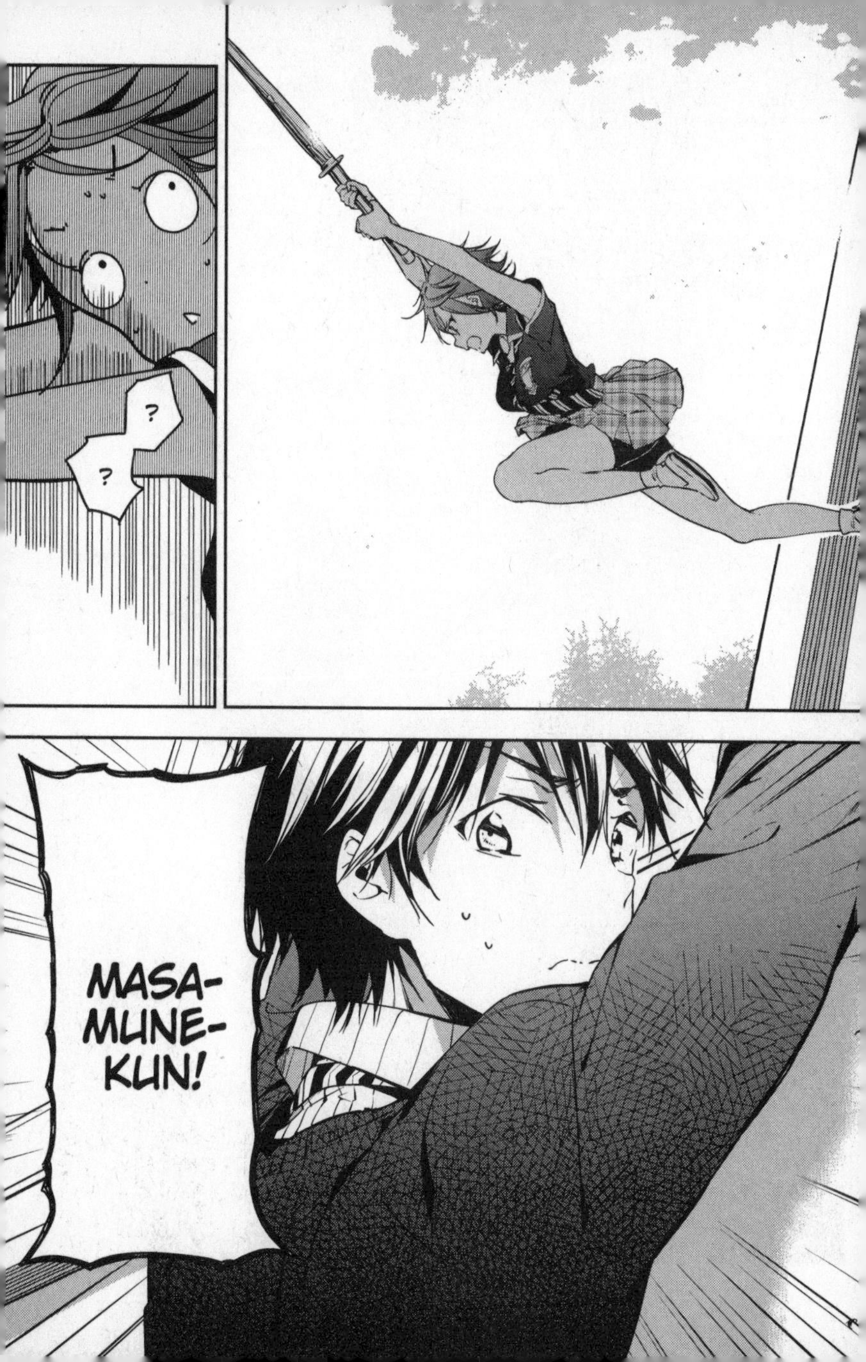
?
?
MASA-MUNE-KUN!

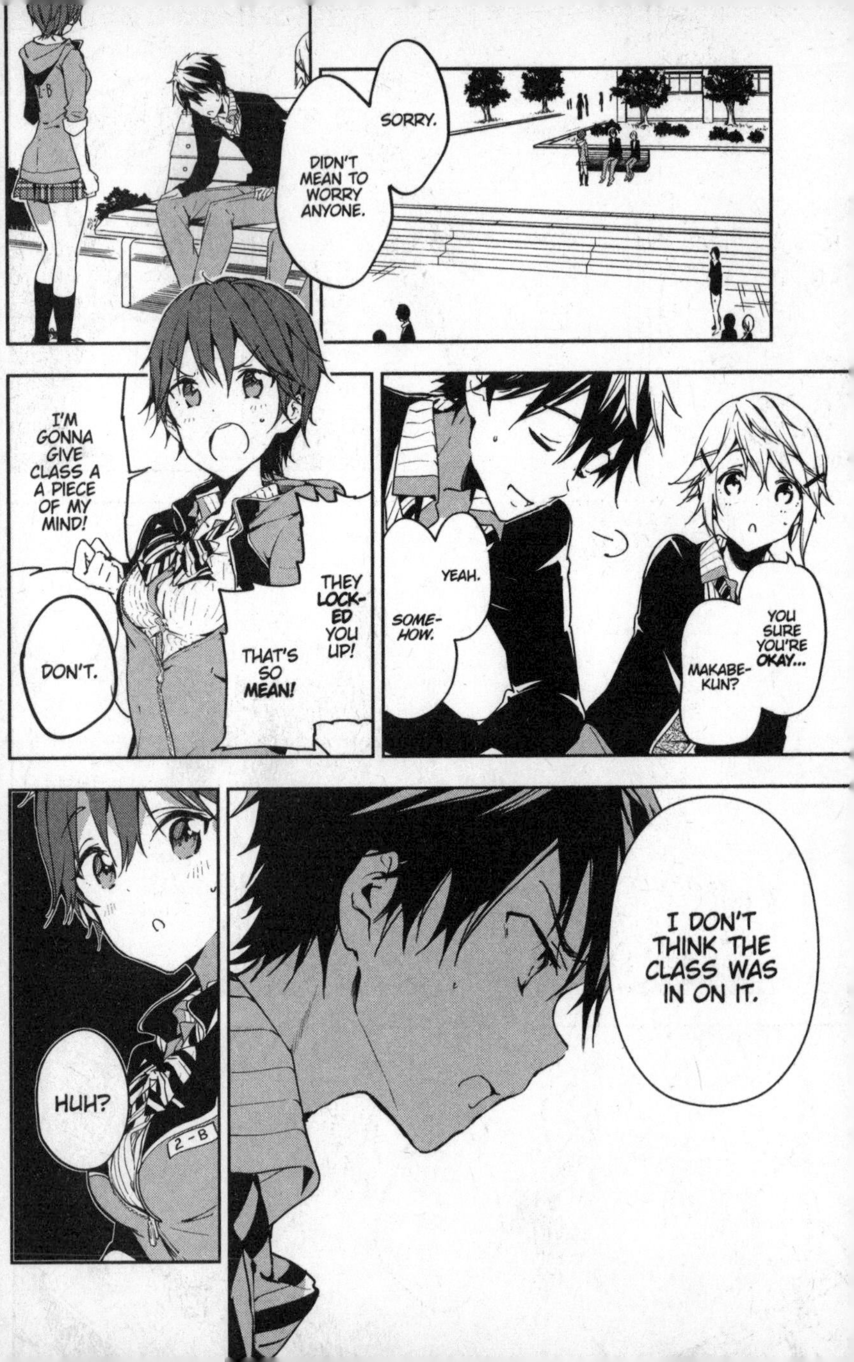
SORRY.
DIDN'T MEAN TO WORRY ANYONE.
YOU SURE YOU'RE OKAY... MAKABE-KUN?
YEAH. SOME-HOW.
THEY LOCKED-ED YOU UP! THAT'S SO MEAN!
I'M GONNA GIVE CLASS A A PIECE OF MY MIND!
DON'T.
I DON'T THINK THE CLASS WAS IN ON IT.
HUH?
2-B

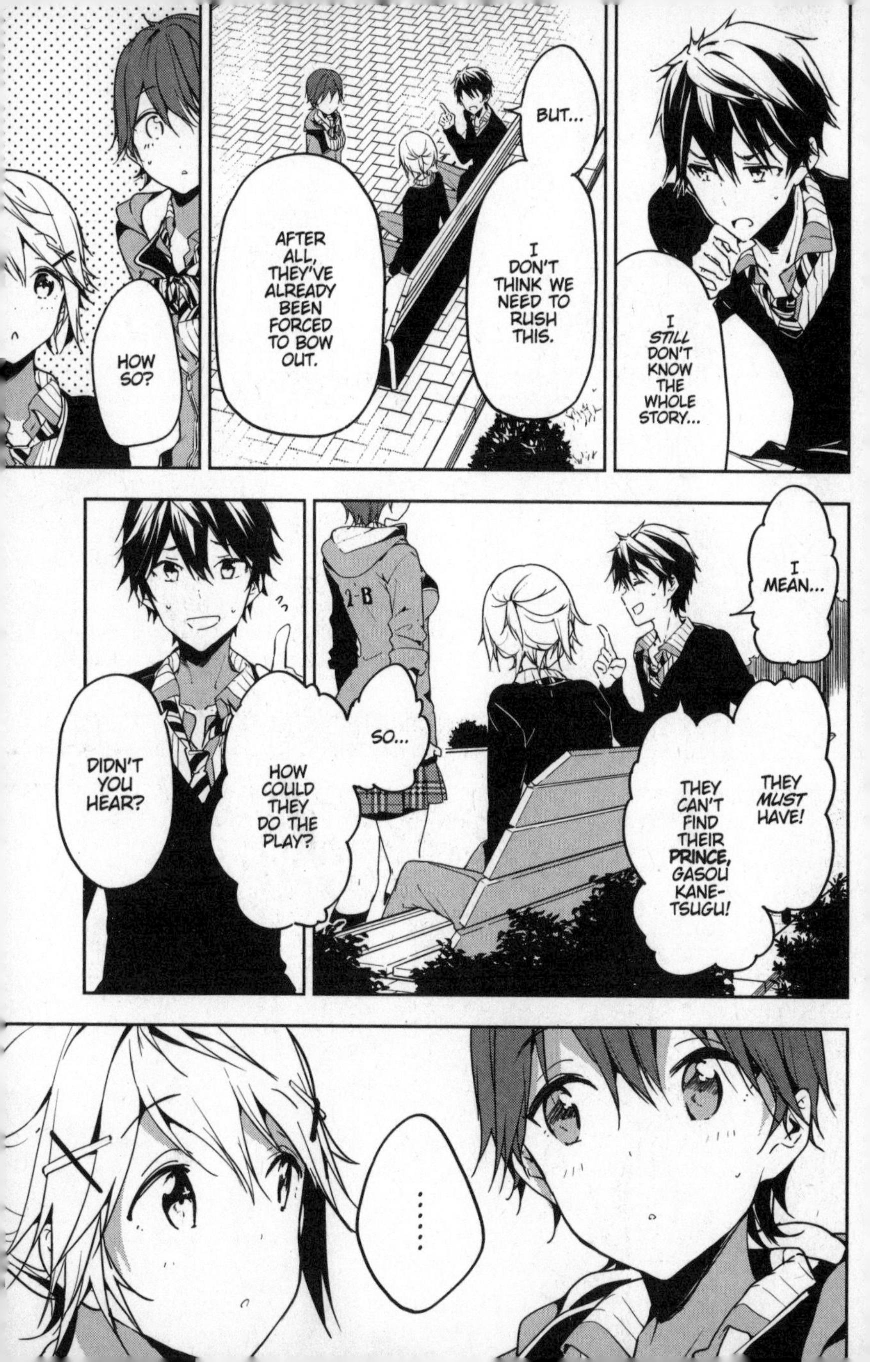
I *STILL* DON'T KNOW THE WHOLE STORY...
BUT...
I DON'T THINK WE NEED TO RUSH THIS.
AFTER ALL, THEY'VE ALREADY BEEN FORCED TO BOW OUT.
HOW SO?
I MEAN...
THEY *MUST* HAVE!
THEY CAN'T FIND THEIR **PRINCE**, GASOU KANE-TSUGU!
SO...
HOW COULD THEY DO THE PLAY?
DIDN'T YOU HEAR?
......

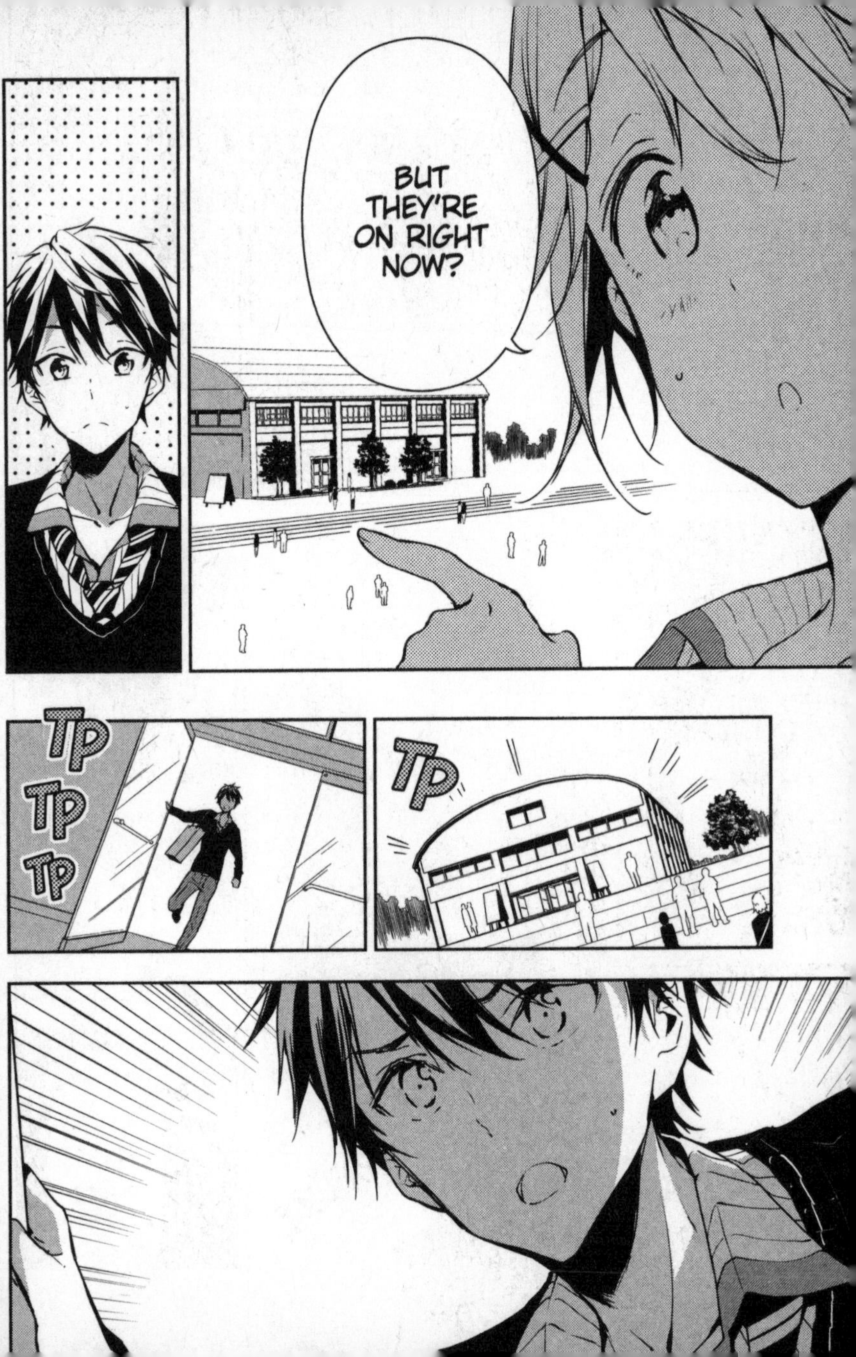
BUT THEY'RE ON RIGHT NOW?
TP
TP TP TP TP

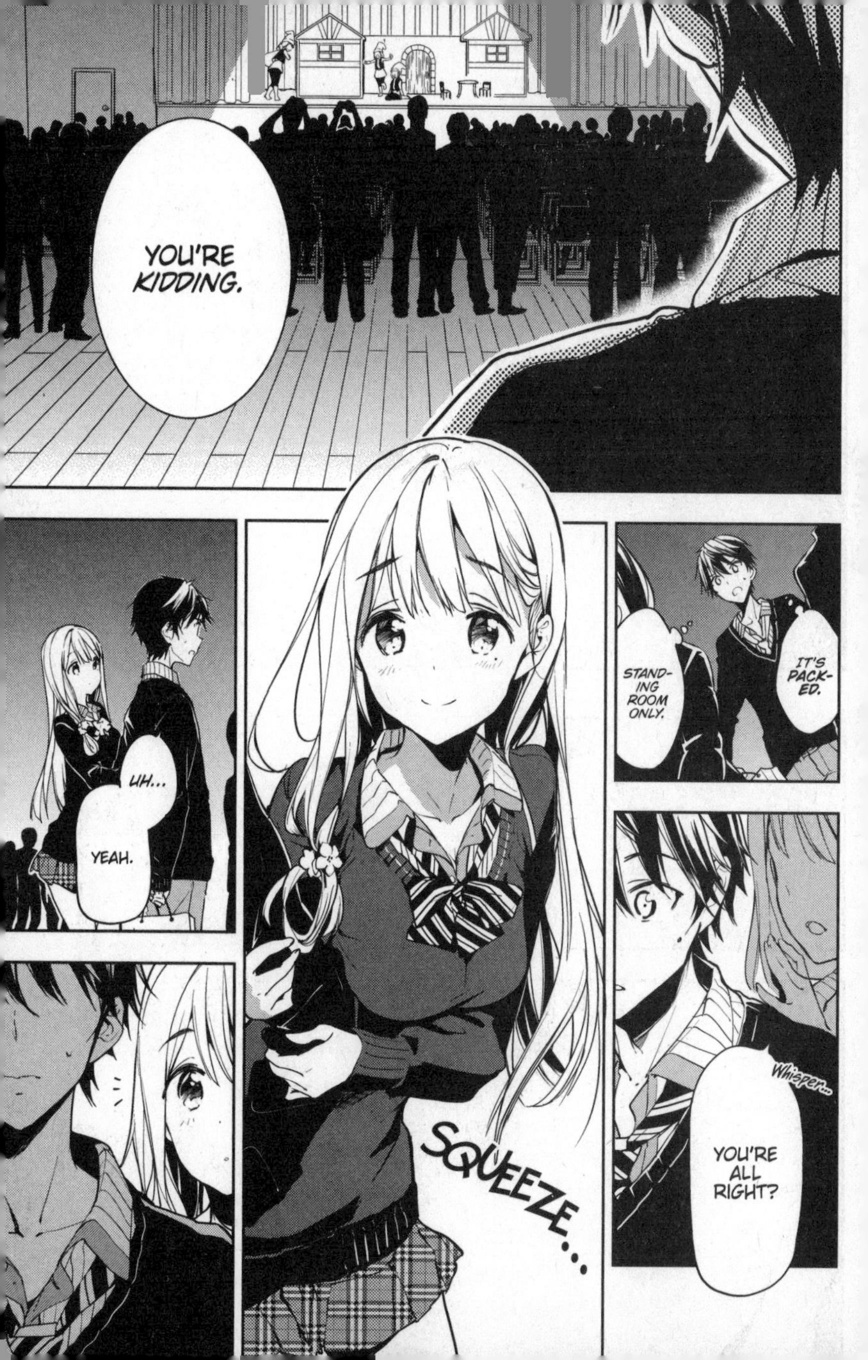
YOU'RE KIDDING.
IT'S PACK-ED.
STAND-ING ROOM ONLY.
Whisper...
YOU'RE ALL RIGHT?
SQUEEZE...
UH...
YEAH.

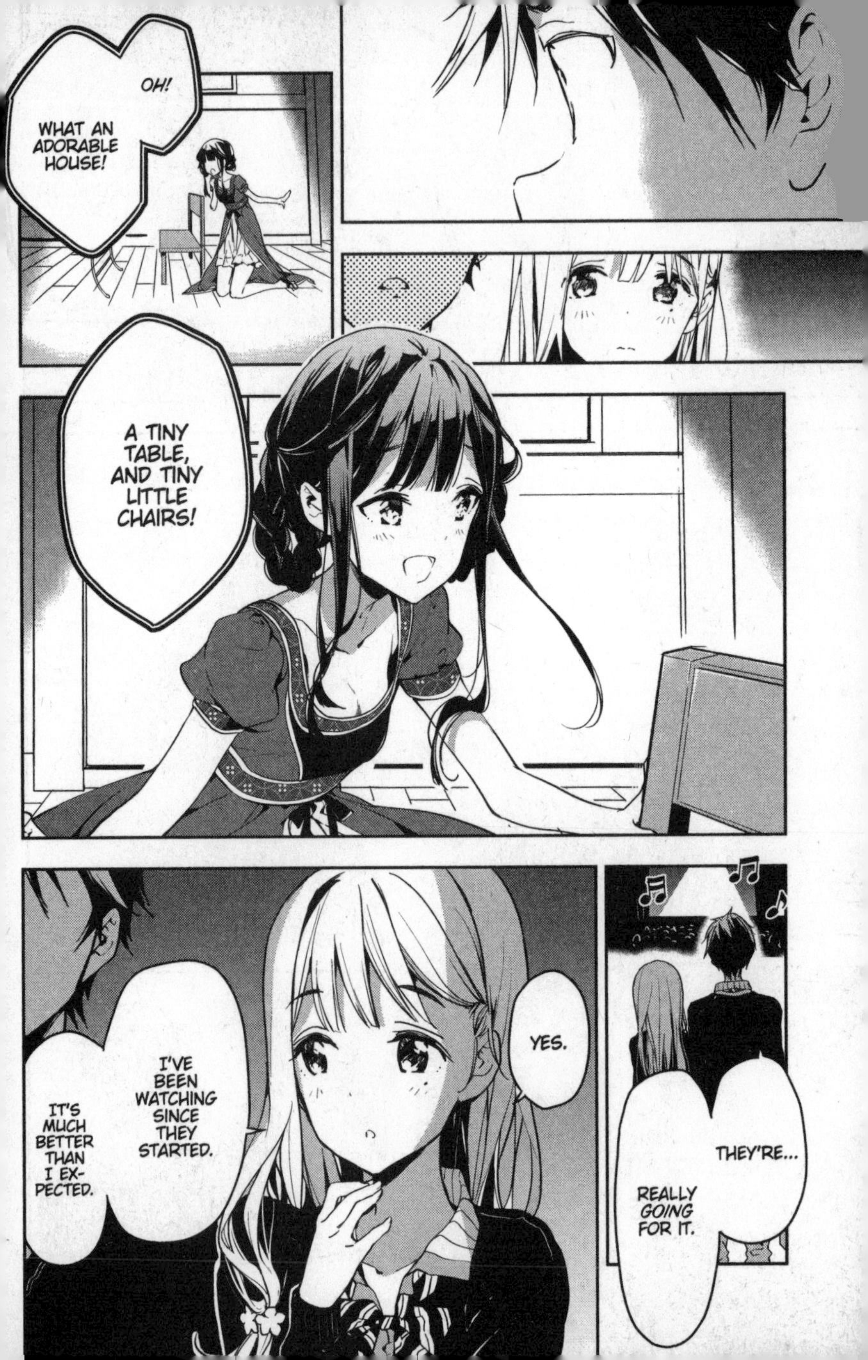
OH!
WHAT AN ADORABLE HOUSE!
A TINY TABLE, AND TINY LITTLE CHAIRS!
THEY'RE...
REALLY GOING FOR IT.
YES.
I'VE BEEN WATCHING SINCE THEY STARTED.
IT'S MUCH BETTER THAN I EXPECTED.

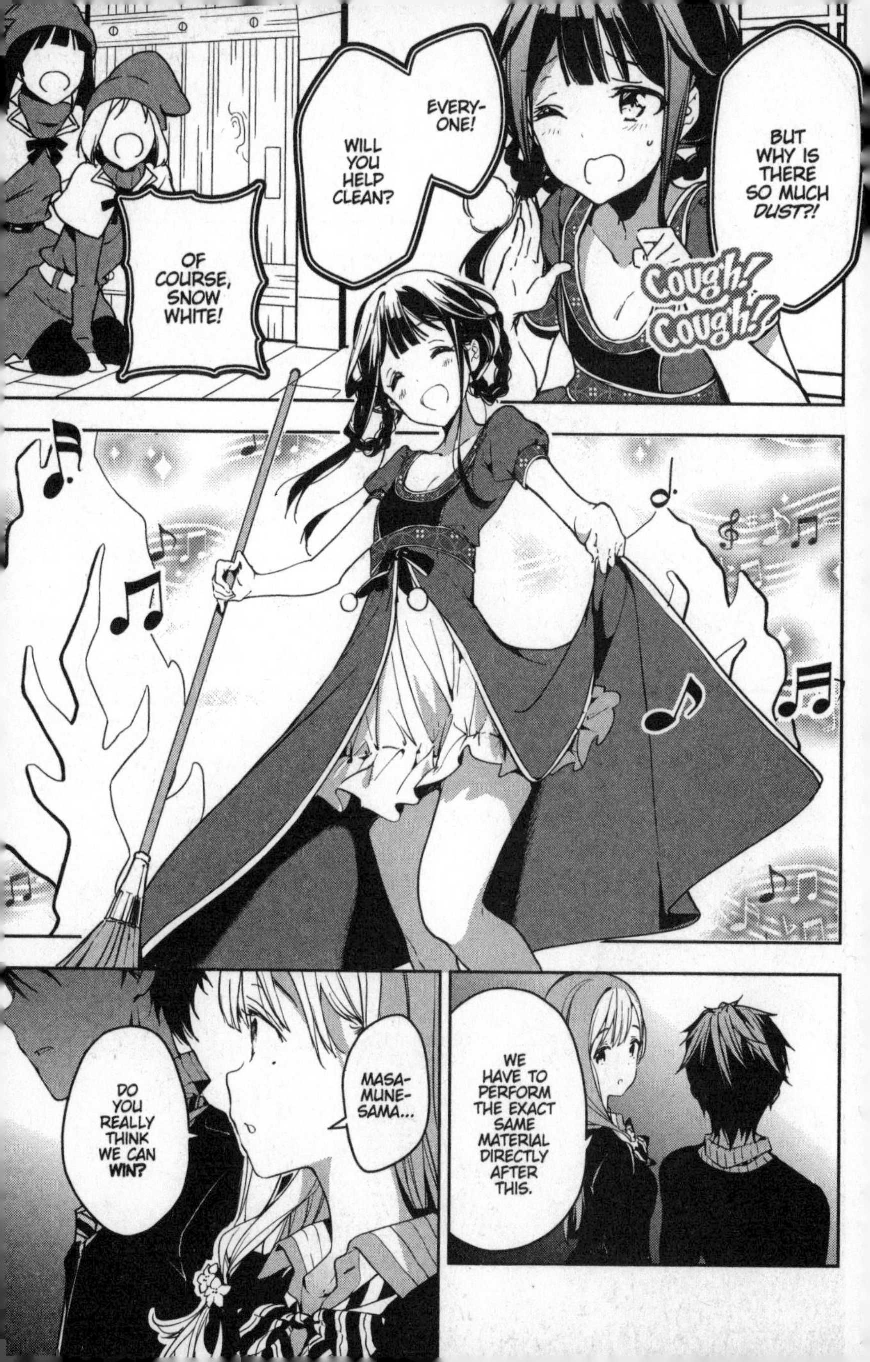
BUT WHY IS THERE SO MUCH DUST?!
Cough! Cough!
EVERYONE!
WILL YOU HELP CLEAN?
OF COURSE, SNOW WHITE!
WE HAVE TO PERFORM THE EXACT SAME MATERIAL DIRECTLY AFTER THIS.
MASAMUNE-SAMA...
DO YOU REALLY THINK WE CAN WIN?

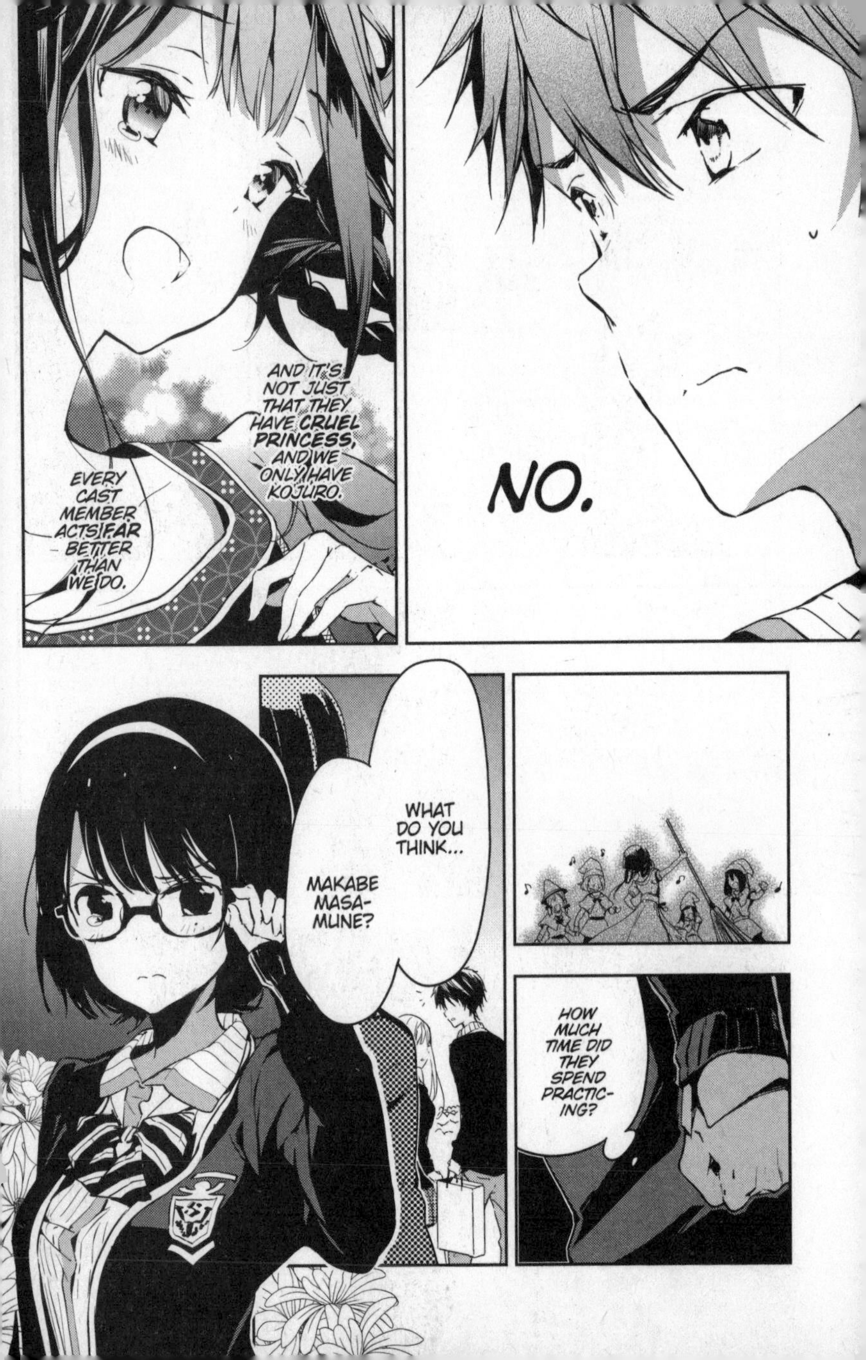
NO.
AND IT'S NOT JUST THAT THEY HAVE CRUEL PRINCESS, AND WE ONLY HAVE KOJURO.
EVERY CAST MEMBER ACTS FAR BETTER THAN WE DO.
HOW MUCH TIME DID THEY SPEND PRACTIC-ING?
WHAT DO YOU THINK...
MAKABE MASA-MUNE?

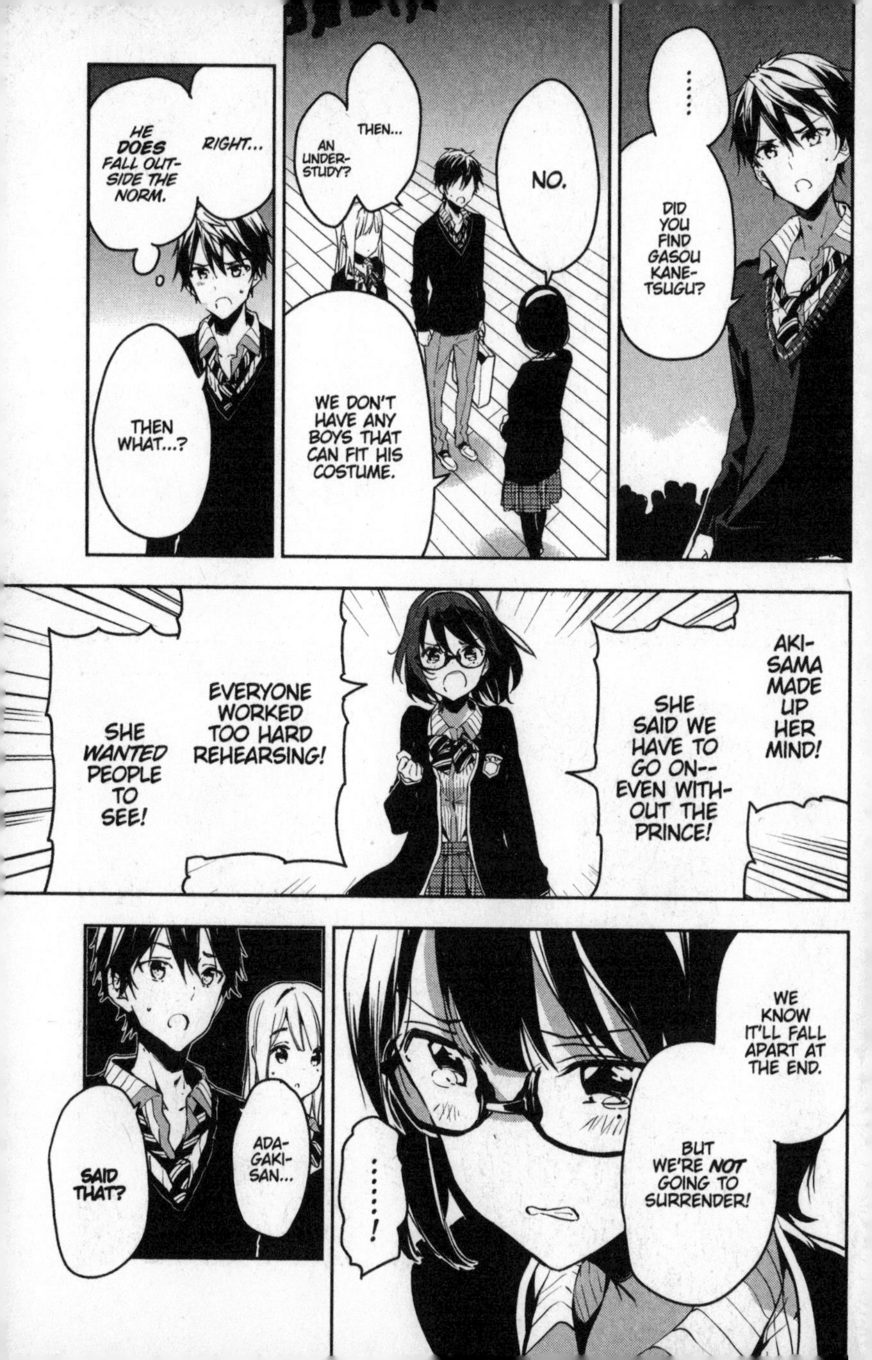
......
DID YOU FIND GASOU KANETSUGU?
NO.
THEN...
AN UNDERSTUDY?
WE DON'T HAVE ANY BOYS THAT CAN FIT HIS COSTUME.
RIGHT...
HE DOES FALL OUTSIDE THE NORM.
THEN WHAT...?
AKI-SAMA MADE UP HER MIND!
SHE SAID WE HAVE TO GO ON-- EVEN WITHOUT THE PRINCE!
EVERYONE WORKED TOO HARD REHEARSING!
SHE WANTED PEOPLE TO SEE!
WE KNOW IT'LL FALL APART AT THE END.
BUT WE'RE NOT GOING TO SURRENDER!
......!
ADAGAKI-SAN...
SAID THAT?

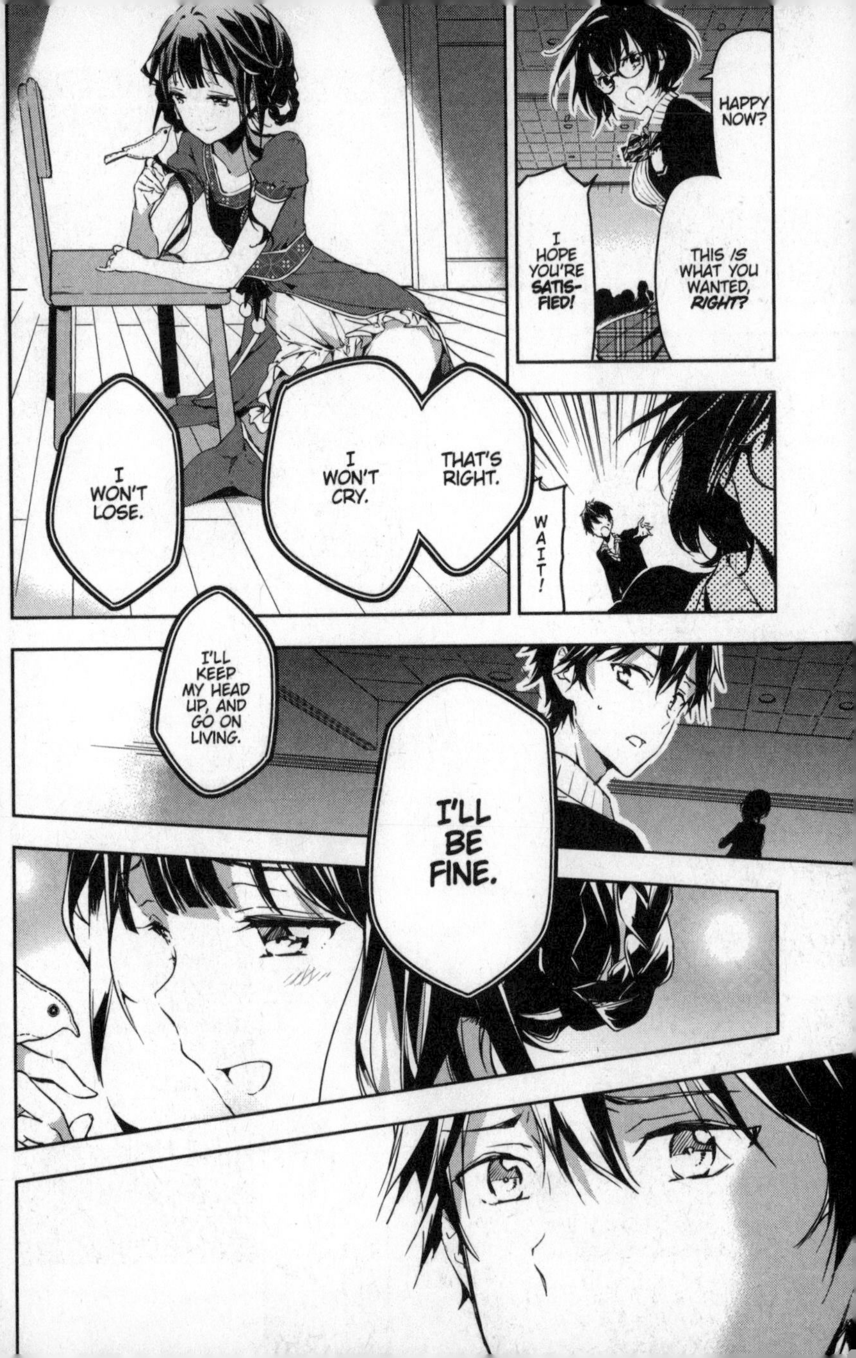
HAPPY NOW?
THIS *IS* WHAT YOU WANTED, ***RIGHT?***
I HOPE YOU'RE **SATISFIED!**
WAIT!
THAT'S RIGHT.
I WON'T CRY.
I WON'T LOSE.
I'LL KEEP MY HEAD UP, AND GO ON LIVING.
I'LL BE FINE.

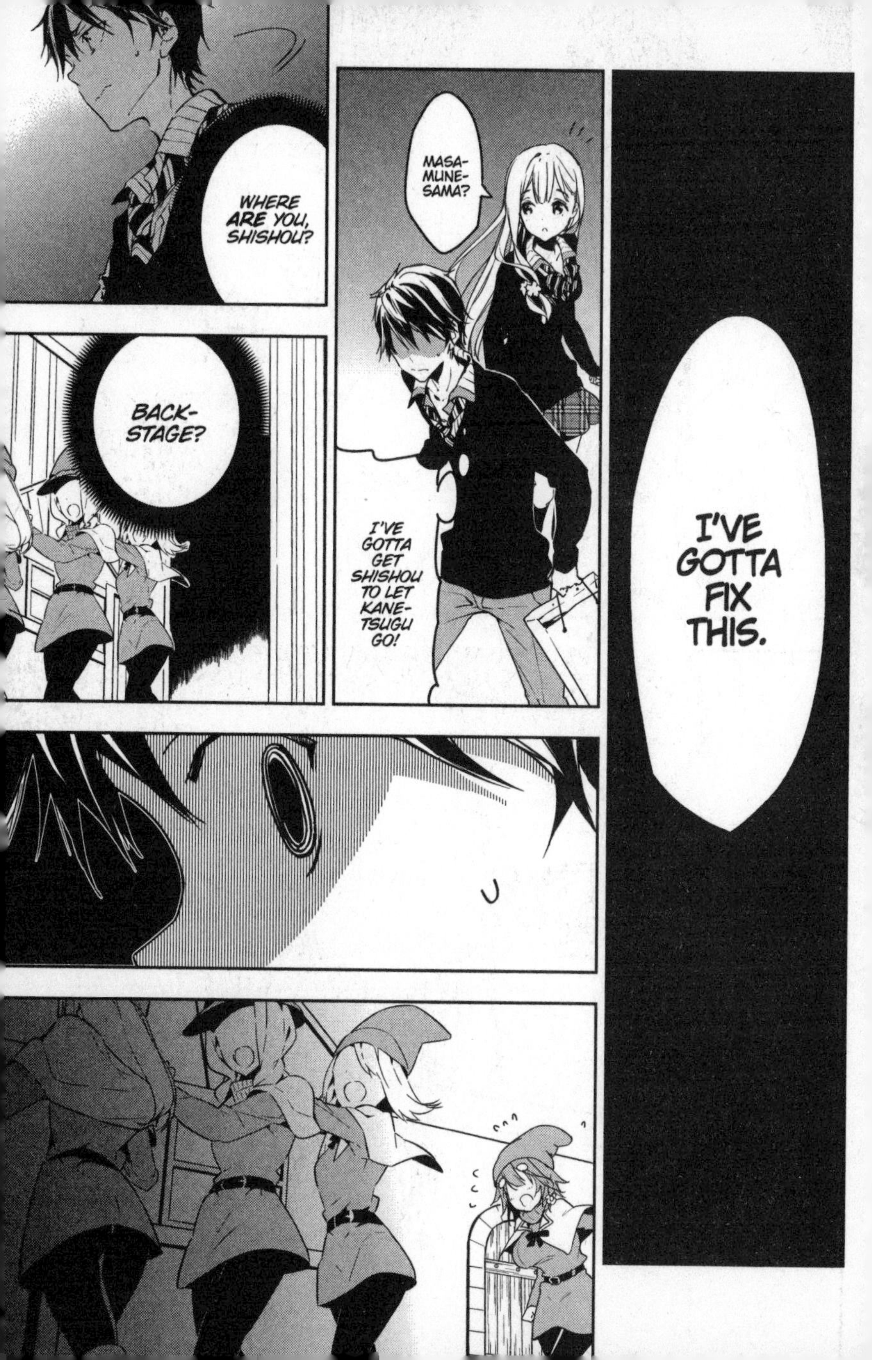
I'VE GOTTA FIX THIS.
MASA-MUNE-SAMA?
I'VE GOTTA GET SHISHOU TO LET KANE-TSUGU GO!
WHERE ARE YOU, SHISHOU?
BACK-STAGE?

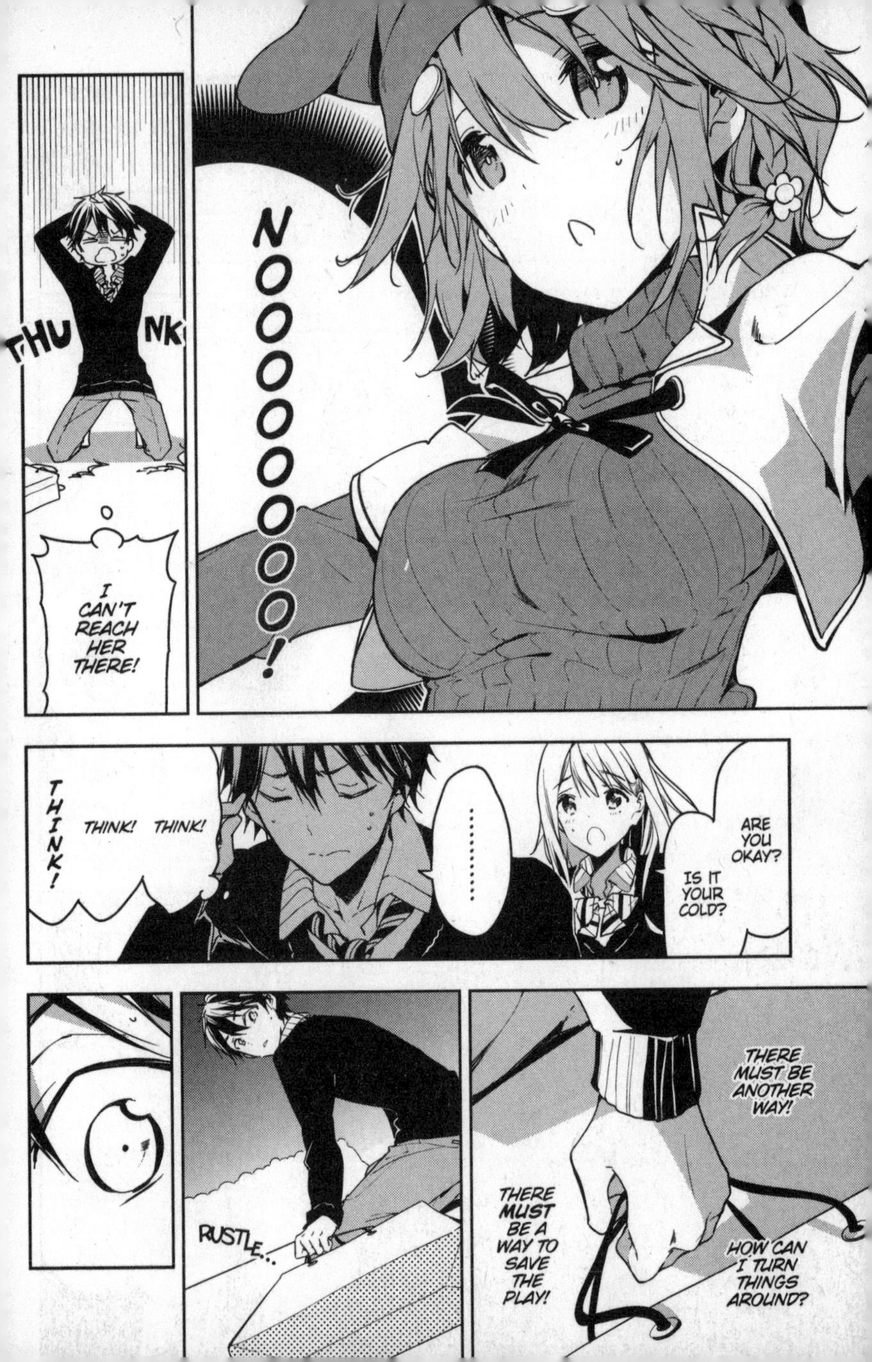
NOOOOOOOO!
THUNK
I CAN'T REACH HER THERE!
ARE YOU OKAY?
IS IT YOUR COLD?
......
THINK! THINK! THINK!
THERE MUST BE ANOTHER WAY!
HOW CAN I TURN THINGS AROUND?
THERE MUST BE A WAY TO SAVE THE PLAY!
RUSTLE...

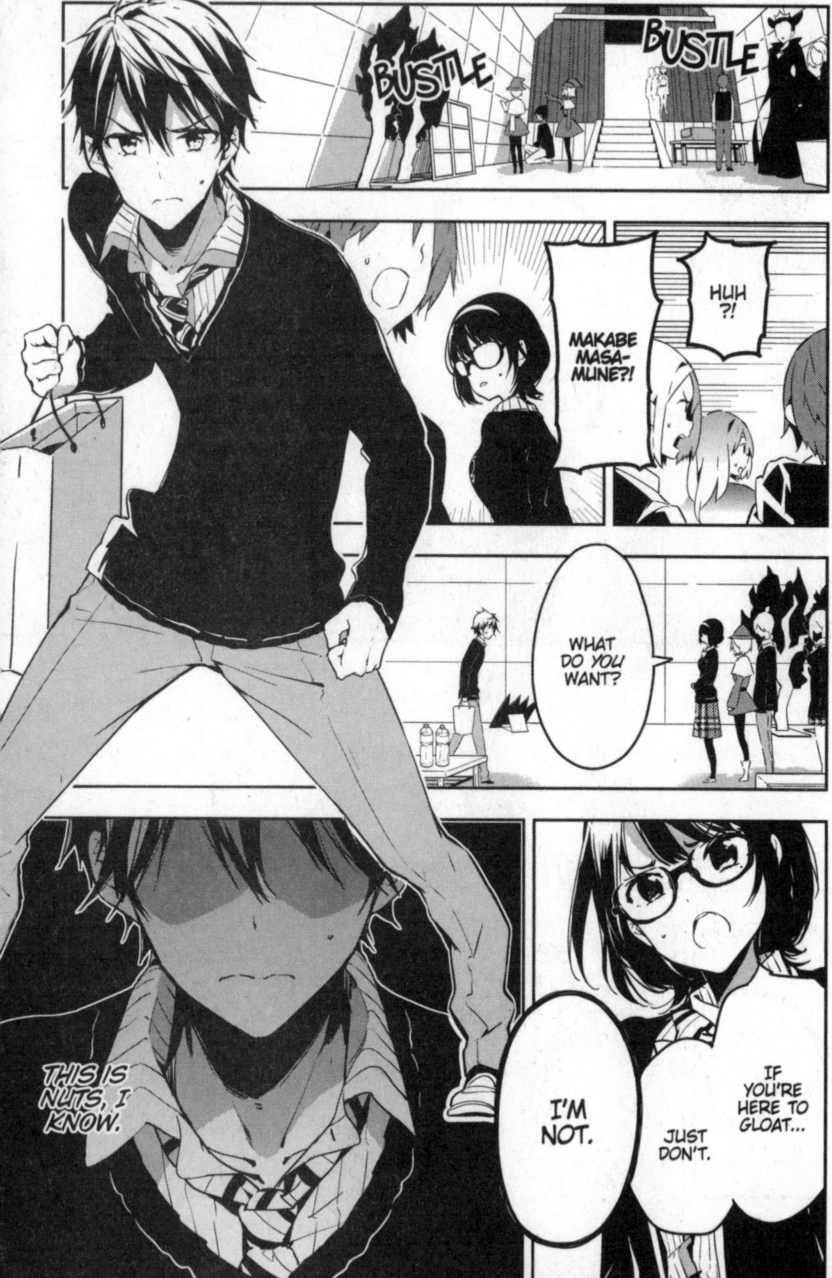
BUSTLE
BUSTLE
HUH ?!
MAKABE MASA-MUNE?!
WHAT DO YOU WANT?
IF YOU'RE HERE TO GLOAT...
JUST DON'T.
I'M NOT.
THIS IS NUTS, I KNOW.

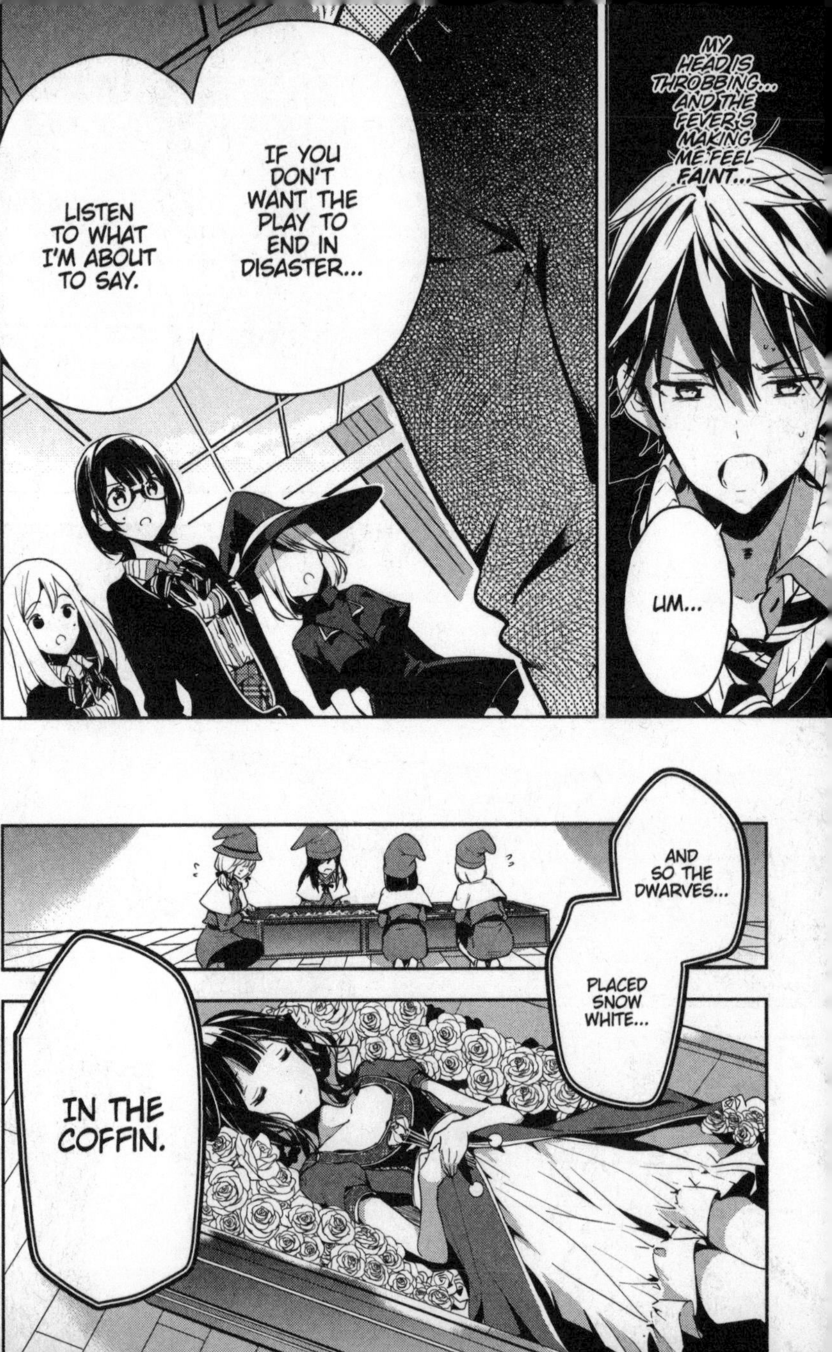
MY HEAD IS THROBBING... AND THE FEVER'S MAKING ME FEEL FAINT...
UM...
IF YOU DON'T WANT THE PLAY TO END IN DISASTER...
LISTEN TO WHAT I'M ABOUT TO SAY.
AND SO THE DWARVES...
PLACED SNOW WHITE...
IN THE COFFIN.

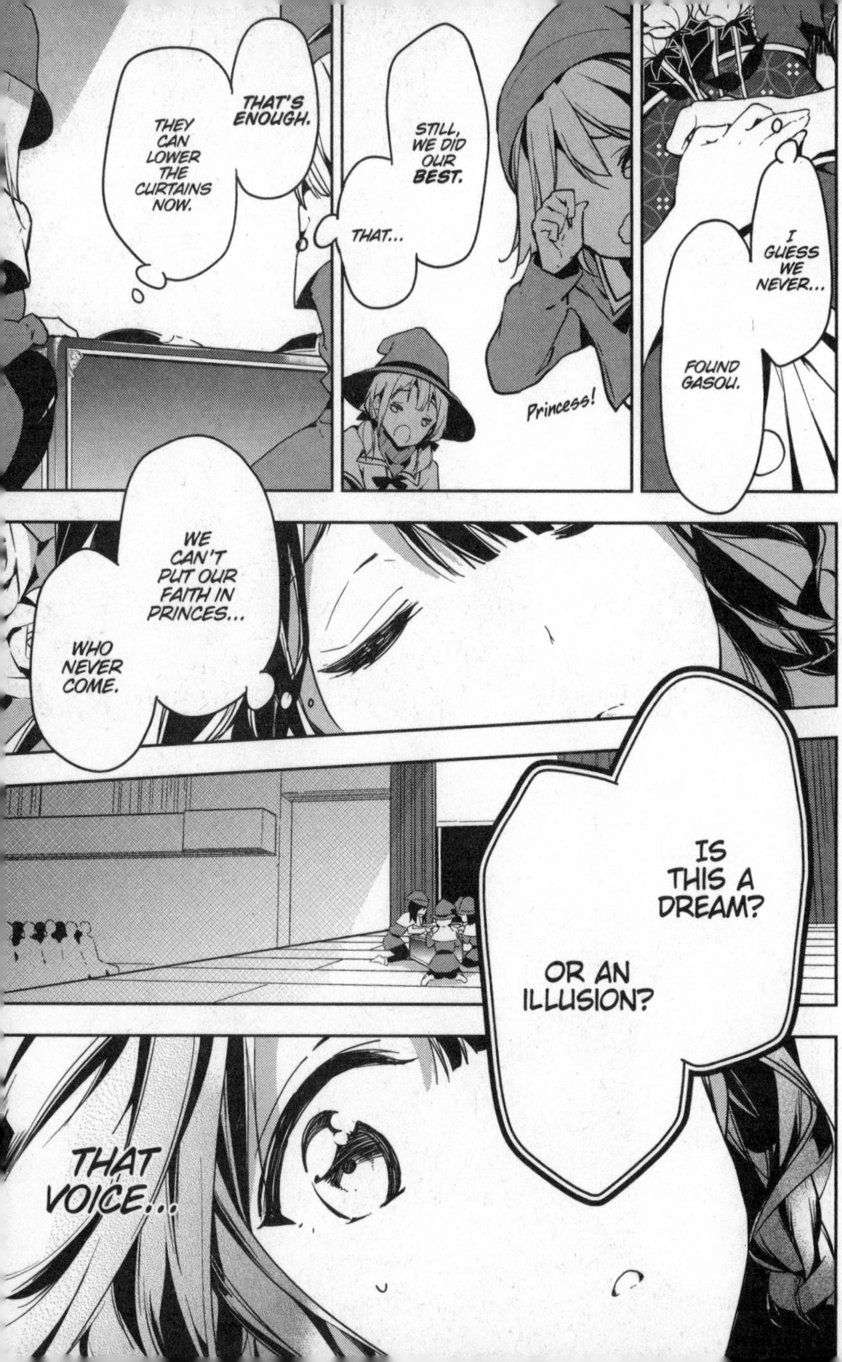
I GUESS WE NEVER...
FOUND GASOU.
STILL, WE DID OUR BEST.
THAT...
Princess!
THAT'S ENOUGH.
THEY CAN LOWER THE CURTAINS NOW.
WE CAN'T PUT OUR FAITH IN PRINCES...
WHO NEVER COME.
IS THIS A DREAM?
OR AN ILLUSION?
THAT VOICE...

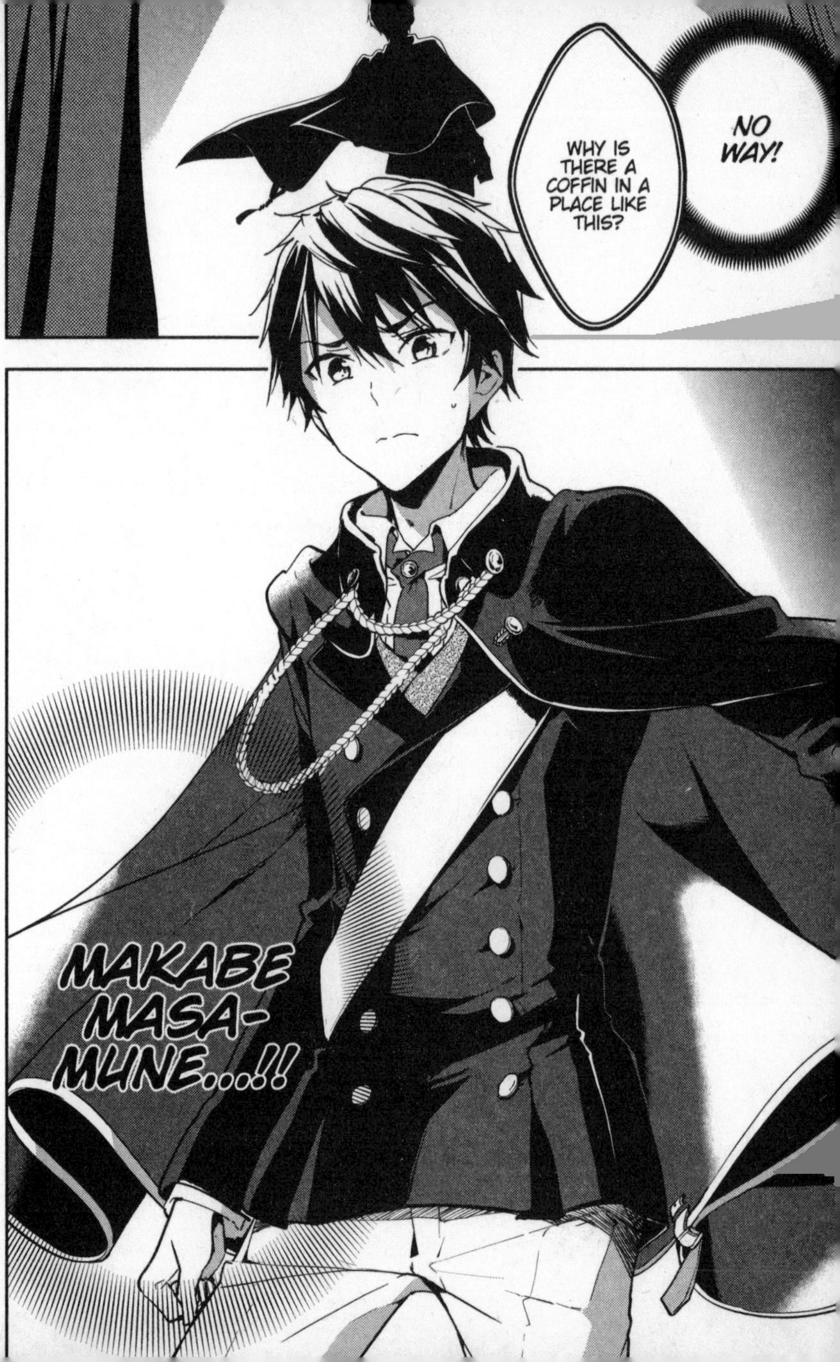
NO WAY!
WHY IS THERE A COFFIN IN A PLACE LIKE THIS?
MAKABE MASA-MUNE...!!

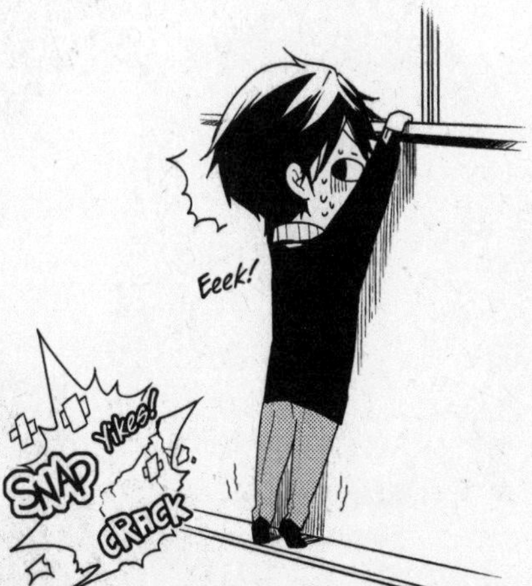
Eeek!
Yikes!
SNAP
CRACK

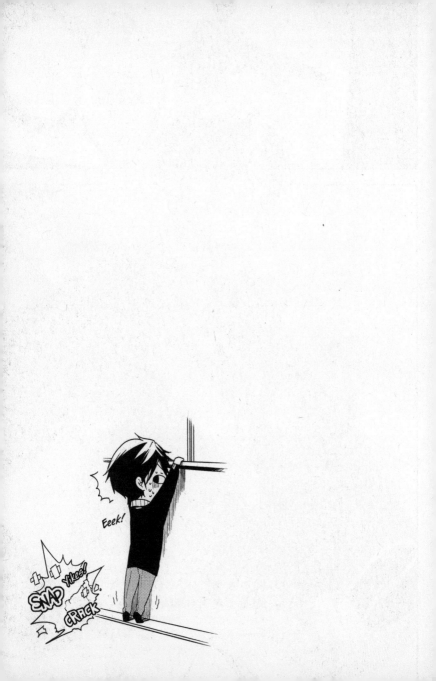

6

Masamune-kun's
REVENGE

Presented by Hazuki Takeoka & TIV

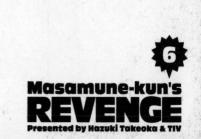

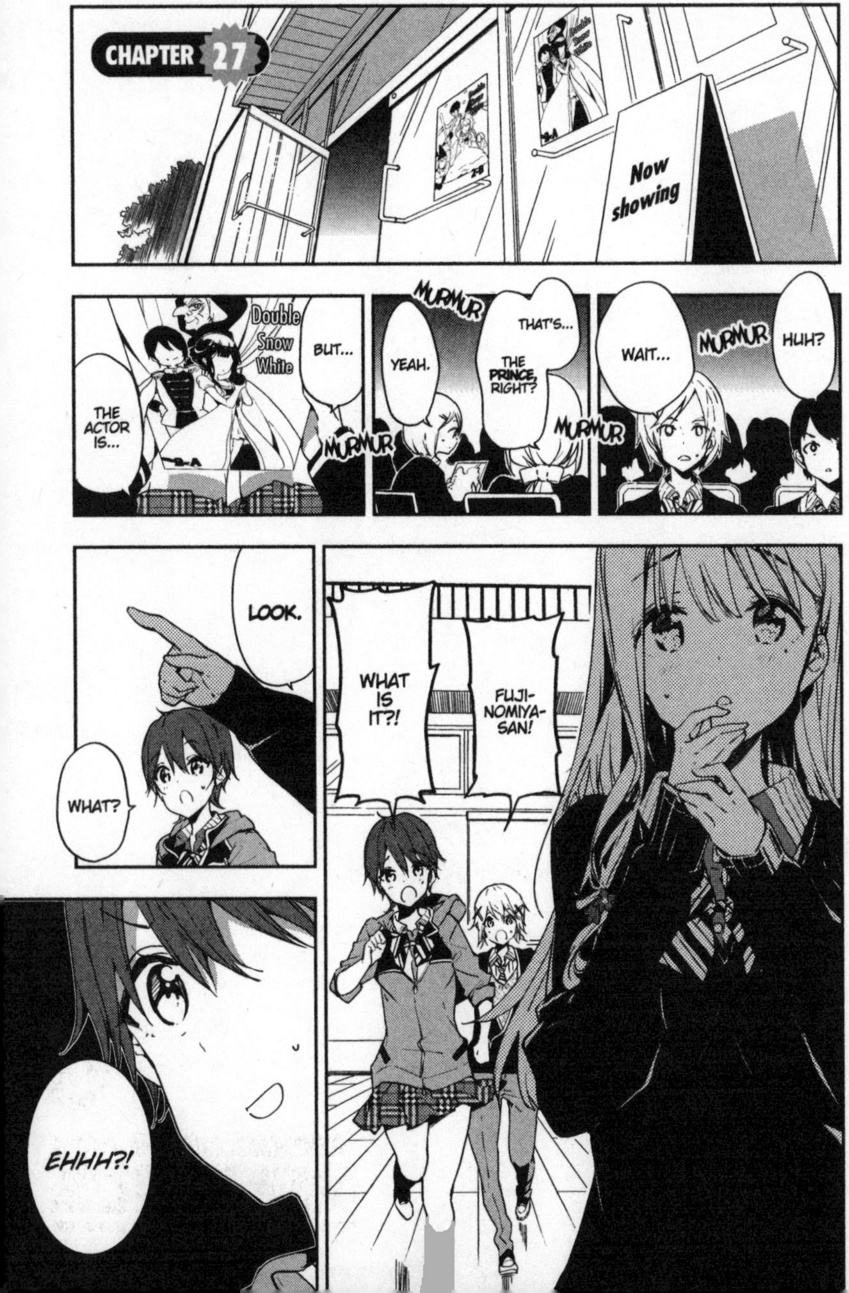
CHAPTER 27
Double Snow White
Now showing
HUH?
MURMUR
WAIT...
THAT'S...
THE PRINCE, RIGHT?
MURMUR
MURMUR
YEAH.
BUT...
Double Snow White
THE ACTOR IS...
MURMUR
FUJI-NOMIYA-SAN!
WHAT IS IT?!
LOOK.
WHAT?
EHHH?!

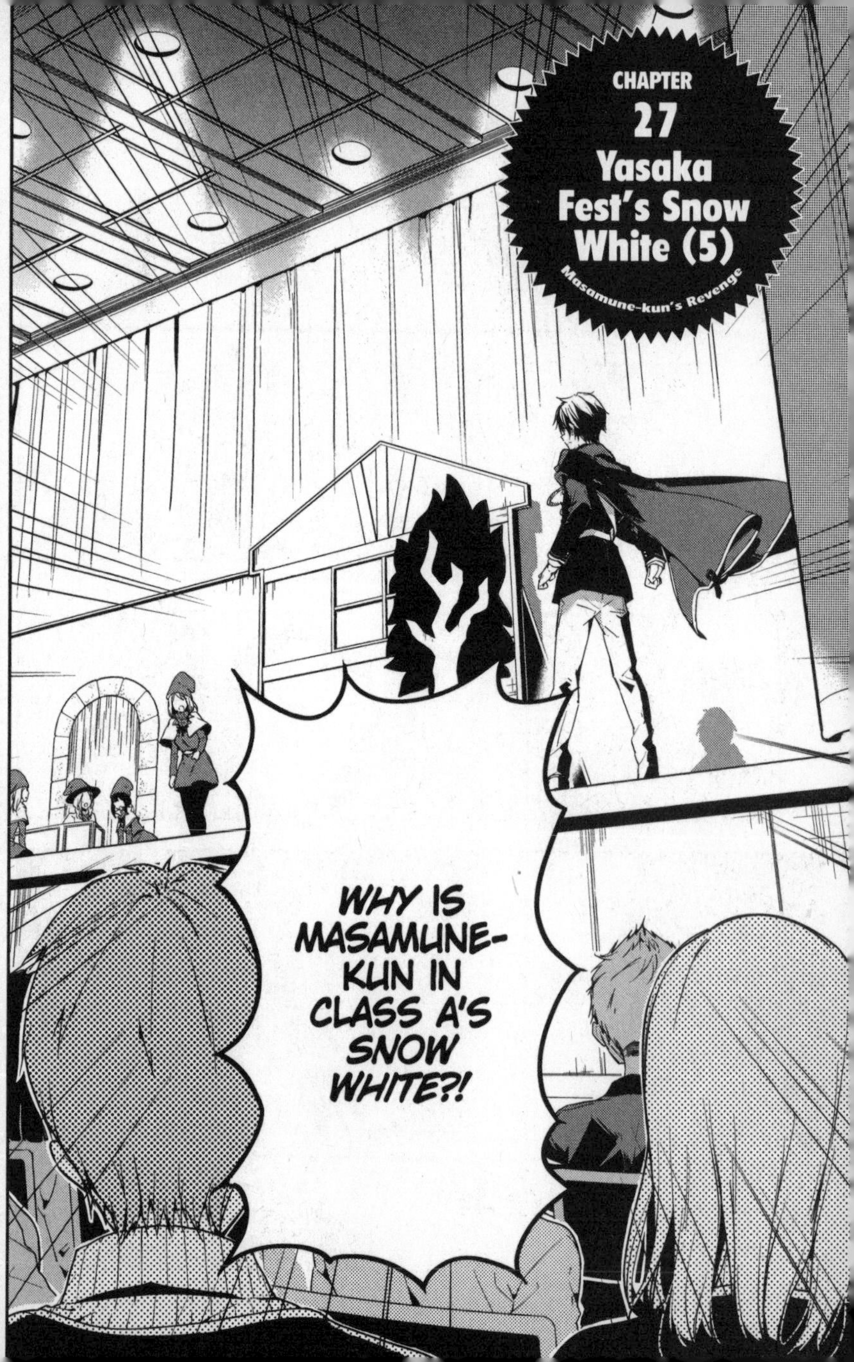
CHAPTER
27
Yasaka Fest's Snow White (5)
Masamune-kun's Revenge
WHY IS MASAMUNE-KUN IN CLASS A'S SNOW WHITE?!

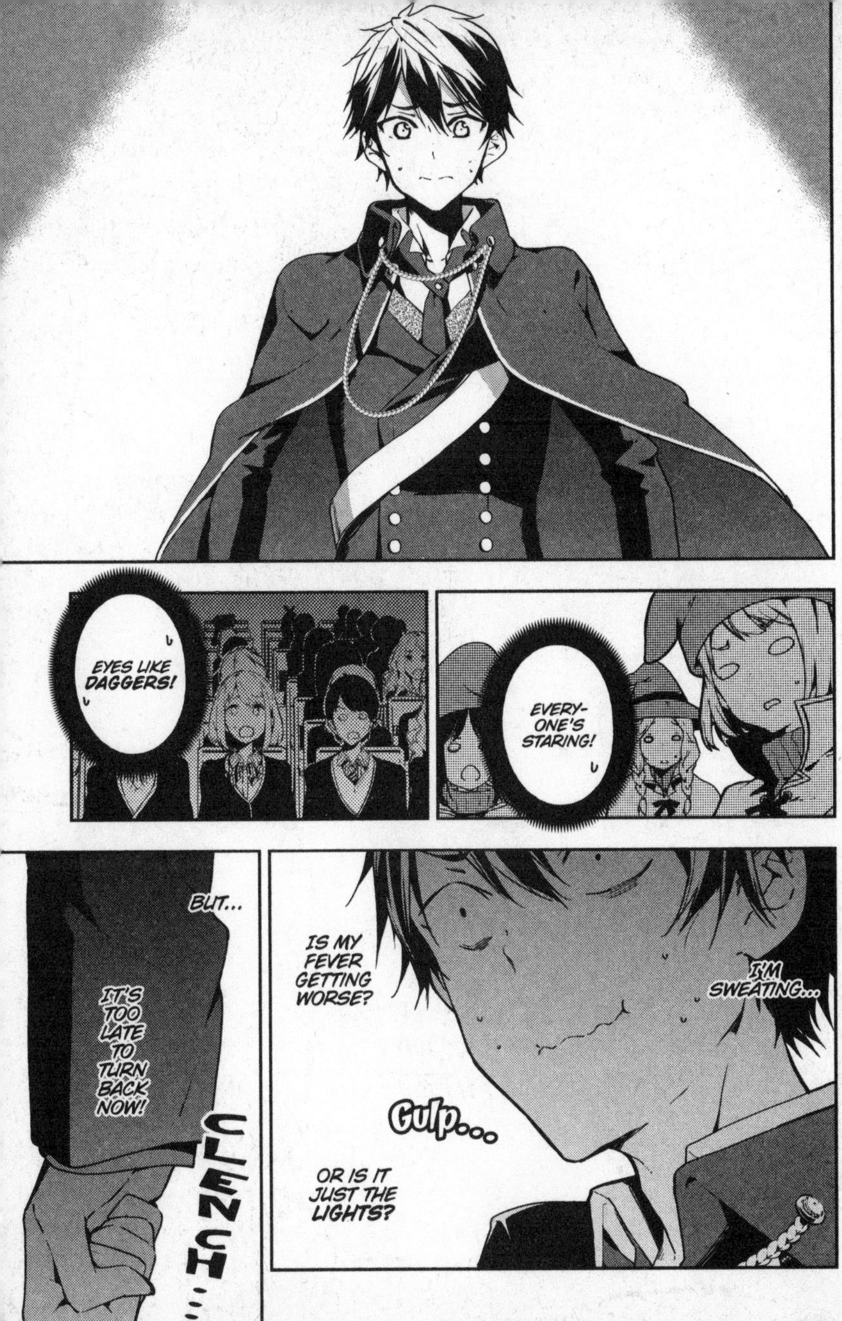
EVERY-ONE'S STARING!
EYES LIKE DAGGERS!
I'M SWEATING...
IS MY FEVER GETTING WORSE?
Gulp...
OR IS IT JUST THE LIGHTS?
BUT...
IT'S TOO LATE TO TURN BACK NOW!
CLENCH...

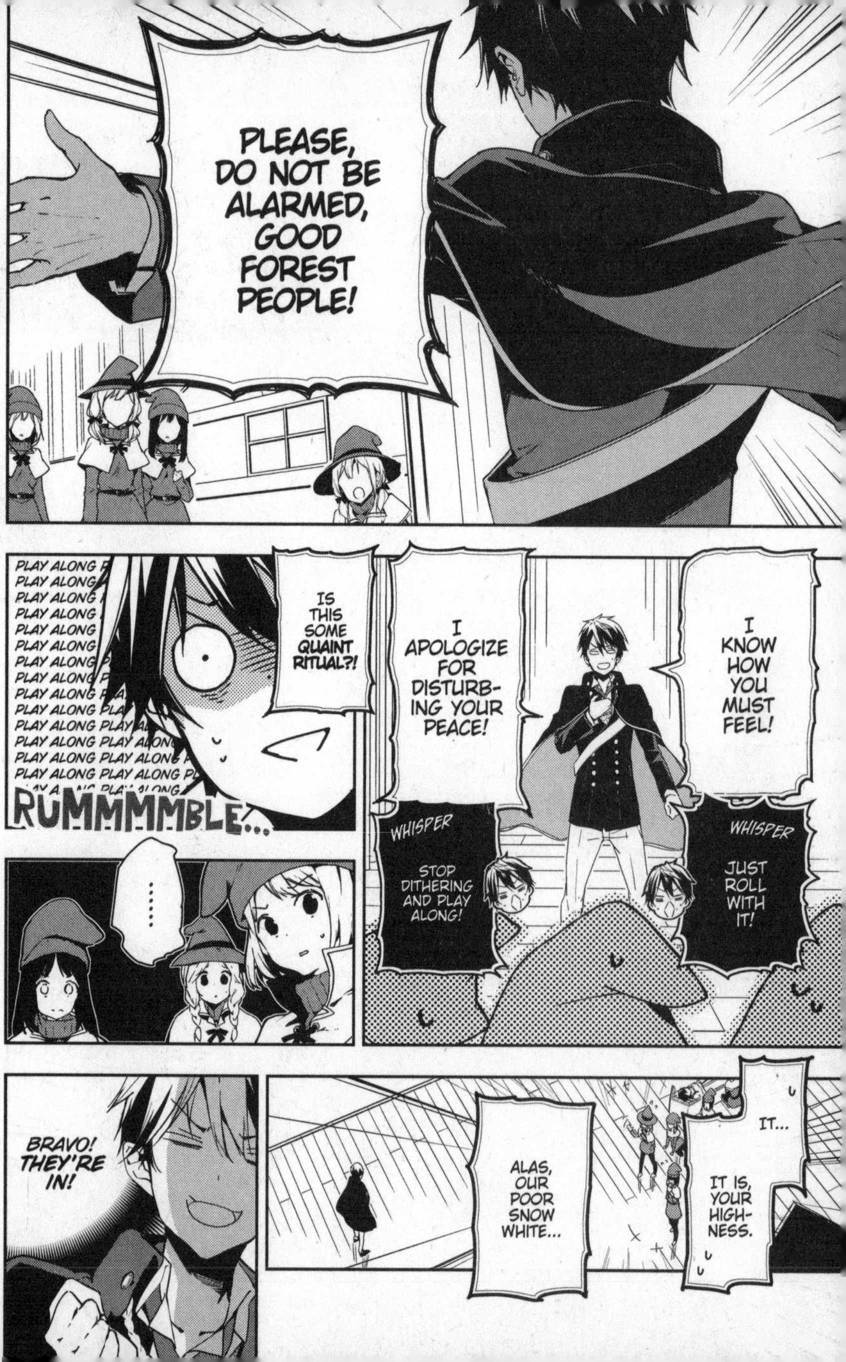
PLEASE, DO NOT BE ALARMED, GOOD FOREST PEOPLE!
I KNOW HOW YOU MUST FEEL!
I APOLOGIZE FOR DISTURBING YOUR PEACE!
WHISPER
JUST ROLL WITH IT!
WHISPER
STOP DITHERING AND PLAY ALONG!
IS THIS SOME QUAINT RITUAL?!
PLAY ALONG PLAY ALONG
RUMMMMBLE...
......
IT...
IT IS, YOUR HIGHNESS.
ALAS, OUR POOR SNOW WHITE...
BRAVO! THEY'RE IN!

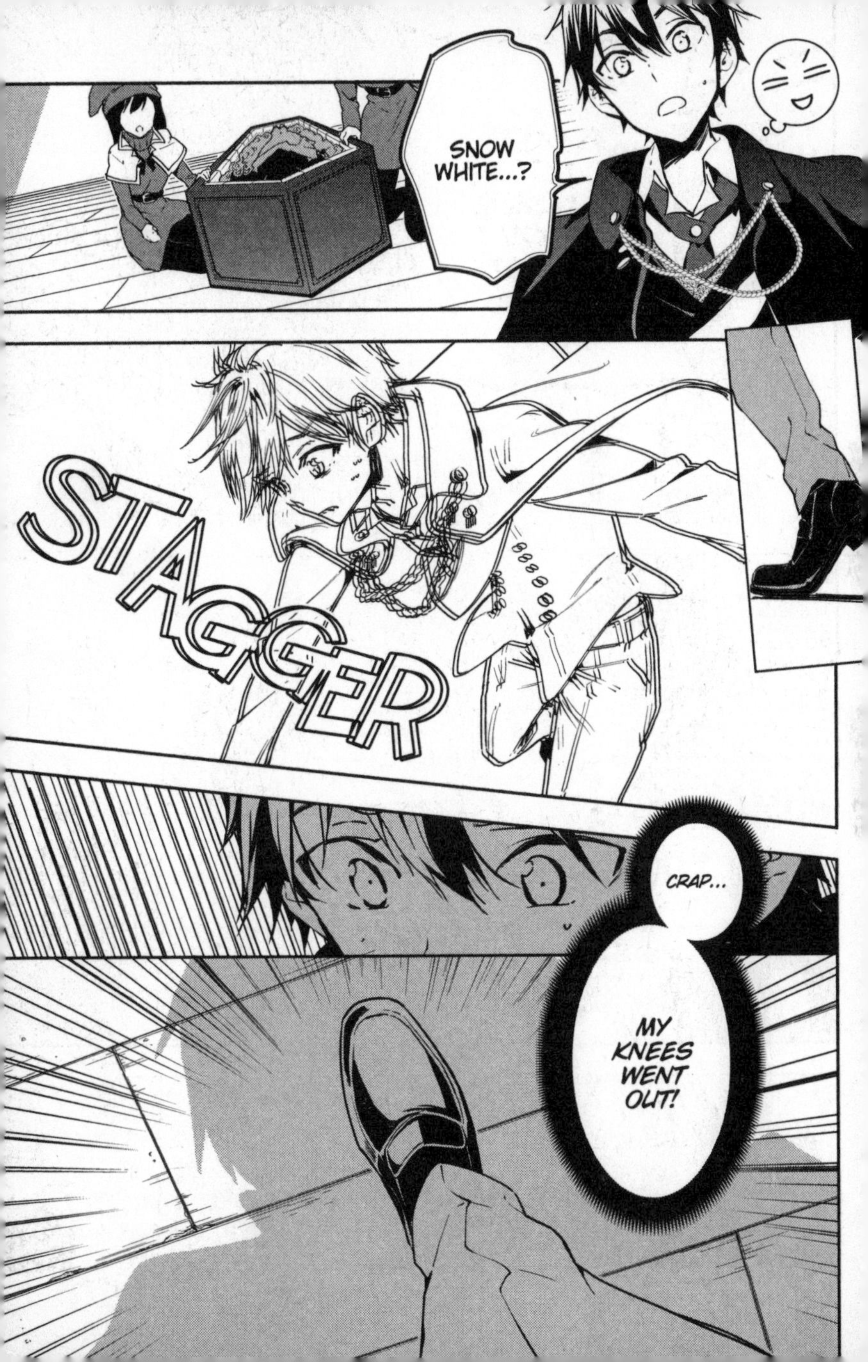
SNOW WHITE...?
STAGGER
CRAP...
MY KNEES WENT OUT!

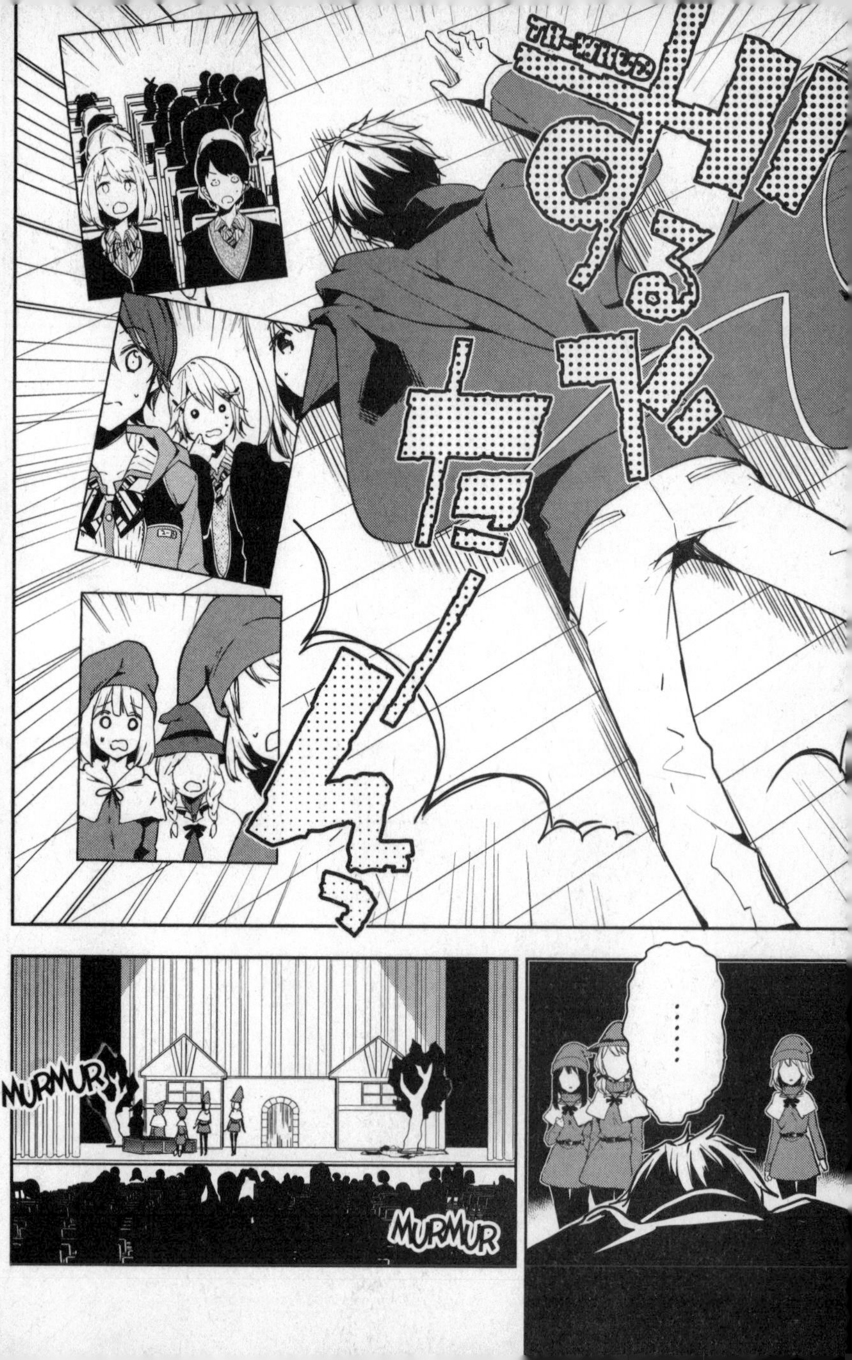
……
MURMUR
MURMUR

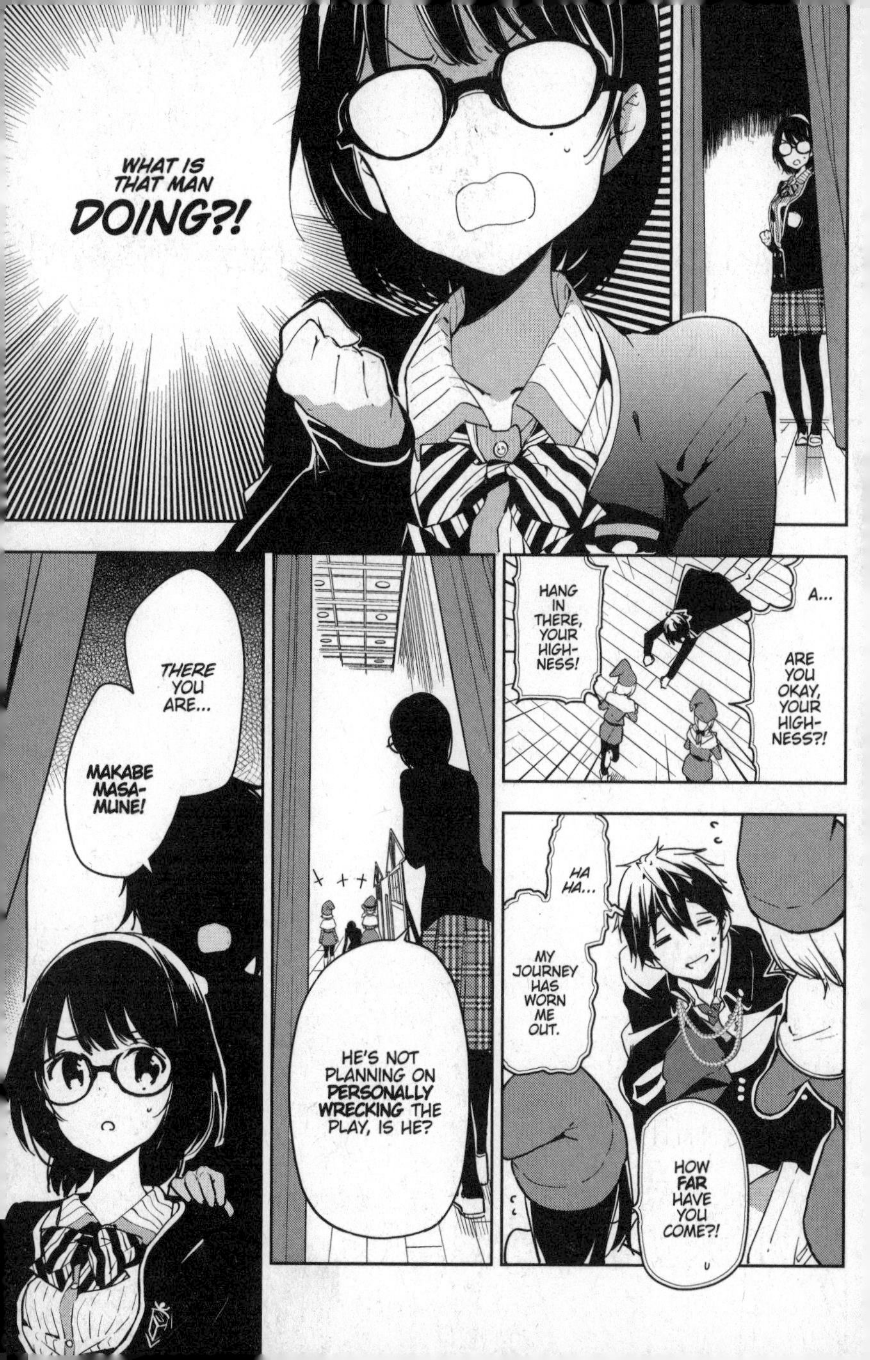
WHAT IS THAT MAN DOING?!
A... ARE YOU OKAY, YOUR HIGHNESS?!
HANG IN THERE, YOUR HIGHNESS!
HA HA... MY JOURNEY HAS WORN ME OUT.
HOW FAR HAVE YOU COME?!
HE'S NOT PLANNING ON PERSONALLY WRECKING THE PLAY, IS HE?
THERE YOU ARE... MAKABE MASAMUNE!

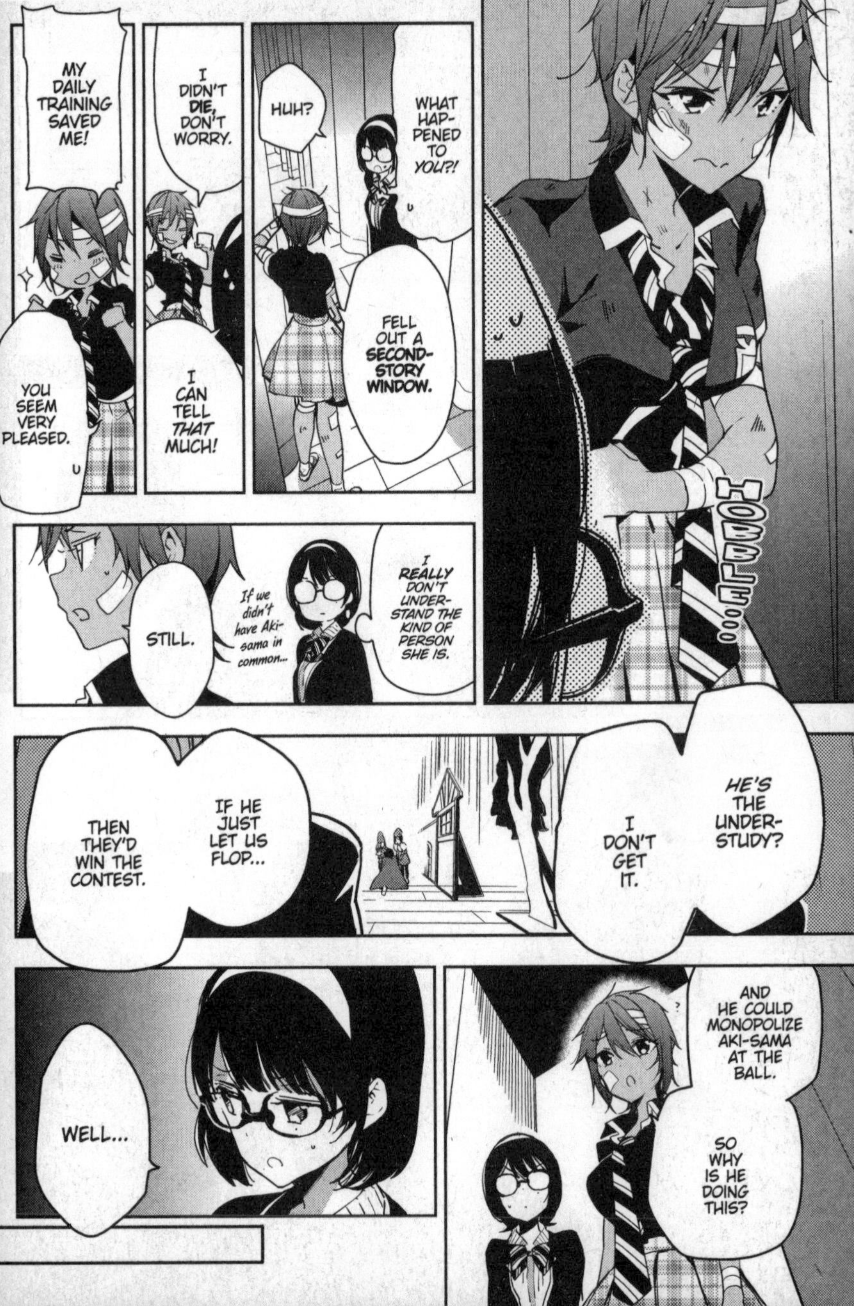
HOBBLE...
WHAT HAPPENED TO YOU?!
HUH?
FELL OUT A SECOND-STORY WINDOW.
I DIDN'T DIE, DON'T WORRY.
I CAN TELL THAT MUCH!
MY DAILY TRAINING SAVED ME!
YOU SEEM VERY PLEASED.
I REALLY DON'T UNDERSTAND THE KIND OF PERSON SHE IS.
If we didn't have Aki-sama in common...
STILL.
HE'S THE UNDERSTUDY?
I DON'T GET IT.
IF HE JUST LET US FLOP...
THEN THEY'D WIN THE CONTEST.
AND HE COULD MONOPOLIZE AKI-SAMA AT THE BALL.
SO WHY IS HE DOING THIS?
WELL...

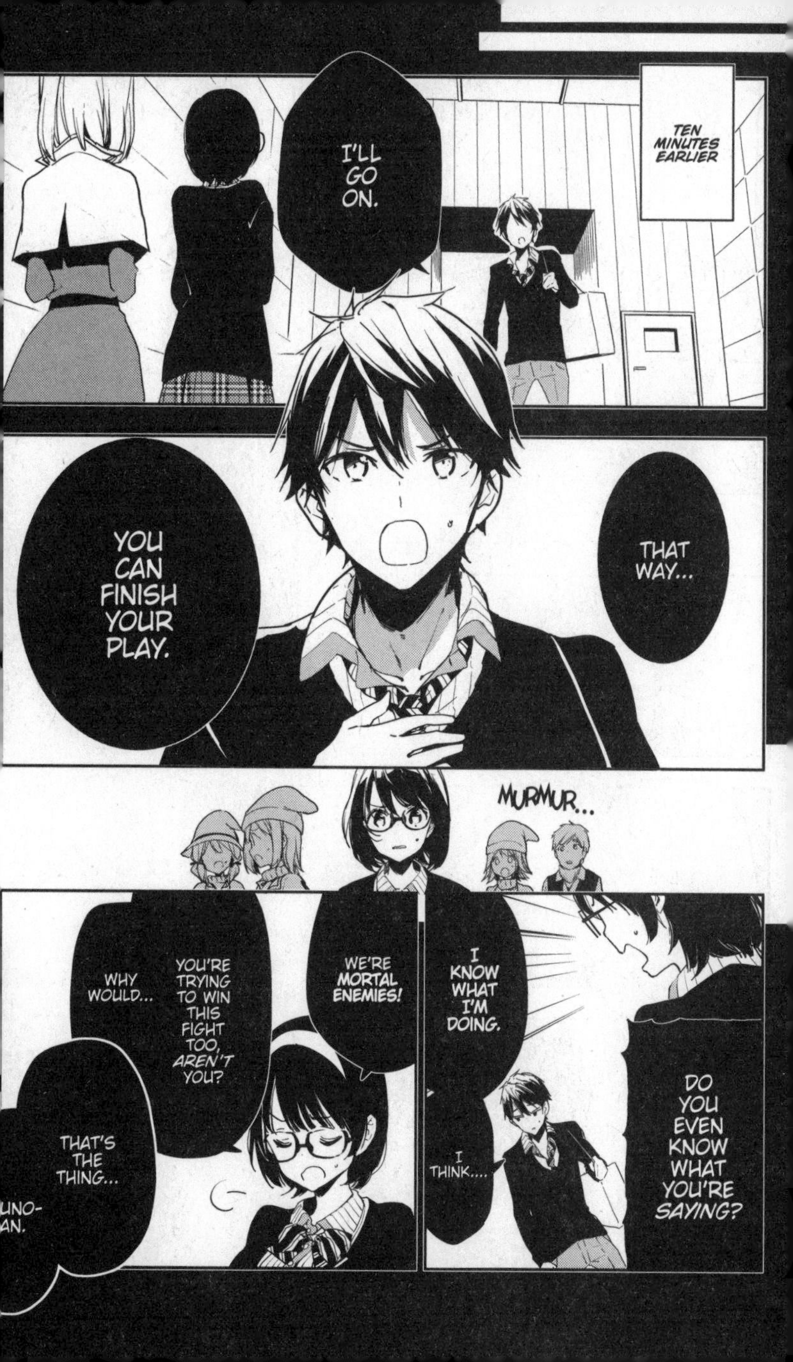

TEN MINUTES EARLIER
I'LL GO ON.
THAT WAY...
YOU CAN FINISH YOUR PLAY.
MURMUR...
DO YOU EVEN KNOW WHAT YOU'RE SAYING?
I KNOW WHAT I'M DOING.
I THINK....
WE'RE MORTAL ENEMIES!
YOU'RE TRYING TO WIN THIS FIGHT TOO, AREN'T YOU?
WHY WOULD...
THAT'S THE THING...
UNO-AN.

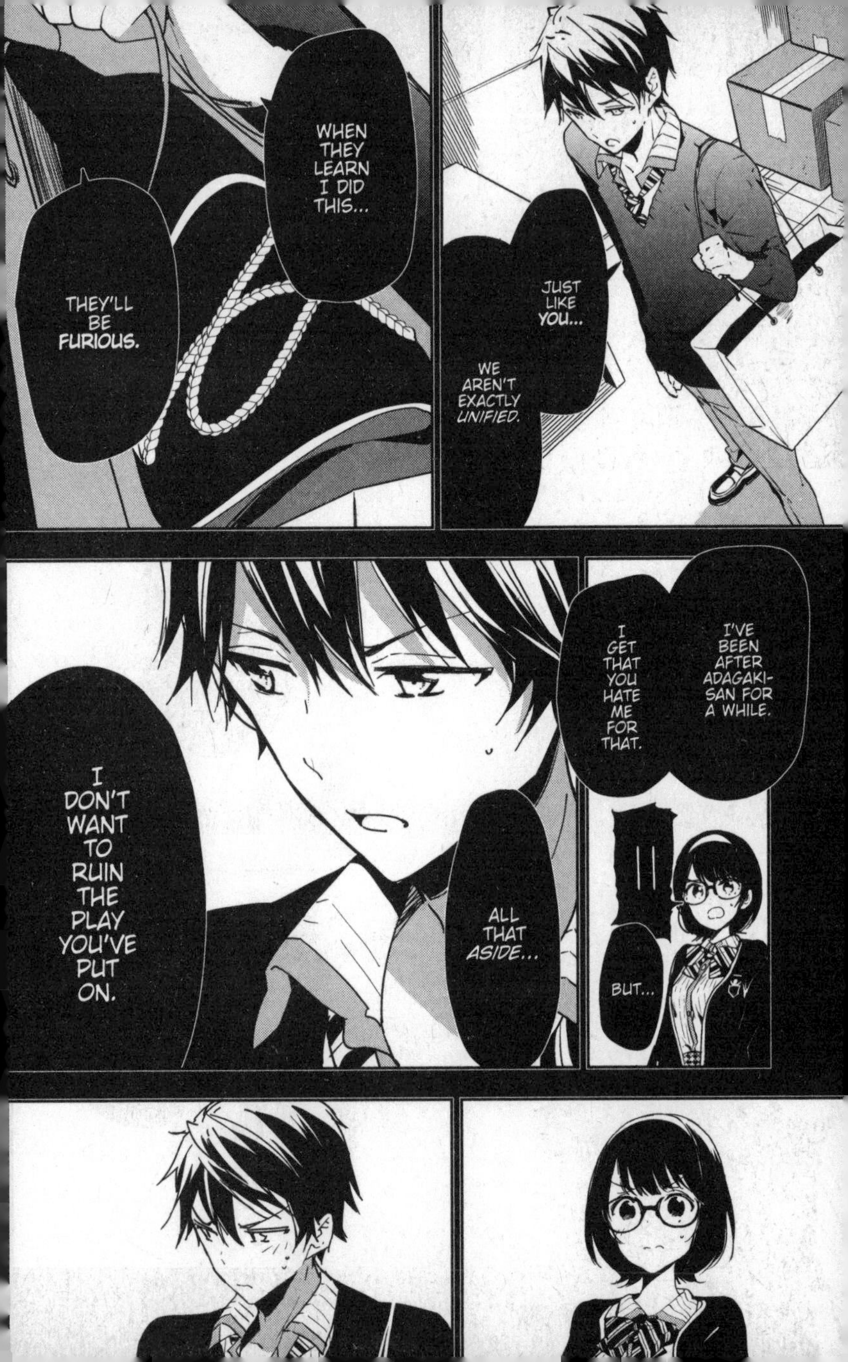
JUST LIKE YOU...
WE AREN'T EXACTLY UNIFIED.
WHEN THEY LEARN I DID THIS...
THEY'LL BE FURIOUS.
I'VE BEEN AFTER ADAGAKI-SAN FOR A WHILE.
I GET THAT YOU HATE ME FOR THAT.
BUT...
ALL THAT ASIDE...
I DON'T WANT TO RUIN THE PLAY YOU'VE PUT ON.

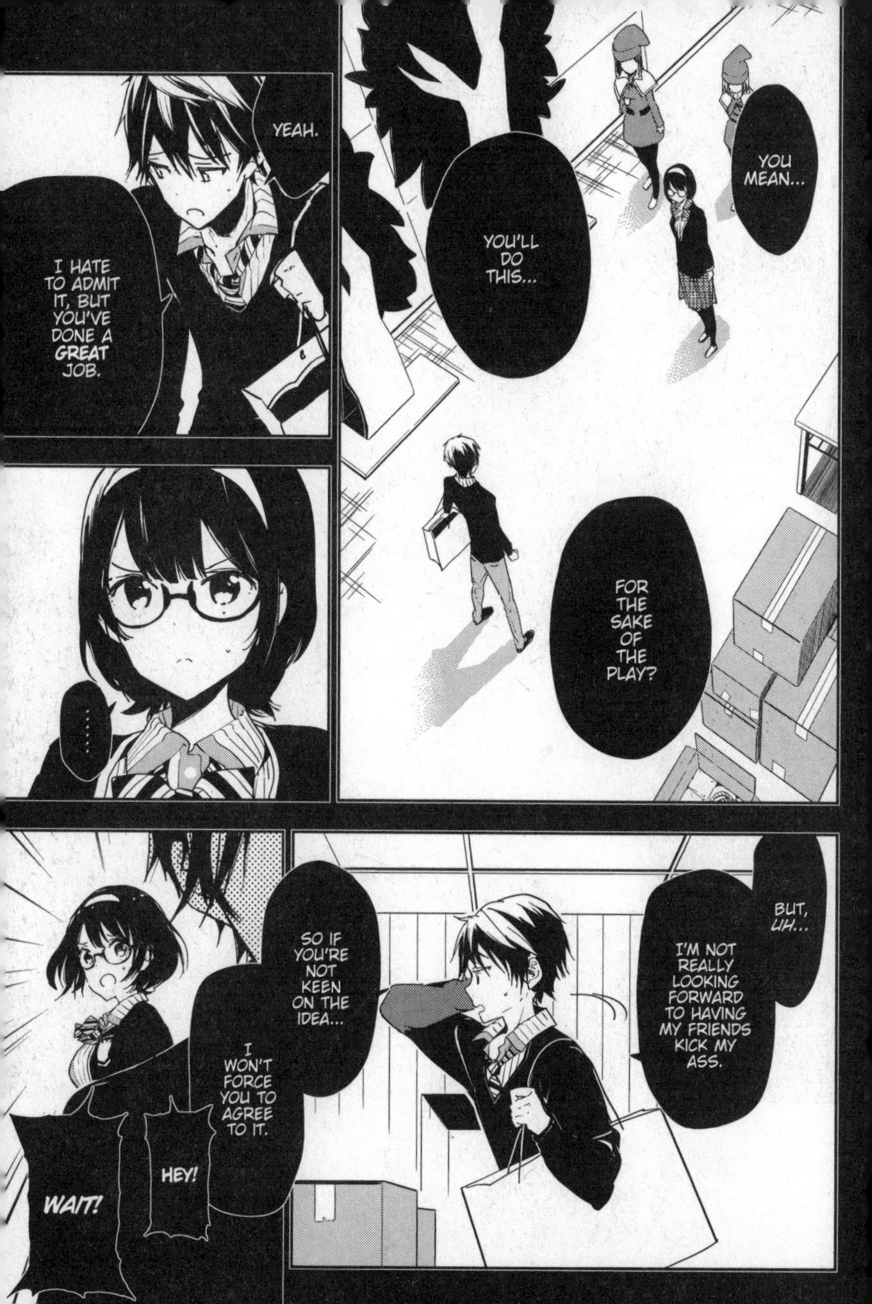
YOU MEAN...
YOU'LL DO THIS...
FOR THE SAKE OF THE PLAY?
YEAH.
I HATE TO ADMIT IT, BUT YOU'VE DONE A **GREAT** JOB.
......
BUT, *UH*...
I'M NOT REALLY LOOKING FORWARD TO HAVING MY FRIENDS KICK MY ASS.
SO IF YOU'RE NOT KEEN ON THE IDEA...
I WON'T FORCE YOU TO AGREE TO IT.
HEY!
WAIT!

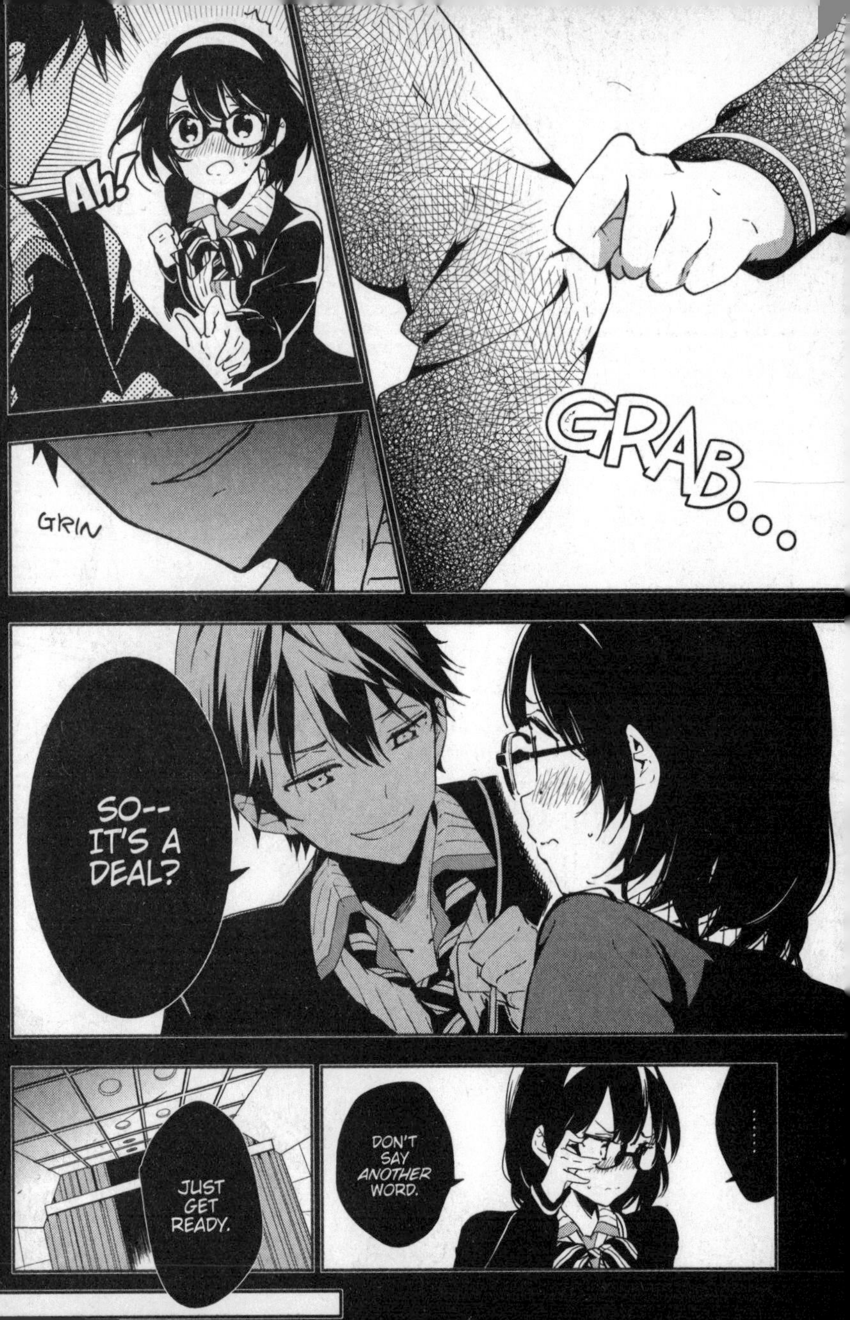
GRAB...
Ah!
GRIN
SO--
IT'S A
DEAL?
DON'T
SAY
ANOTHER
WORD.
JUST
GET
READY.

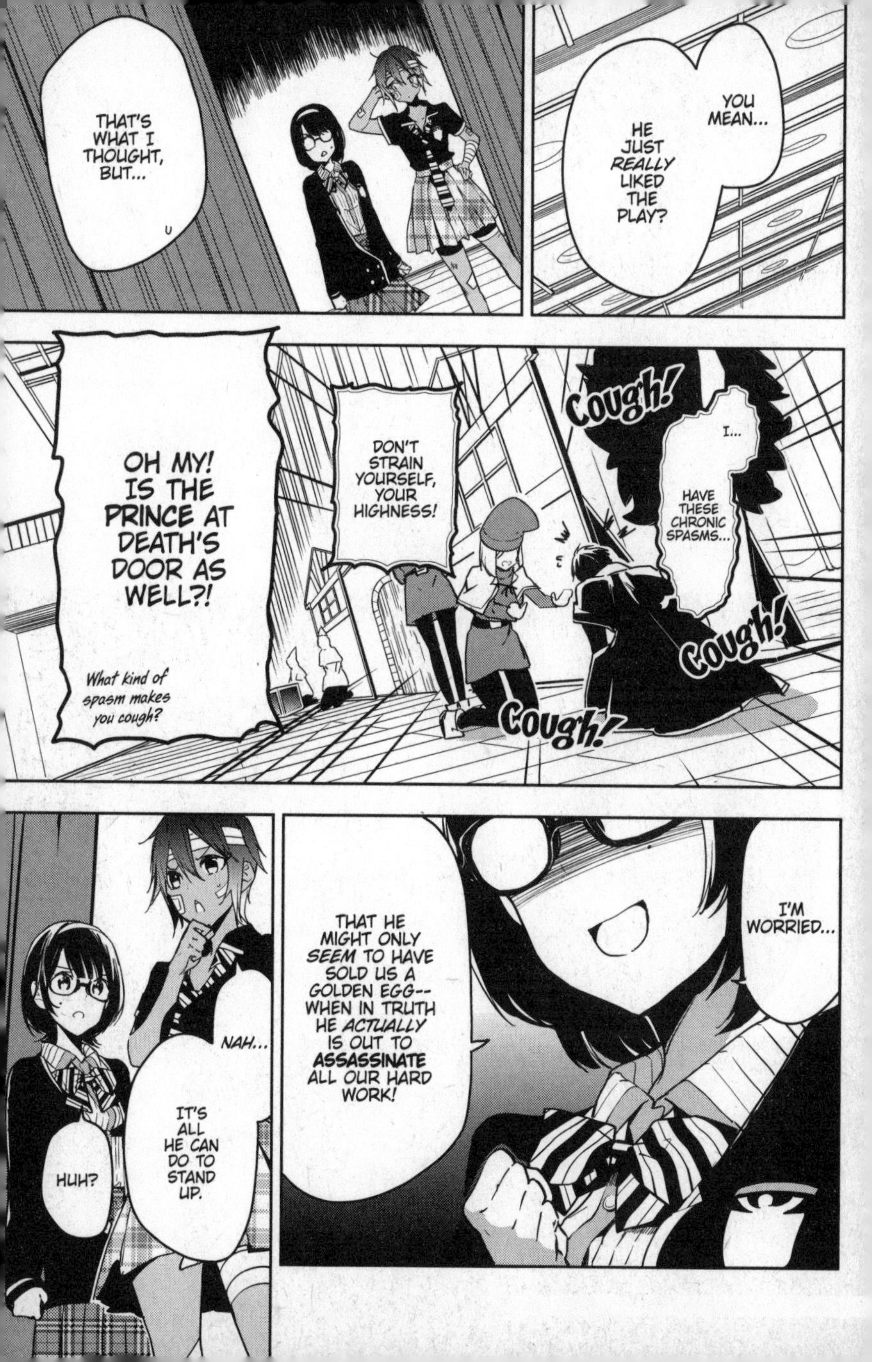
YOU MEAN... HE JUST REALLY LIKED THE PLAY?
THAT'S WHAT I THOUGHT, BUT...
Cough!
I... HAVE THESE CHRONIC SPASMS...
Cough!
Cough!
DON'T STRAIN YOURSELF, YOUR HIGHNESS!
OH MY! IS THE PRINCE AT DEATH'S DOOR AS WELL?!
What kind of spasm makes you cough?
I'M WORRIED...
THAT HE MIGHT ONLY SEEM TO HAVE SOLD US A GOLDEN EGG-- WHEN IN TRUTH HE ACTUALLY IS OUT TO ASSASSINATE ALL OUR HARD WORK!
NAH...
IT'S ALL HE CAN DO TO STAND UP.
HUH?

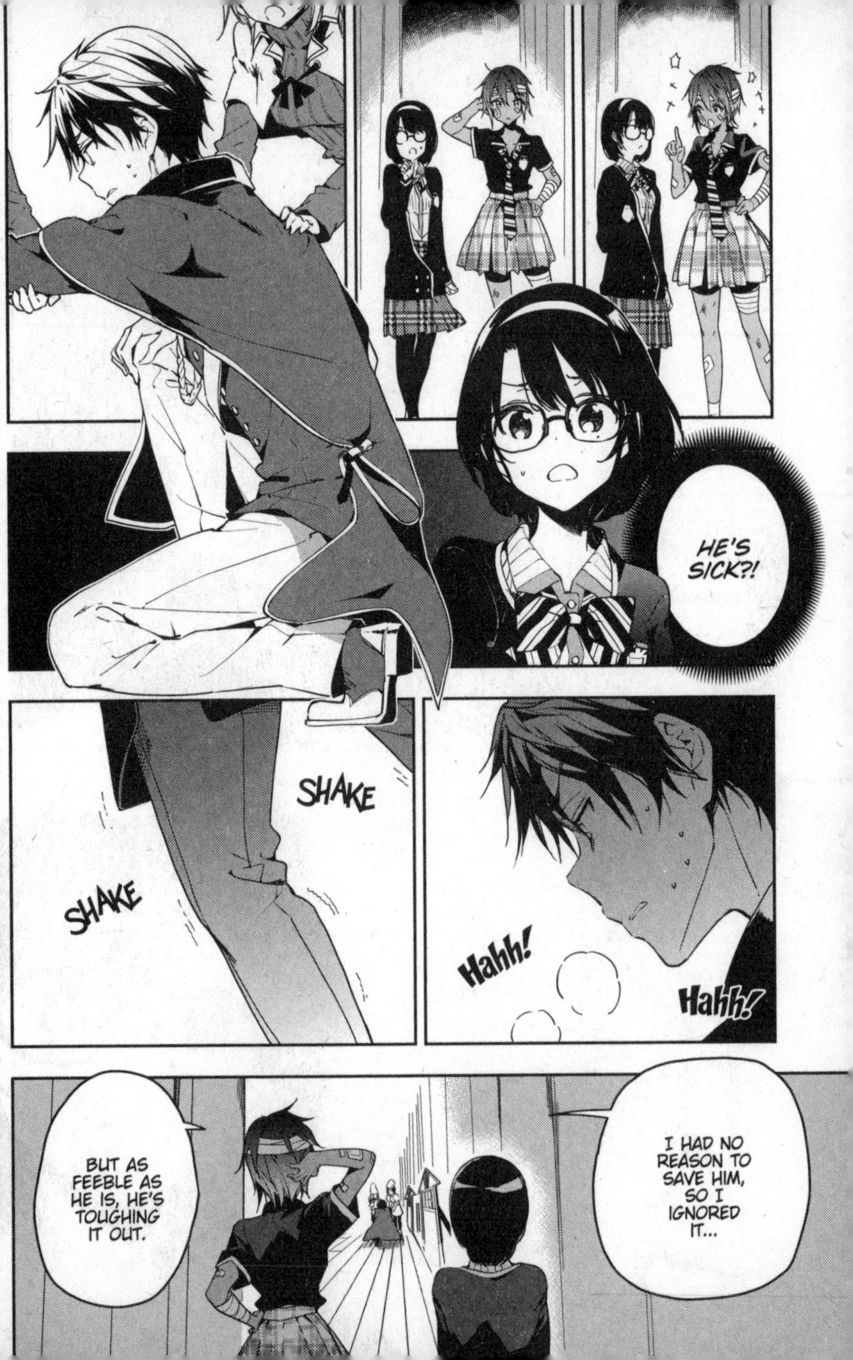
HE'S SICK?!
Hahh!
Hahh!
SHAKE
SHAKE
I HAD NO REASON TO SAVE HIM, SO I IGNORED IT...
BUT AS FEEBLE AS HE IS, HE'S TOUGHING IT OUT.

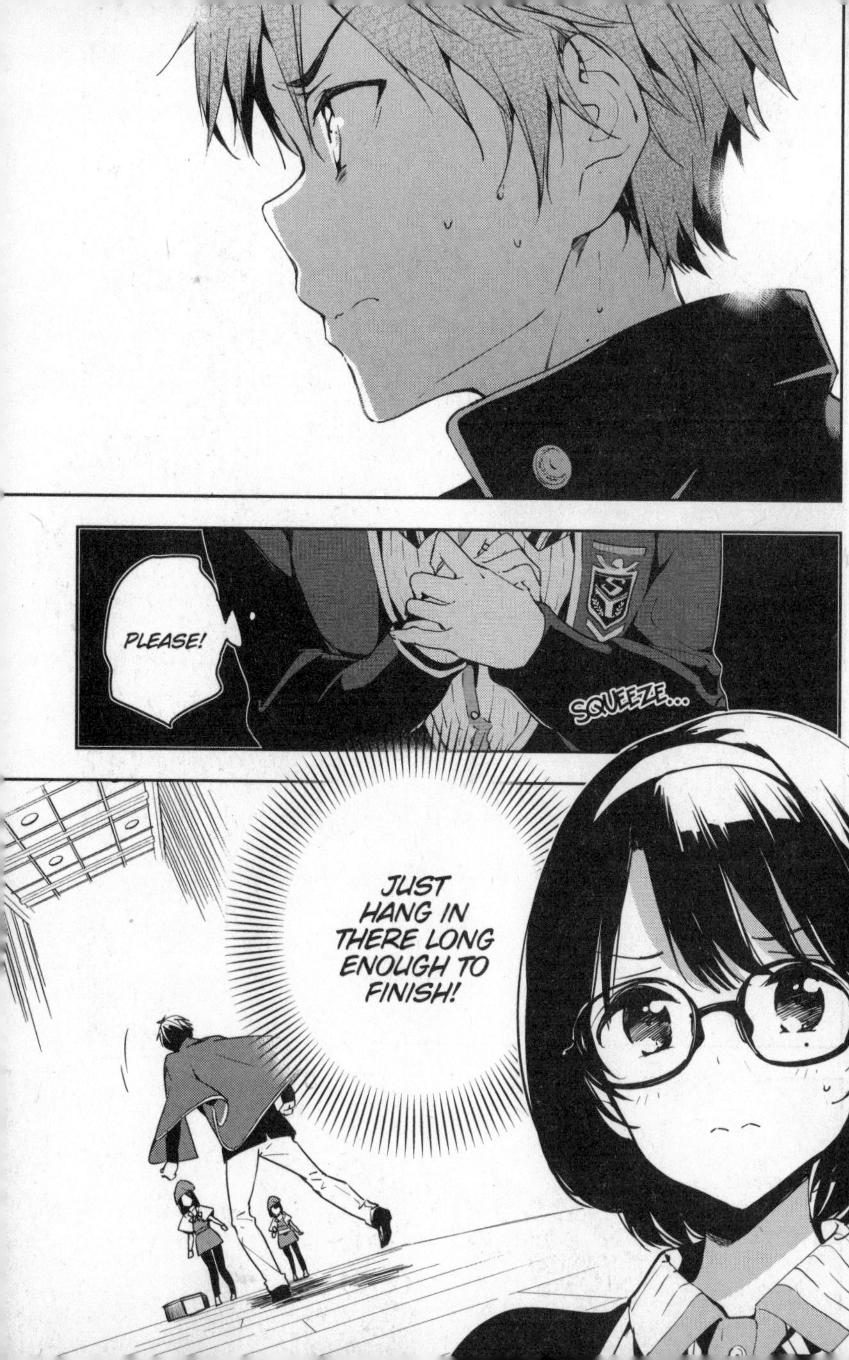
PLEASE!
SQUEEZE...
JUST HANG IN THERE LONG ENOUGH TO FINISH!

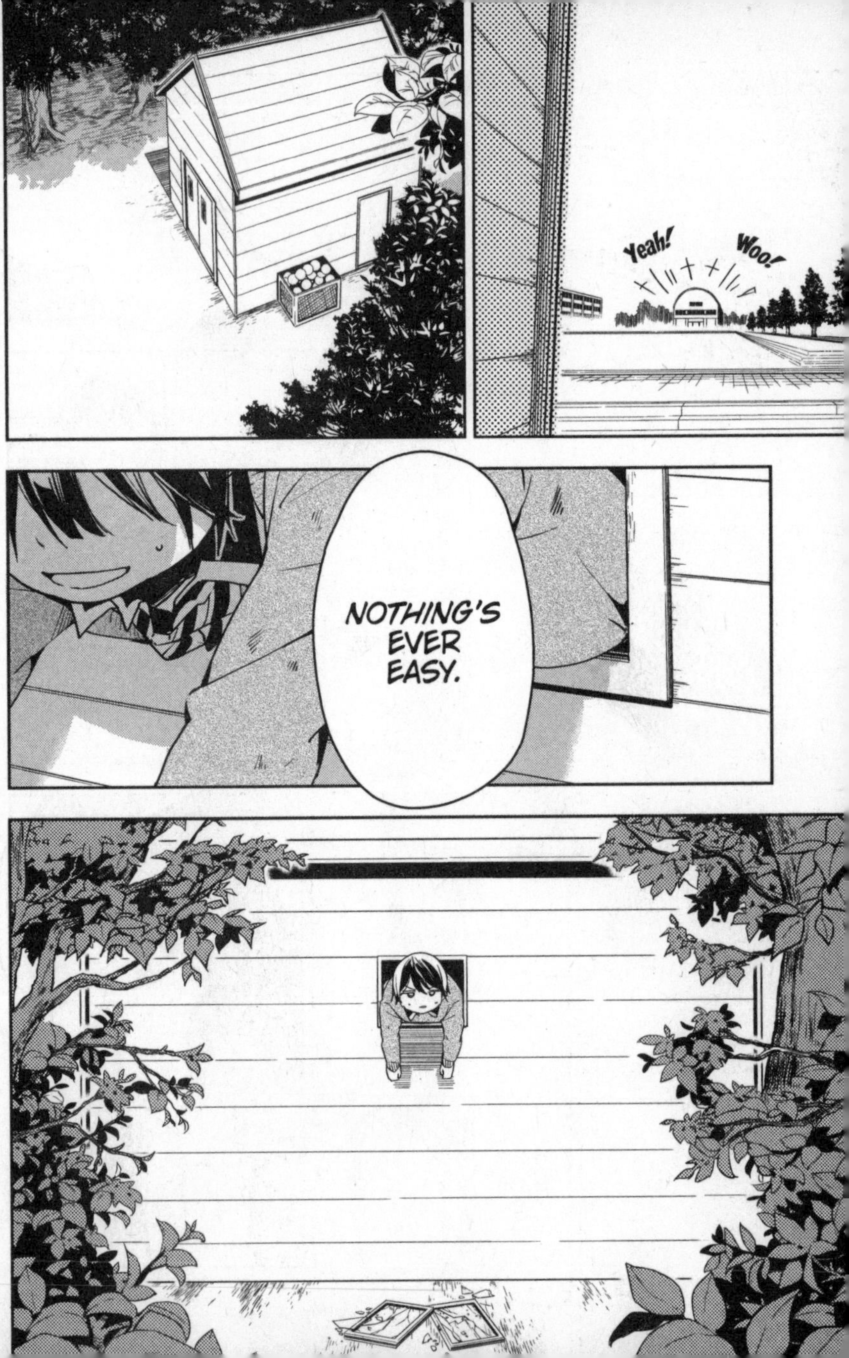
Woo!
Yeah!
NOTHING'S EVER EASY.

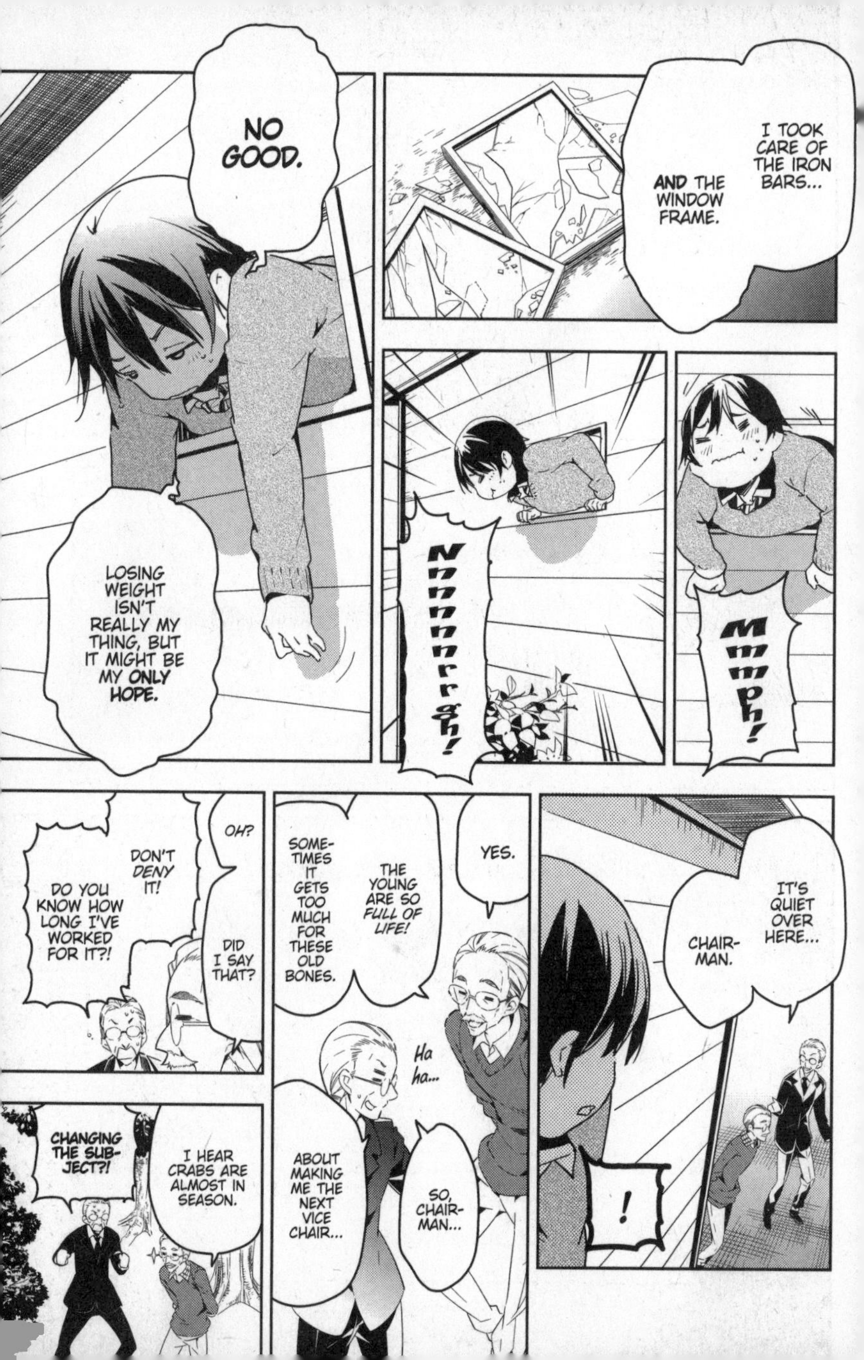
I TOOK CARE OF THE IRON BARS...
AND THE WINDOW FRAME.
Mmmph!
Nnnnnrrgh!
NO GOOD.
LOSING WEIGHT ISN'T REALLY MY THING, BUT IT MIGHT BE MY ONLY HOPE.
IT'S QUIET OVER HERE...
CHAIRMAN.
!
YES.
THE YOUNG ARE SO FULL OF LIFE!
SOMETIMES IT GETS TOO MUCH FOR THESE OLD BONES.
Ha ha...
SO, CHAIRMAN...
ABOUT MAKING ME THE NEXT VICE CHAIR...
OH?
DID I SAY THAT?
DON'T DENY IT!
DO YOU KNOW HOW LONG I'VE WORKED FOR IT?!
I HEAR CRABS ARE ALMOST IN SEASON.
CHANGING THE SUBJECT?!

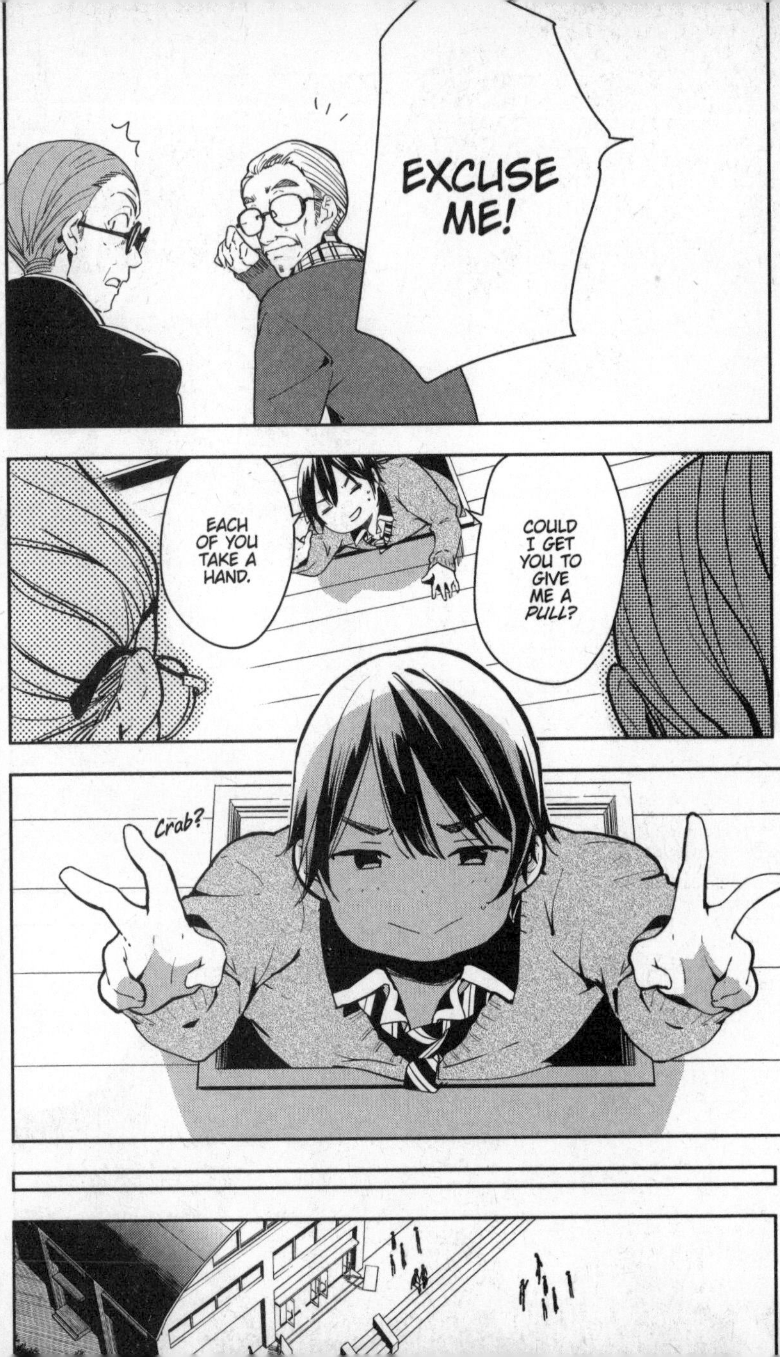
EXCUSE ME!
COULD I GET YOU TO GIVE ME A *PULL?*
EACH OF YOU TAKE A HAND.
Crab?

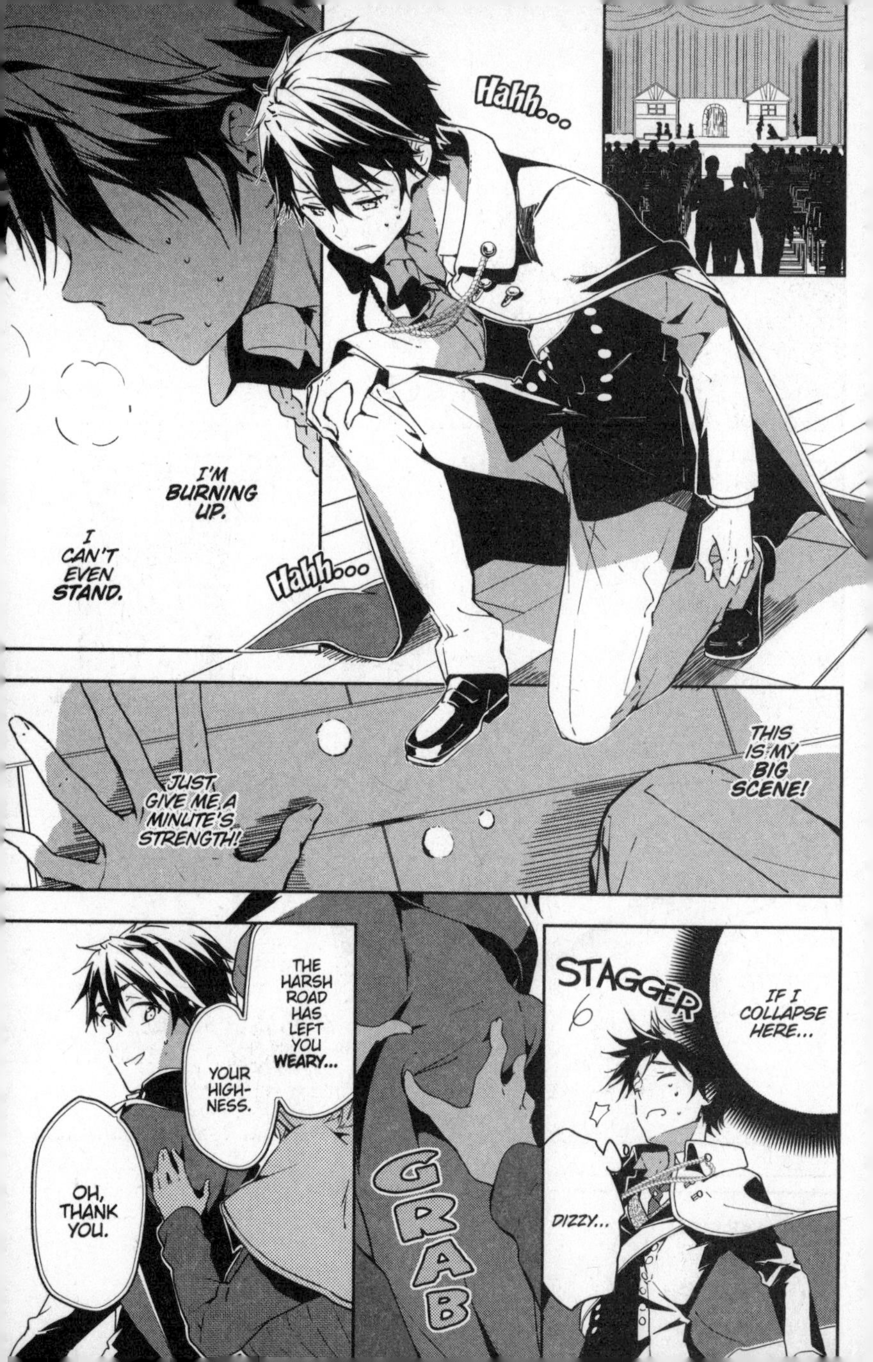
Hahh...
I'M BURNING UP.
I CAN'T EVEN STAND.
Hahh...
THIS IS MY BIG SCENE!
JUST GIVE ME A MINUTE'S STRENGTH!
STAGGER
IF I COLLAPSE HERE...
DIZZY...
GRAB
THE HARSH ROAD HAS LEFT YOU WEARY...
YOUR HIGHNESS.
OH, THANK YOU.

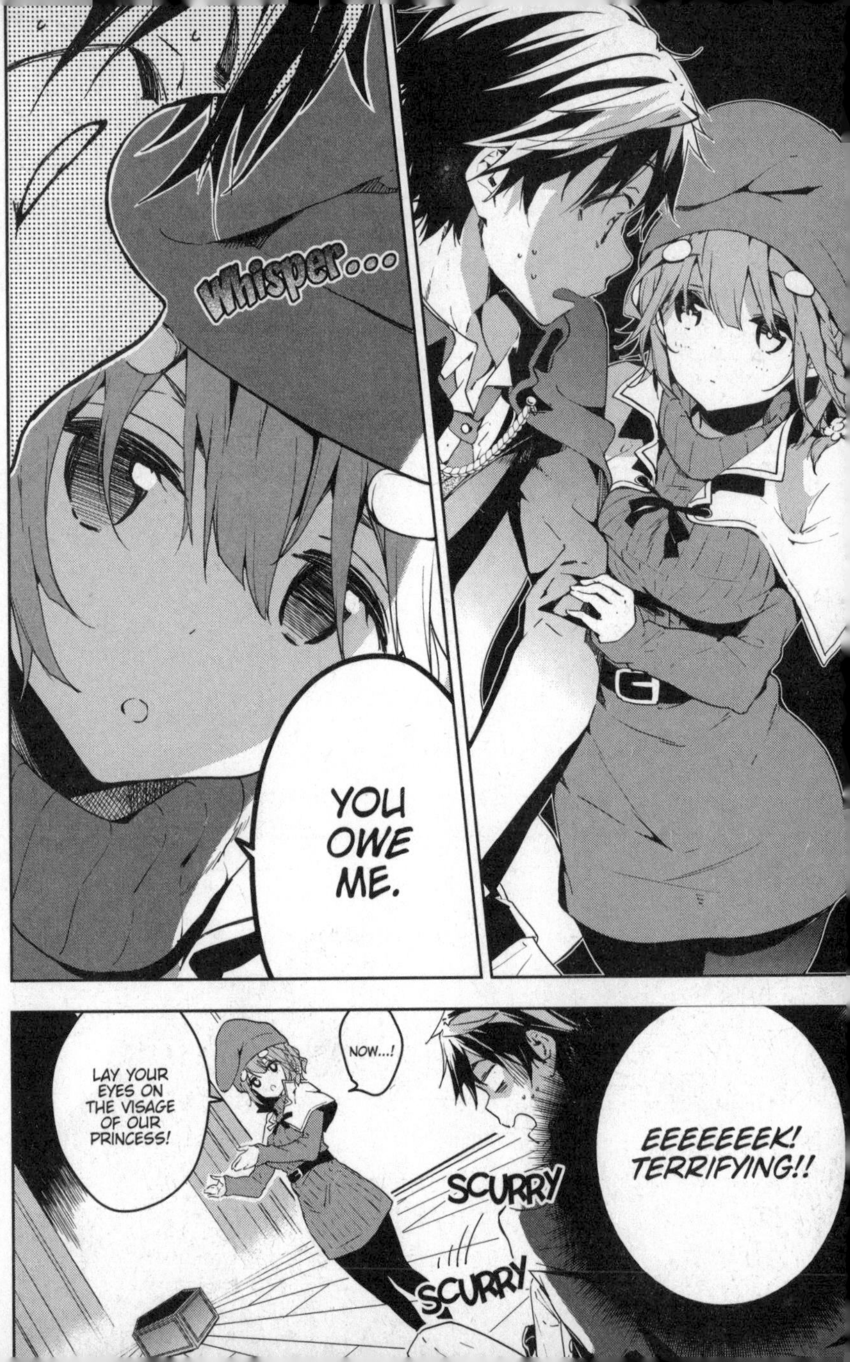
whisper...
YOU OWE ME.
EEEEEEEK! TERRIFYING!!
SCURRY
SCURRY
NOW...!
LAY YOUR EYES ON THE VISAGE OF OUR PRINCESS!

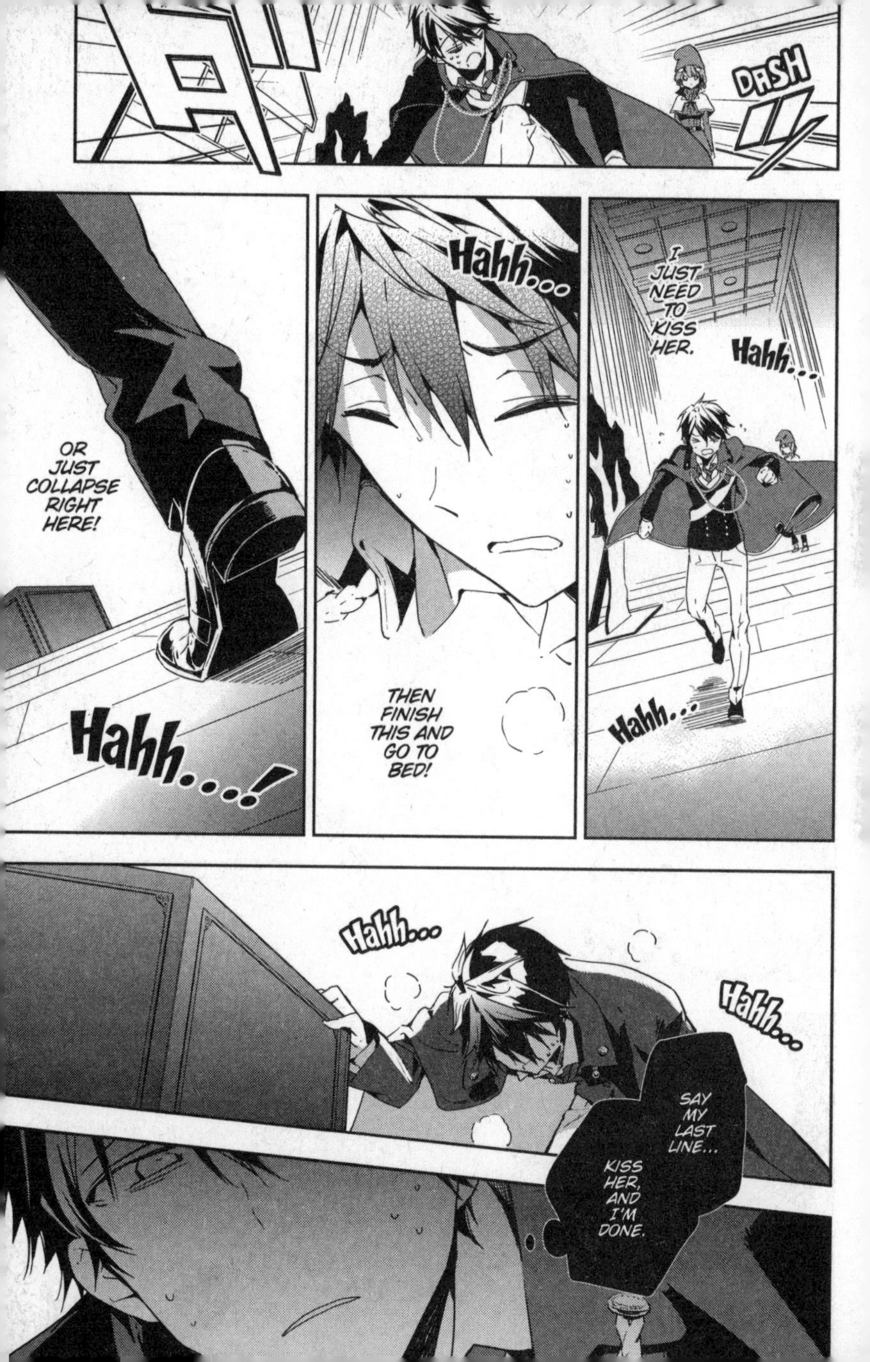
DASH
I JUST NEED TO KISS HER.
Hahh...
Hahh...
Hahh...
THEN FINISH THIS AND GO TO BED!
OR JUST COLLAPSE RIGHT HERE!
Hahh...!
Hahh...
SAY MY LAST LINE...
KISS HER, AND I'M DONE.
Hahh...

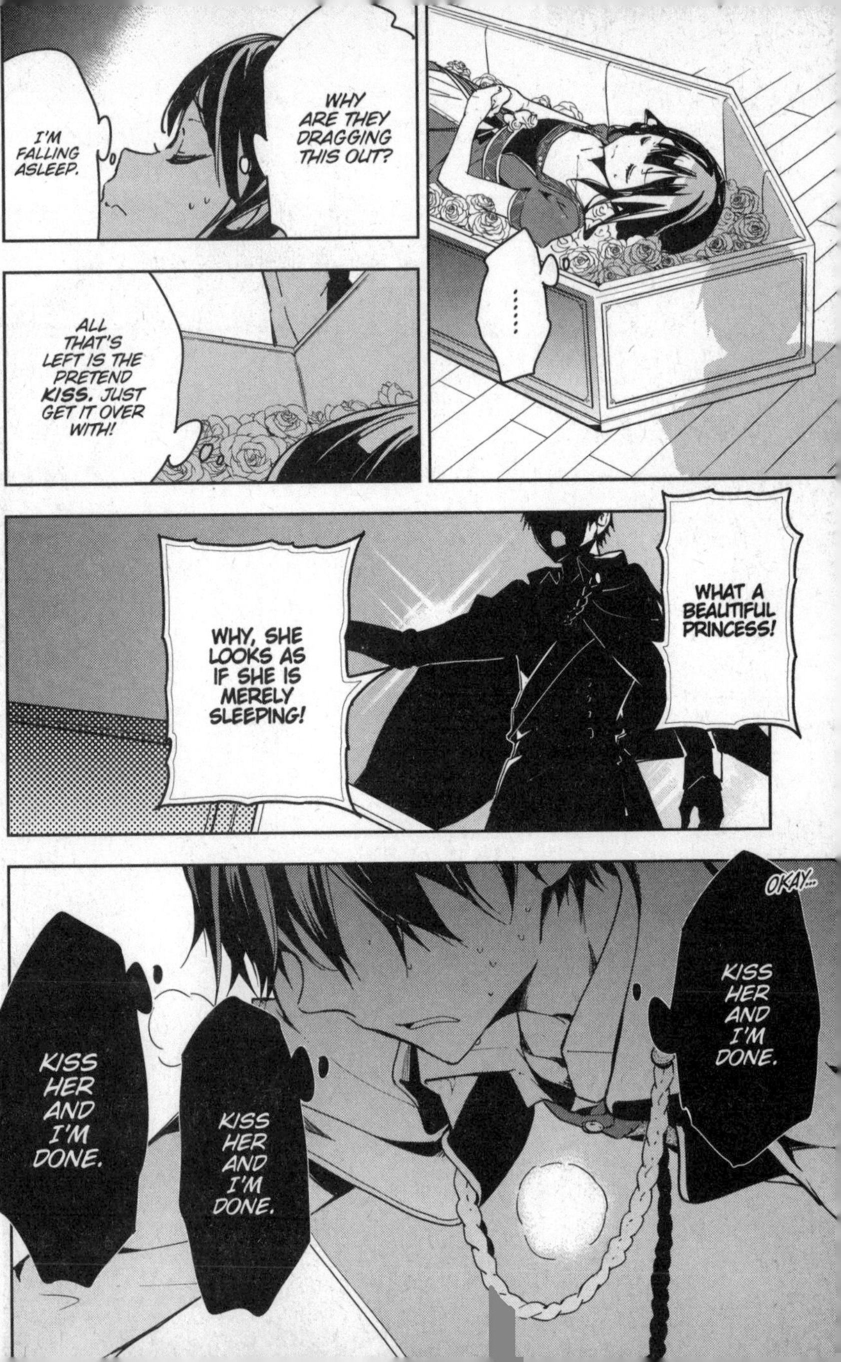
......
WHY ARE THEY DRAGGING THIS OUT?
I'M FALLING ASLEEP.
ALL THAT'S LEFT IS THE PRETEND **KISS.** JUST GET IT OVER WITH!
WHAT A BEAUTIFUL PRINCESS!
WHY, SHE LOOKS AS IF SHE IS MERELY SLEEPING!
OKAY...
KISS HER AND I'M DONE.
KISS HER AND I'M DONE.
KISS HER AND I'M DONE.

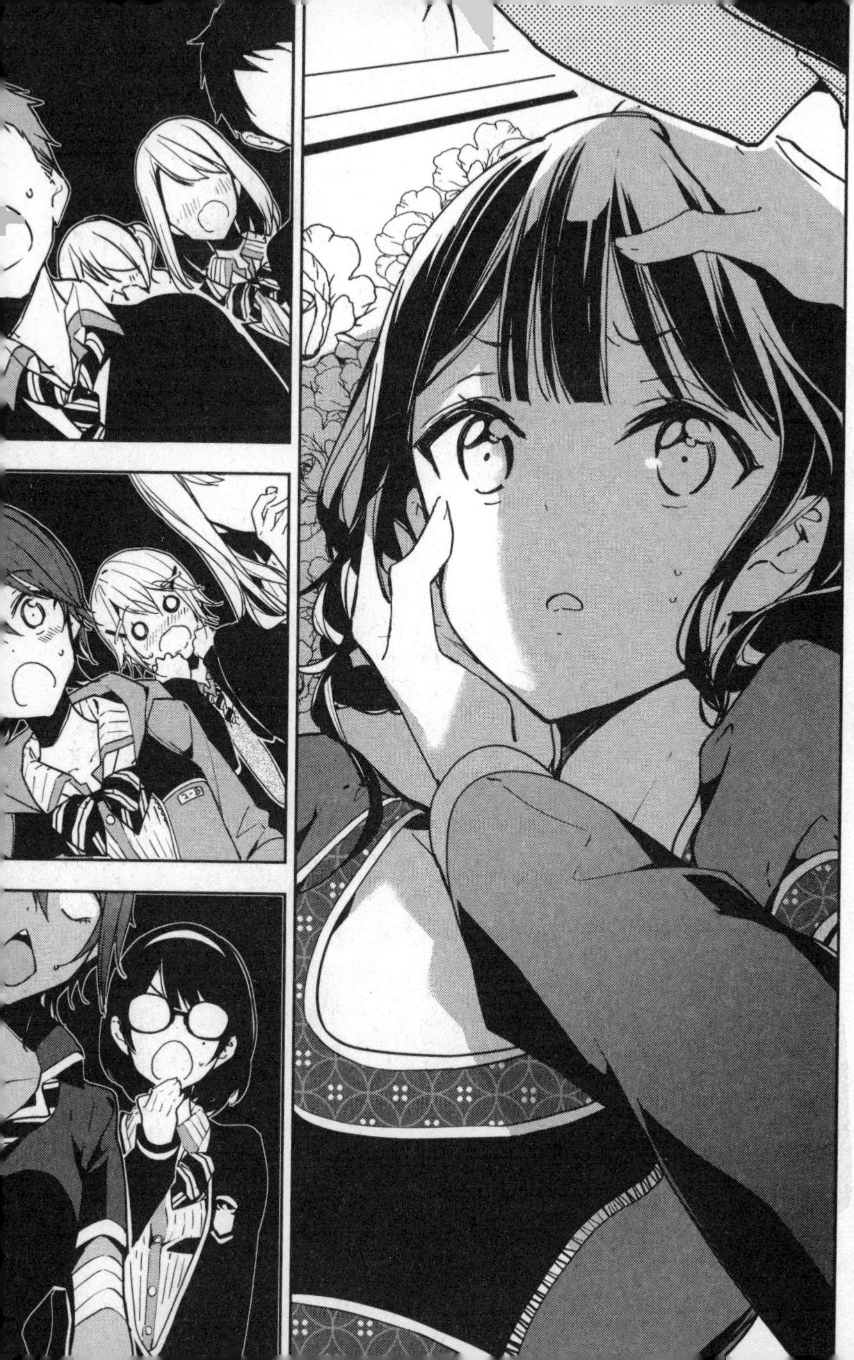

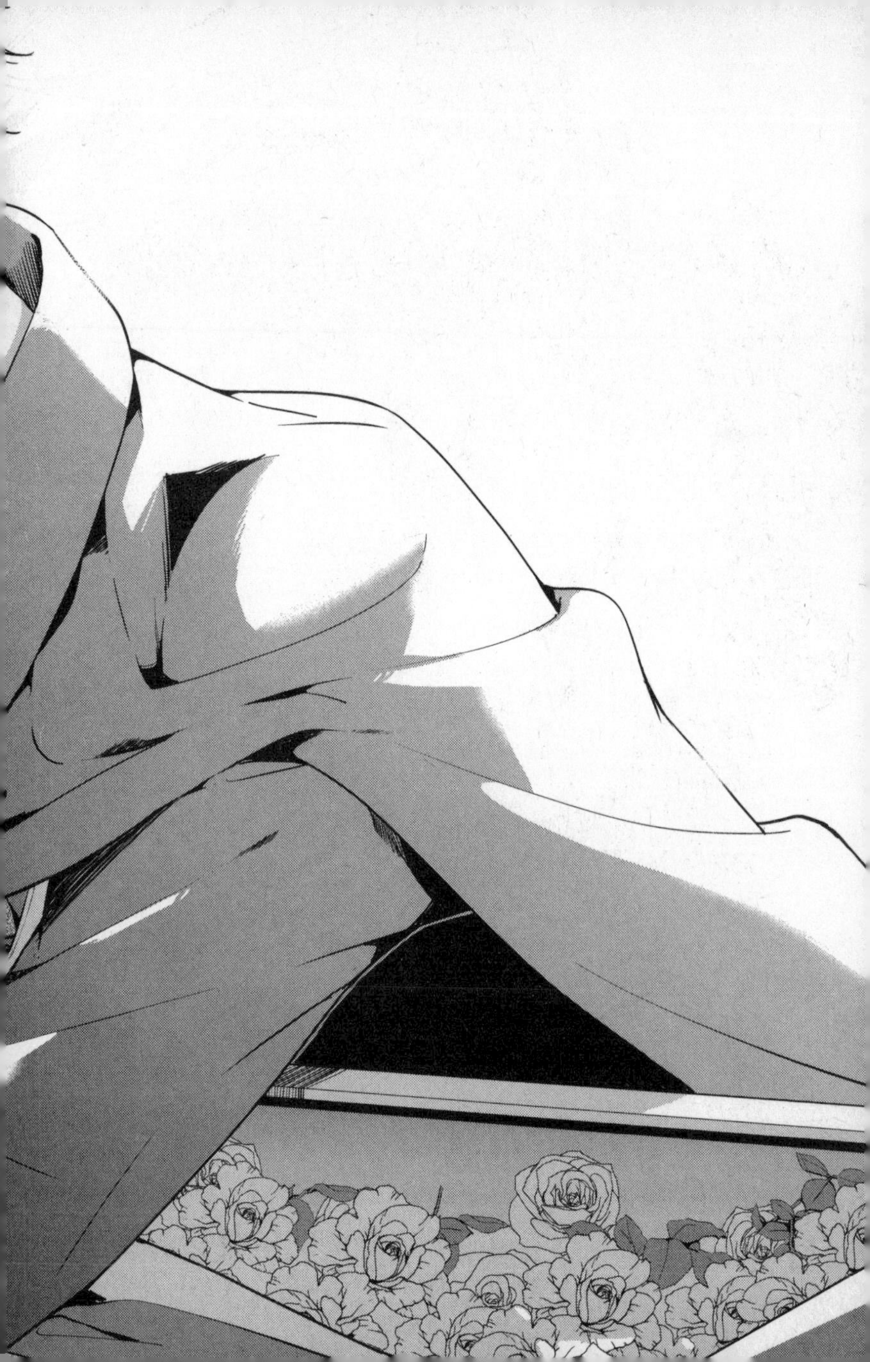

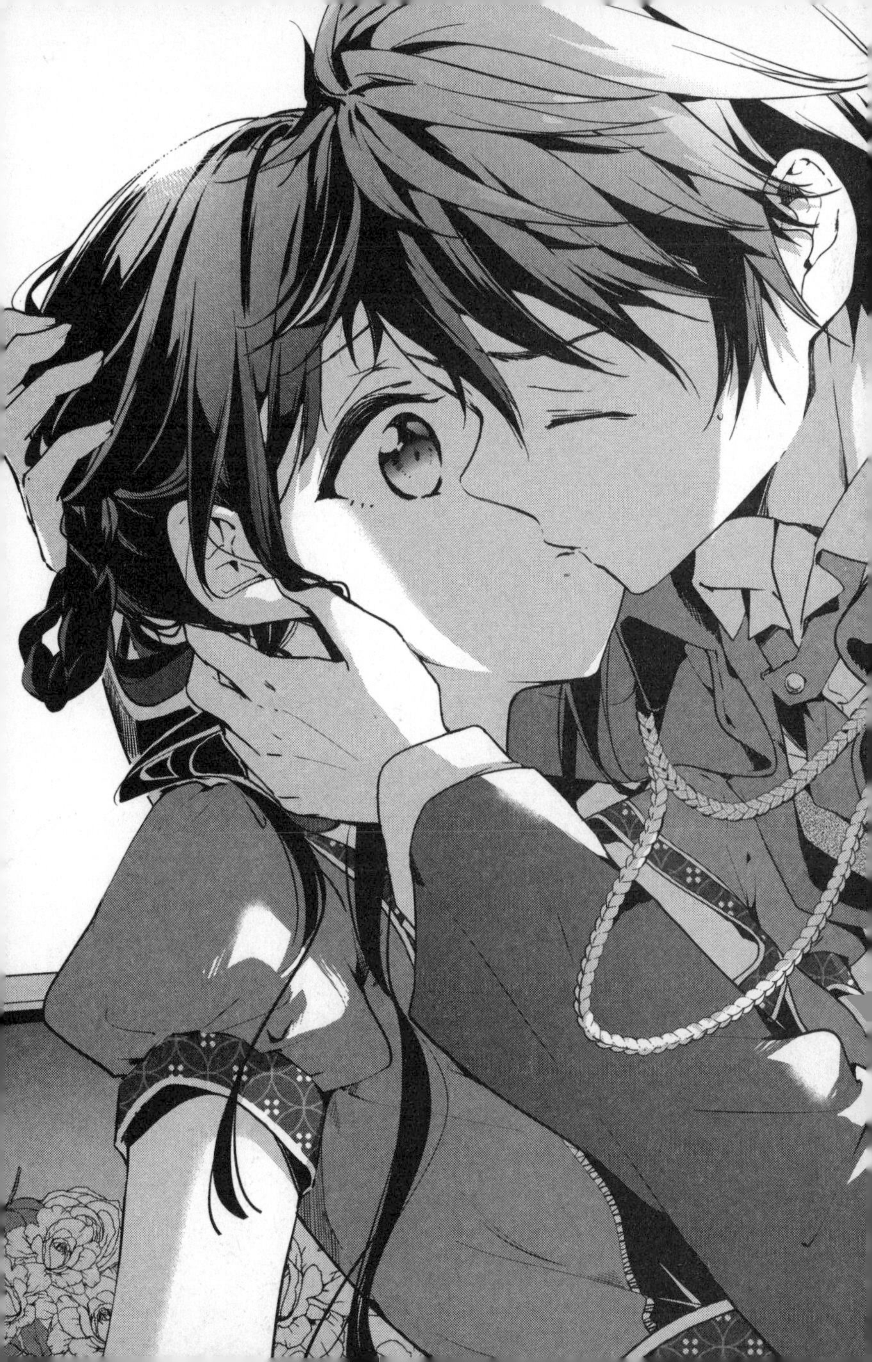

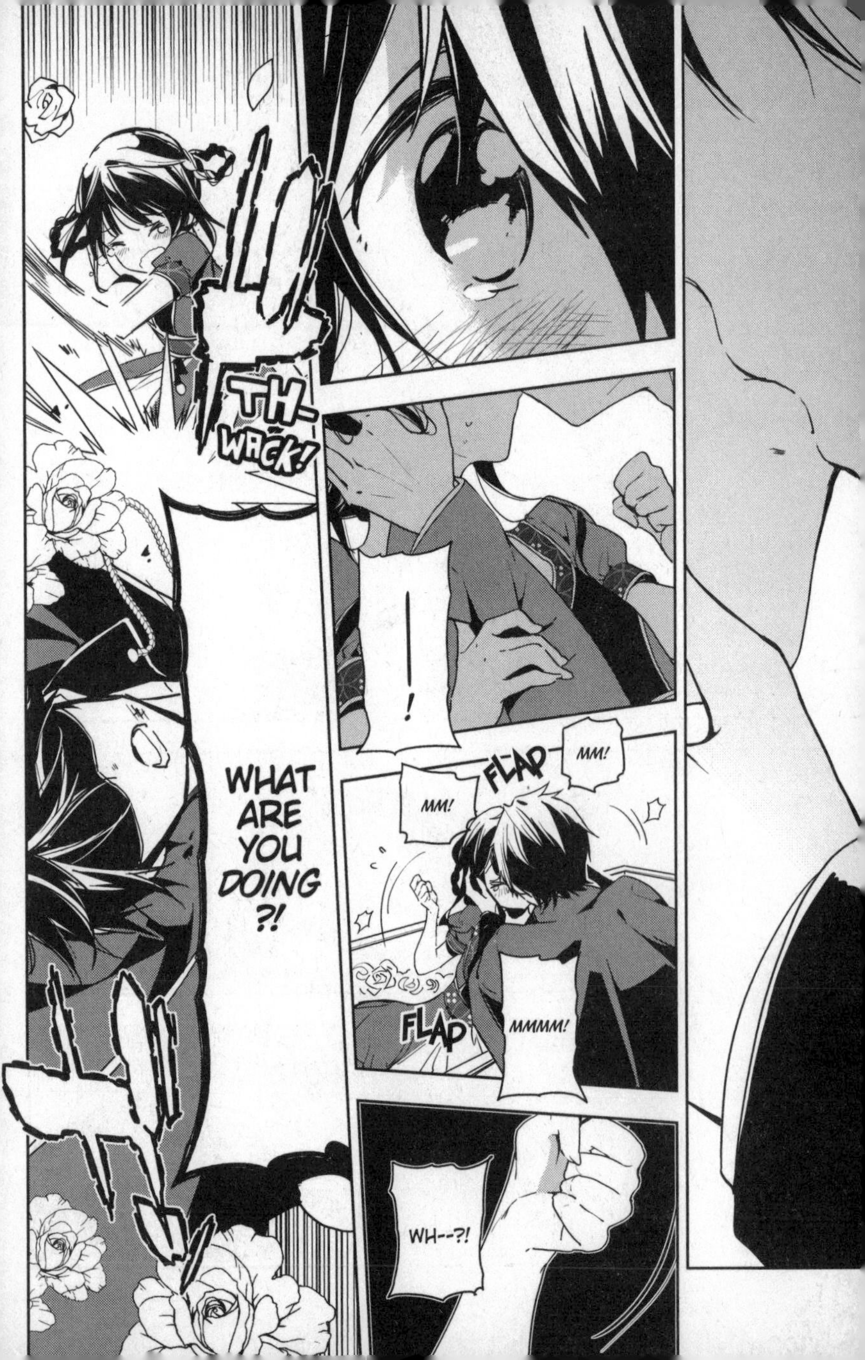
!
MM!
FLAP
MM!
MMMMM!
FLAP
WH--?!
TH-WACK!
WHAT ARE YOU DOING?!

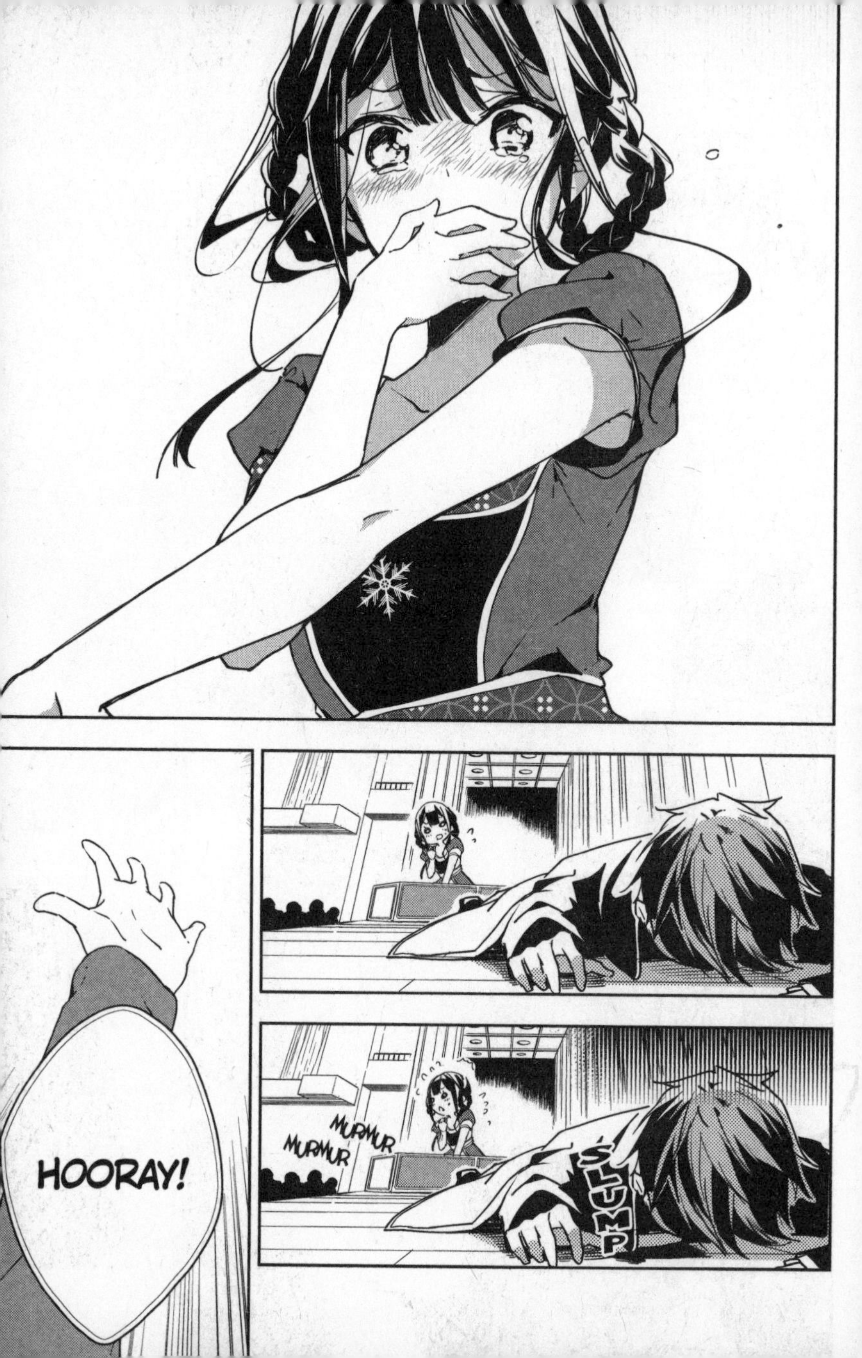
SLUMP
MURMUR
MURMUR
HOORAY!

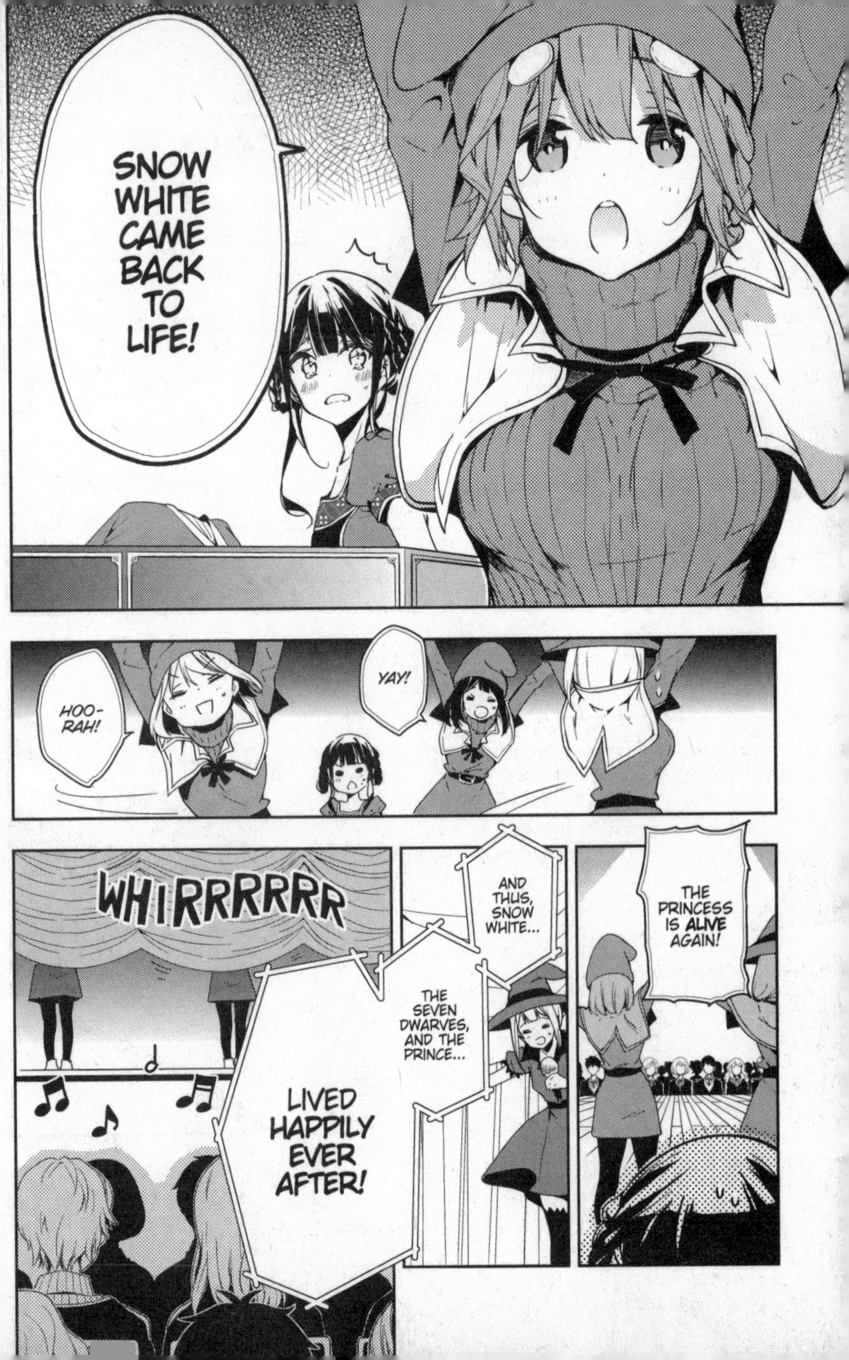
SNOW WHITE CAME BACK TO LIFE!
YAY!
HOO-RAH!
THE PRINCESS IS ALIVE AGAIN!
AND THUS, SNOW WHITE...
THE SEVEN DWARVES, AND THE PRINCE...
LIVED HAPPILY EVER AFTER!
WHIRRRRRRR

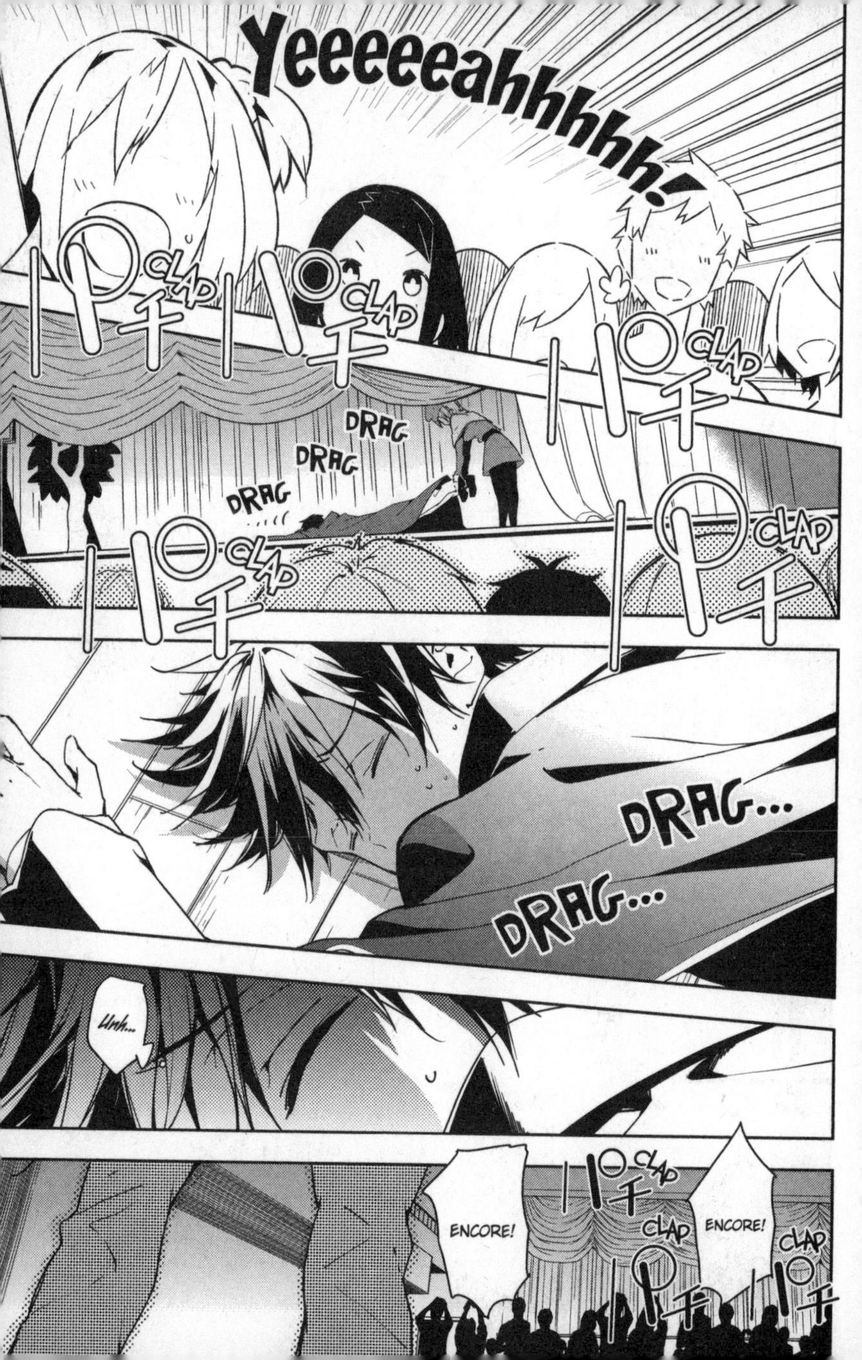
Yeeeeeahhhhh!
パチ CLAP
パチ CLAP
パチ CLAP
DRAG
DRAG
DRAG
パチ CLAP
パチ CLAP
DRAG...
DRAG...
Unh...
ENCORE!
ENCORE!
パチ CLAP
パチ CLAP
パチ CLAP

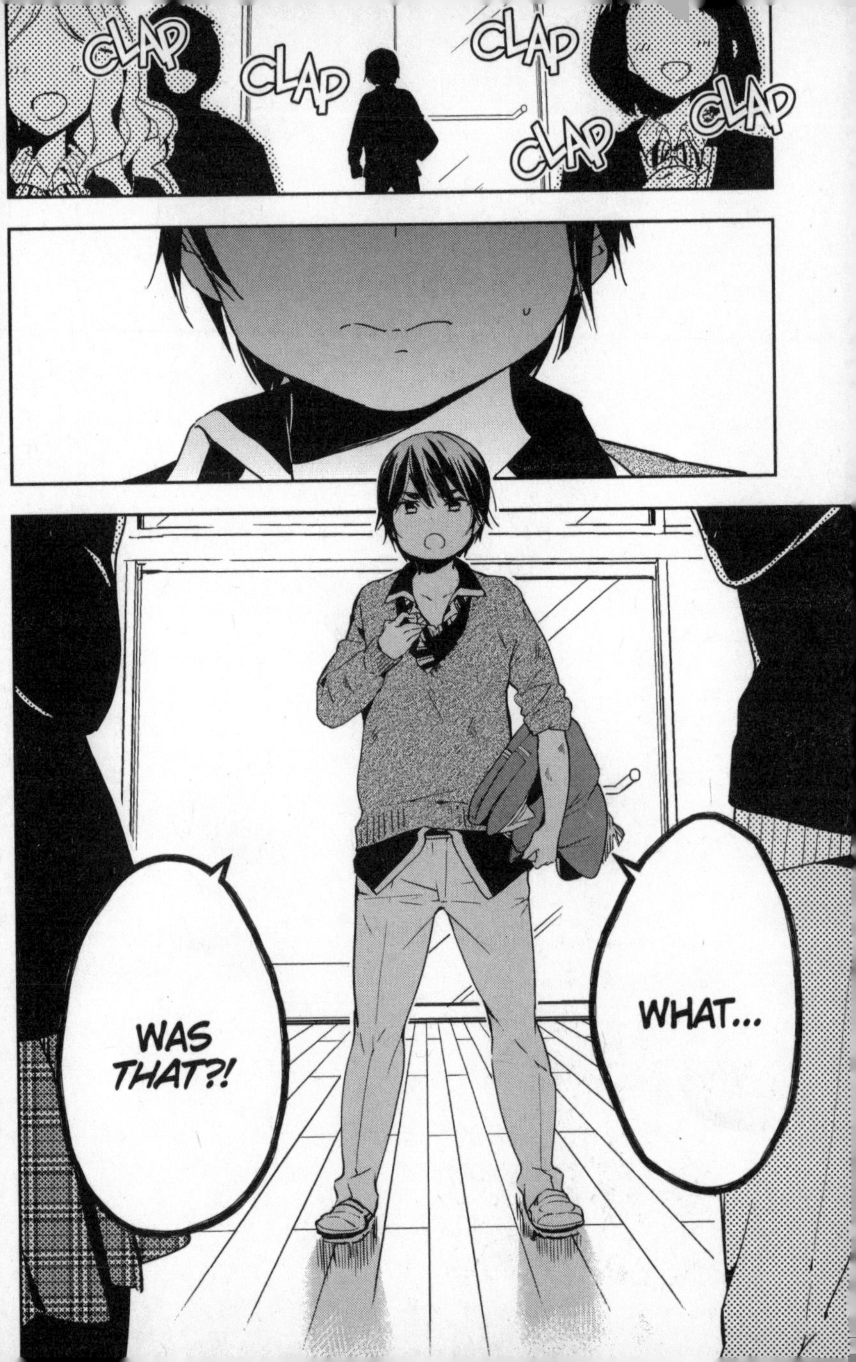
CLAP
CLAP
CLAP
CLAP
CLAP
WHAT...
WAS THAT?!

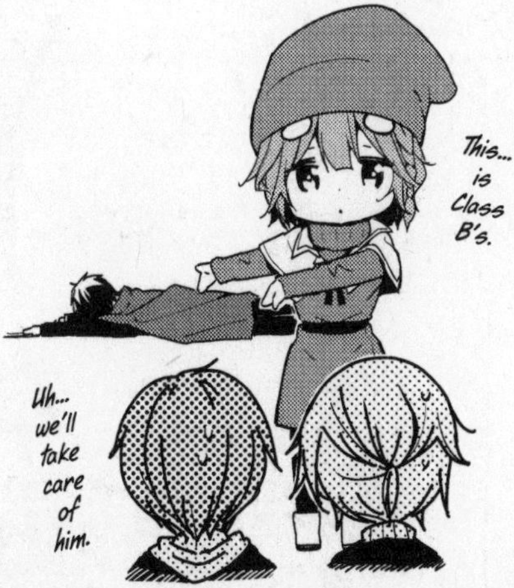
This... is Class B's.
Uh... we'll take care of him.

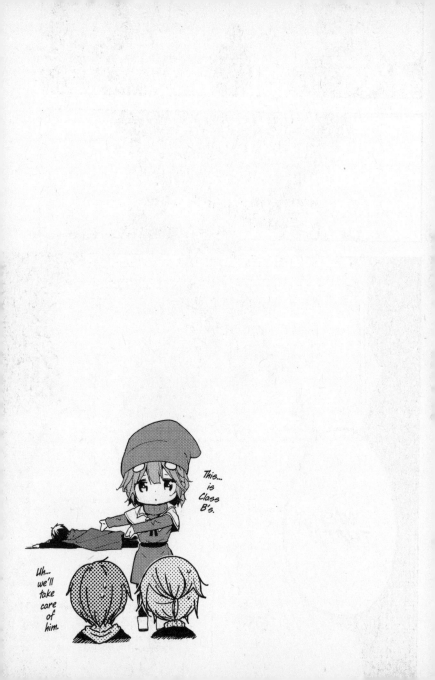

Masamune-kun's
REVENGE
Presented by Hazuki Takeoka & TIV

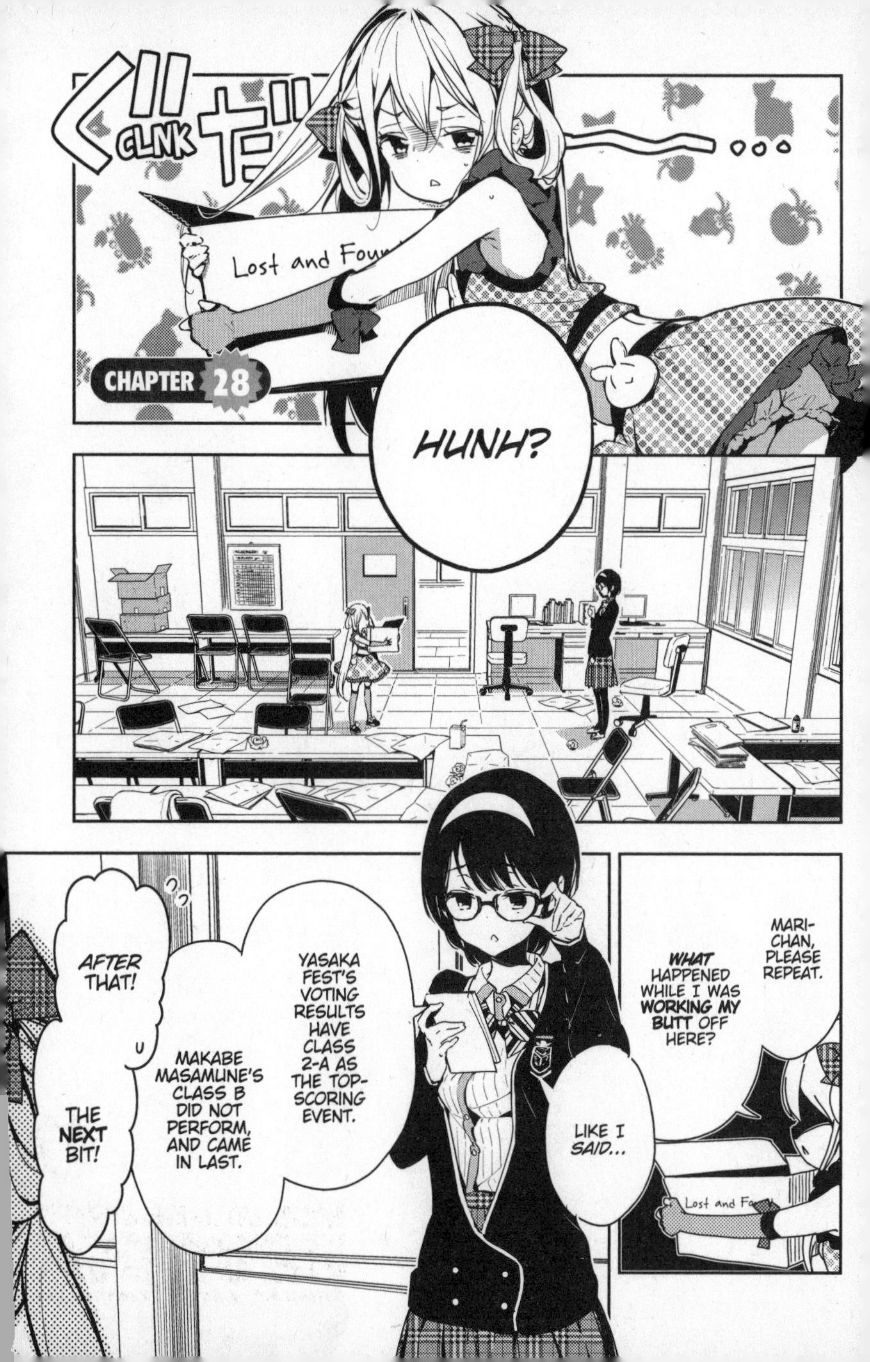
CLNK
Lost and Found
CHAPTER 28
HUNH?
MARI-CHAN, PLEASE REPEAT.
WHAT HAPPENED WHILE I WAS WORKING MY BUTT OFF HERE?
Lost and Found
LIKE I SAID...
YASAKA FEST'S VOTING RESULTS HAVE CLASS 2-A AS THE TOP-SCORING EVENT.
MAKABE MASAMUNE'S CLASS B DID NOT PERFORM, AND CAME IN LAST.
AFTER THAT!
THE NEXT BIT!

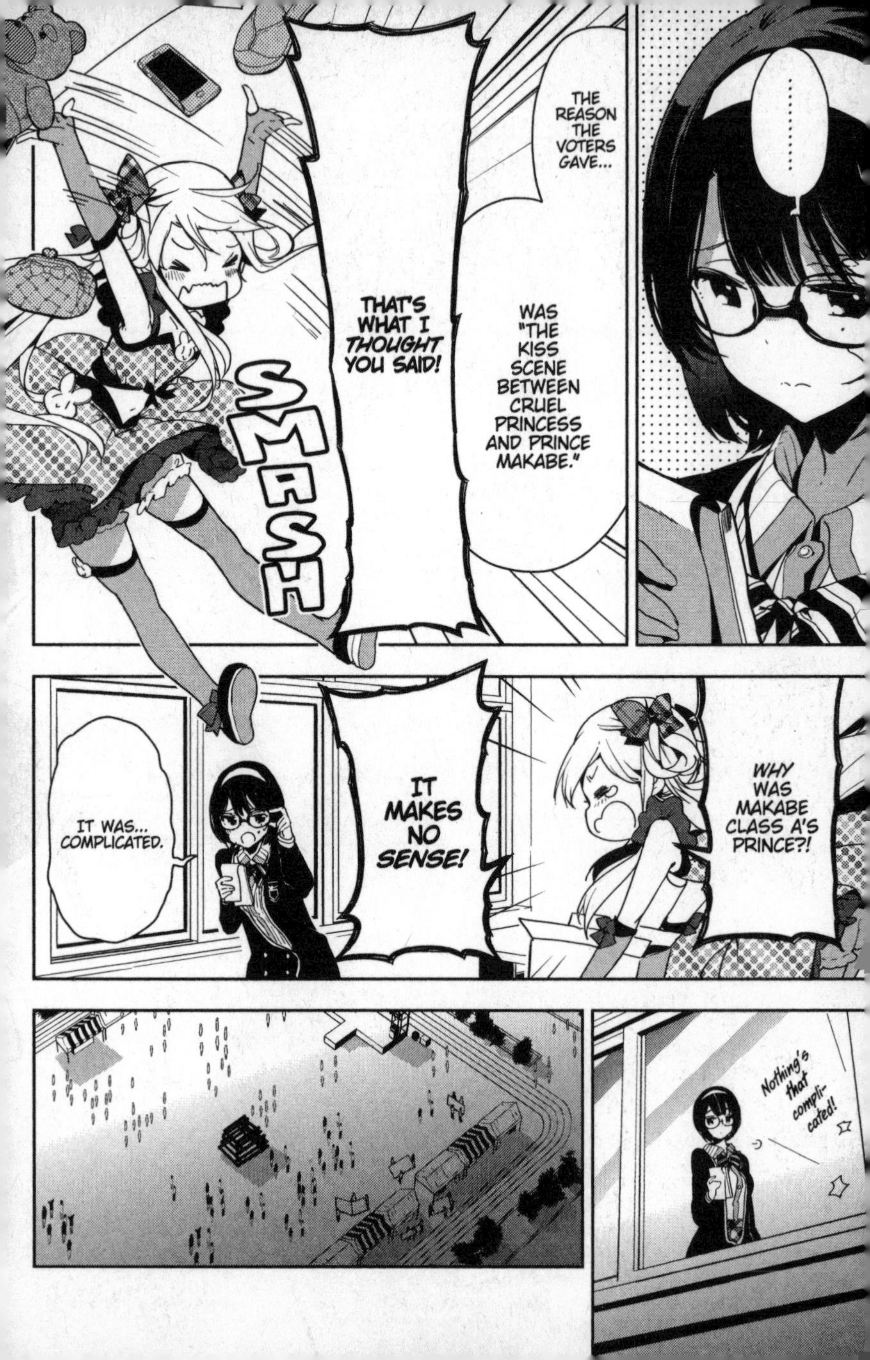
......
THE REASON THE VOTERS GAVE...
WAS "THE KISS SCENE BETWEEN CRUEL PRINCESS AND PRINCE MAKABE."
THAT'S WHAT I *THOUGHT* YOU SAID!
SMASH
WHY WAS MAKABE CLASS A'S PRINCE?!
IT MAKES NO *SENSE!*
IT WAS... COMPLICATED.
Nothing's that compli-cated!

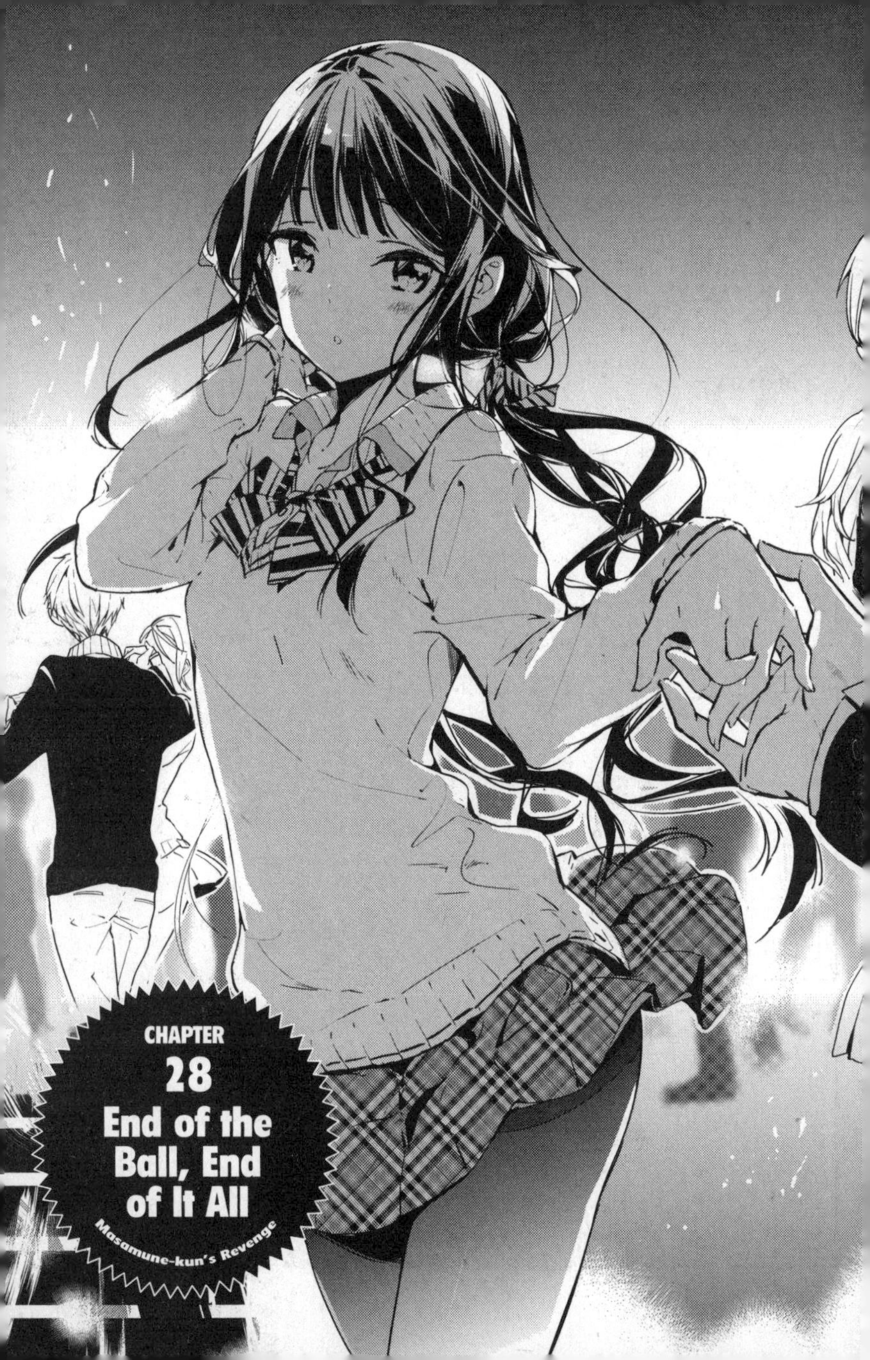
CHAPTER
28
End of the Ball, End of It All
Masamune-kun's Revenge

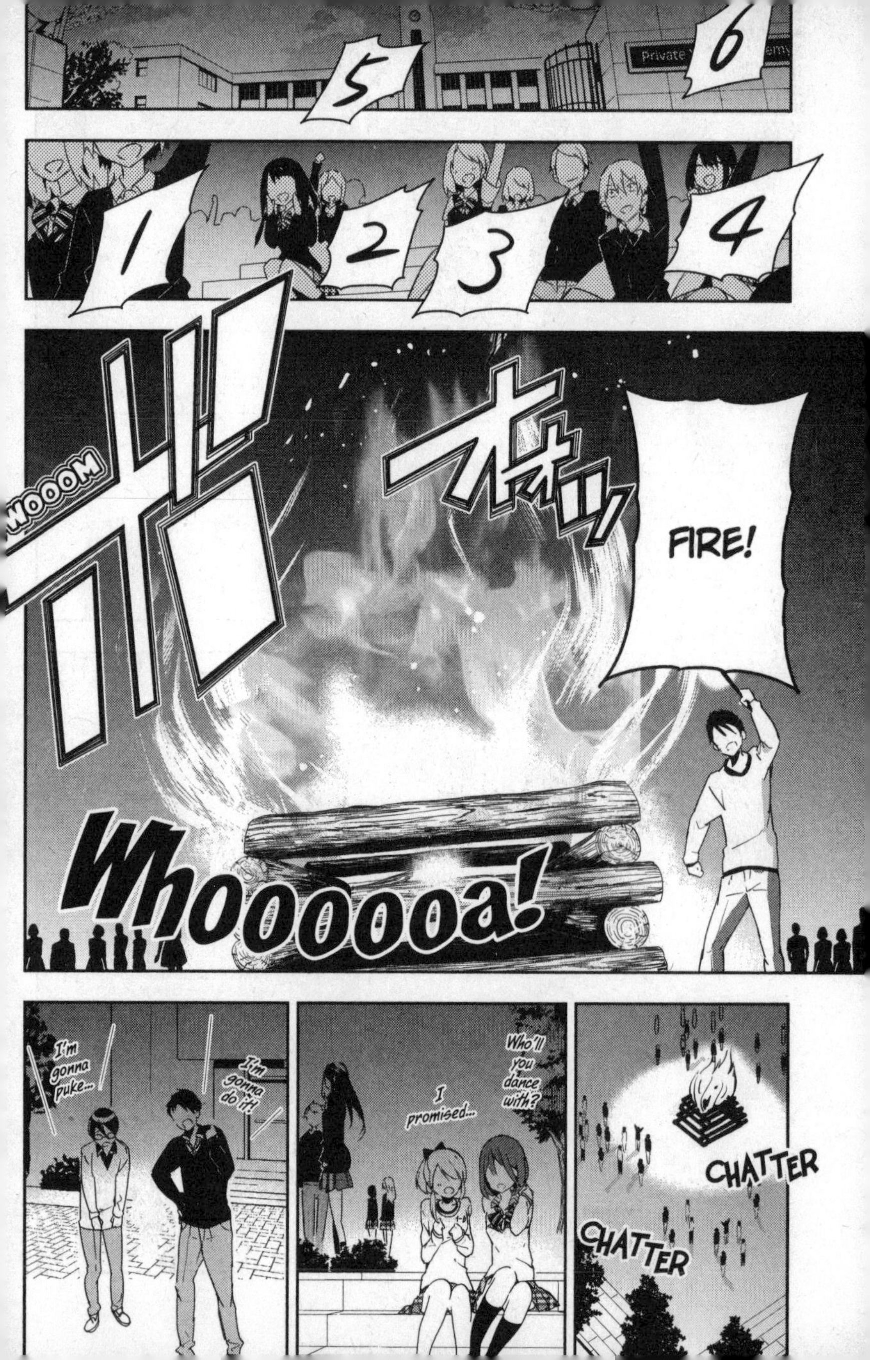

6
Private
5
4
3
2
1
FIRE!
WOOOM
Whooooa!
CHATTER
CHATTER
Who'll you dance with?
I promised...
I'm gonna do it!
I'm gonna puke...

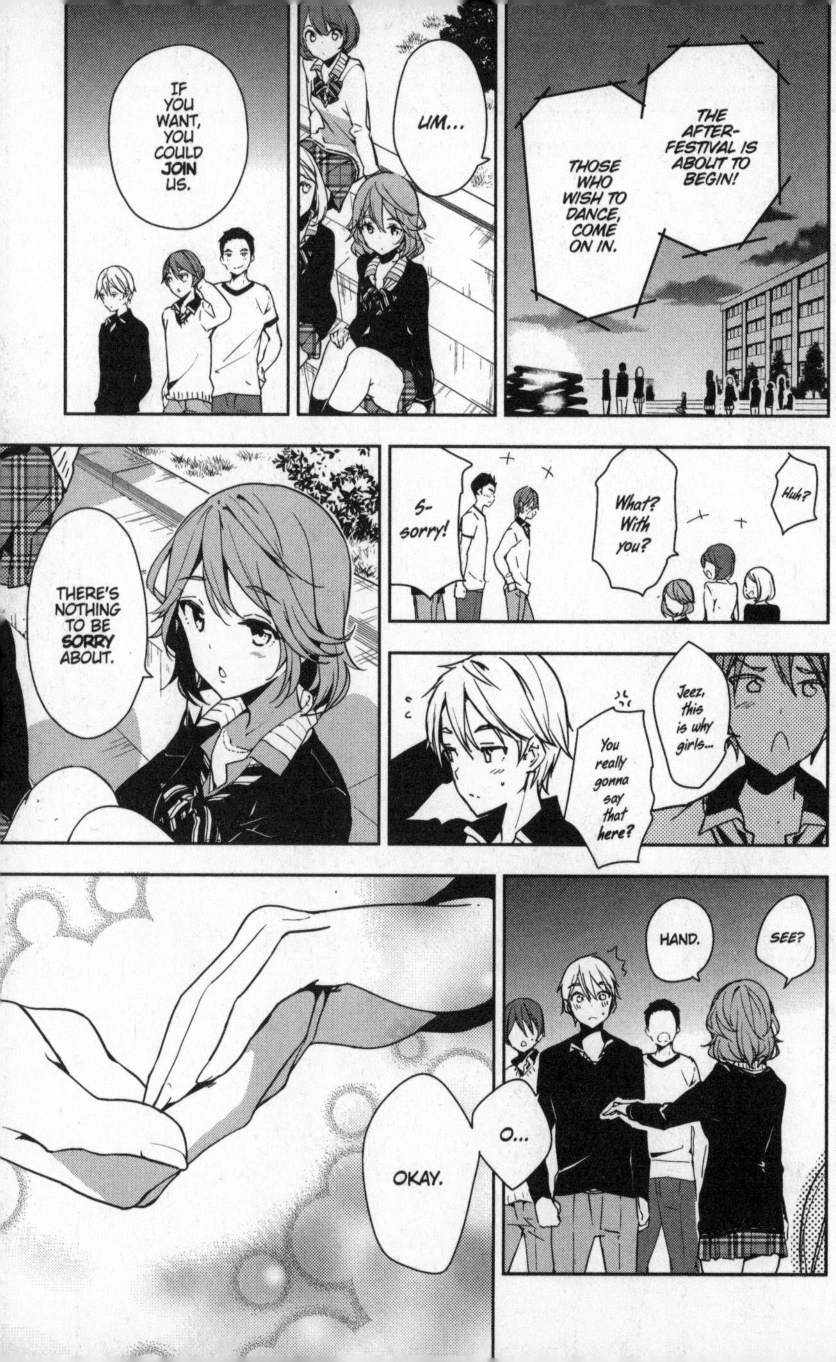
THE AFTER-FESTIVAL IS ABOUT TO BEGIN!
THOSE WHO WISH TO DANCE, COME ON IN.
UM...
IF YOU WANT, YOU COULD **JOIN** US.
Huh?
What? With you?
S-sorry!
Jeez, this is why girls...
You really gonna say that *here*?
THERE'S NOTHING TO BE **SORRY** ABOUT.
SEE?
HAND.
O... OKAY.

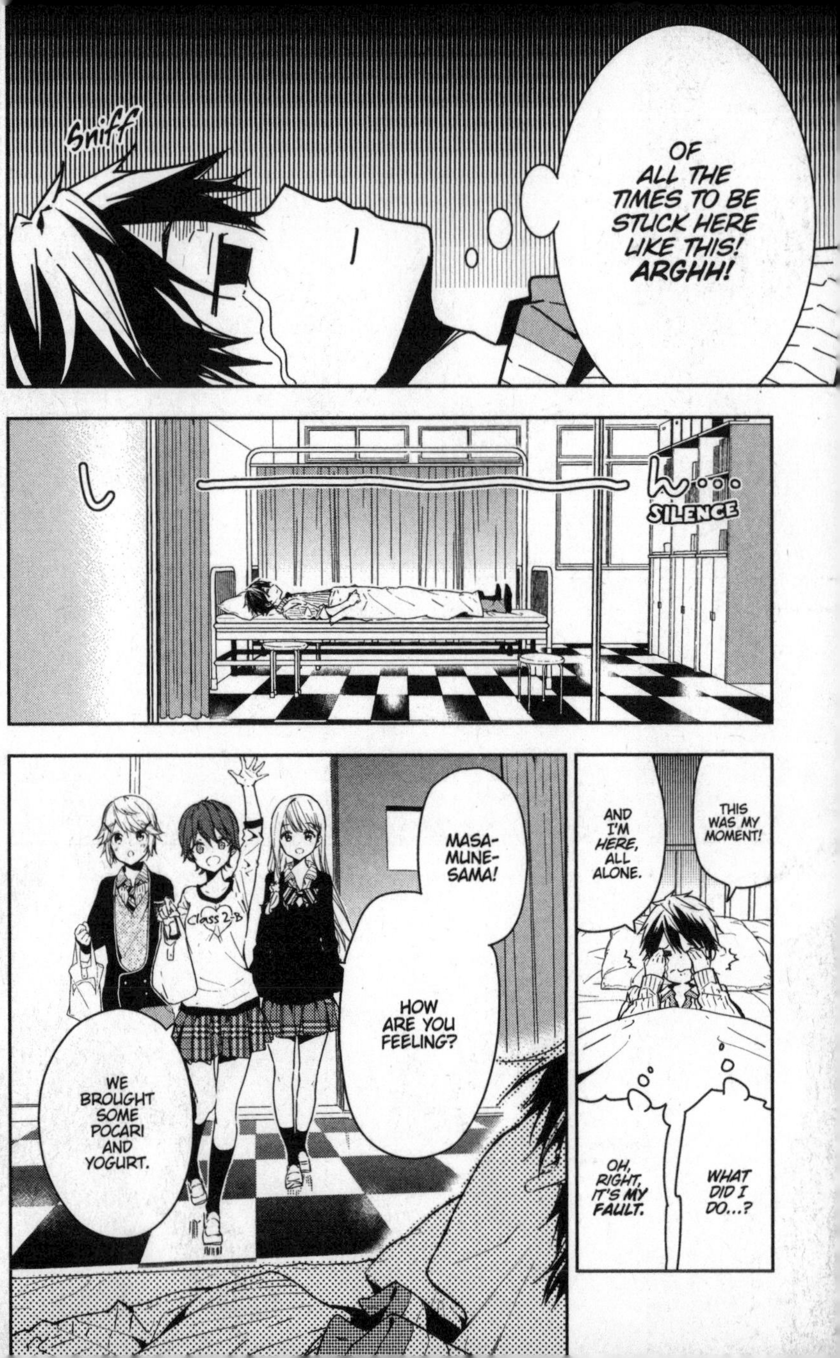
OF ALL THE TIMES TO BE STUCK HERE LIKE THIS! ARGHH!
Sniff
し～～ん…
SILENCE
THIS WAS MY MOMENT!
AND I'M HERE, ALL ALONE.
WHAT DID I DO...?
OH, RIGHT, IT'S MY FAULT.
MASA-MUNE-SAMA!
HOW ARE YOU FEELING?
WE BROUGHT SOME POCARI AND YOGURT.

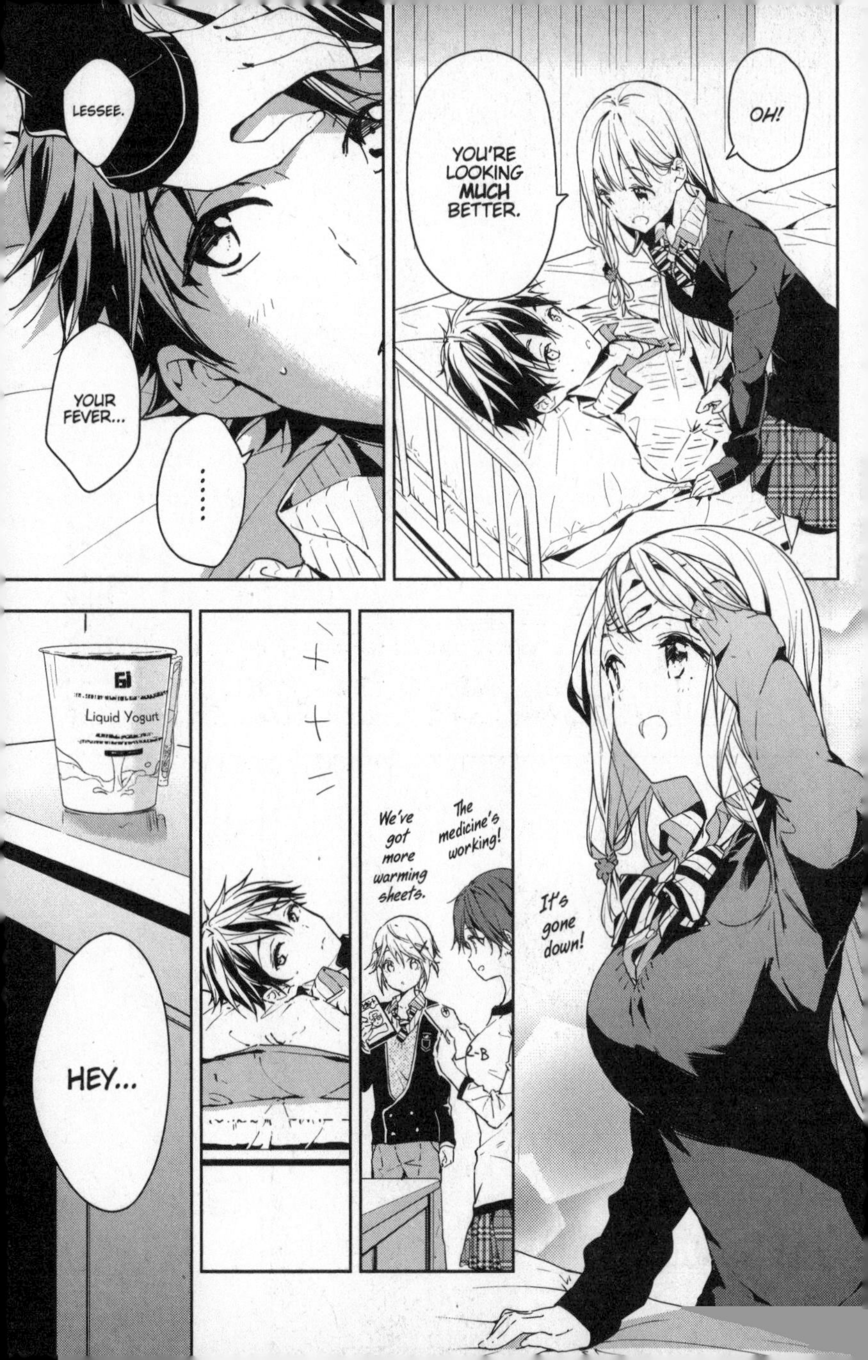
OH!
YOU'RE LOOKING MUCH BETTER.
LESSEE.
YOUR FEVER...
......
It's gone down!
The medicine's working!
We've got more warming sheets.
2-B
Liquid Yogurt
HEY...

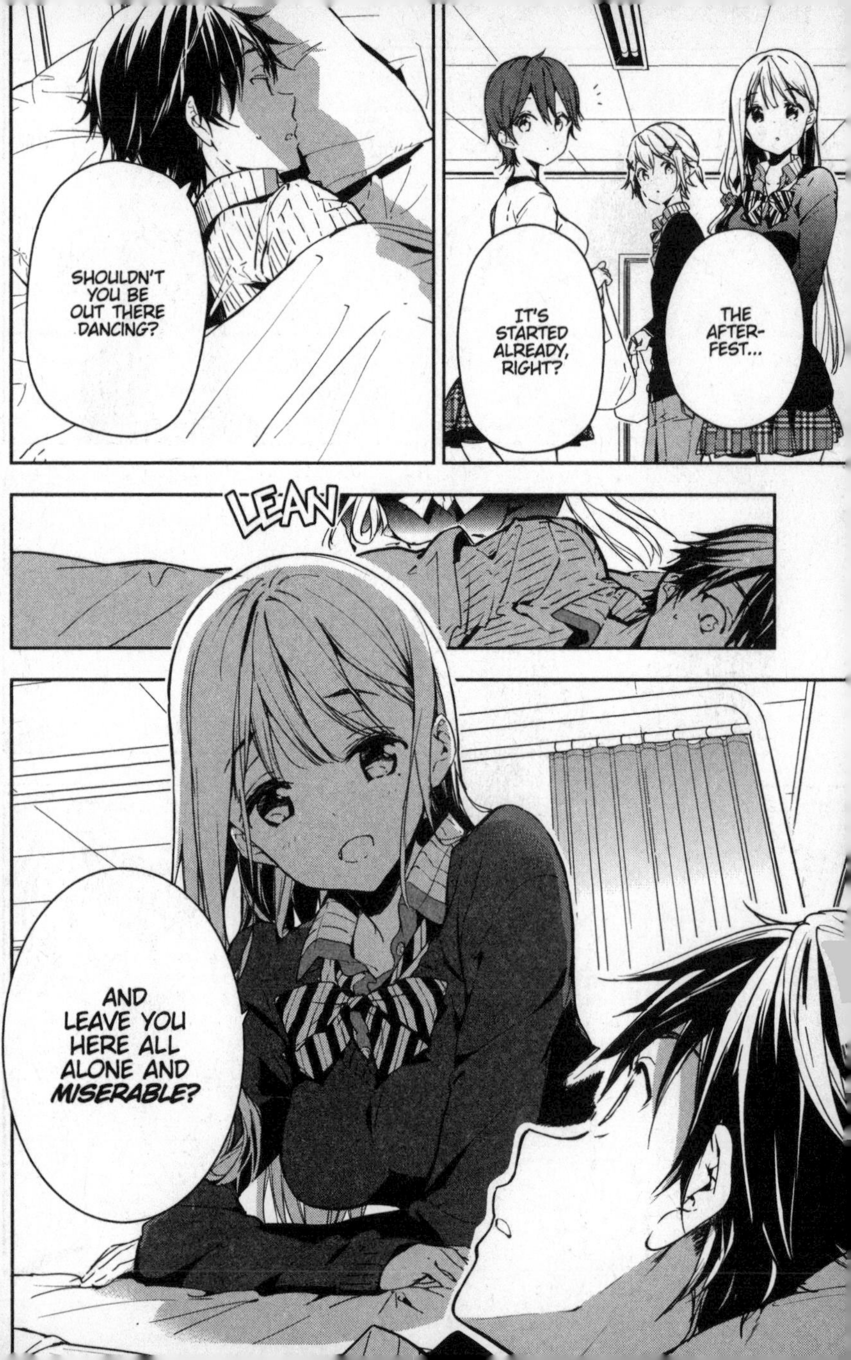
THE AFTER-FEST...
IT'S STARTED ALREADY, RIGHT?
SHOULDN'T YOU BE OUT THERE DANCING?
LEAN
AND LEAVE YOU HERE ALL ALONE AND *MISERABLE?*

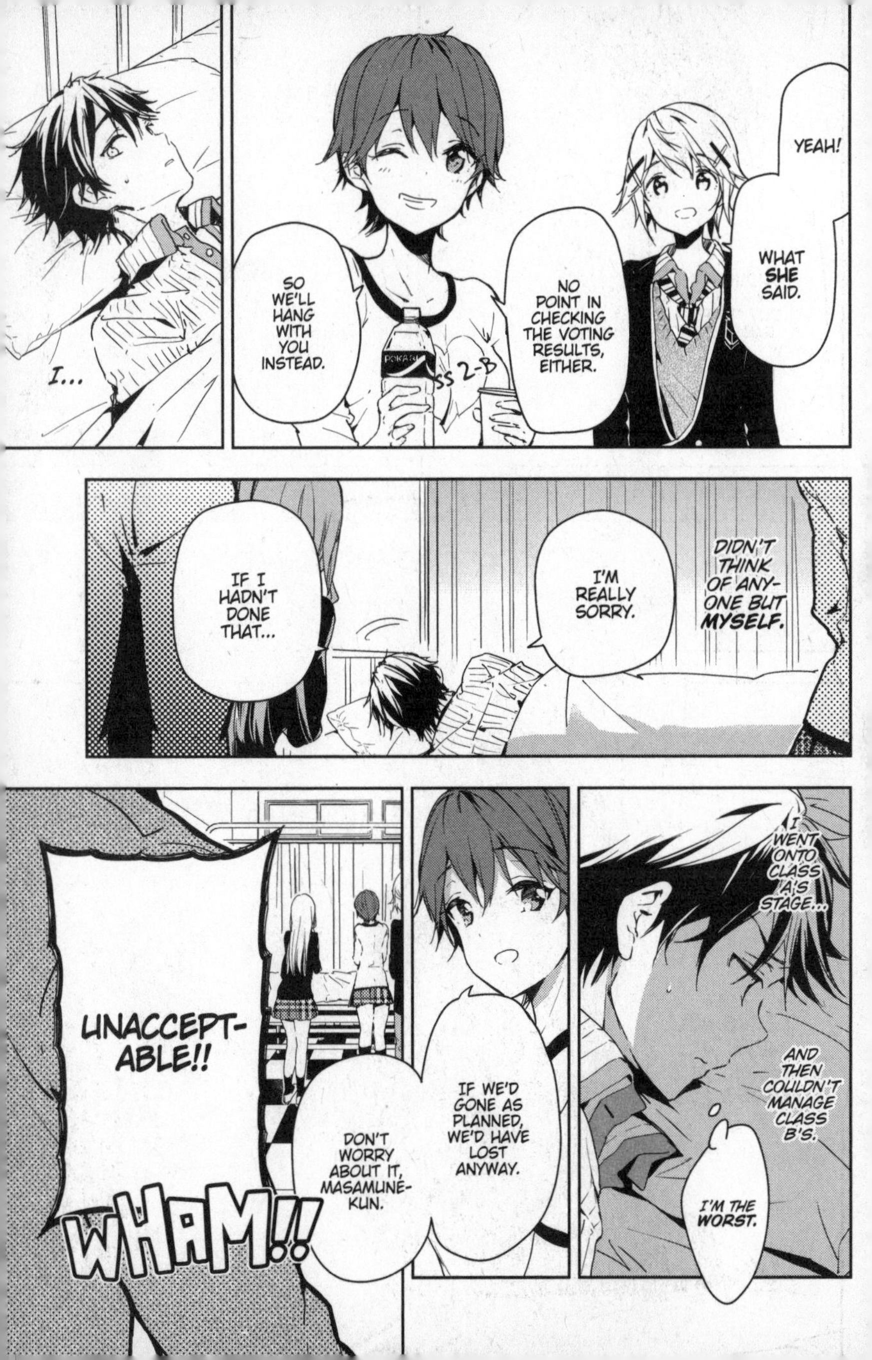
YEAH!
WHAT SHE SAID.
NO POINT IN CHECKING THE VOTING RESULTS, EITHER.
SO WE'LL HANG WITH YOU INSTEAD.
I...
DIDN'T THINK OF ANYONE BUT MYSELF.
I'M REALLY SORRY.
IF I HADN'T DONE THAT...
I WENT ONTO CLASS A'S STAGE...
AND THEN COULDN'T MANAGE CLASS B'S.
I'M THE WORST.
IF WE'D GONE AS PLANNED, WE'D HAVE LOST ANYWAY.
DON'T WORRY ABOUT IT, MASAMUNE-KUN.
UNACCEPTABLE!!
WHAM!!

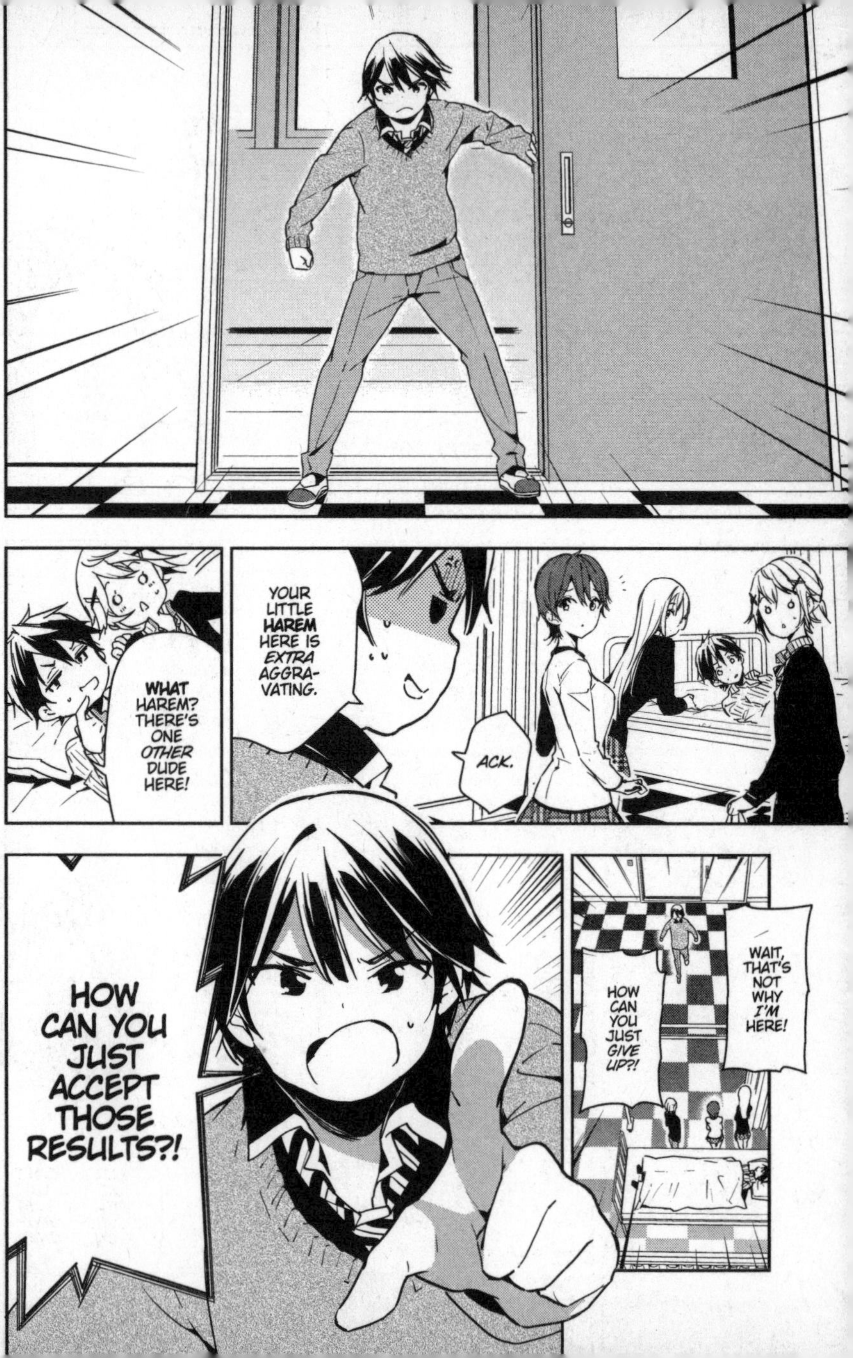
ACK.
YOUR LITTLE HAREM HERE IS EXTRA AGGRAVATING.
WHAT HAREM? THERE'S ONE OTHER DUDE HERE!
WAIT, THAT'S NOT WHY I'M HERE!
HOW CAN YOU JUST GIVE UP?!
HOW CAN YOU JUST ACCEPT THOSE RESULTS?!

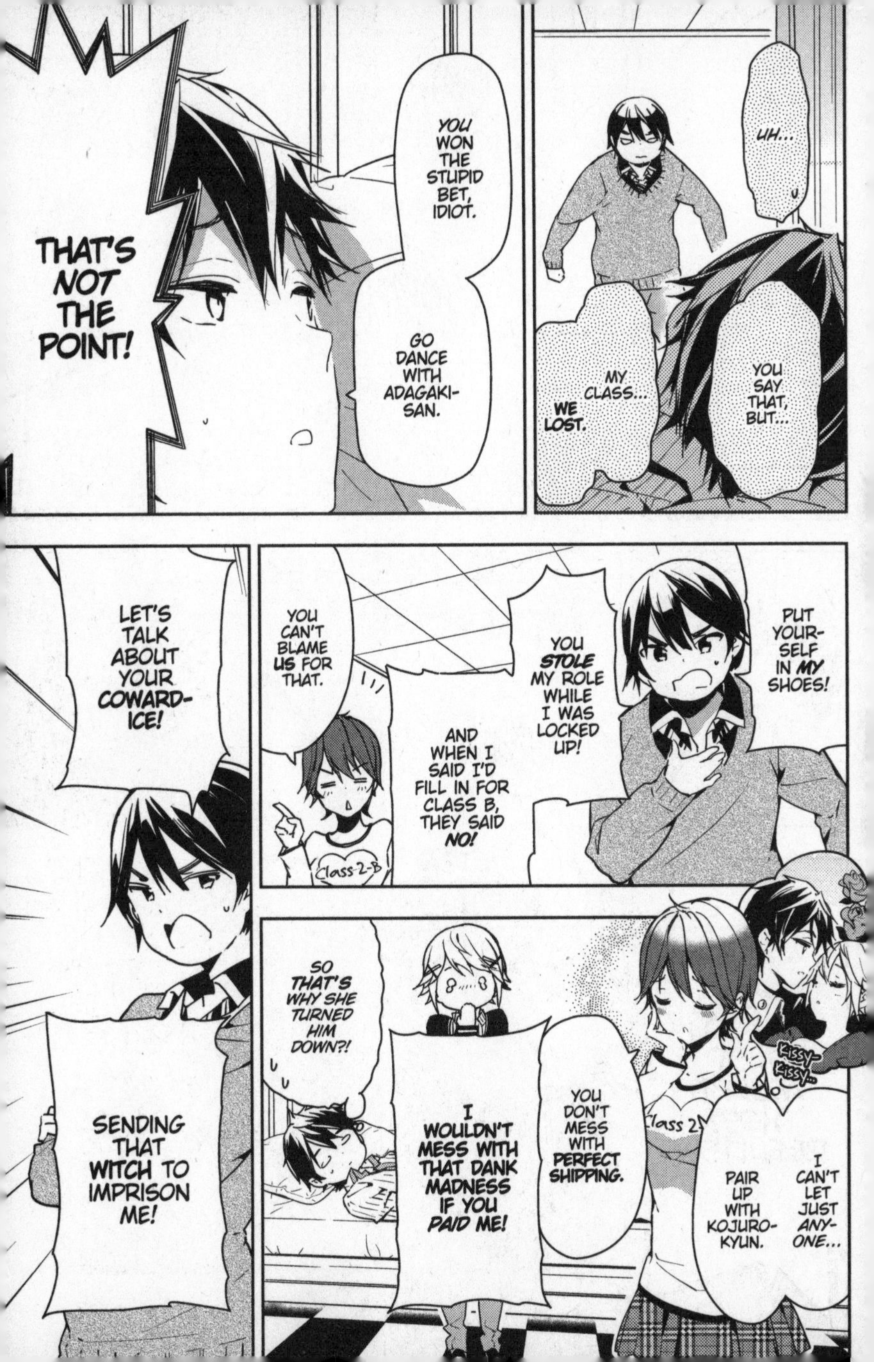
UH...
YOU SAY THAT, BUT...
MY CLASS... WE LOST.
YOU WON THE STUPID BET, IDIOT.
GO DANCE WITH ADAGAKI-SAN.
THAT'S NOT THE POINT!
PUT YOURSELF IN MY SHOES!
YOU STOLE MY ROLE WHILE I WAS LOCKED UP!
AND WHEN I SAID I'D FILL IN FOR CLASS B, THEY SAID NO!
YOU CAN'T BLAME US FOR THAT.
Class-2-B
I CAN'T LET JUST ANY-ONE...
PAIR UP WITH KOJURO-KYUN.
KISSY-KISSY...
YOU DON'T MESS WITH PERFECT SHIPPING.
Class 2
I WOULDN'T MESS WITH THAT DANK MADNESS IF YOU PAID ME!
SO THAT'S WHY SHE TURNED HIM DOWN?!
LET'S TALK ABOUT YOUR COWARD-ICE!
SENDING THAT WITCH TO IMPRISON ME!

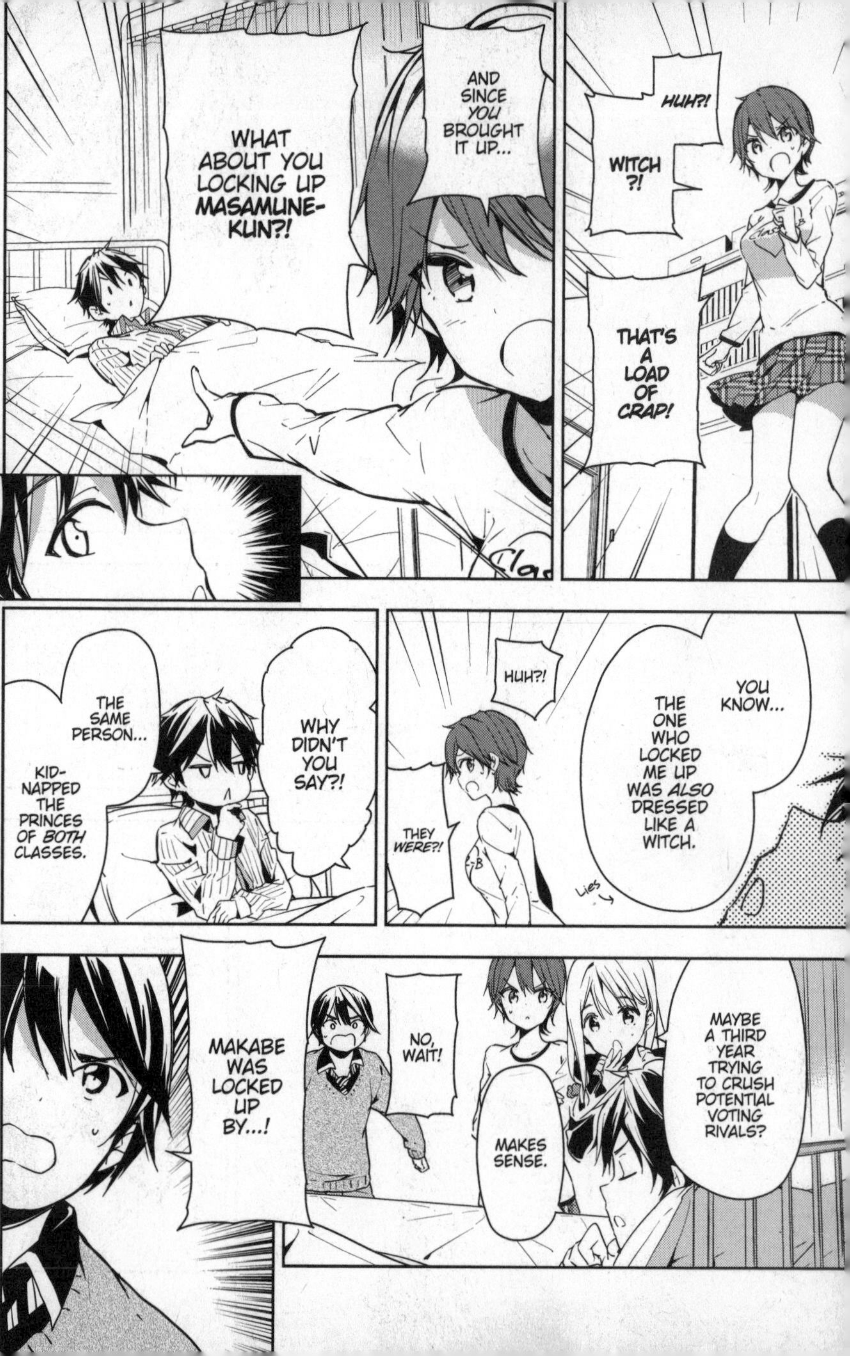
HUH?!
WITCH ?!
THAT'S A LOAD OF *CRAP!*
AND SINCE *YOU* BROUGHT IT UP...
WHAT ABOUT YOU LOCKING UP MASAMUNE-KUN?!
YOU KNOW...
THE ONE WHO LOCKED ME UP WAS *ALSO* DRESSED LIKE A WITCH.
Lies
HUH?!
THEY *WERE?!*
WHY DIDN'T YOU SAY?!
THE SAME PERSON...
KID-NAPPED THE PRINCES OF *BOTH* CLASSES.
MAYBE A THIRD YEAR TRYING TO CRUSH POTENTIAL VOTING RIVALS?
MAKES SENSE.
NO, WAIT!
MAKABE WAS LOCKED UP BY...!

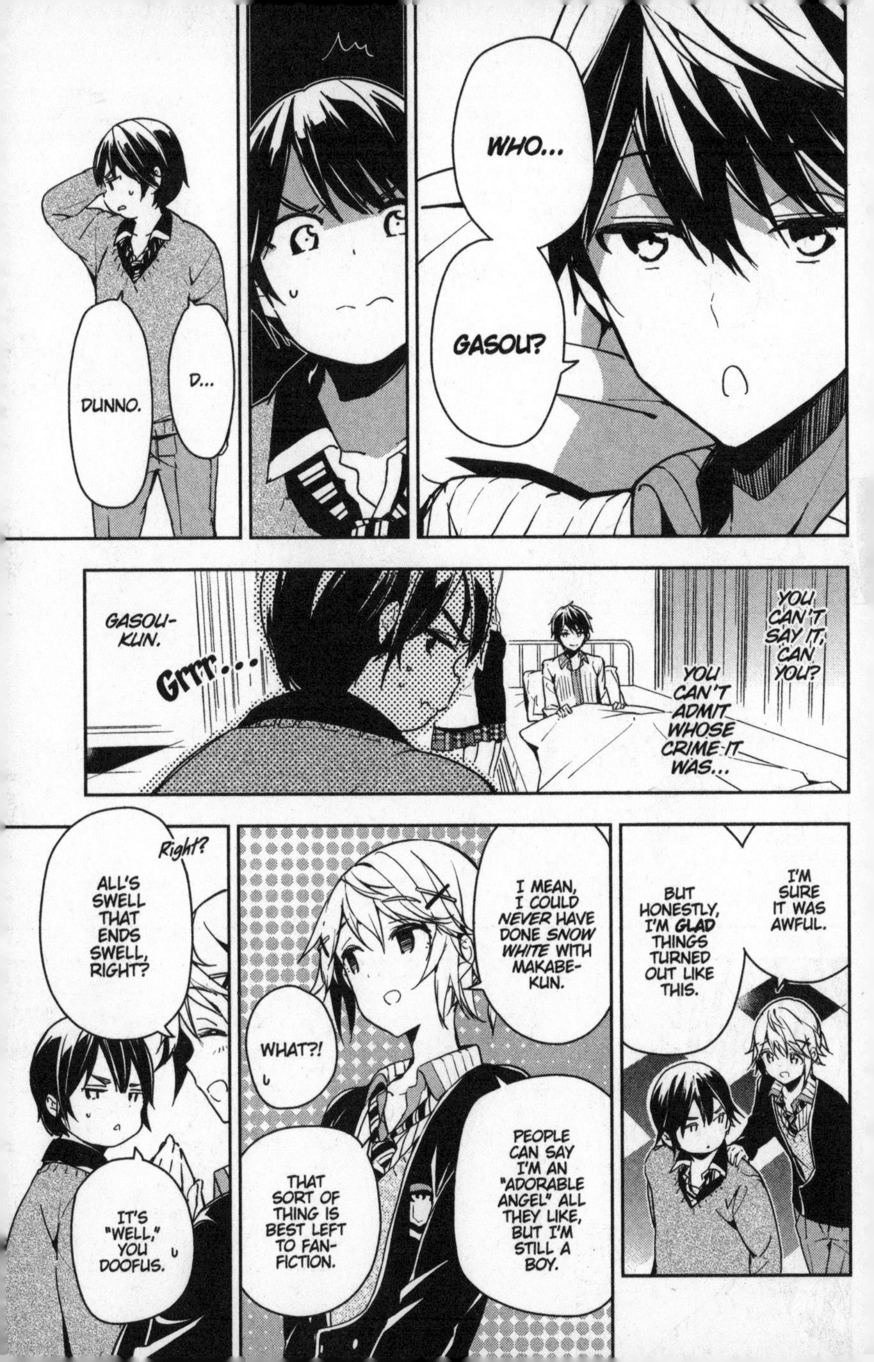
WHO...
GASOU?
D...
DUNNO.
YOU CAN'T SAY IT, CAN YOU?
YOU CAN'T ADMIT WHOSE CRIME IT WAS...
Grrr...
GASOU-KUN.
I'M SURE IT WAS AWFUL.
BUT HONESTLY, I'M GLAD THINGS TURNED OUT LIKE THIS.
I MEAN, I COULD NEVER HAVE DONE SNOW WHITE WITH MAKABE-KUN.
WHAT?!
PEOPLE CAN SAY I'M AN "ADORABLE ANGEL" ALL THEY LIKE, BUT I'M STILL A BOY.
THAT SORT OF THING IS BEST LEFT TO FAN-FICTION.
Right?
ALL'S SWELL THAT ENDS SWELL, RIGHT?
IT'S "WELL," YOU DOOFUS.

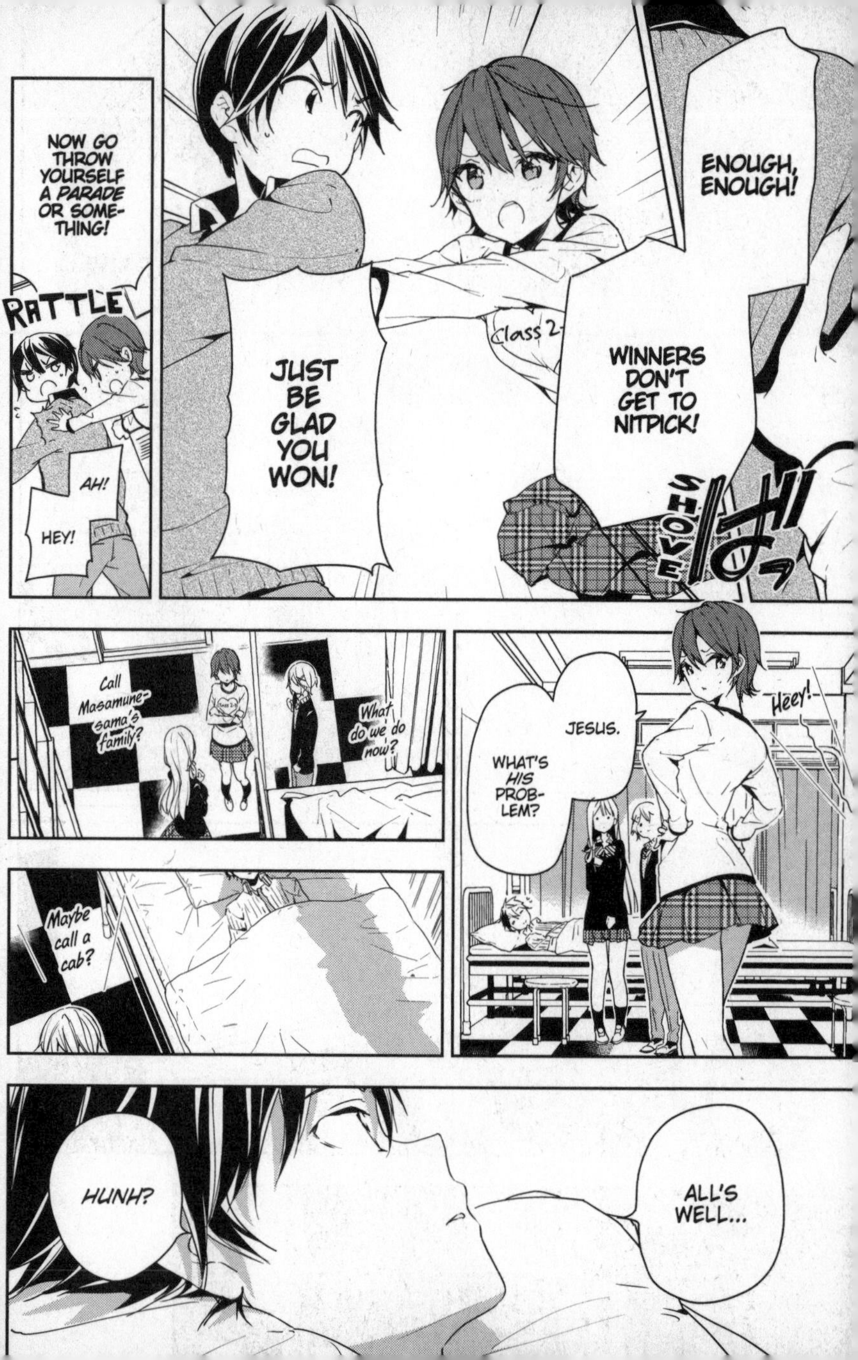
ENOUGH, ENOUGH!
WINNERS DON'T GET TO NITPICK!
Class 2-
JUST BE GLAD YOU WON!
SHOVE
NOW GO THROW YOURSELF A *PARADE* OR SOME-THING!
RATTLE
AH!
HEY!
Heey!
JESUS.
WHAT'S *HIS* PROB-LEM?
What do we do now?
Call Masamune-sama's family?
Maybe call a cab?
ALL'S WELL...
HUNH?

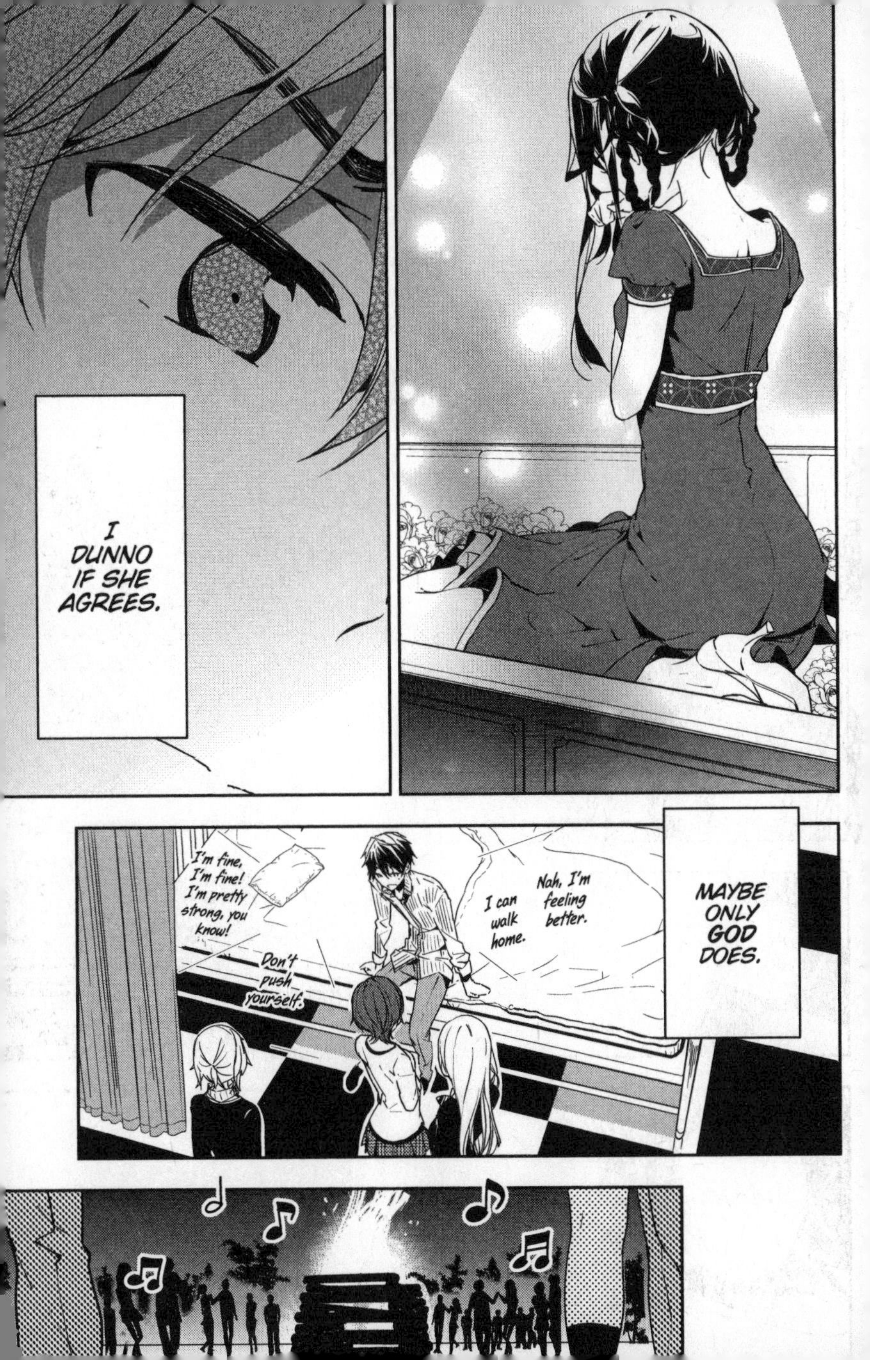
I DUNNO IF SHE AGREES.
MAYBE ONLY GOD DOES.
Nah, I'm feeling better.
I can walk home.
I'm fine, I'm fine! I'm pretty strong, you know!
Don't push yourself.

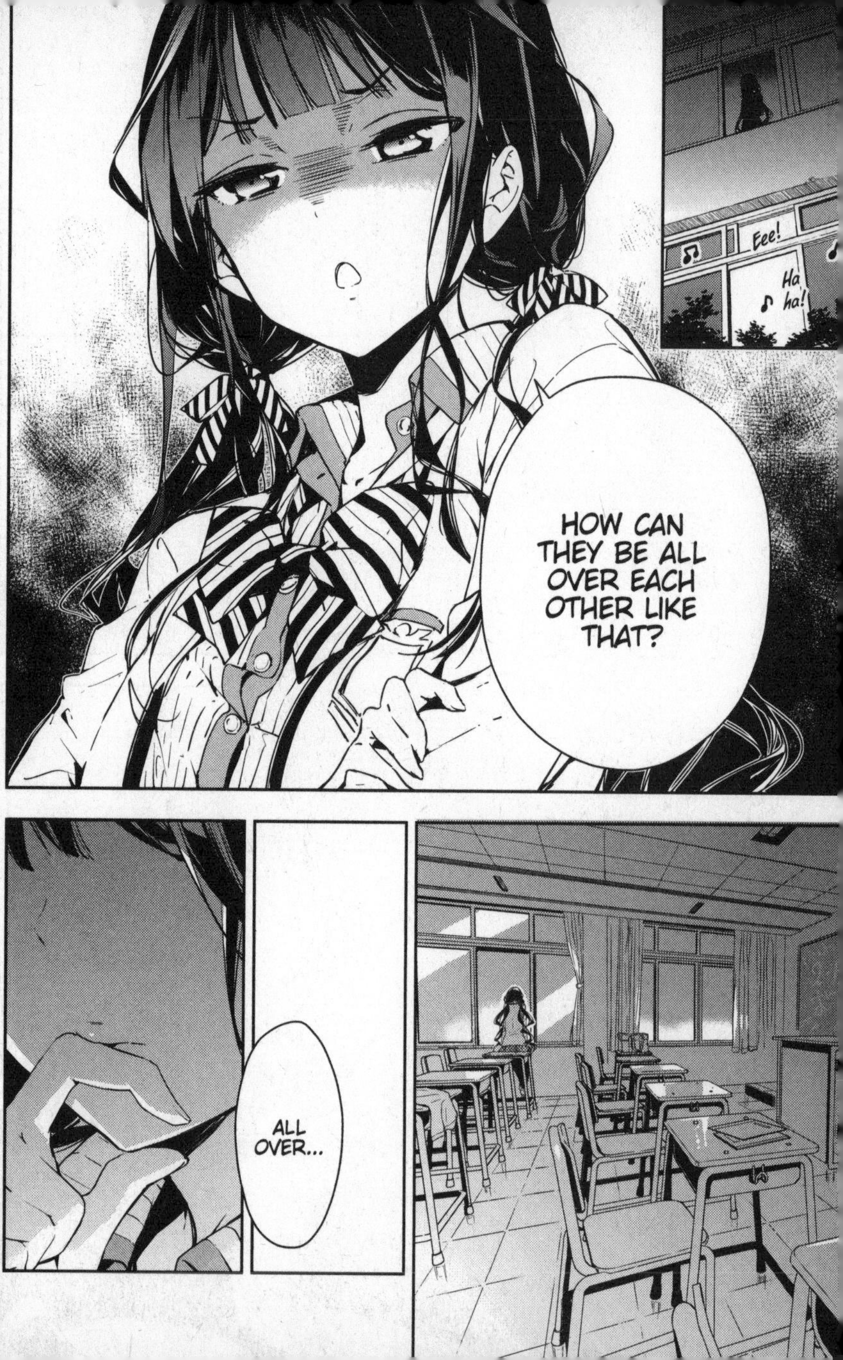
Eee!
Ha ha!
HOW CAN THEY BE ALL OVER EACH OTHER LIKE THAT?
ALL OVER...

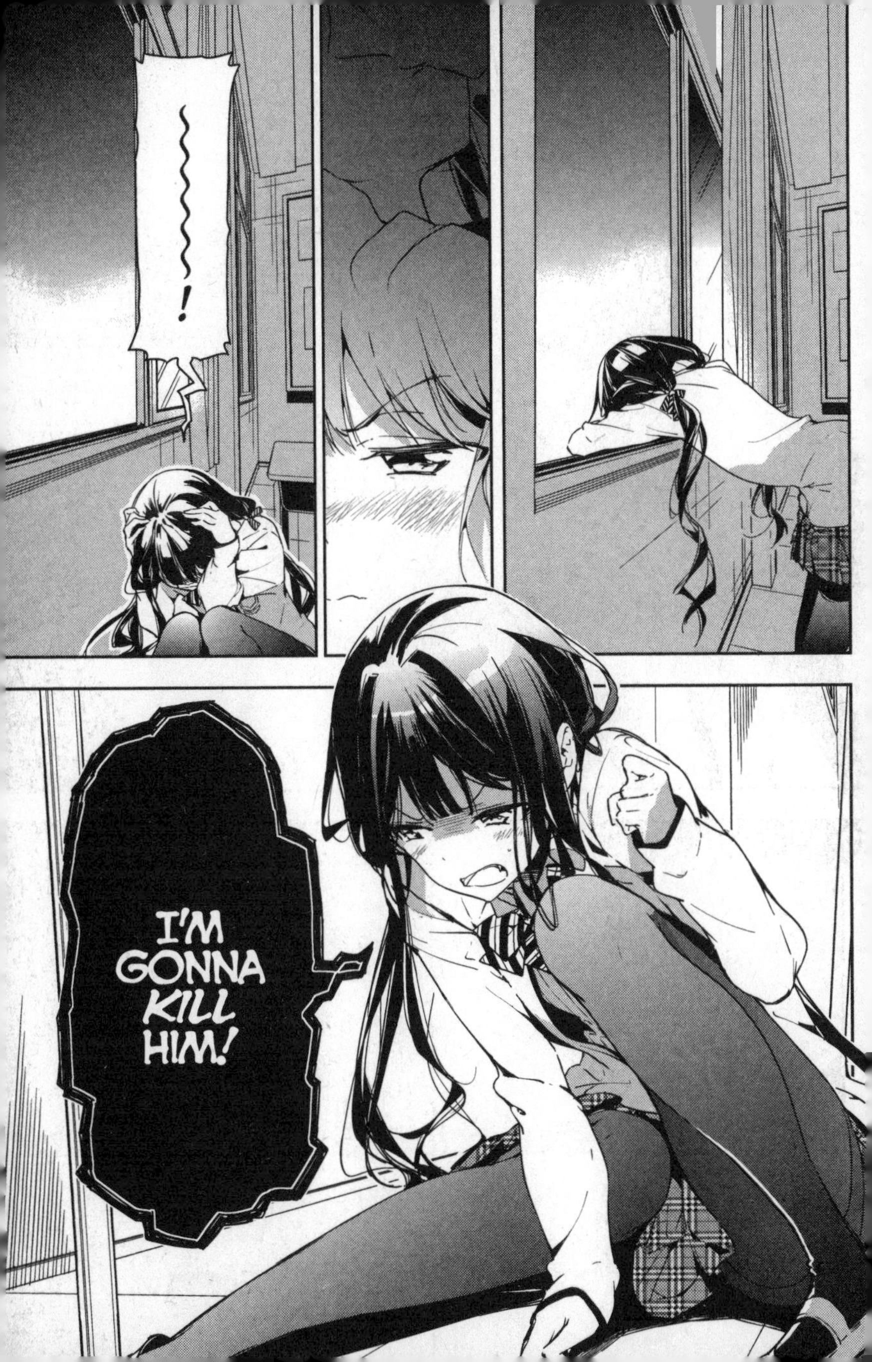

I'M GONNA KILL HIM!

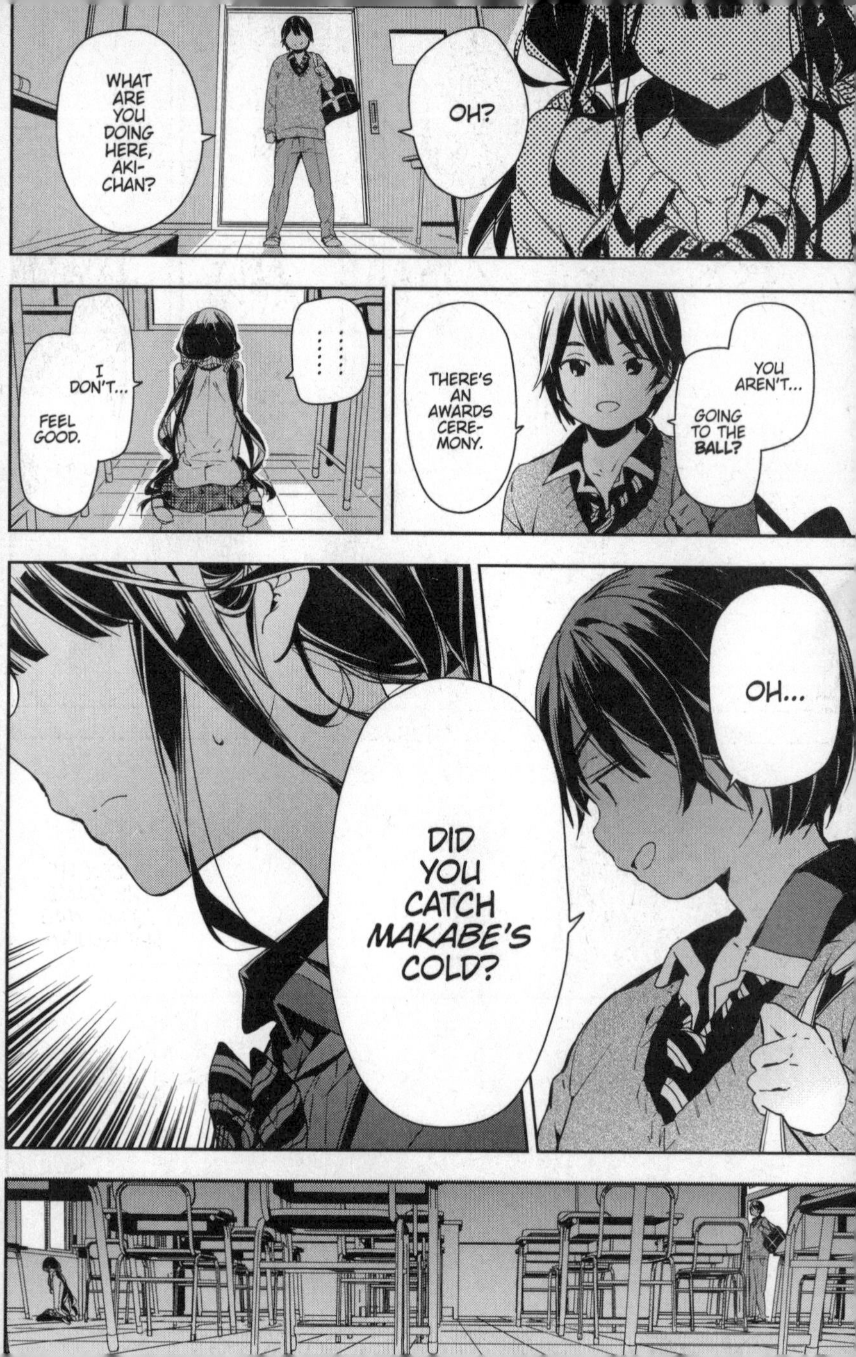
OH?
WHAT ARE YOU DOING HERE, AKI-CHAN?
YOU AREN'T... GOING TO THE BALL?
THERE'S AN AWARDS CERE-MONY.
......
I DON'T... FEEL GOOD.
OH...
DID YOU CATCH *MAKABE'S* COLD?

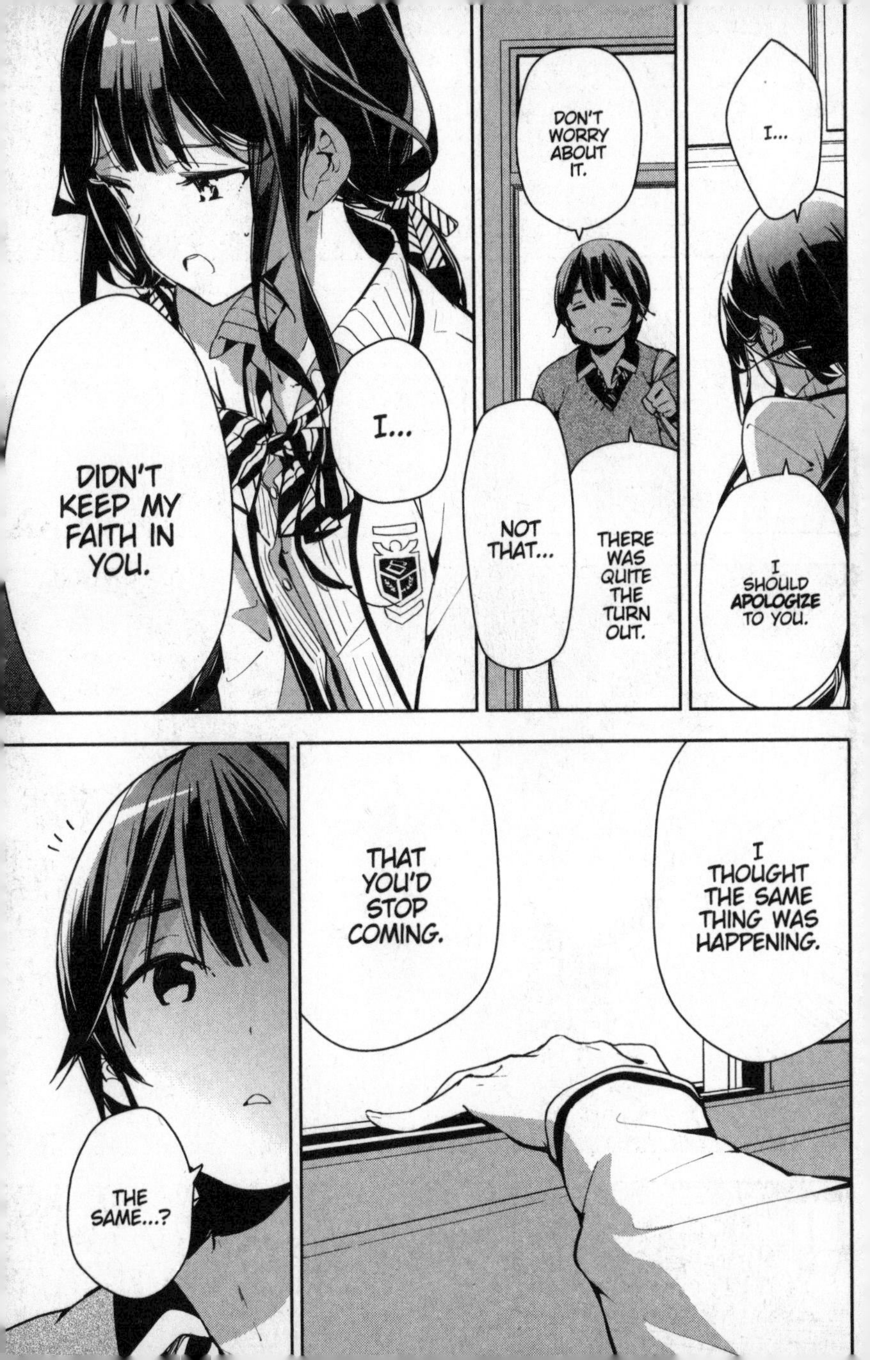
I...
I SHOULD APOLOGIZE TO YOU.
DON'T WORRY ABOUT IT.
THERE WAS QUITE THE TURN OUT.
NOT THAT...
I...
DIDN'T KEEP MY FAITH IN YOU.
I THOUGHT THE SAME THING WAS HAPPENING.
THAT YOU'D STOP COMING.
THE SAME...?

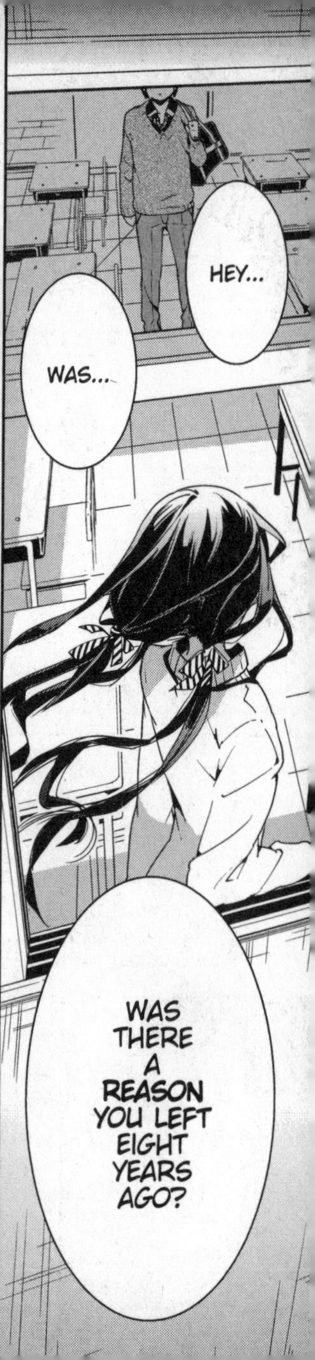
HEY...
WAS...
WAS THERE A REASON YOU LEFT EIGHT YEARS AGO?
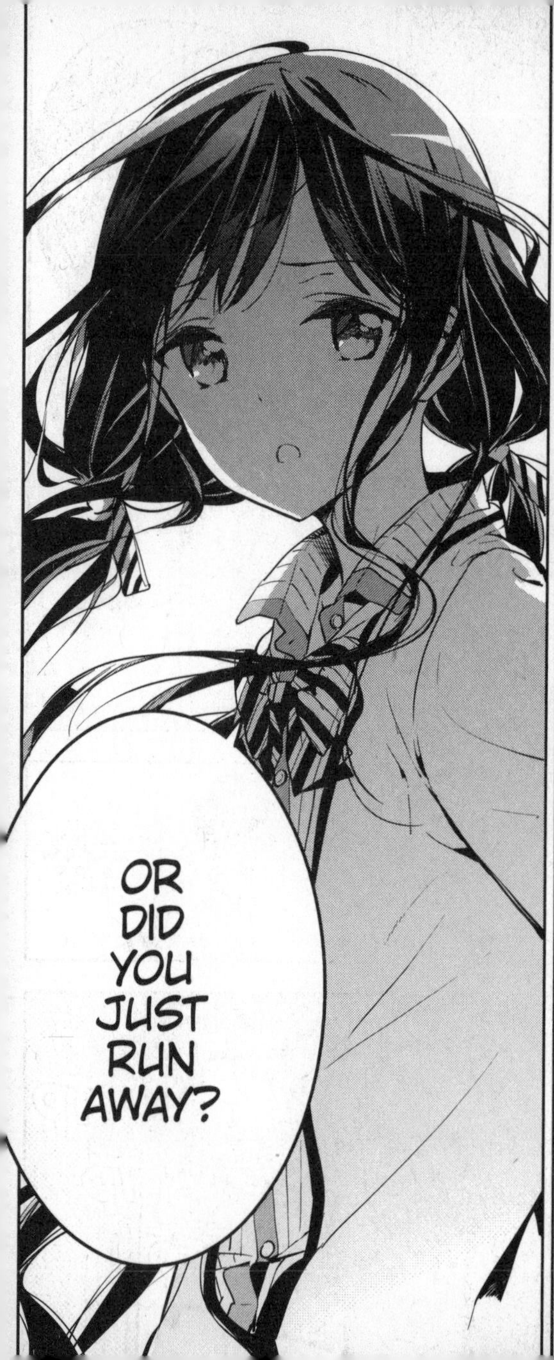
OR DID YOU JUST RUN AWAY?

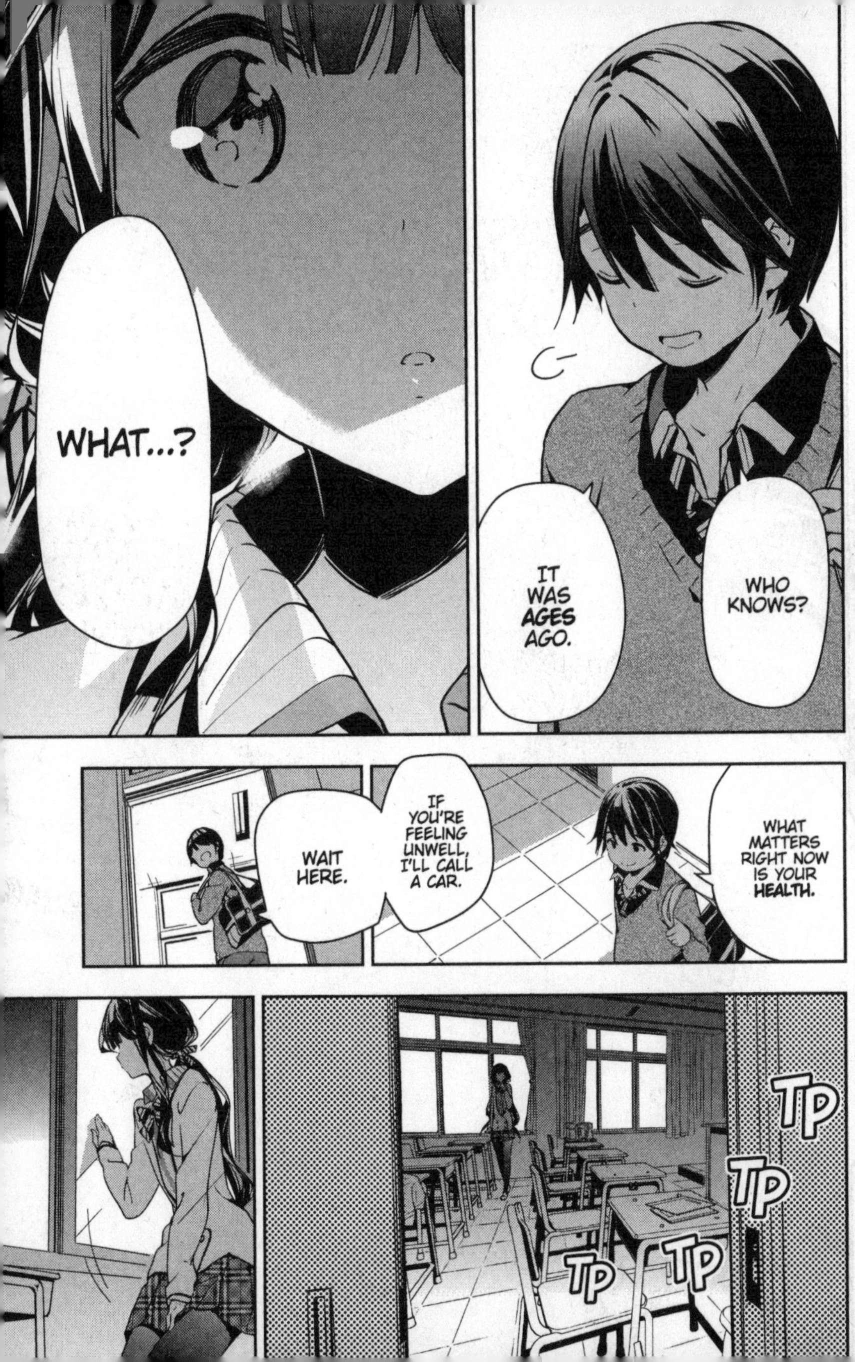
WHO KNOWS?
IT WAS AGES AGO.
WHAT...?
WHAT MATTERS RIGHT NOW IS YOUR HEALTH.
IF YOU'RE FEELING UNWELL, I'LL CALL A CAR.
WAIT HERE.
TP
TP
TP
TP

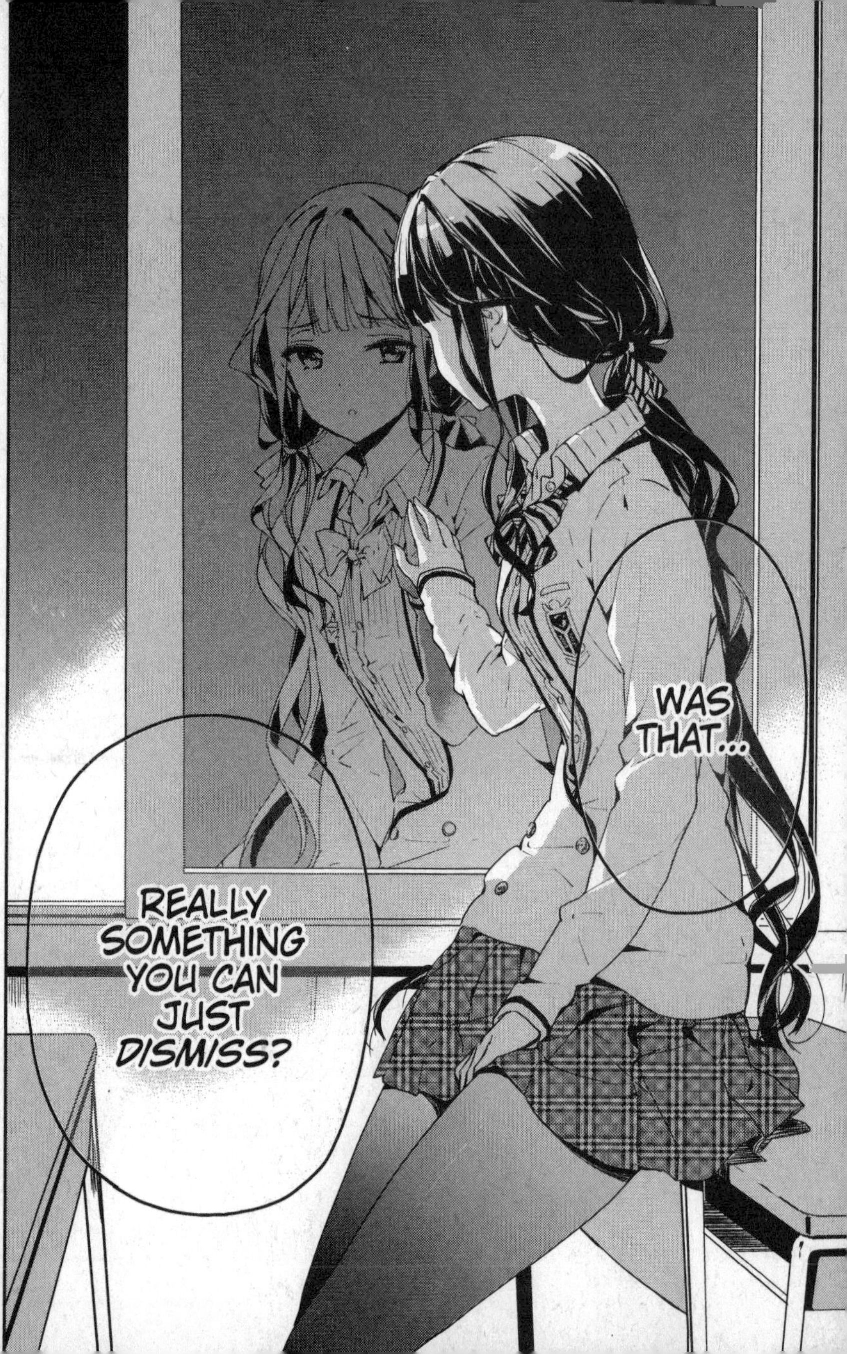
WAS THAT...
REALLY SOMETHING YOU CAN JUST DISMISS?

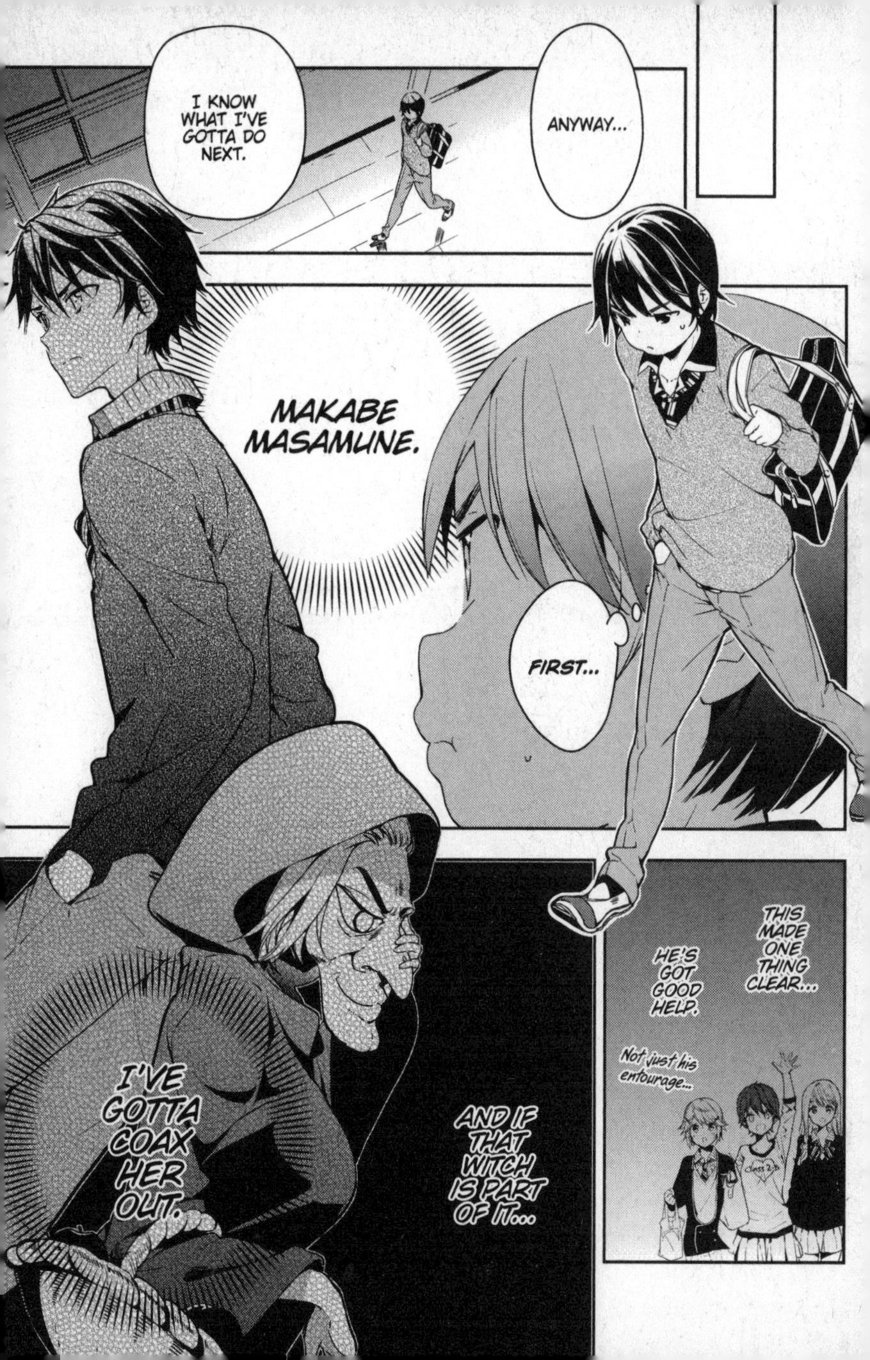
ANYWAY...
I KNOW WHAT I'VE GOTTA DO NEXT.
FIRST...
MAKABE MASAMUNE.
THIS MADE ONE THING CLEAR...
HE'S GOT GOOD HELP.
Not just his entourage...
AND IF THAT WITCH IS PART OF IT...
I'VE GOTTA COAX HER OUT.

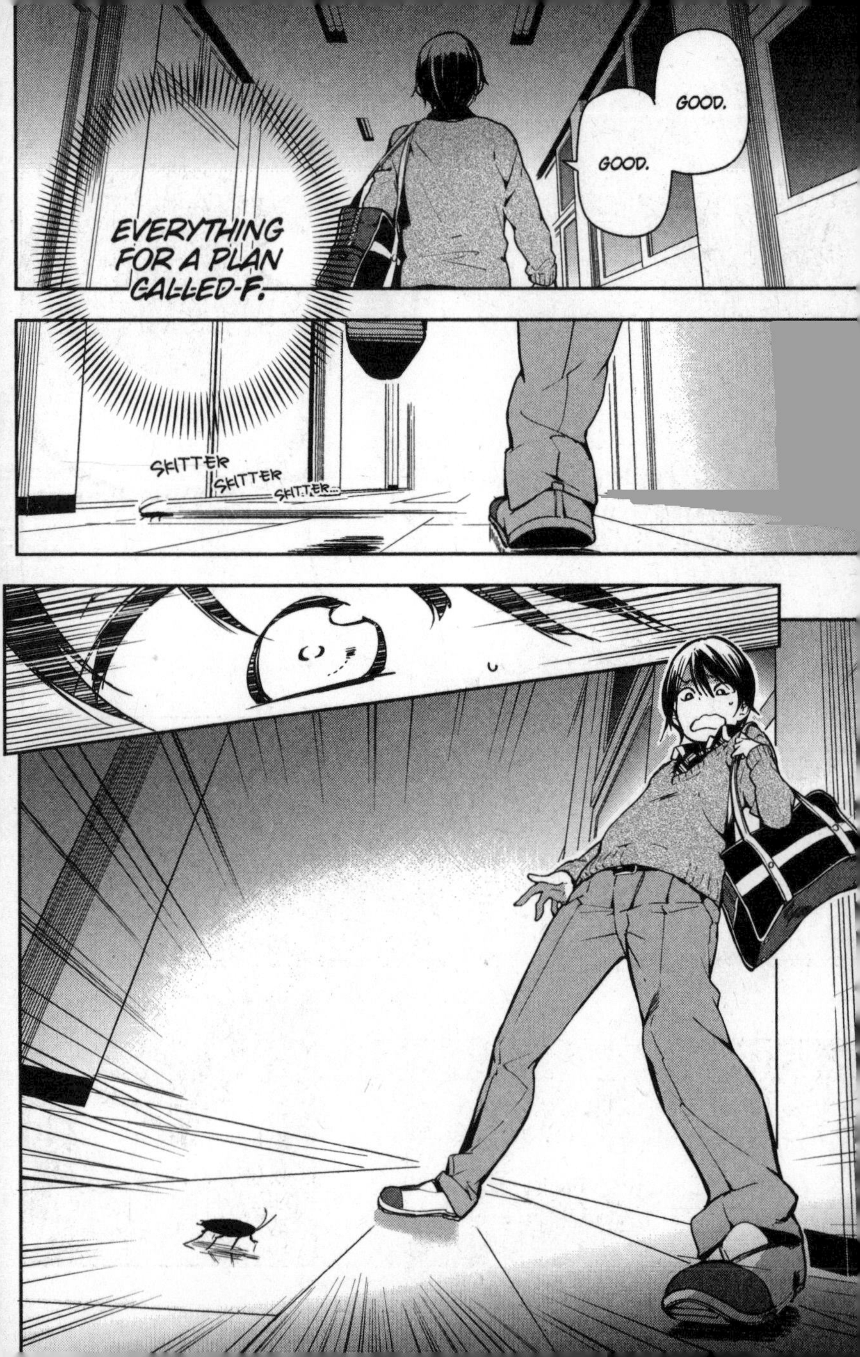
GOOD.
GOOD.
EVERYTHING FOR A PLAN CALLED-F.
SKITTER SKITTER SKITTER...

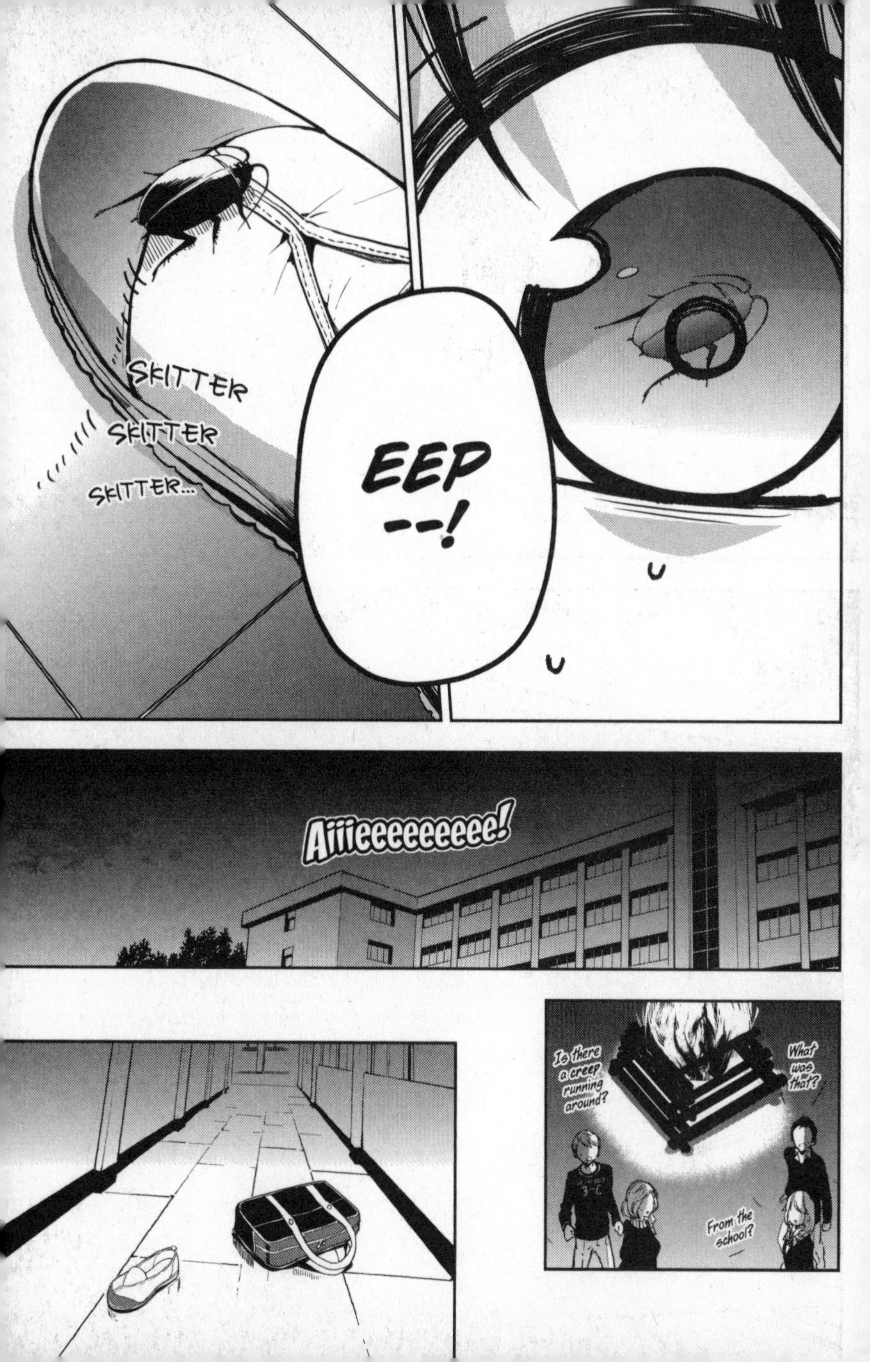
EEP --!
SKITTER
SKITTER
SKITTER...
Aiiieeeeeeeeee!
What was that?
Is there a creep running around?
From the school?

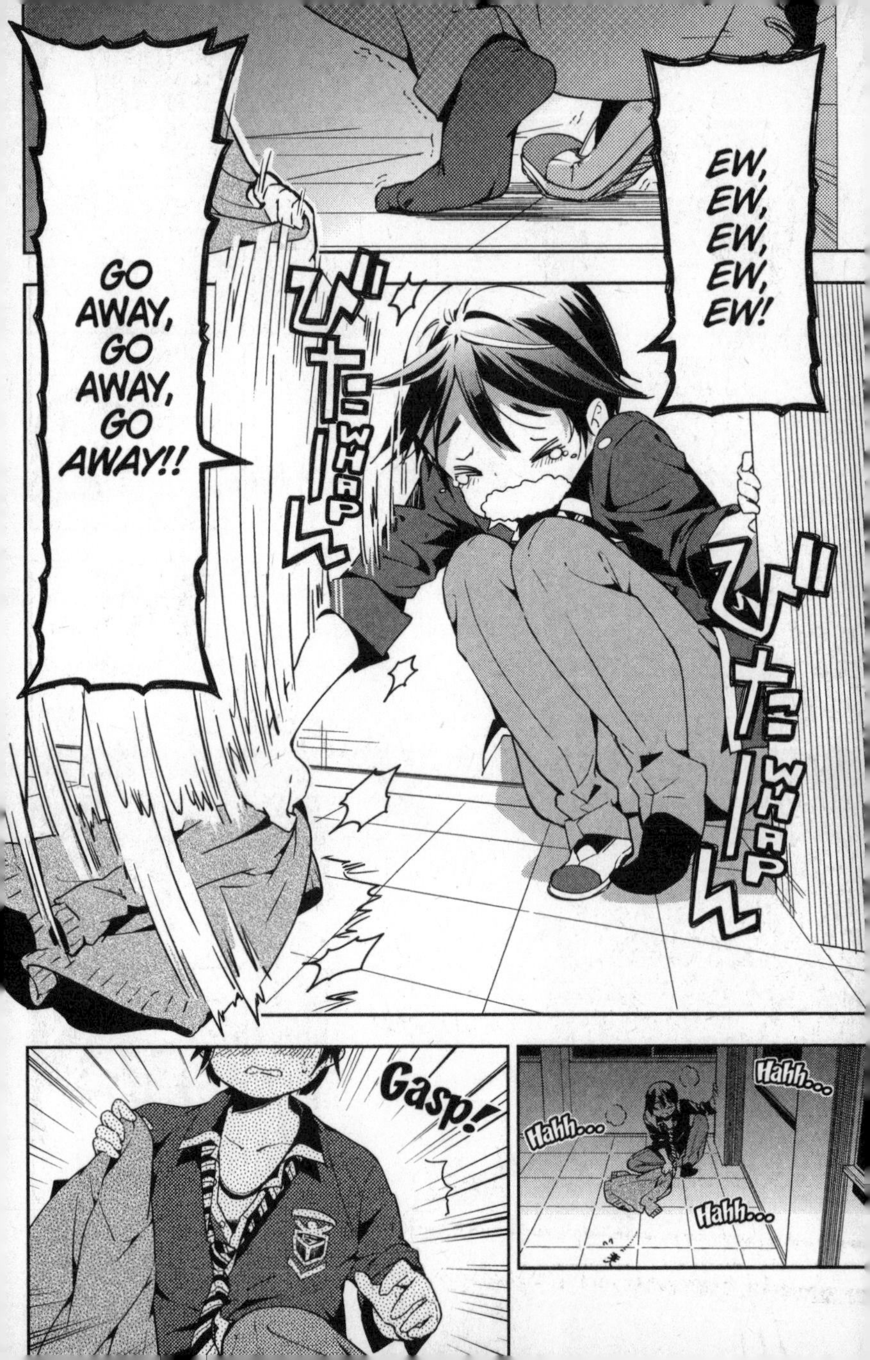
EW, EW, EW, EW, EW!
WHAP
GO AWAY, GO AWAY, GO AWAY!!
WHAP
Hahh...
Hahh...
Hahh...
Gasp!

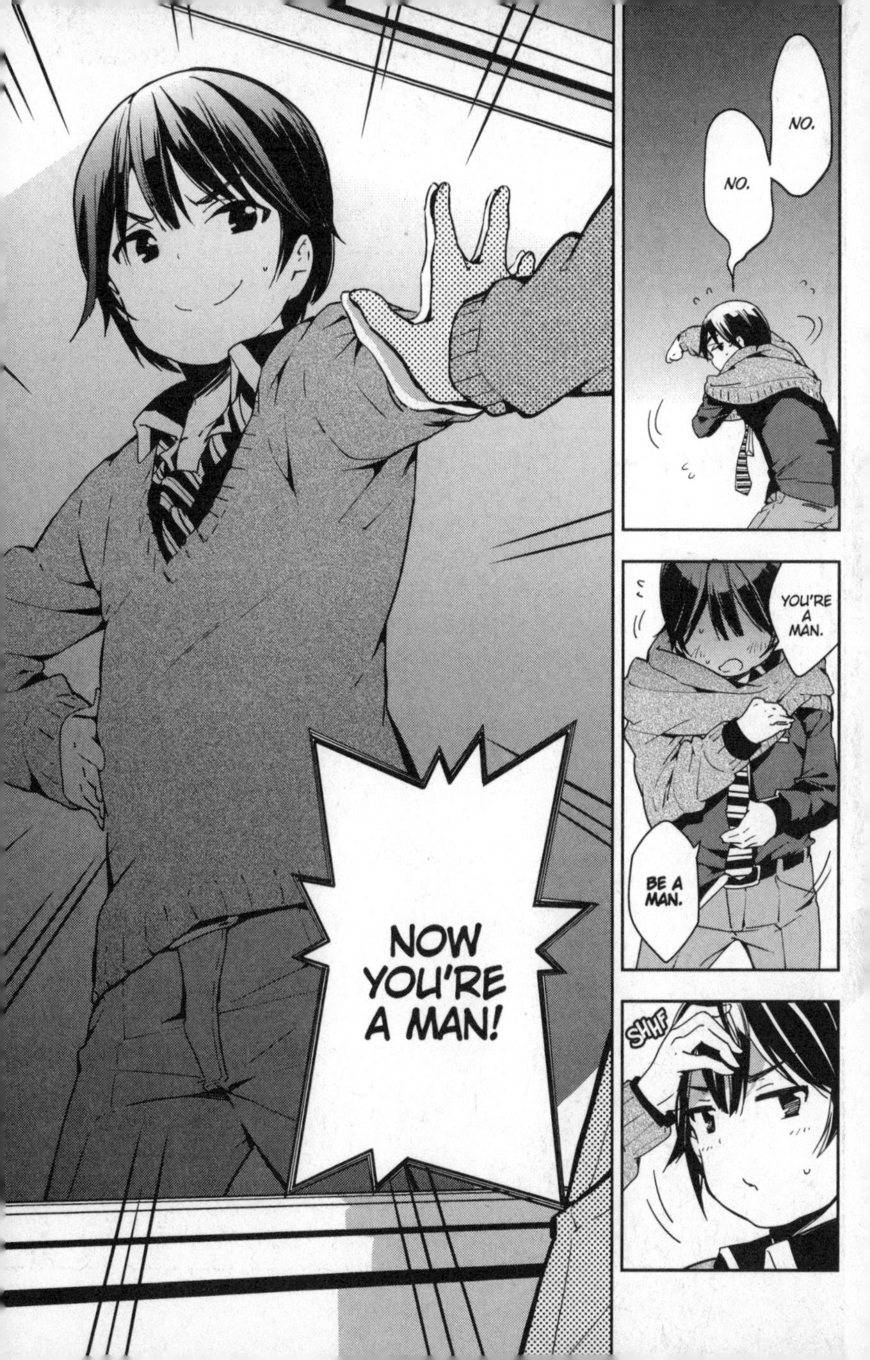
NO.
NO.
YOU'RE A MAN.
BE A MAN.
SHHF
NOW YOU'RE A MAN!

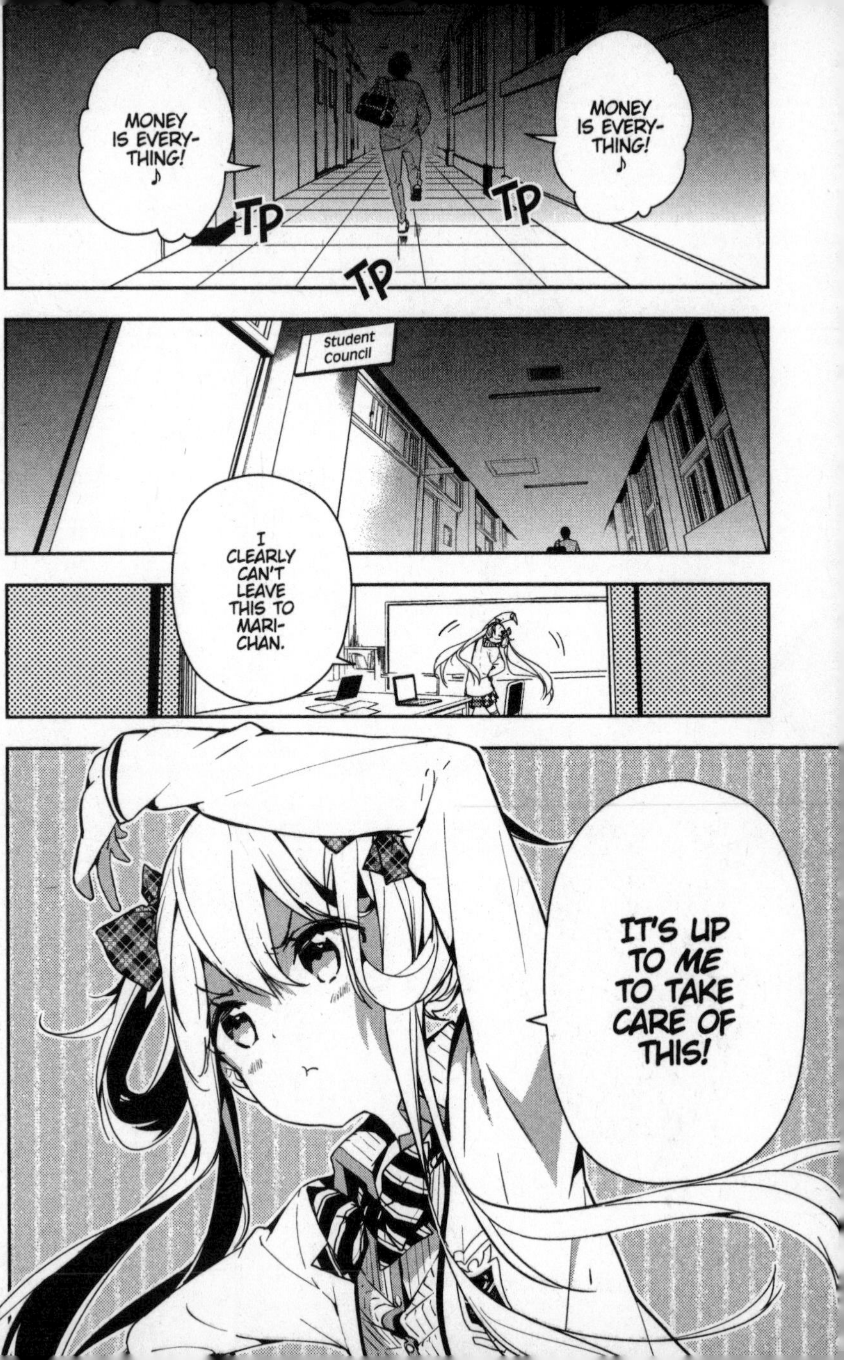
MONEY IS EVERY-THING! ♪
TP
TP
MONEY IS EVERY-THING! ♪
TP
Student Council
I CLEARLY CAN'T LEAVE THIS TO MARI-CHAN.
IT'S UP TO *ME* TO TAKE CARE OF THIS!

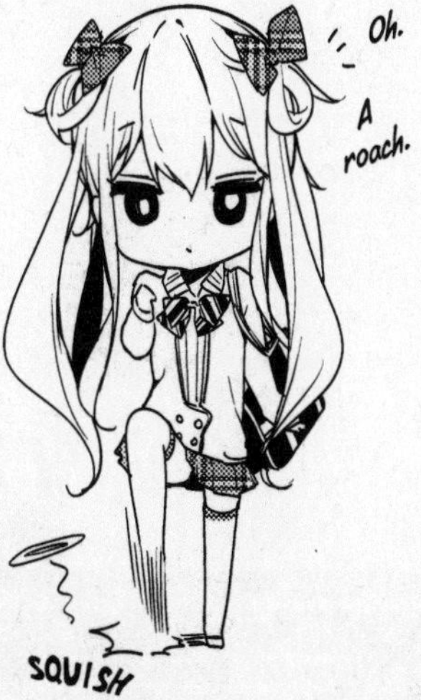
Oh.
A roach.
SQUISH

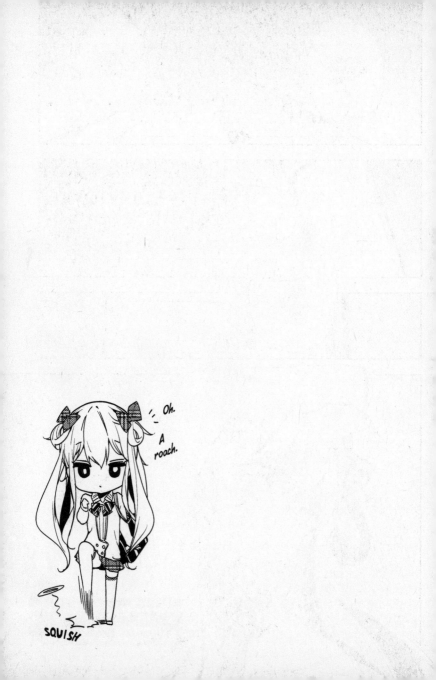

6

Masamune-kun's
REVENGE
Presented by Hazuki Takeoka & TIV

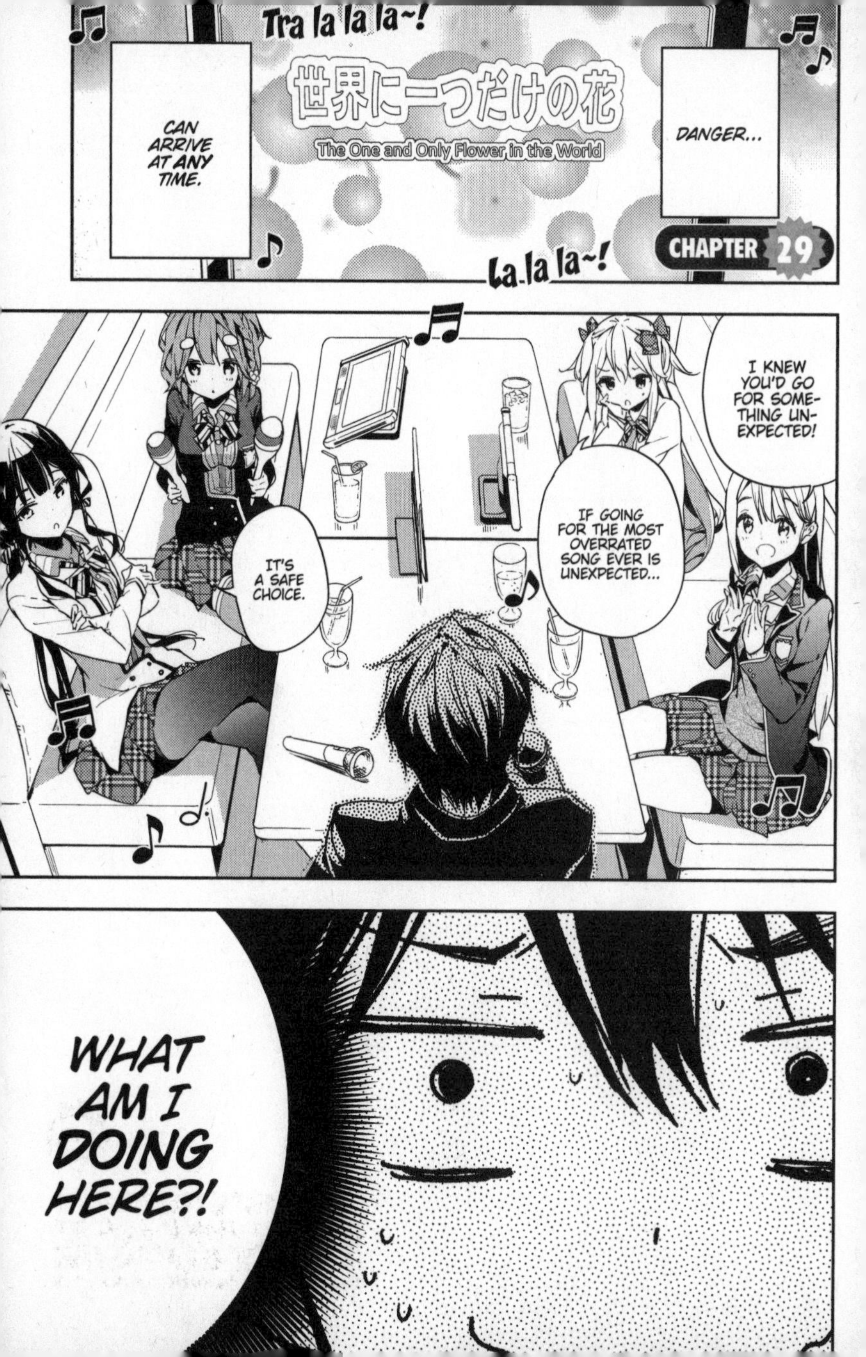
Tra la la la~!
DANGER...
世界に一つだけの花
The One and Only Flower in the World
CAN ARRIVE AT ANY TIME.
CHAPTER 29
La la la~!
I KNEW YOU'D GO FOR SOME-THING UN-EXPECTED!
IF GOING FOR THE MOST OVERRATED SONG EVER IS UNEXPECTED...
IT'S A SAFE CHOICE.
WHAT AM I DOING HERE?!

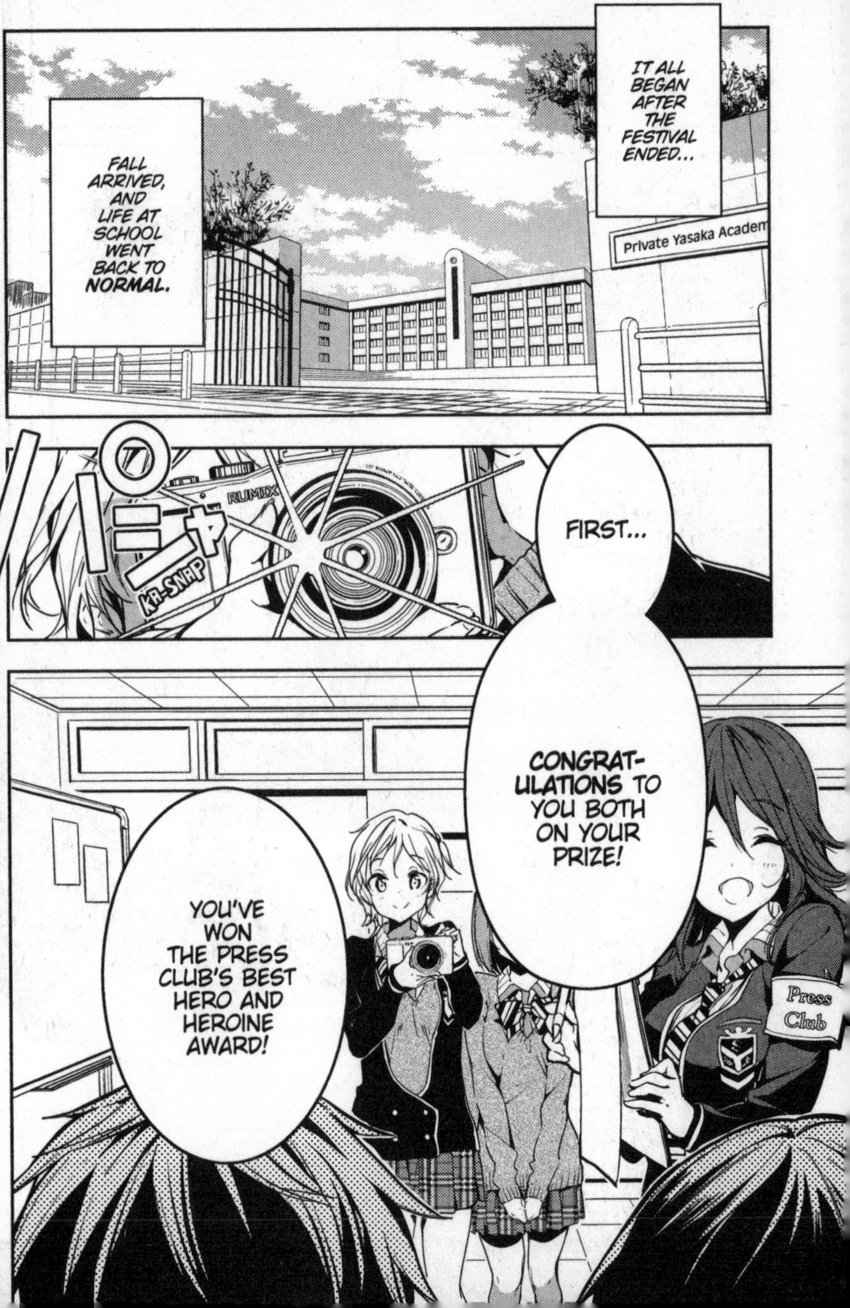
IT ALL BEGAN AFTER THE FESTIVAL ENDED...
FALL ARRIVED, AND LIFE AT SCHOOL WENT BACK TO NORMAL.
Private Yasaka Academ
FIRST...
RUMIX
KA-SNAP
CONGRAT-ULATIONS TO YOU BOTH ON YOUR PRIZE!
YOU'VE WON THE PRESS CLUB'S BEST HERO AND HEROINE AWARD!
Press Club

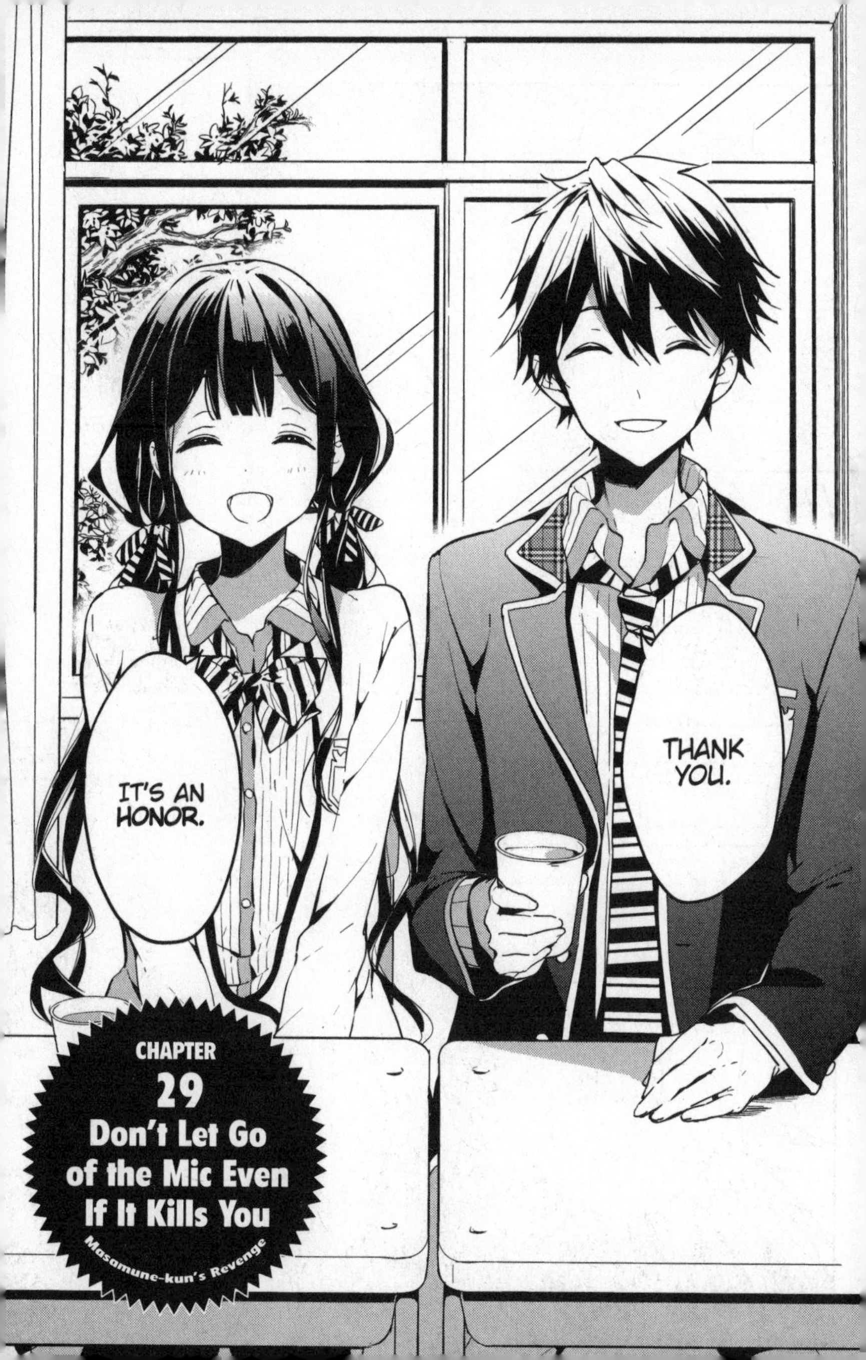
THANK YOU.
IT'S AN HONOR.
CHAPTER 29
Don't Let Go of the Mic Even If It Kills You
Masamune-kun's Revenge

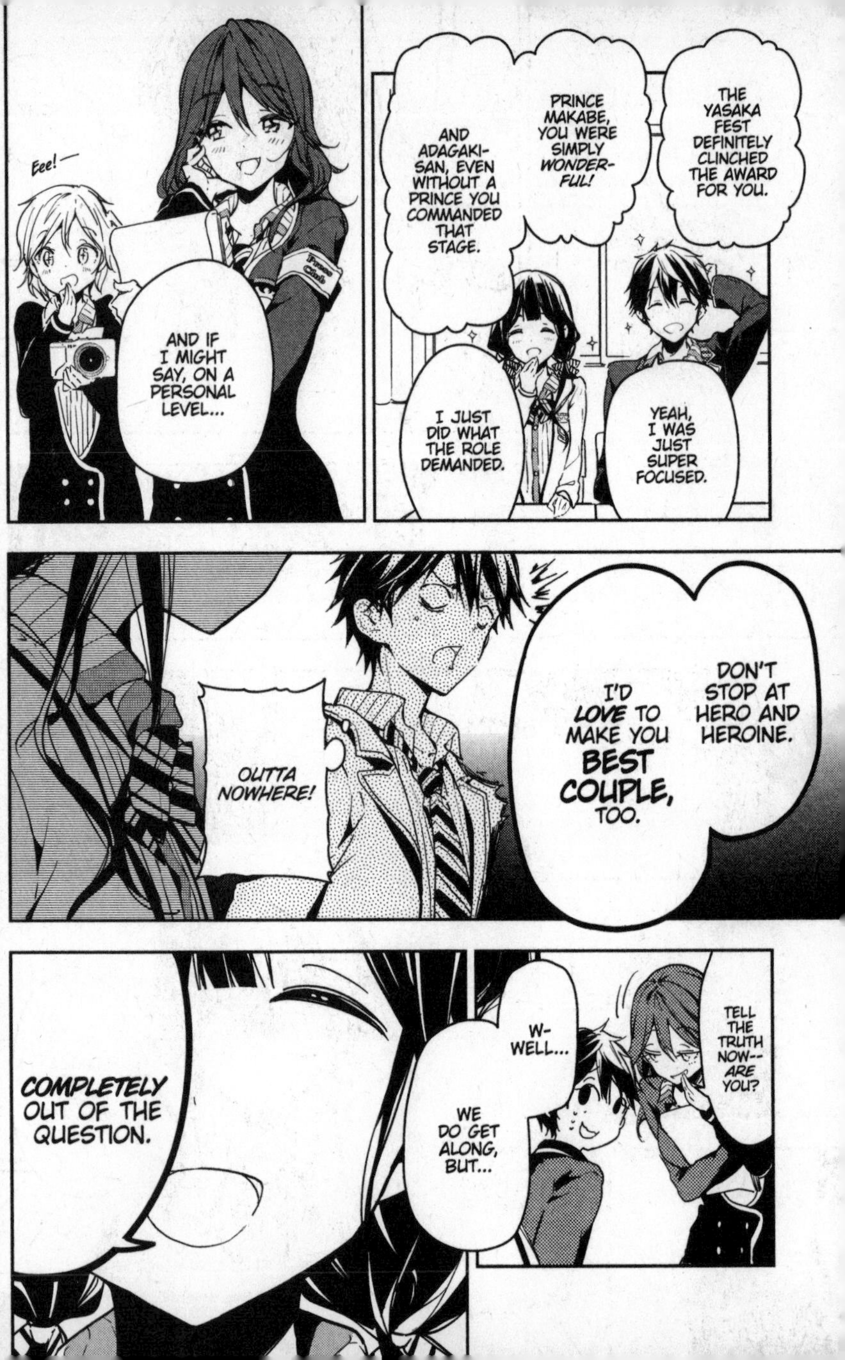
THE YASAKA FEST DEFINITELY CLINCHED THE AWARD FOR YOU.
PRINCE MAKABE, YOU WERE SIMPLY *WONDERFUL!*
AND ADAGAKI-SAN, EVEN WITHOUT A PRINCE YOU COMMANDED THAT STAGE.
YEAH, I WAS JUST SUPER FOCUSED.
I JUST DID WHAT THE ROLE DEMANDED.
Eee!—
AND IF I MIGHT SAY, ON A PERSONAL LEVEL...
DON'T STOP AT HERO AND HEROINE.
I'D *LOVE* TO MAKE YOU **BEST COUPLE,** TOO.
OUTTA NOWHERE!
TELL THE TRUTH NOW-- *ARE* YOU?
W-WELL...
WE DO GET ALONG, BUT...
COMPLETELY OUT OF THE QUESTION.

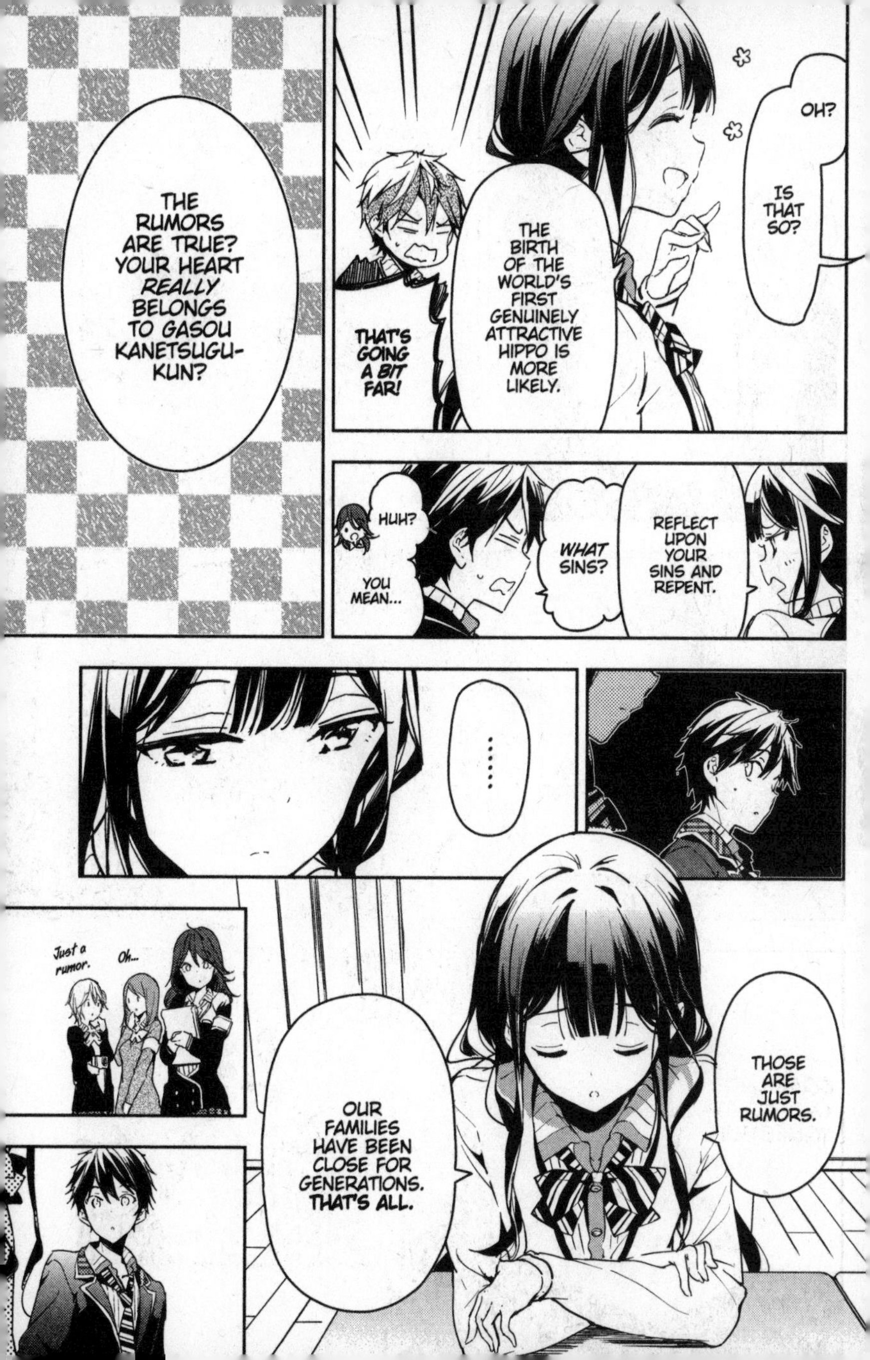
OH?
IS THAT SO?
THE BIRTH OF THE WORLD'S FIRST GENUINELY ATTRACTIVE HIPPO IS MORE LIKELY.
THAT'S GOING A *BIT* FAR!
REFLECT UPON YOUR SINS AND REPENT.
WHAT SINS?
HUH?
YOU MEAN...
THE RUMORS ARE TRUE? YOUR HEART *REALLY* BELONGS TO GASOU KANETSUGU-KUN?
......
THOSE ARE JUST RUMORS.
OUR FAMILIES HAVE BEEN CLOSE FOR GENERATIONS. THAT'S ALL.
Just a rumor.
Oh...

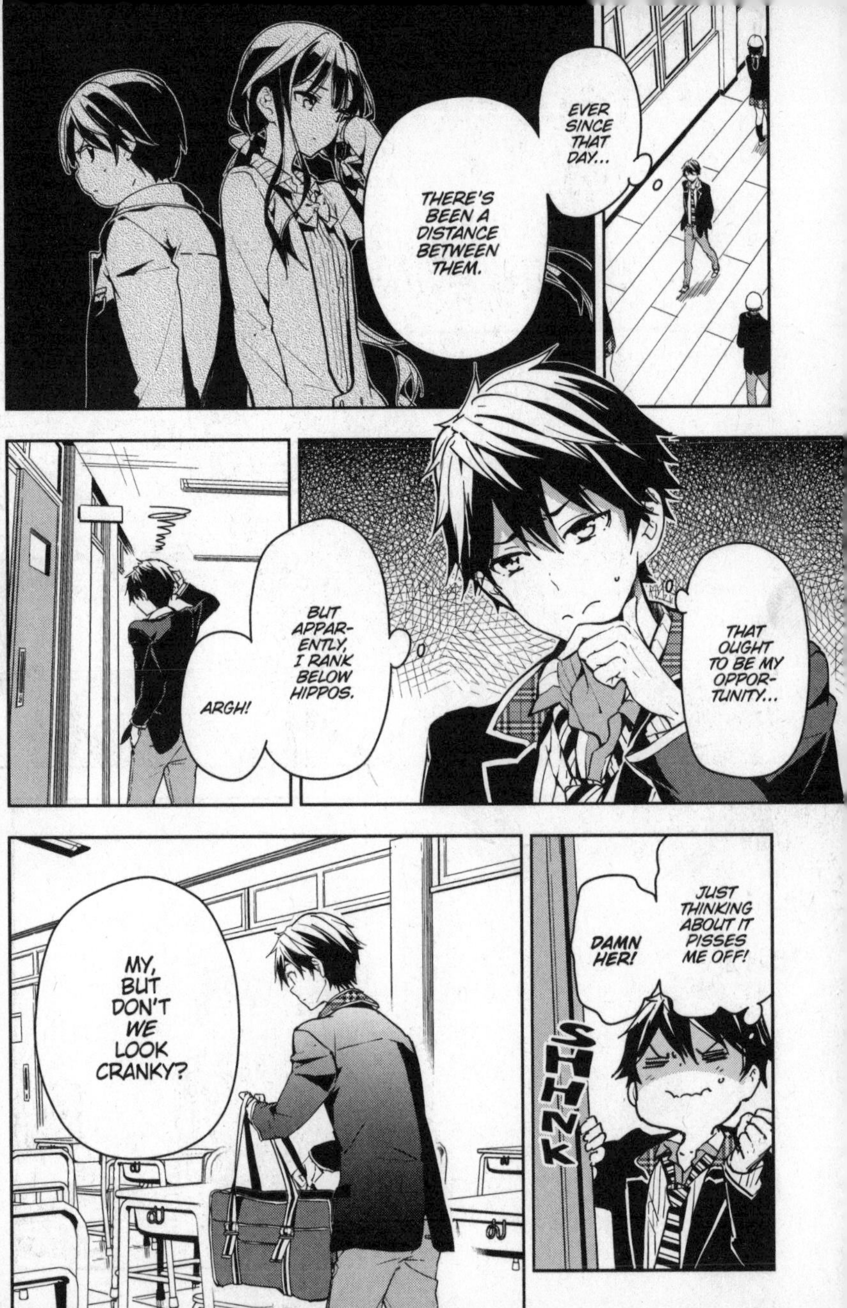
EVER SINCE THAT DAY...
THERE'S BEEN A DISTANCE BETWEEN THEM.
THAT OUGHT TO BE MY OPPORTUNITY...
BUT APPARENTLY, I RANK BELOW HIPPOS.
ARGH!
JUST THINKING ABOUT IT PISSES ME OFF!
DAMN HER!
SHHNK
MY, BUT DON'T WE LOOK CRANKY?

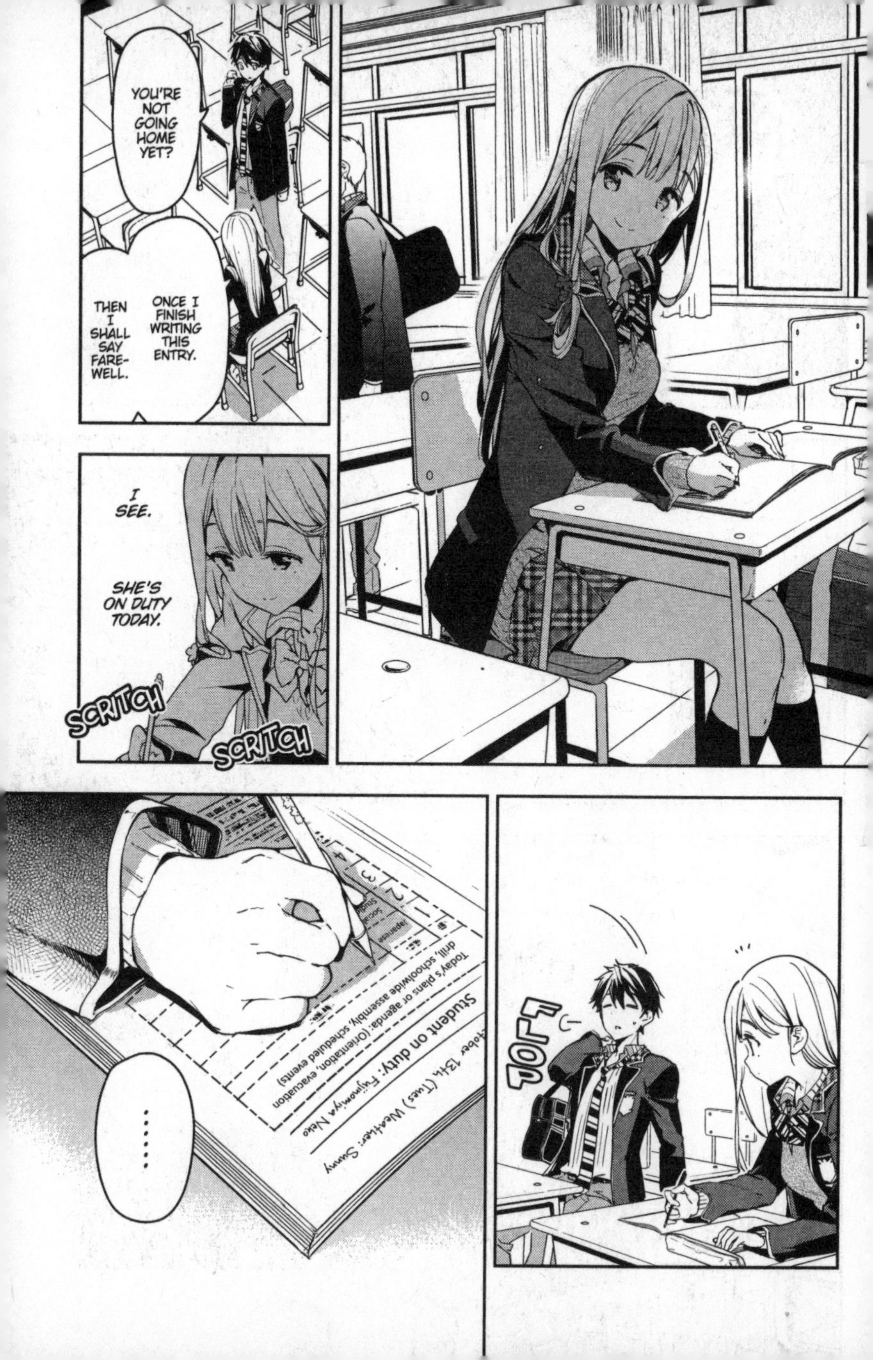
YOU'RE NOT GOING HOME YET?
ONCE I FINISH WRITING THIS ENTRY.
THEN I SHALL SAY FARE-WELL.
I SEE.
SHE'S ON DUTY TODAY.
SCRITCH
SCRITCH
FLOP
tober 13th (Tues) Weather: Sunny
Student on duty: Fujimiya Neko
Today's plans or agenda: (Orientation, evacuation drill, schoolwide assembly, scheduled events)
......

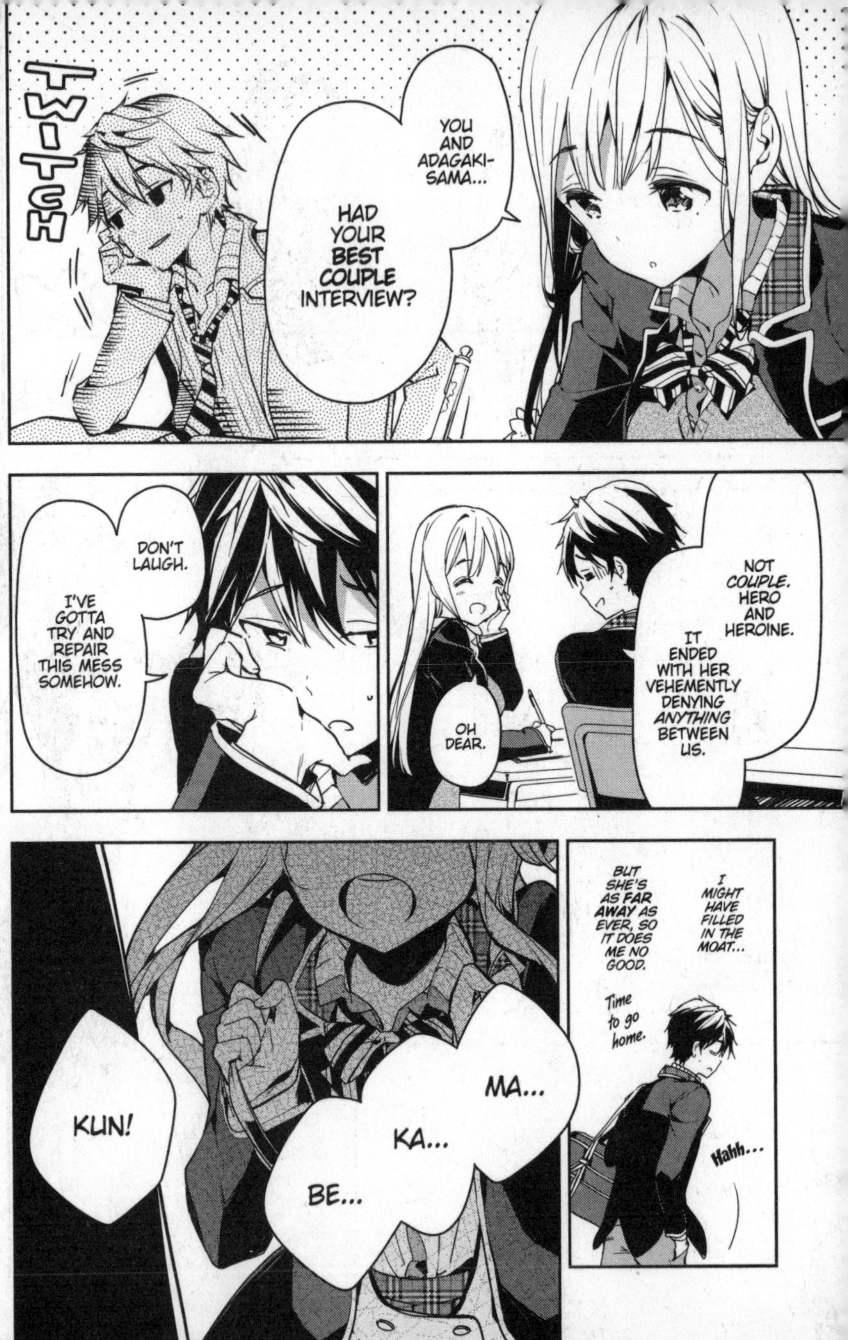
YOU AND ADAGAKI-SAMA...
HAD YOUR BEST COUPLE INTERVIEW?
TWITCH
NOT COUPLE. HERO AND HEROINE.
IT ENDED WITH HER VEHEMENTLY DENYING *ANYTHING* BETWEEN US.
OH DEAR.
DON'T LAUGH.
I'VE GOTTA TRY AND REPAIR THIS MESS SOMEHOW.
I MIGHT HAVE FILLED IN THE MOAT...
BUT SHE'S AS **FAR AWAY** AS EVER, SO IT DOES ME NO GOOD.
Time to go home.
Hahh...
MA...
KA...
BE...
KUN!

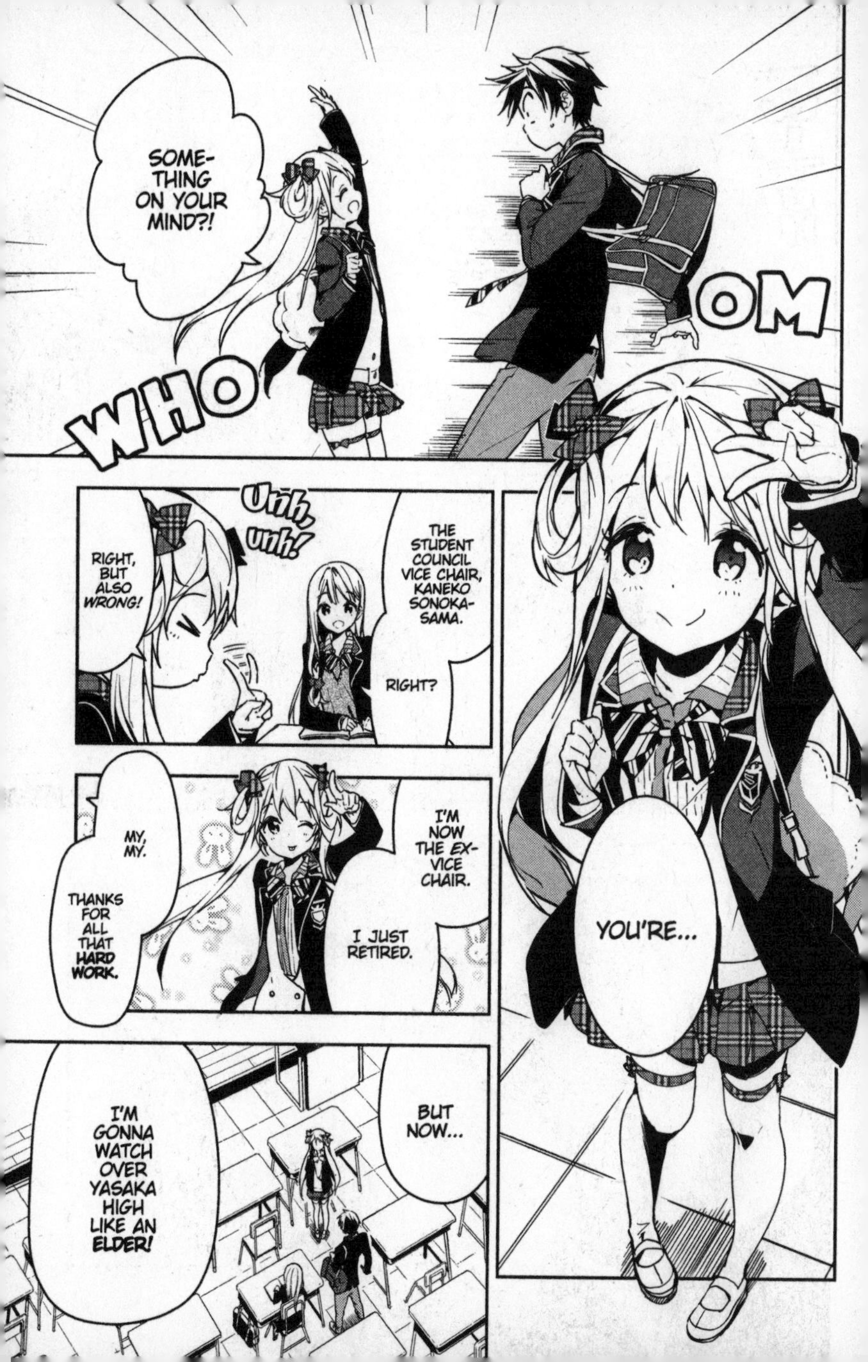
SOMETHING ON YOUR MIND?!
WHOOM
YOU'RE...
THE STUDENT COUNCIL VICE CHAIR, KANEKO SONOKA-SAMA.
RIGHT?
Unh, unh!
RIGHT, BUT ALSO WRONG!
I'M NOW THE EX-VICE CHAIR.
I JUST RETIRED.
MY, MY.
THANKS FOR ALL THAT HARD WORK.
BUT NOW...
I'M GONNA WATCH OVER YASAKA HIGH LIKE AN ELDER!

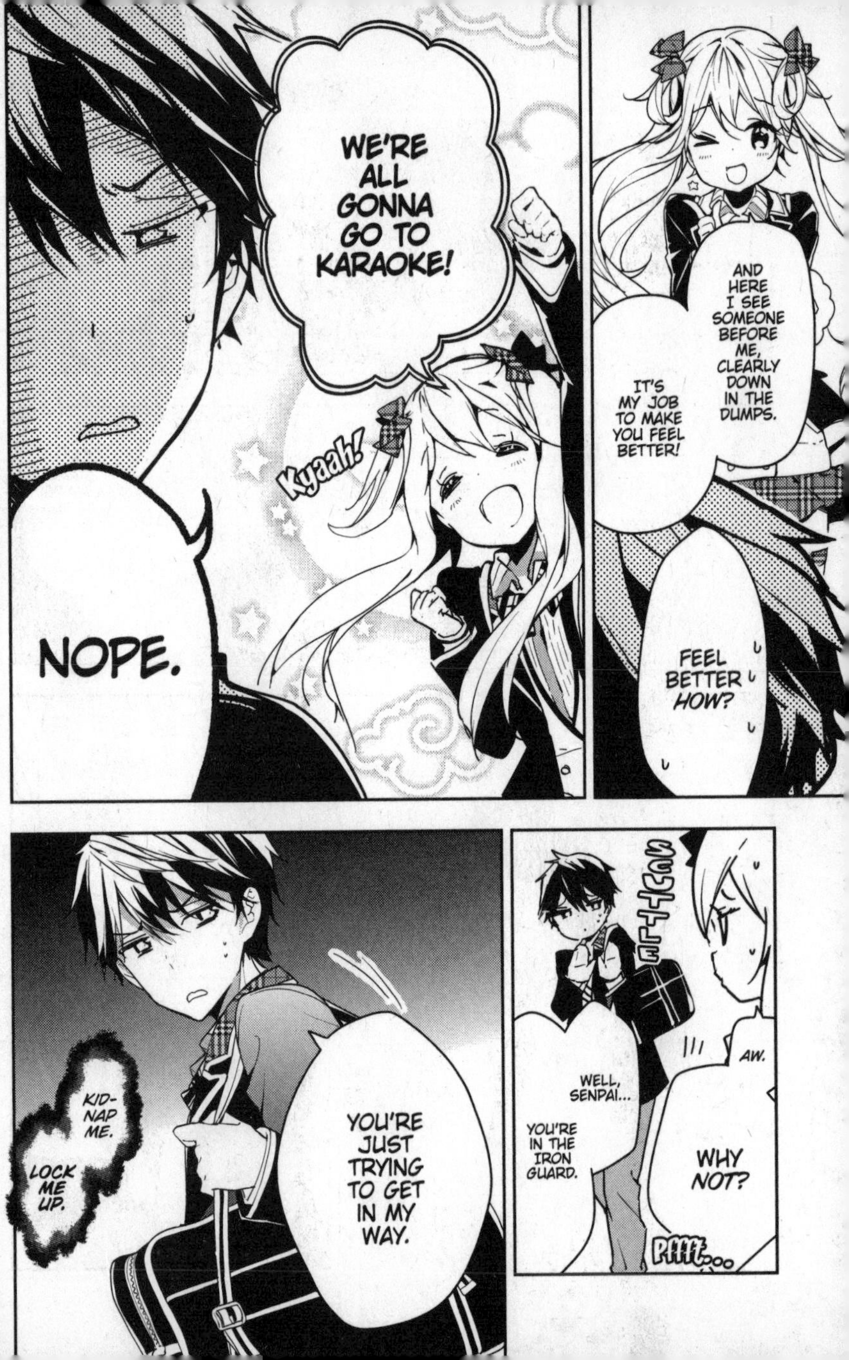
AND HERE I SEE SOMEONE BEFORE ME, CLEARLY DOWN IN THE DUMPS.
IT'S MY JOB TO MAKE YOU FEEL BETTER!
FEEL BETTER *HOW?*
WE'RE ALL GONNA GO TO KARAOKE!
Kyaah!
NOPE.
SCUTTLE
AW.
WHY *NOT?*
WELL, SENPAI...
YOU'RE IN THE IRON GUARD.
Pffft...
YOU'RE JUST TRYING TO GET IN MY WAY.
KID-NAP ME.
LOCK ME UP.

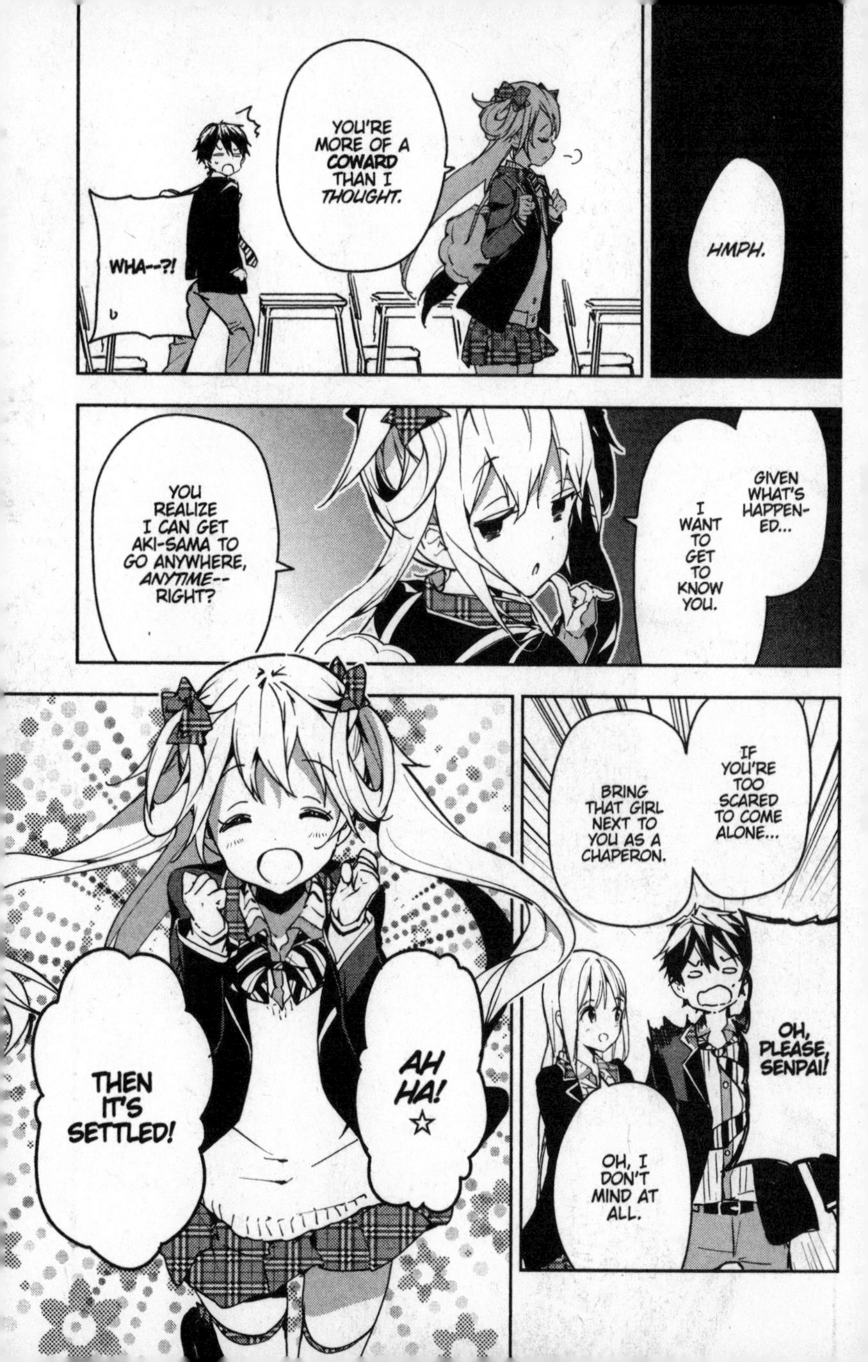
HMPH.
YOU'RE MORE OF A COWARD THAN I THOUGHT.
WHA--?!
GIVEN WHAT'S HAPPENED... I WANT TO GET TO KNOW YOU.
YOU REALIZE I CAN GET AKI-SAMA TO GO ANYWHERE, ANYTIME--RIGHT?
IF YOU'RE TOO SCARED TO COME ALONE...
BRING THAT GIRL NEXT TO YOU AS A CHAPERON.
OH, PLEASE, SENPAI!
OH, I DON'T MIND AT ALL.
AH HA! ☆
THEN IT'S SETTLED!

I'LL JUST POP BY NEXT DOOR... AND TALK AKI-SAMA INTO IT!
HEY...!
......
SHOULD I NOT HAVE AGREED...?
NO... IT'S FINE.
IF YOU'RE THERE, THEY'RE UNLIKELY TO KID-NAP ME.
IT'S JUST KARAOKE.
BUT...
I CAN'T ADMIT IT...

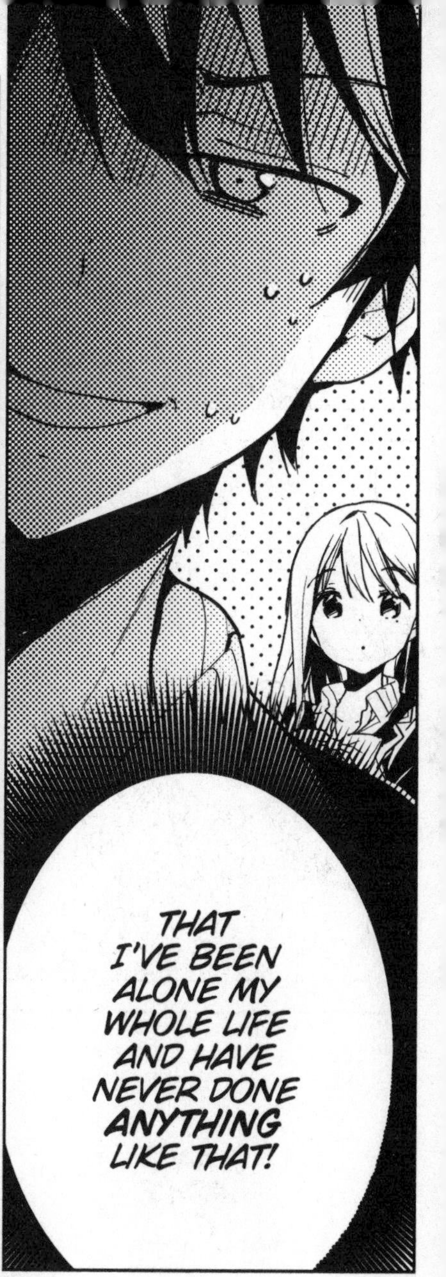
THAT I'VE BEEN ALONE MY WHOLE LIFE AND HAVE NEVER DONE ANYTHING LIKE THAT!

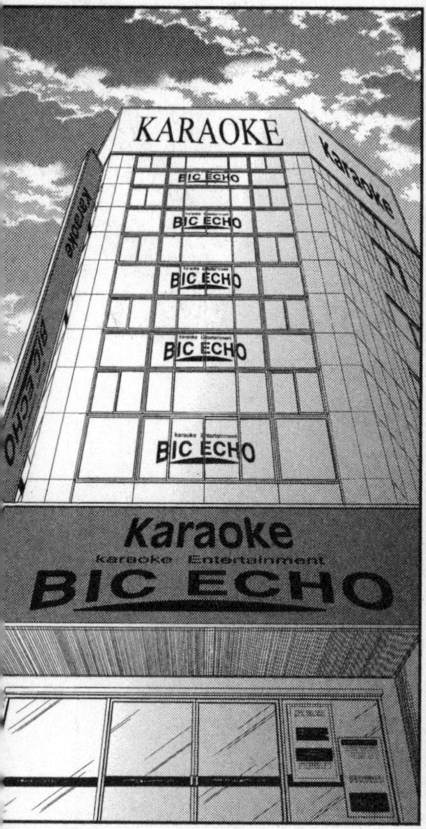
KARAOKE
Karaoke
BIC ECHO
Karaoke
karaoke Entertainment
BIC ECHO

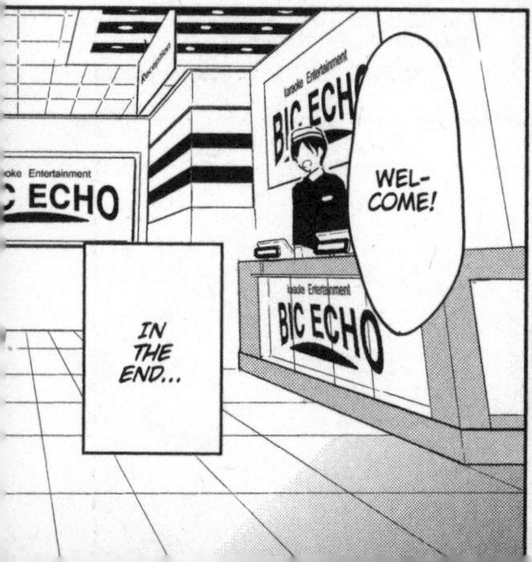
Reception
karaoke Entertainment
BIC ECHO
WEL-COME!
IN THE END...

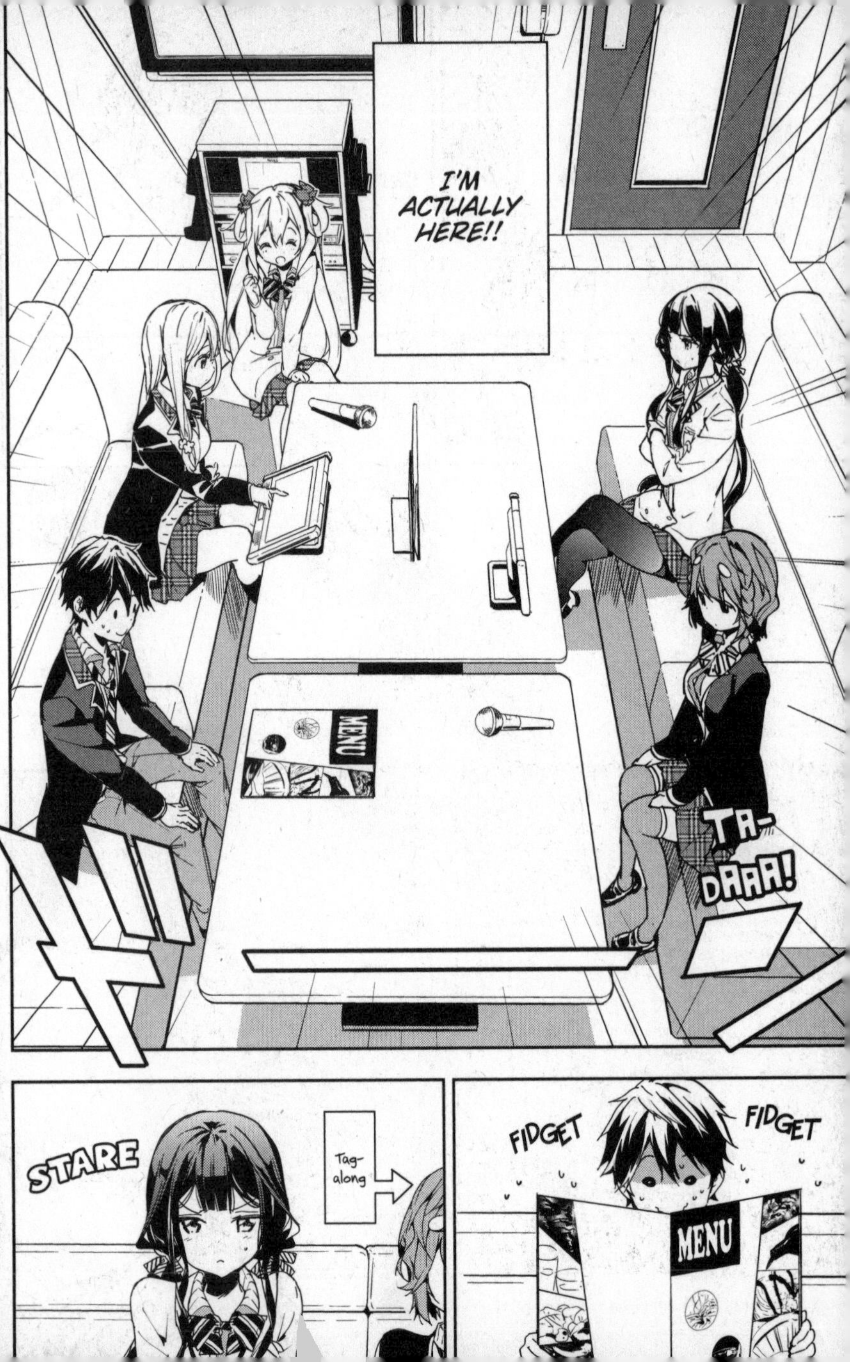
I'M ACTUALLY HERE!!
TA-DAAA!
MENU
FIDGET FIDGET
MENU
STARE
Tag-along

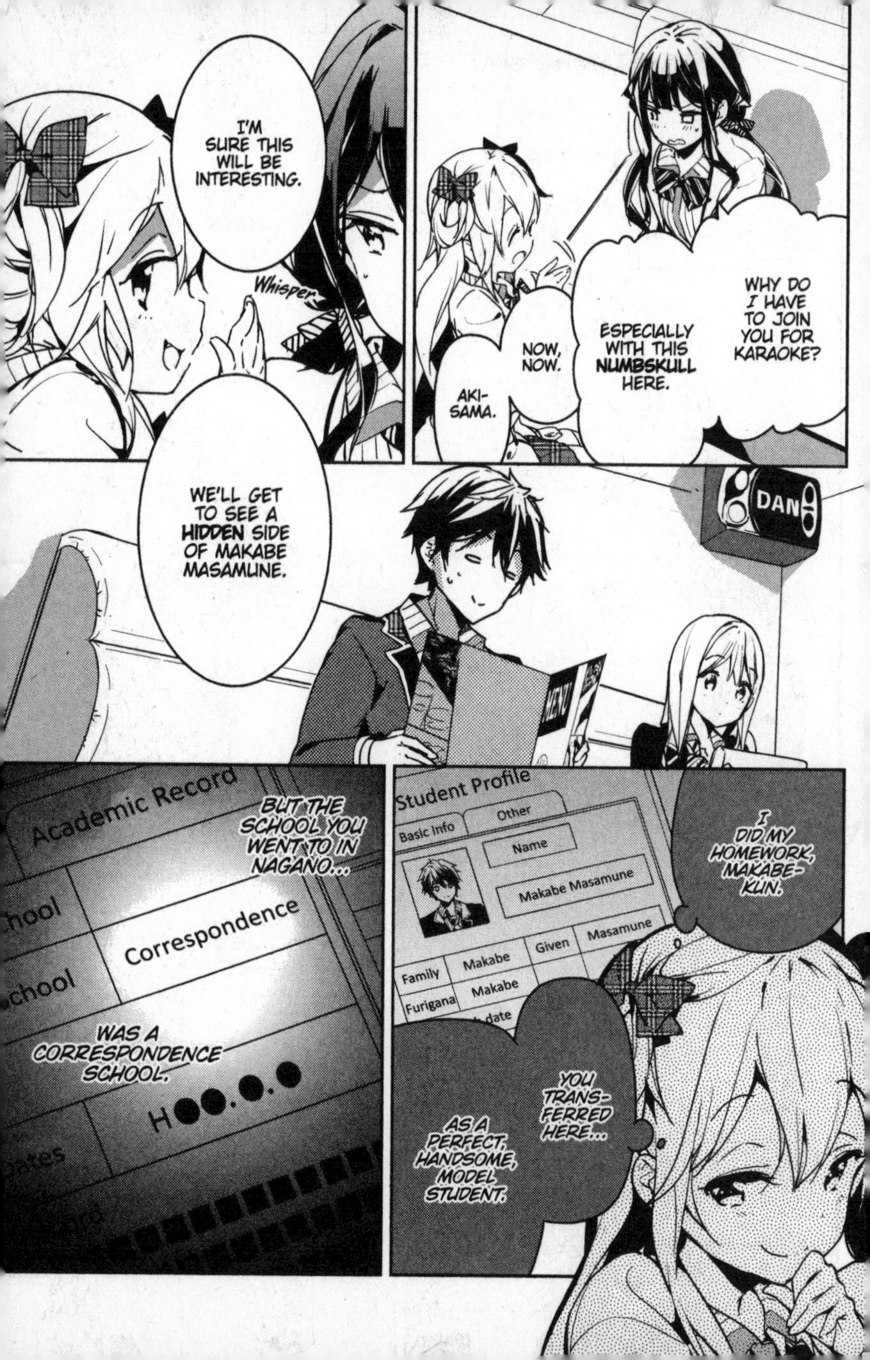
WHY DO I HAVE TO JOIN YOU FOR KARAOKE?
ESPECIALLY WITH THIS **NUMBSKULL** HERE.
NOW, NOW.
AKI-SAMA.
I'M SURE THIS WILL BE INTERESTING.
Whisper
WE'LL GET TO SEE A **HIDDEN** SIDE OF MAKABE MASAMUNE.
DAN
MENU
Student Profile
Basic Info
Other
Name
Makabe Masamune
Family
Makabe
Given
Masamune
Furigana
Makabe
I DID MY HOMEWORK, MAKABE-KUN.
YOU TRANSFERRED HERE...
AS A PERFECT, HANDSOME, MODEL STUDENT.
Academic Record
Correspondence
BUT THE SCHOOL YOU WENT TO IN NAGANO...
WAS A CORRESPONDENCE SCHOOL.

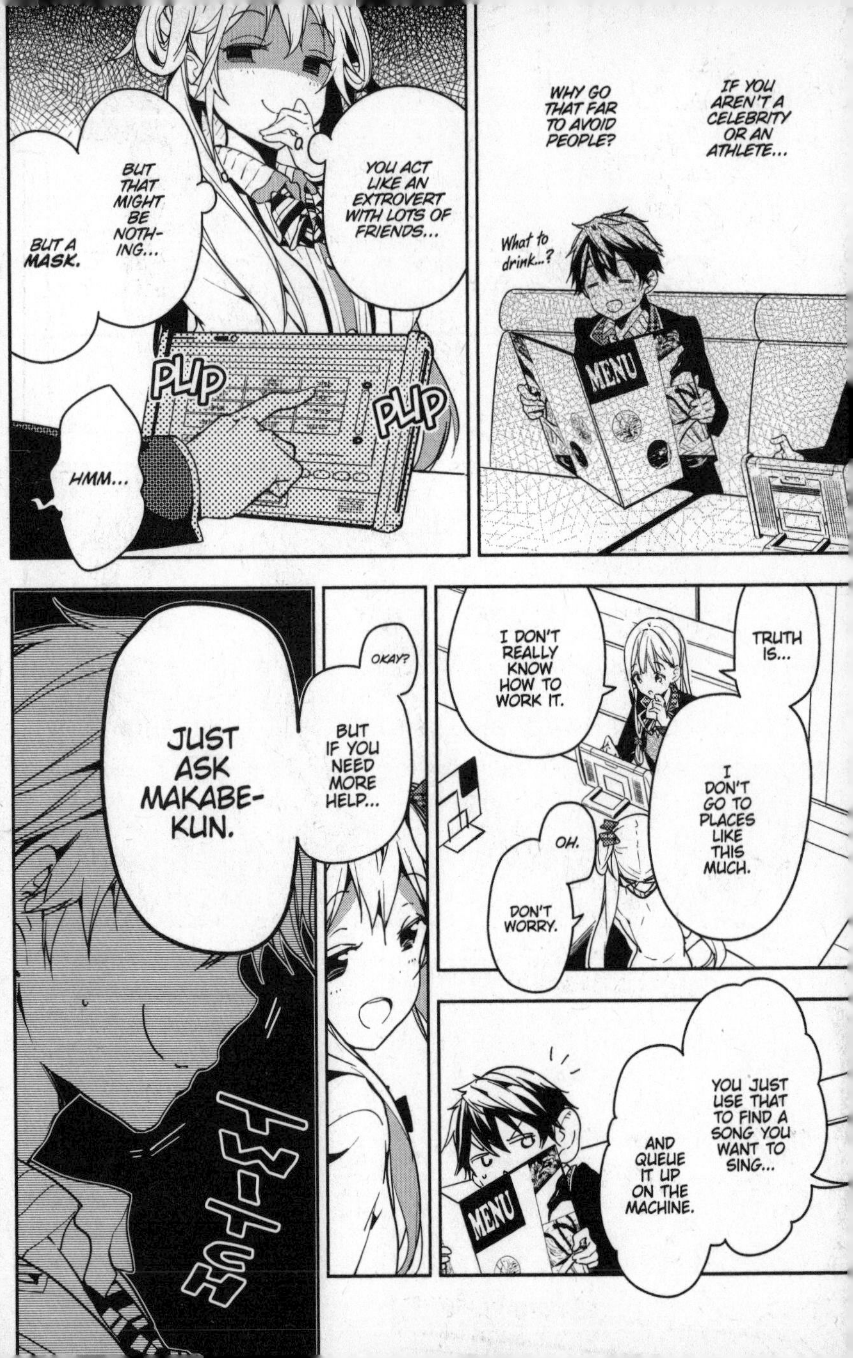
IF YOU AREN'T A CELEBRITY OR AN ATHLETE...
WHY GO THAT FAR TO AVOID PEOPLE?
What to drink...?
YOU ACT LIKE AN EXTROVERT WITH LOTS OF FRIENDS...
BUT THAT MIGHT BE NOTHING...
BUT A MASK.
PLIP
PLIP
HMM...
TRUTH IS...
I DON'T GO TO PLACES LIKE THIS MUCH.
I DON'T REALLY KNOW HOW TO WORK IT.
OH.
DON'T WORRY.
YOU JUST USE THAT TO FIND A SONG YOU WANT TO SING...
AND QUEUE IT UP ON THE MACHINE.
OKAY?
BUT IF YOU NEED MORE HELP...
JUST ASK MAKABE-KUN.

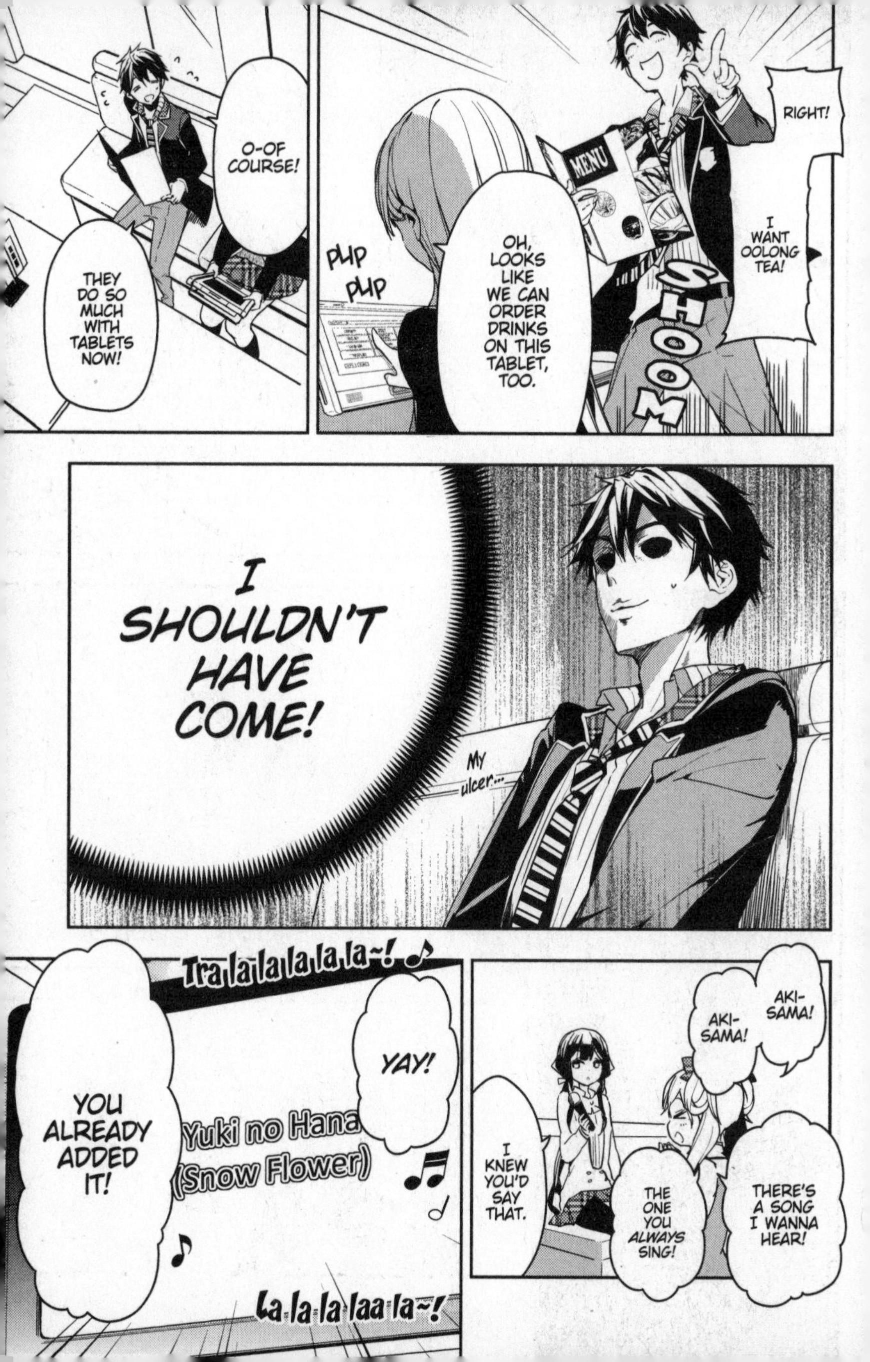
RIGHT!
I WANT OOLONG TEA!
SHOOM
MENU
OH, LOOKS LIKE WE CAN ORDER DRINKS ON THIS TABLET, TOO.
PUP PUP
O-OF COURSE!
THEY DO SO MUCH WITH TABLETS NOW!
I SHOULDN'T HAVE COME!
My ulcer...
AKI-SAMA!
AKI-SAMA!
THERE'S A SONG I WANNA HEAR!
THE ONE YOU ALWAYS SING!
I KNEW YOU'D SAY THAT.
Tra la la la la la~!
YAY!
Yuki no Hana (Snow Flower)
YOU ALREADY ADDED IT!
La la la laa la~!

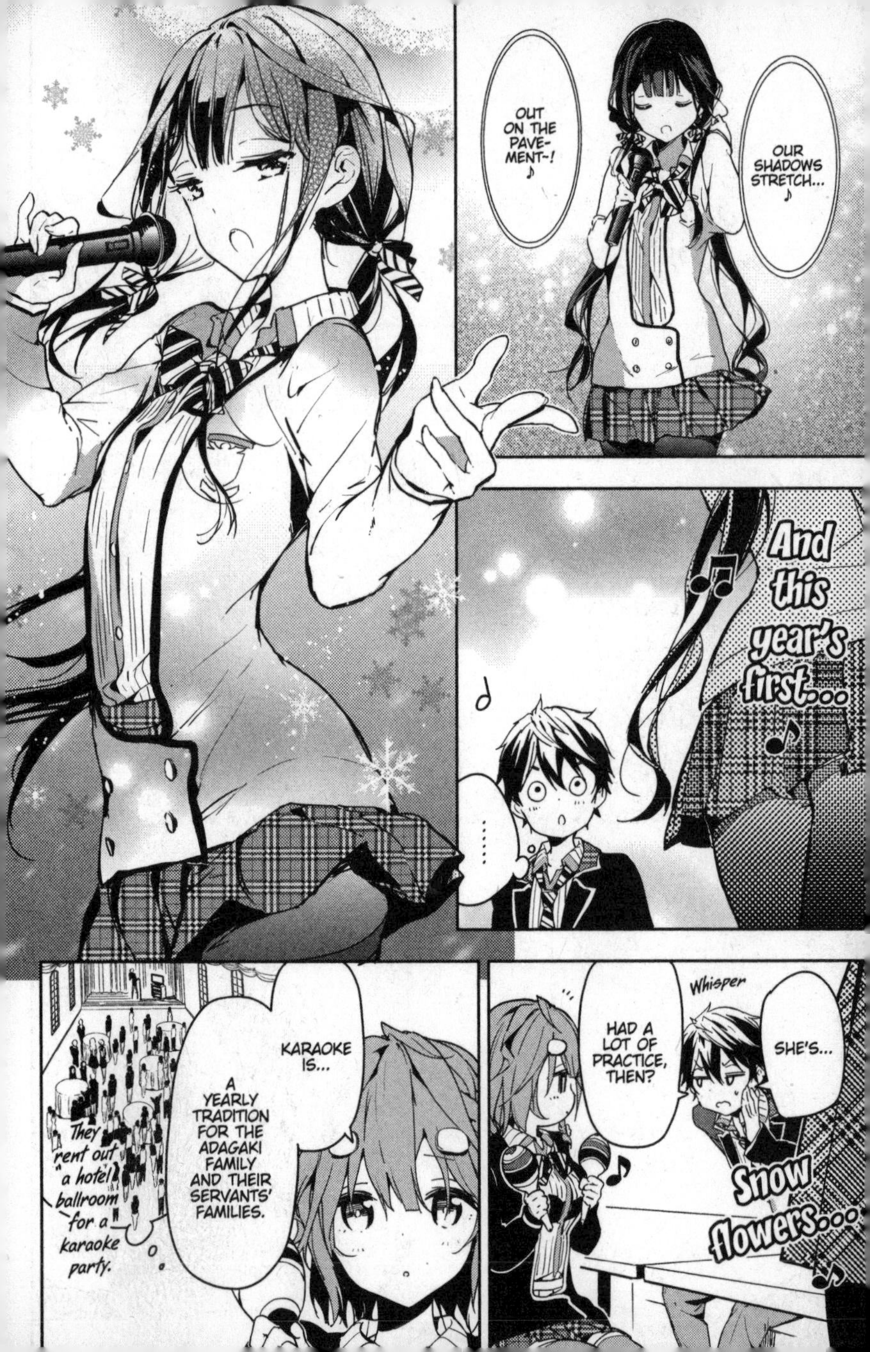
OUR SHADOWS STRETCH... ♪
OUT ON THE PAVE-MENT~! ♪
And this year's first...
......
SHE'S...
Whisper
HAD A LOT OF PRACTICE, THEN?
Snow flowers...
KARAOKE IS...
A YEARLY TRADITION FOR THE ADAGAKI FAMILY AND THEIR SERVANTS' FAMILIES.
They rent out a hotel ballroom for a karaoke party.

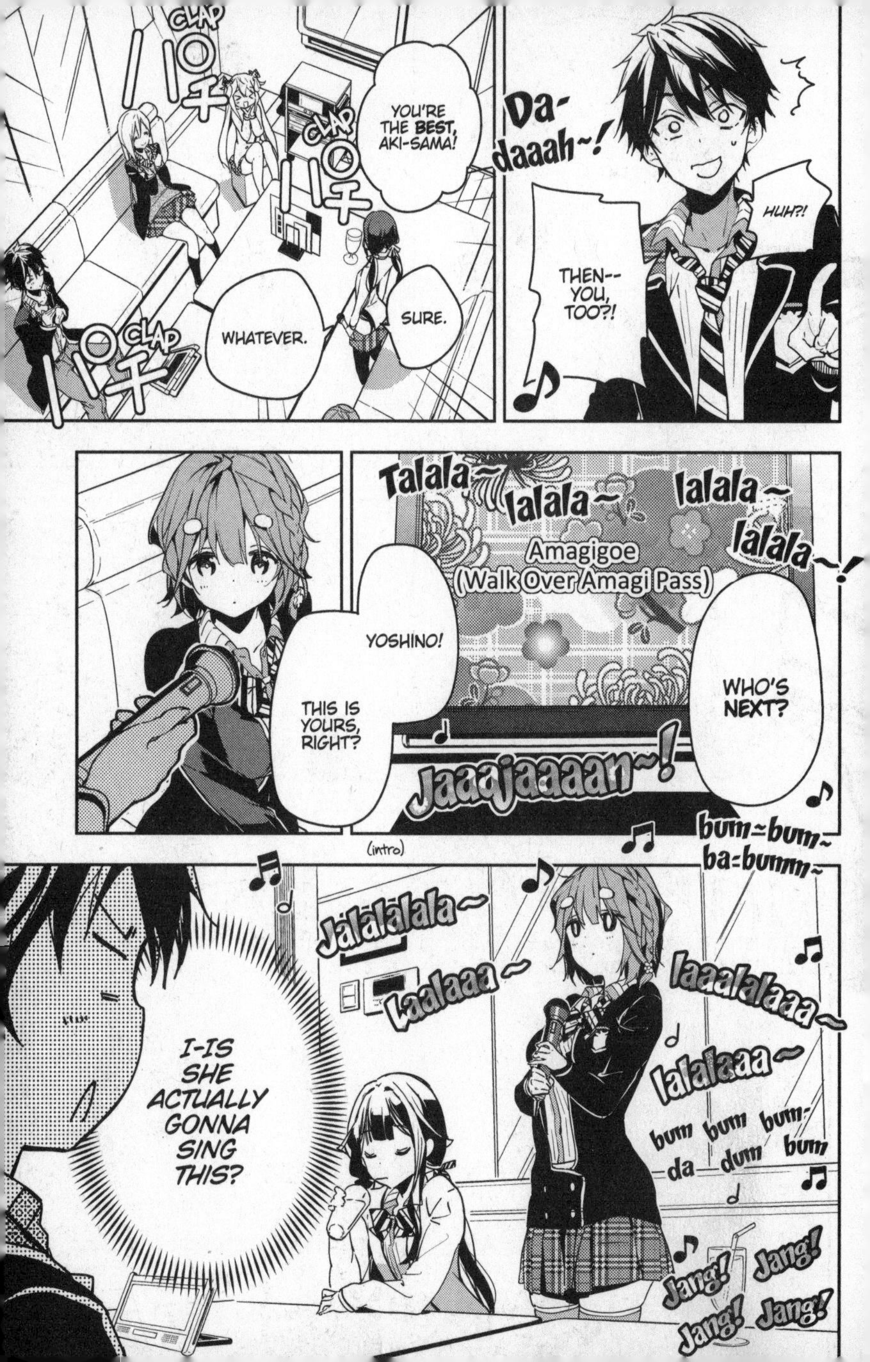
Da-daaah~!
HUH?!
THEN-- YOU, TOO?!
CLAP
YOU'RE THE BEST, AKI-SAMA!
CLAP
SURE.
WHATEVER.
CLAP
Talala~ lalala~ lalala~ lalala~!
Amagigoe (Walk Over Amagi Pass)
WHO'S NEXT?
Jaaajaaaan~!
YOSHINO!
THIS IS YOURS, RIGHT?
(intro)
bum~bum~ ba~bumm~
laaalalaaa~
lalalaaa~
bum bum bum~ da dum bum
Jang! Jang! Jang! Jang!
Jalalalala~
Laalaaa~
I-IS SHE ACTUALLY GONNA SING THIS?

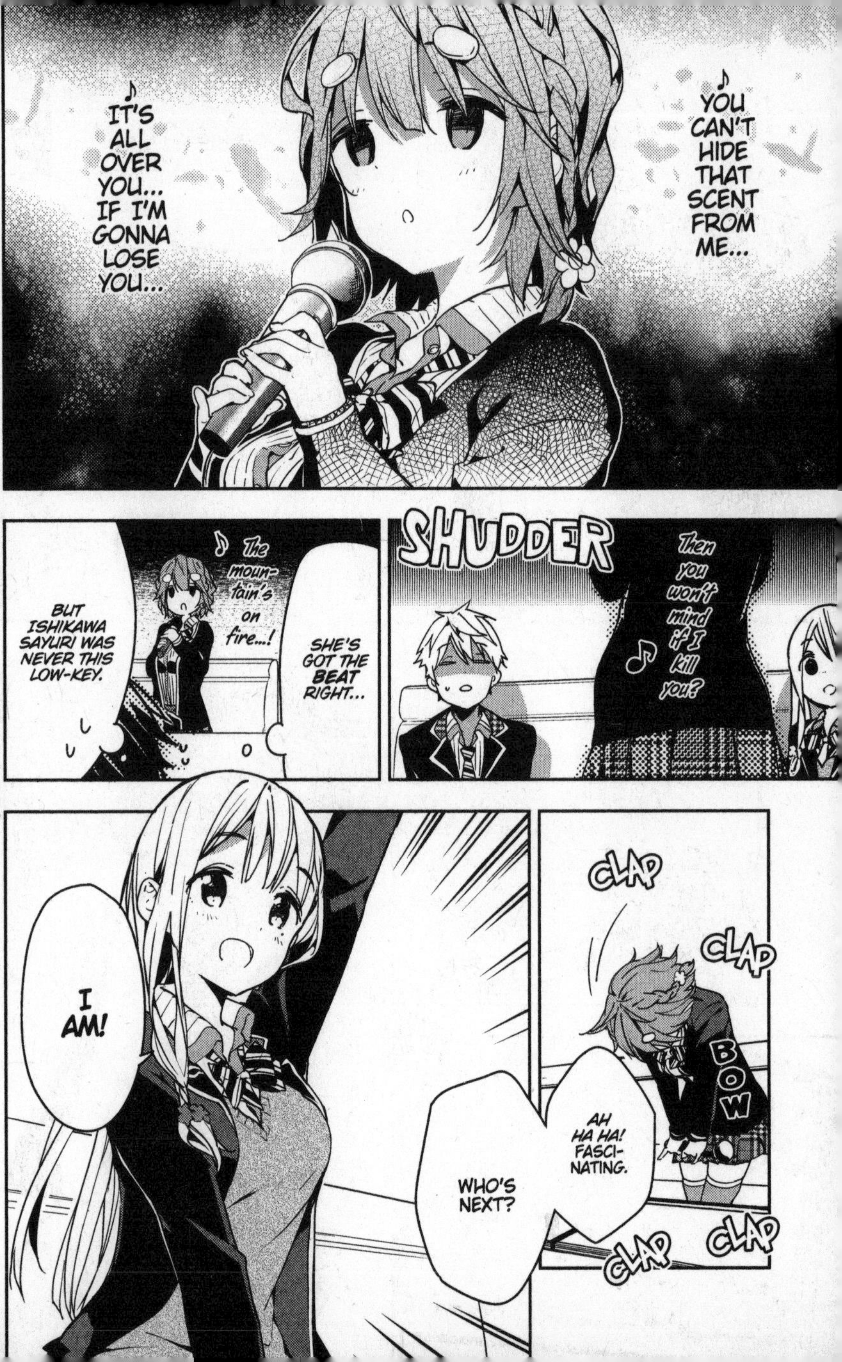
♪ YOU CAN'T HIDE THAT SCENT FROM ME...
♪ IT'S ALL OVER YOU... IF I'M GONNA LOSE YOU...
SHUDDER
Then you won't mind if I kill you? ♪
♪ The moun-tain's on fire...!
SHE'S GOT THE BEAT RIGHT...
BUT ISHIKAWA SAYURI WAS NEVER THIS LOW-KEY.
CLAP
CLAP
BOW
AH HA HA! FASCI-NATING.
WHO'S NEXT?
CLAP
CLAP
I AM!

Ishikawa Sayuri is a Japanese enka singer. Enka is a music genre stylistically similar to traditional Japanese music.

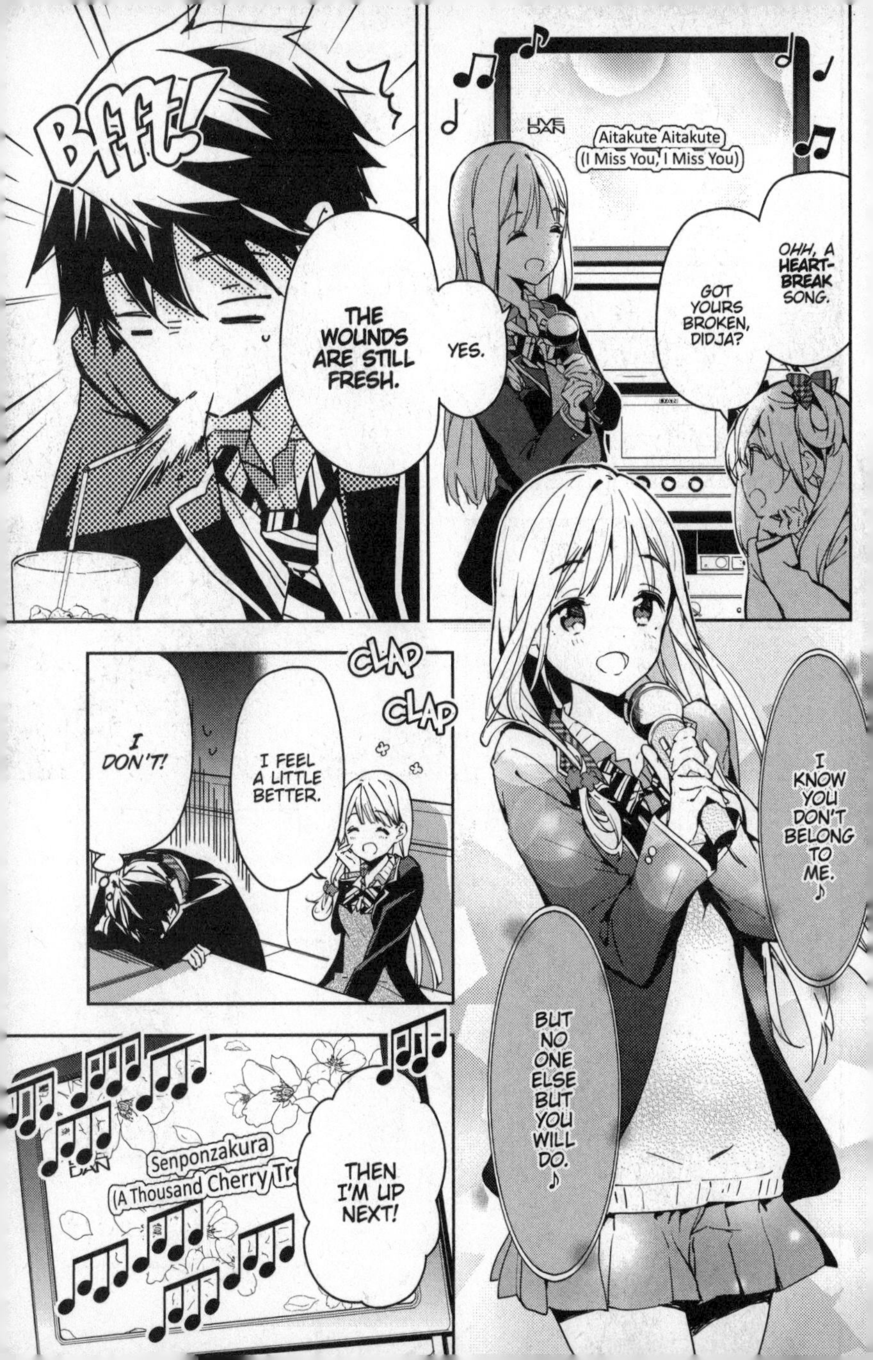
Aitakute Aitakute
(I Miss You, I Miss You)
OHH, A HEARTBREAK SONG.
GOT YOURS BROKEN, DIDJA?
YES.
THE WOUNDS ARE STILL FRESH.
BFFT!
I KNOW YOU DON'T BELONG TO ME. ♪
BUT NO ONE ELSE BUT YOU WILL DO. ♪
CLAP
CLAP
I FEEL A LITTLE BETTER.
I DON'T!
Senponzakura
(A Thousand Cherry Tre
THEN I'M UP NEXT!

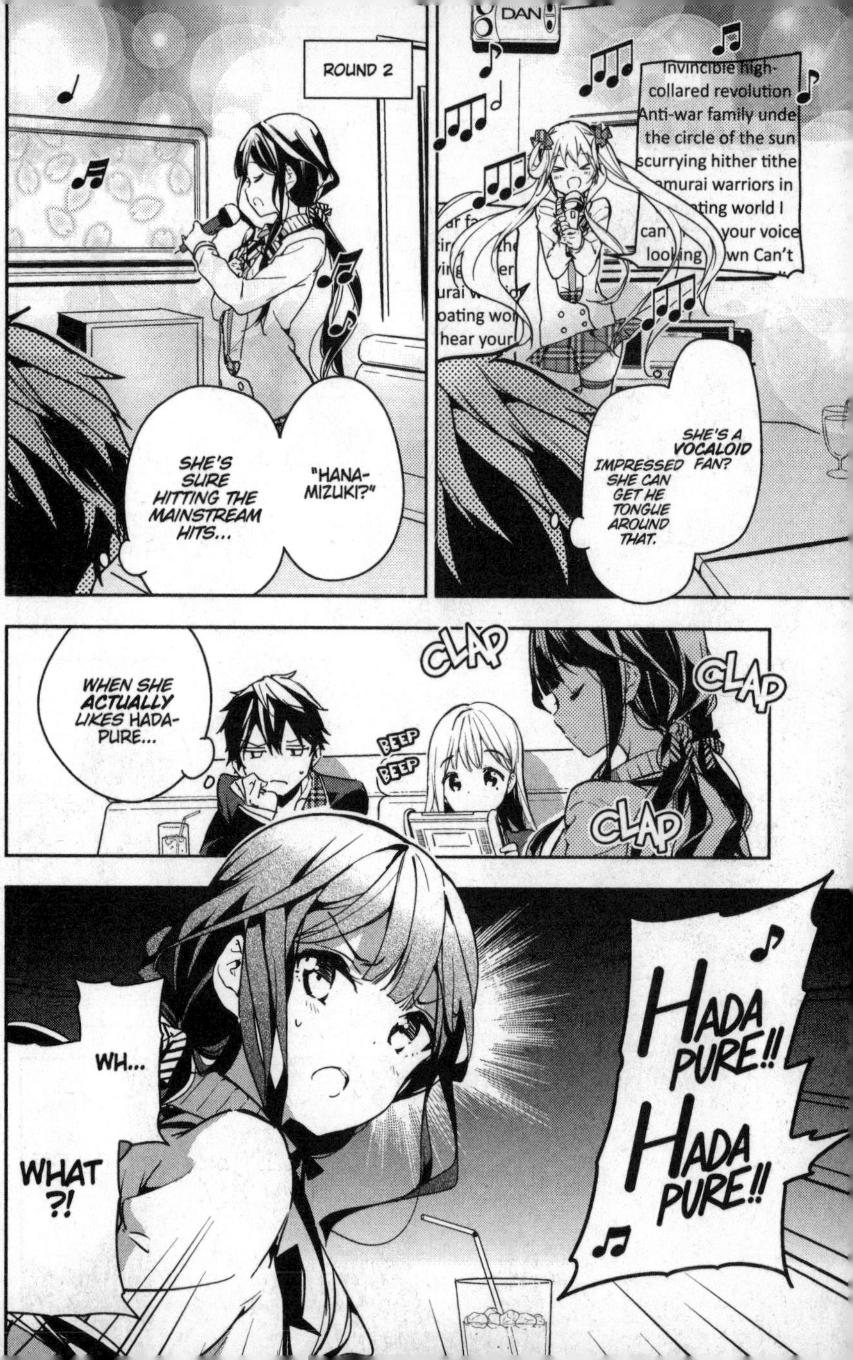
DAN
Invincible high-
collared revolution
Anti-war family unde
the circle of the sun
scurrying hither tithe
emurai warriors in
ating world I
your voice
wn Can't
SHE'S A VOCALOID FAN? IMPRESSED SHE CAN GET HE TONGUE AROUND THAT.
ROUND 2
"HANA-MIZUKI?"
SHE'S SURE HITTING THE MAINSTREAM HITS...
CLAP
CLAP
BEEP BEEP
WHEN SHE ACTUALLY LIKES HADA-PURE...
CLAP
HADA PURE!! HADA PURE!!
WH...
WHAT?!

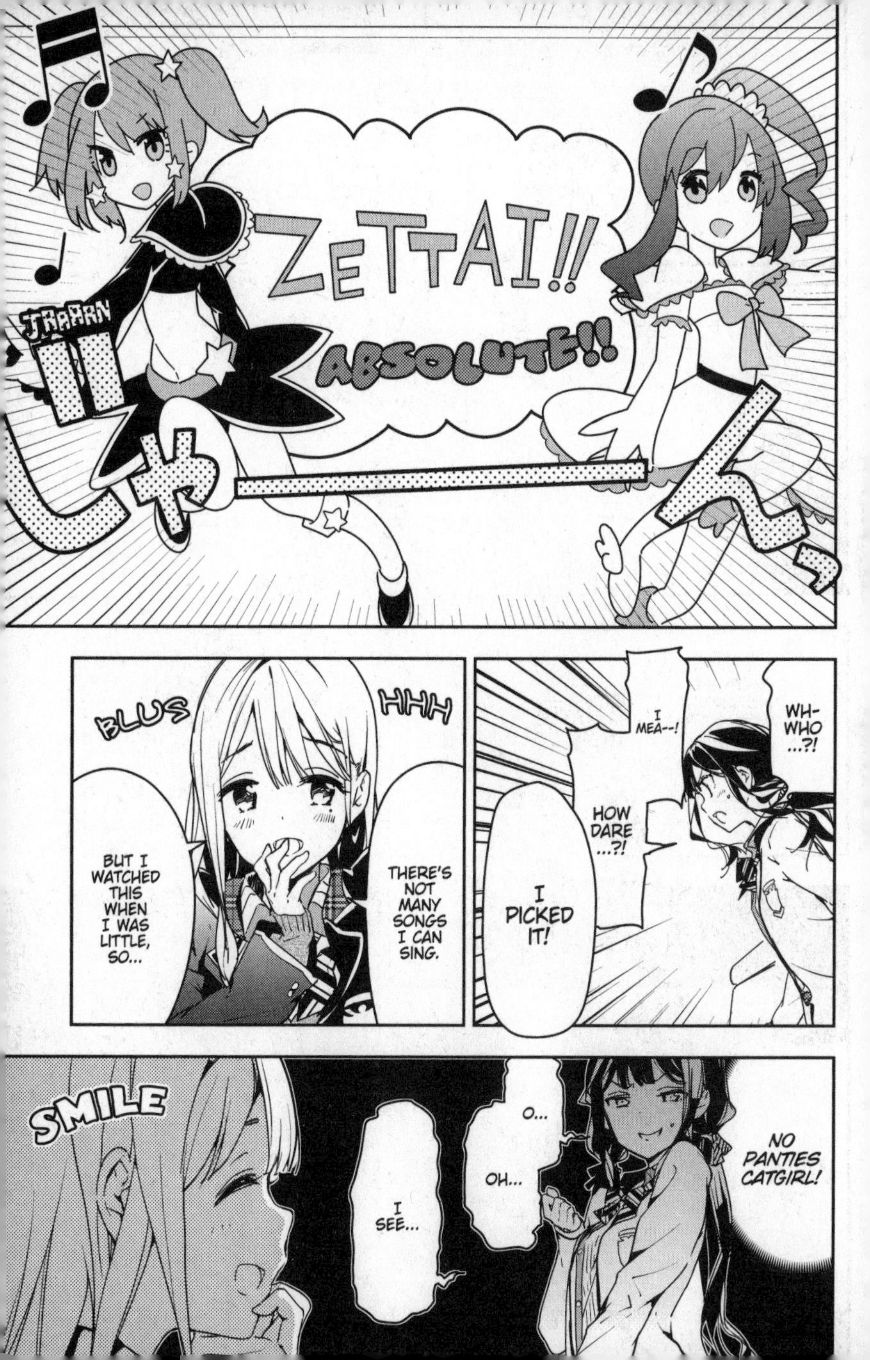
ZETTAI!!
ABSOLUTE!!
JRAAARN
WH-WHO...?!
I MEA--!
HOW DARE...?!
I PICKED IT!
HHH
BLUS
THERE'S NOT MANY SONGS I CAN SING.
BUT I WATCHED THIS WHEN I WAS LITTLE, SO...
NO PANTIES CATGIRL!
O... OH...
I SEE...
SMILE

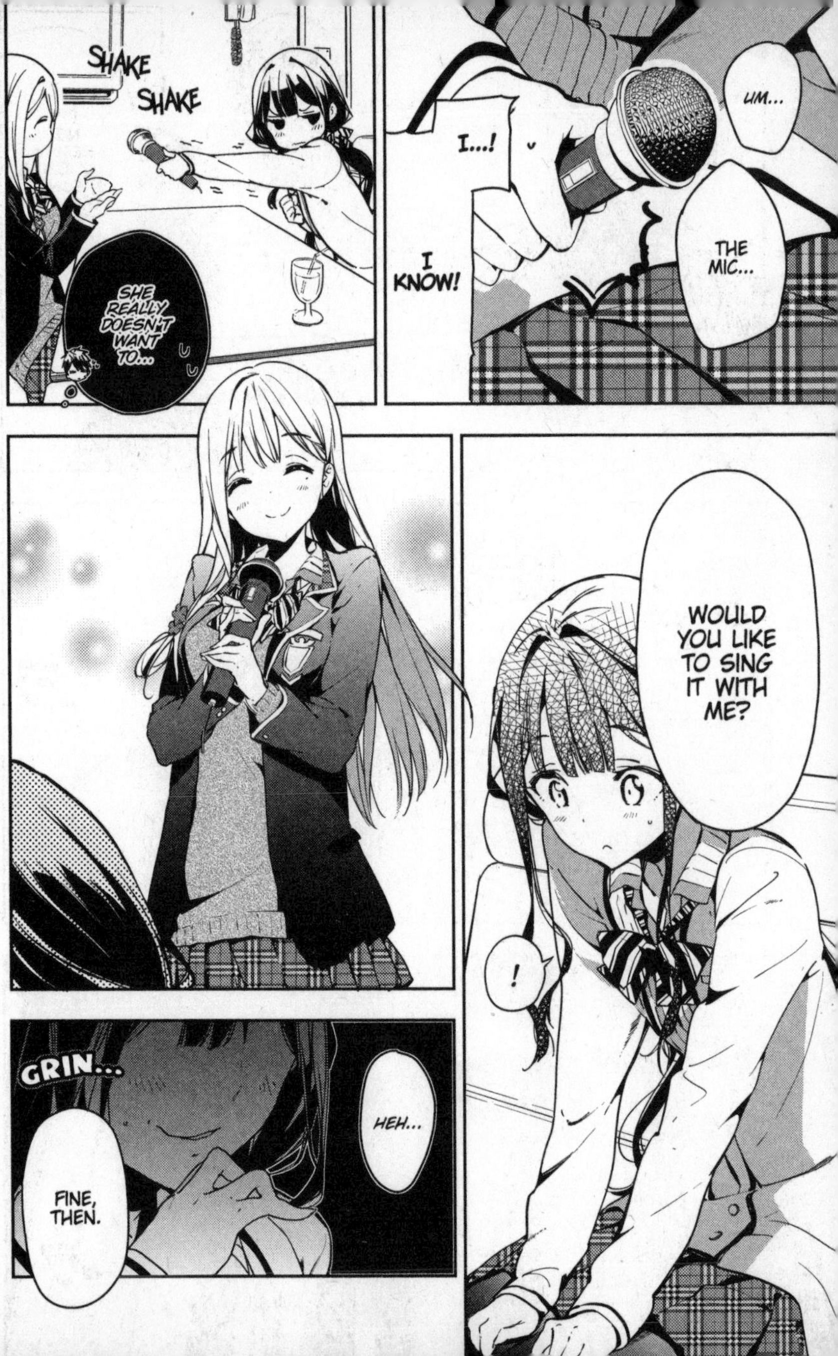
UM...
THE MIC...
I...!
I KNOW!
SHAKE
SHAKE
SHE REALLY DOESN'T WANT TO...
WOULD YOU LIKE TO SING IT WITH ME?
!
GRIN...
HEH...
FINE, THEN.

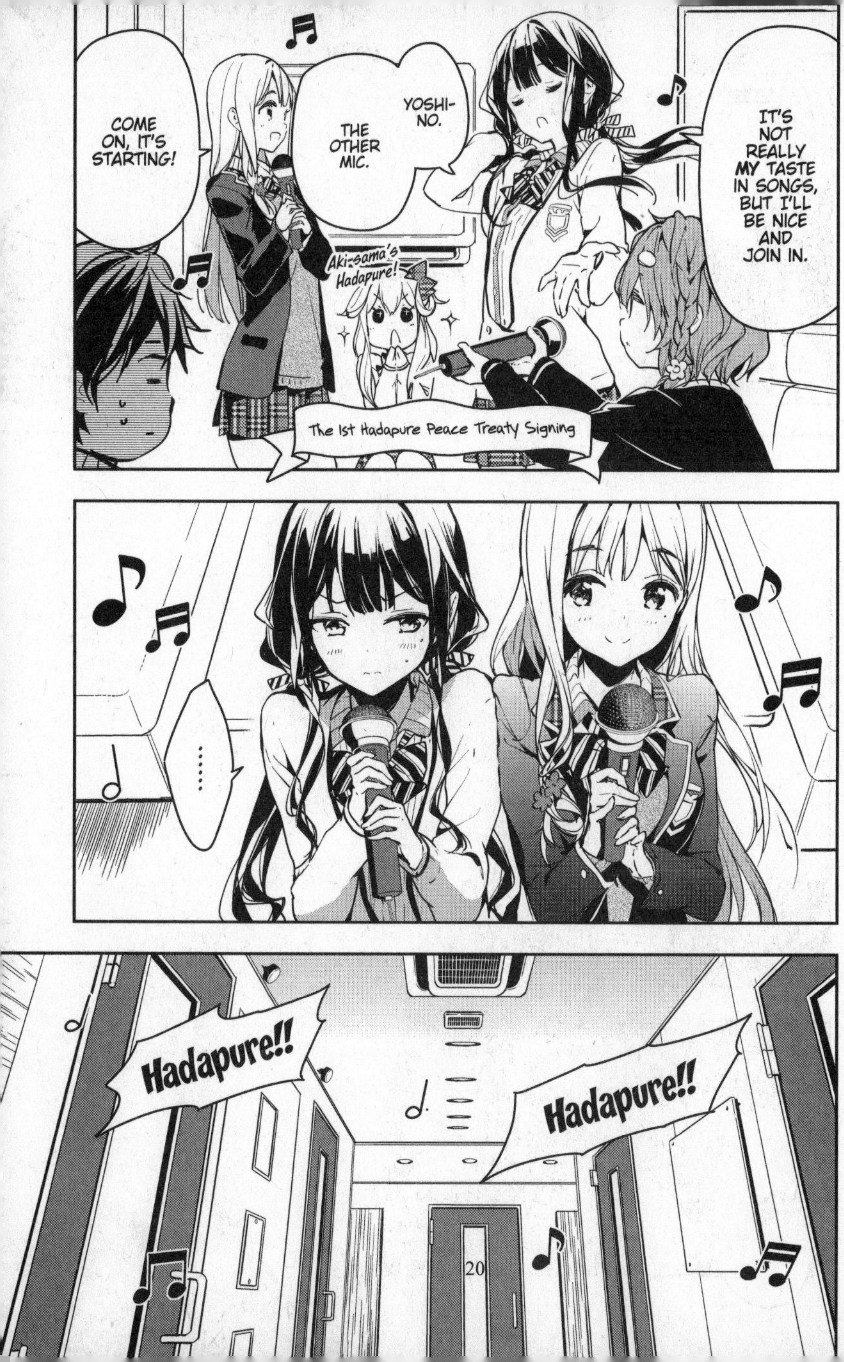
IT'S NOT REALLY MY TASTE IN SONGS, BUT I'LL BE NICE AND JOIN IN.
YOSHI-NO.
THE OTHER MIC.
Aki-sama's Hadapure!
COME ON, IT'S STARTING!
The 1st Hadapure Peace Treaty Signing
......
Hadapure!!
Hadapure!!

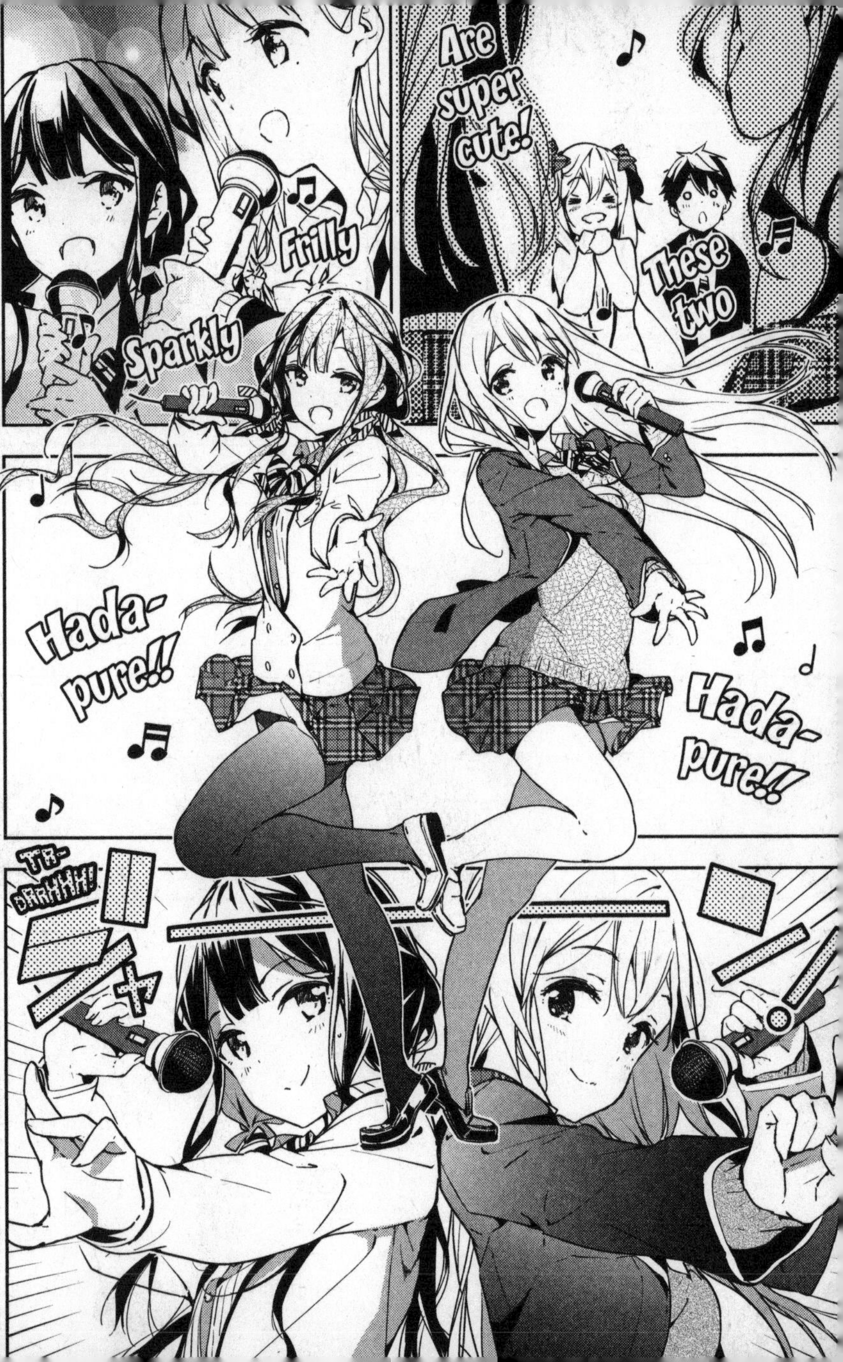
These two
Are super cute!
Frilly
Sparkly
Hada-pure!!
Hada-pure!!
TA-DAHHHH!

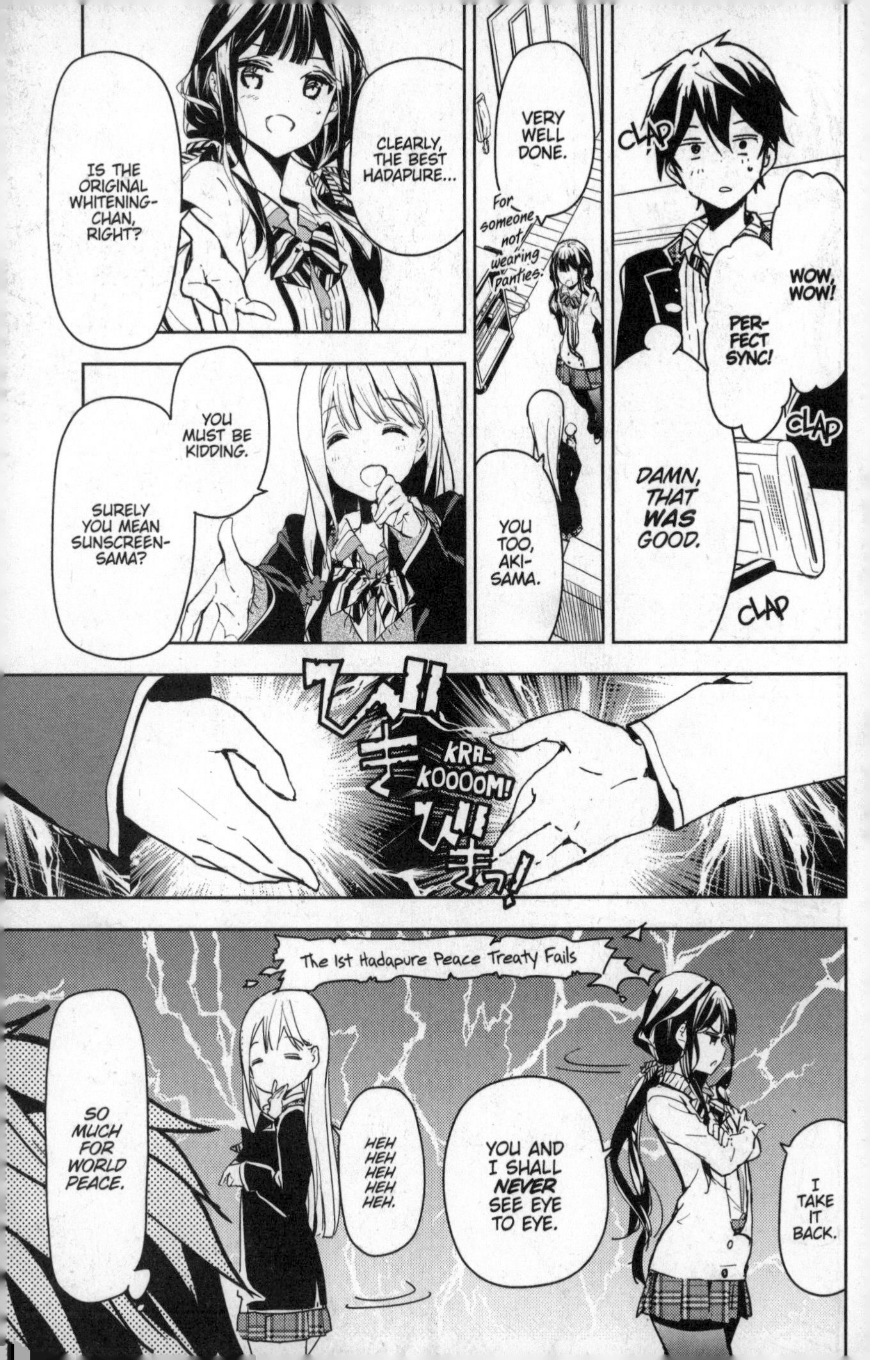

CLAP
WOW, WOW!
PER-FECT SYNC!
CLAP
DAMN, THAT WAS GOOD.
CLAP
VERY WELL DONE.
For someone not wearing panties.
YOU TOO, AKI-SAMA.
CLEARLY, THE BEST HADAPURE...
IS THE ORIGINAL WHITENING-CHAN, RIGHT?
YOU MUST BE KIDDING.
SURELY YOU MEAN SUNSCREEN-SAMA?
KRA-KOOOOM!
The 1st Hadapure Peace Treaty Fails
I TAKE IT BACK.
YOU AND I SHALL NEVER SEE EYE TO EYE.
HEH HEH HEH HEH HEH.
SO MUCH FOR WORLD PEACE.

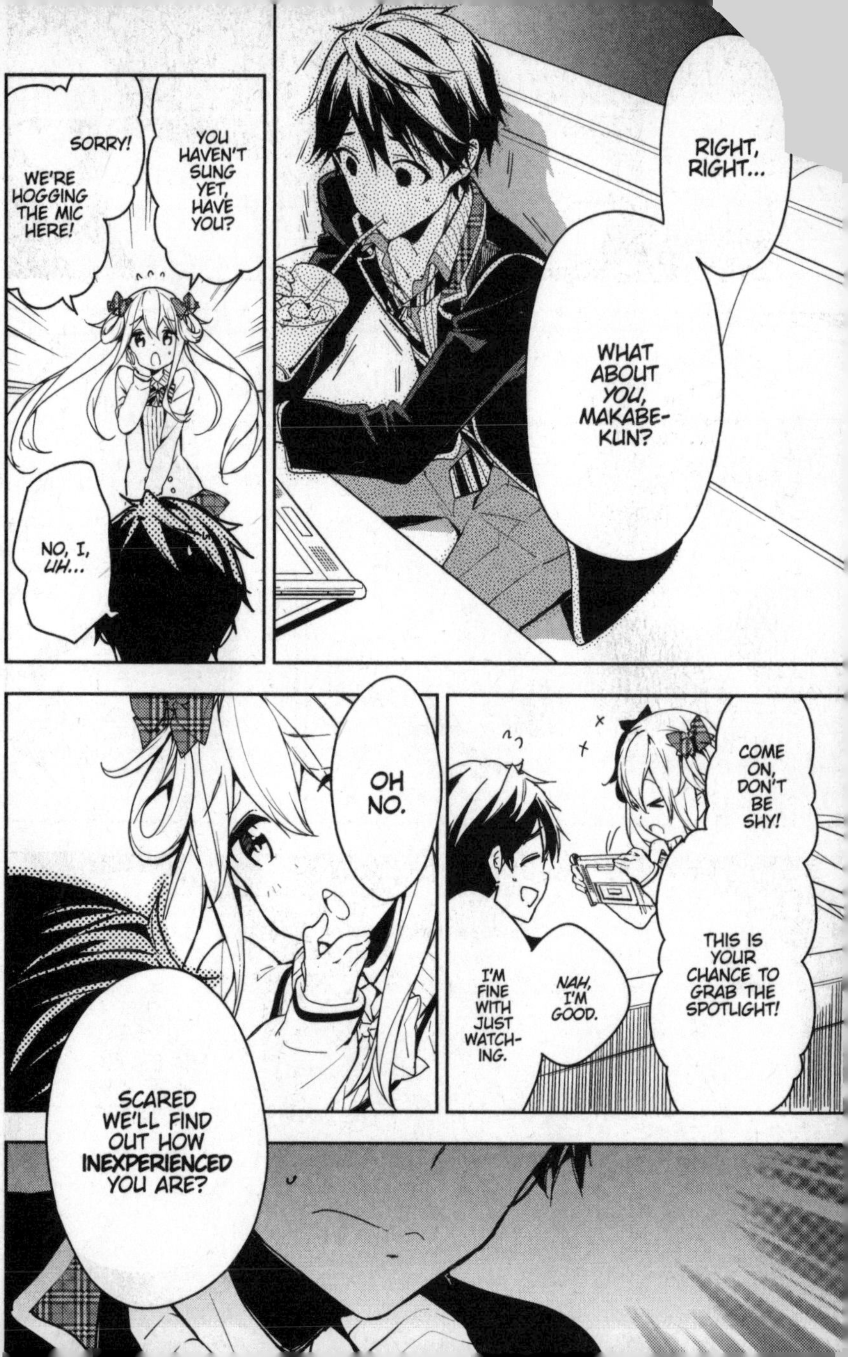
RIGHT, RIGHT...
WHAT ABOUT YOU, MAKABE-KUN?
YOU HAVEN'T SUNG YET, HAVE YOU?
SORRY! WE'RE HOGGING THE MIC HERE!
NO, I, UH...
COME ON, DON'T BE SHY!
THIS IS YOUR CHANCE TO GRAB THE SPOTLIGHT!
NAH, I'M GOOD.
I'M FINE WITH JUST WATCHING.
OH NO.
SCARED WE'LL FIND OUT HOW INEXPERIENCED YOU ARE?

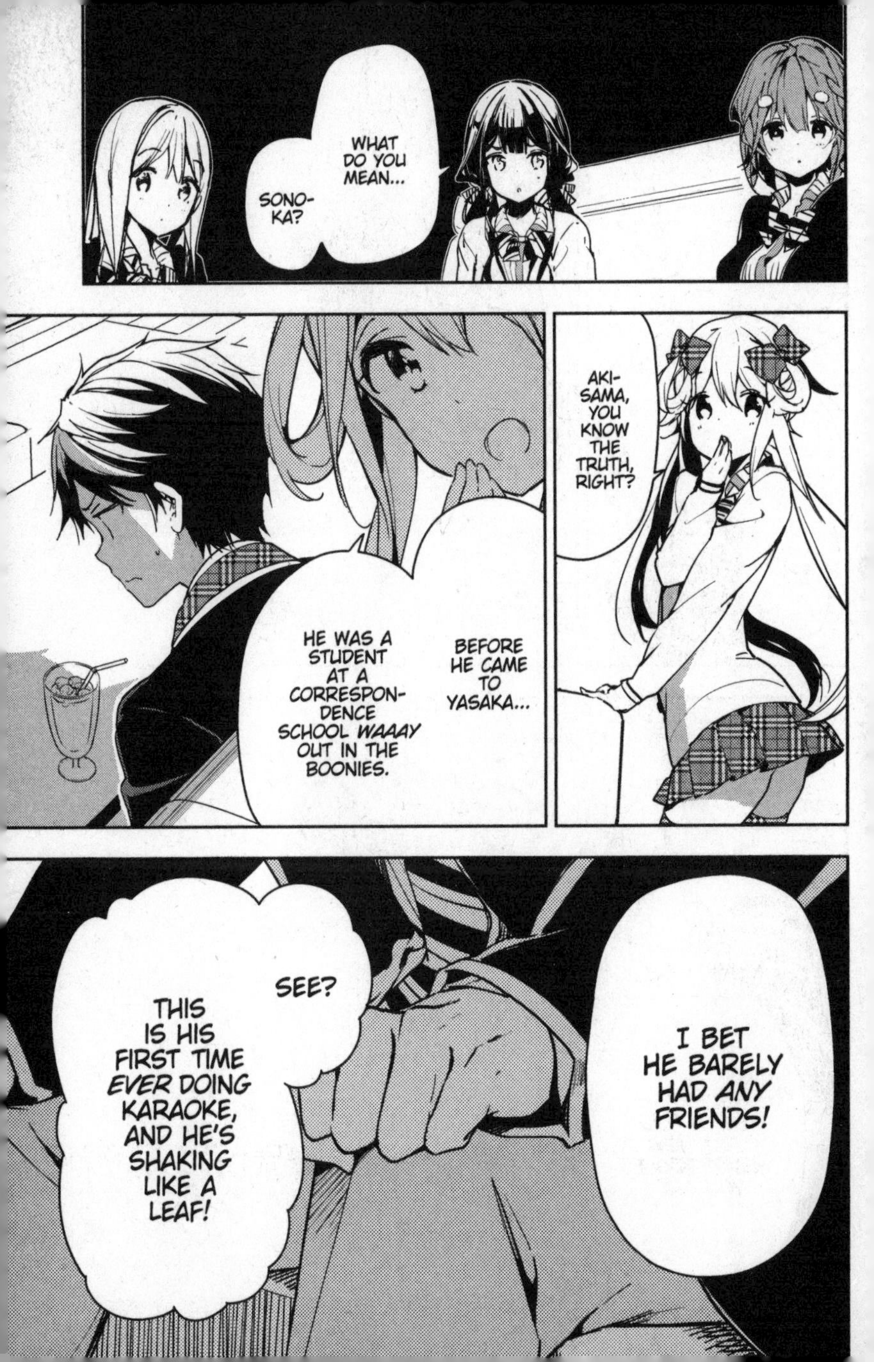
WHAT DO YOU MEAN...
SONO-KA?
AKI-SAMA, YOU KNOW THE TRUTH, RIGHT?
BEFORE HE CAME TO YASAKA...
HE WAS A STUDENT AT A CORRESPONDENCE SCHOOL *WAAAY* OUT IN THE BOONIES.
I BET HE BARELY HAD *ANY* FRIENDS!
SEE?
THIS IS HIS FIRST TIME *EVER* DOING KARAOKE, AND HE'S SHAKING LIKE A LEAF!

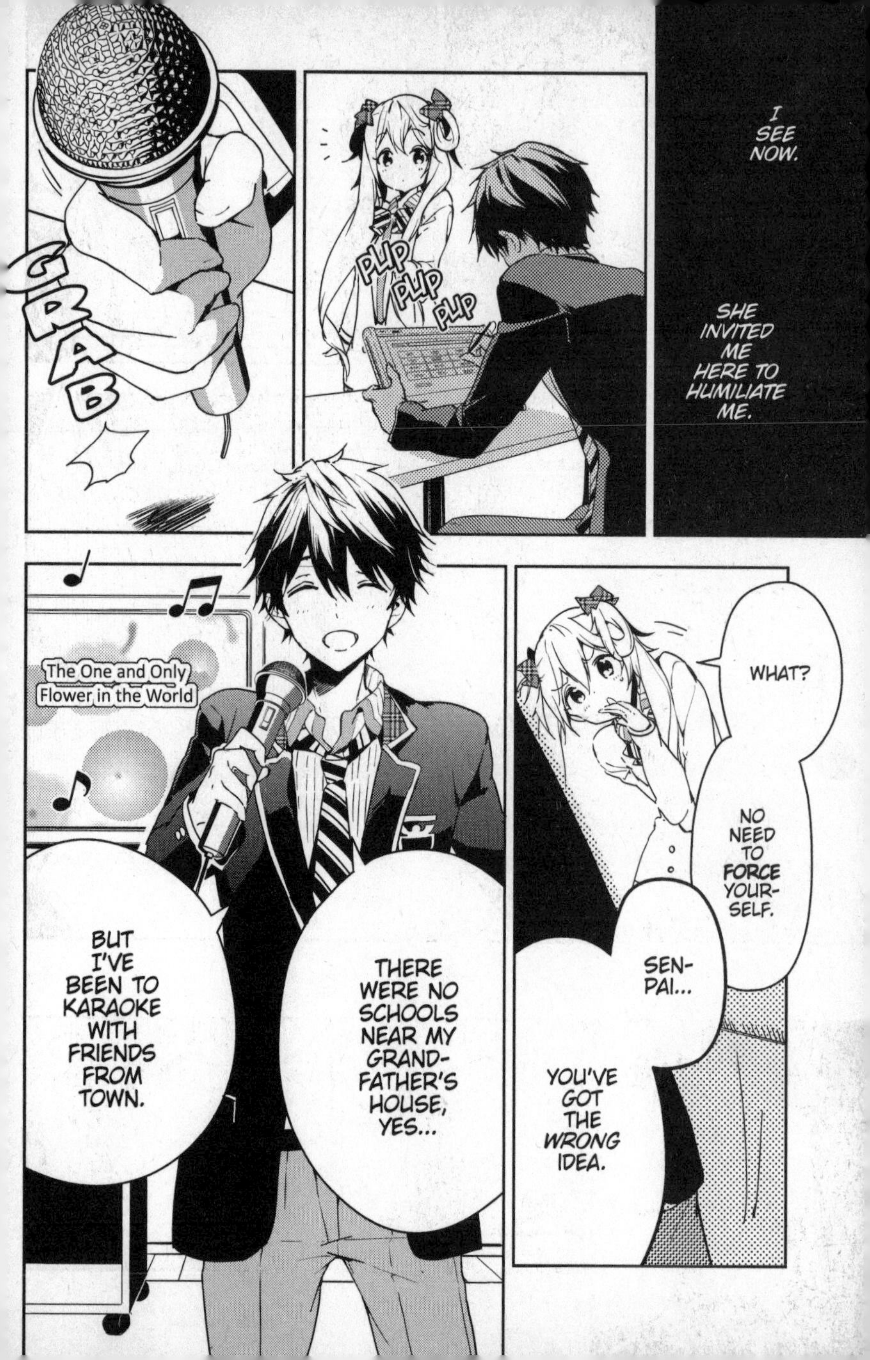
I SEE NOW.
SHE INVITED ME HERE TO HUMILIATE ME.
PLIP PLIP PLIP
GRAB
WHAT?
NO NEED TO FORCE YOURSELF.
SEN-PAI...
YOU'VE GOT THE WRONG IDEA.
The One and Only Flower in the World
THERE WERE NO SCHOOLS NEAR MY GRANDFATHER'S HOUSE, YES...
BUT I'VE BEEN TO KARAOKE WITH FRIENDS FROM TOWN.

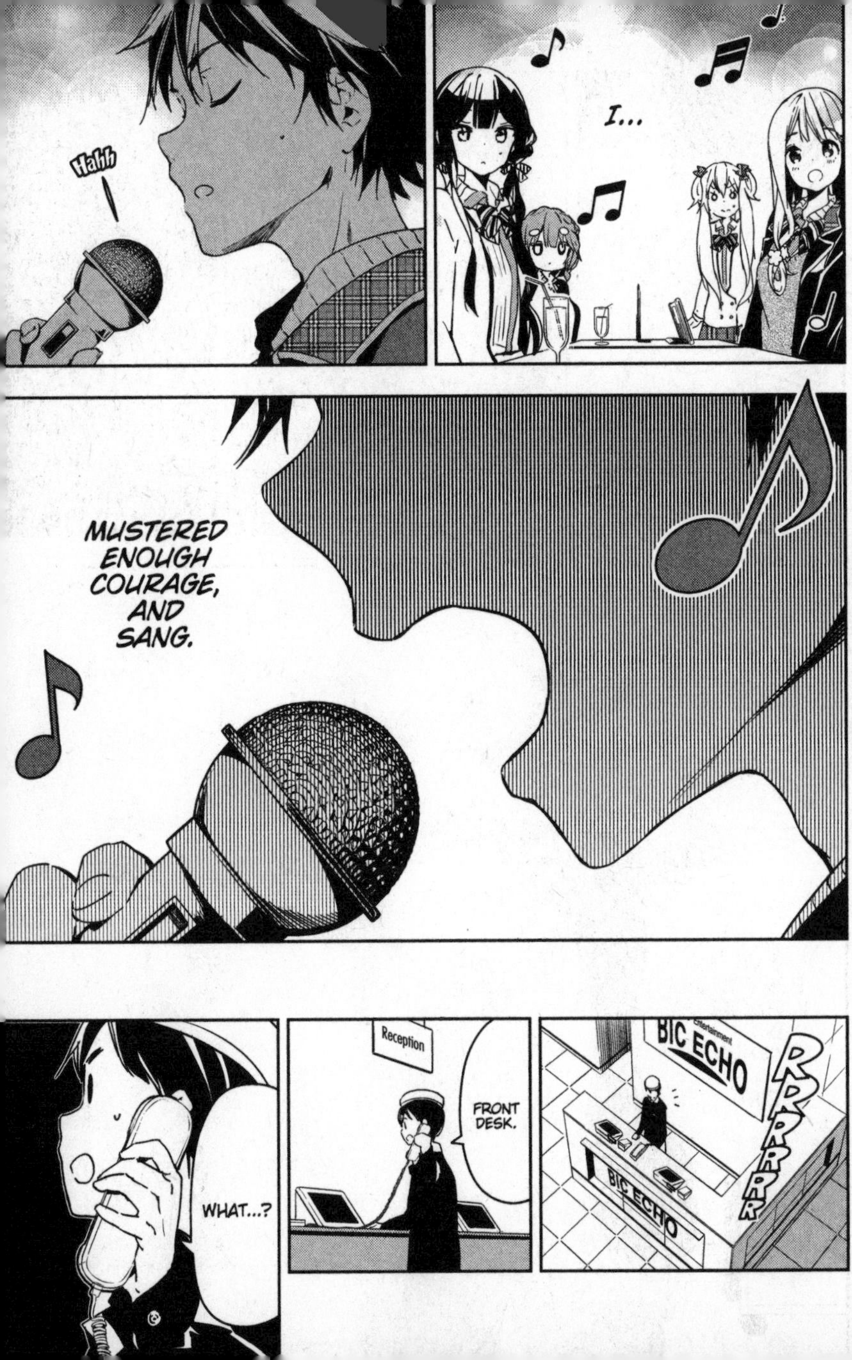
I...
Hahh
MUSTERED ENOUGH COURAGE, AND SANG.
Entertainment
BIC ECHO
RRRRRR
BIC ECHO
Reception
FRONT DESK.
WHAT...?

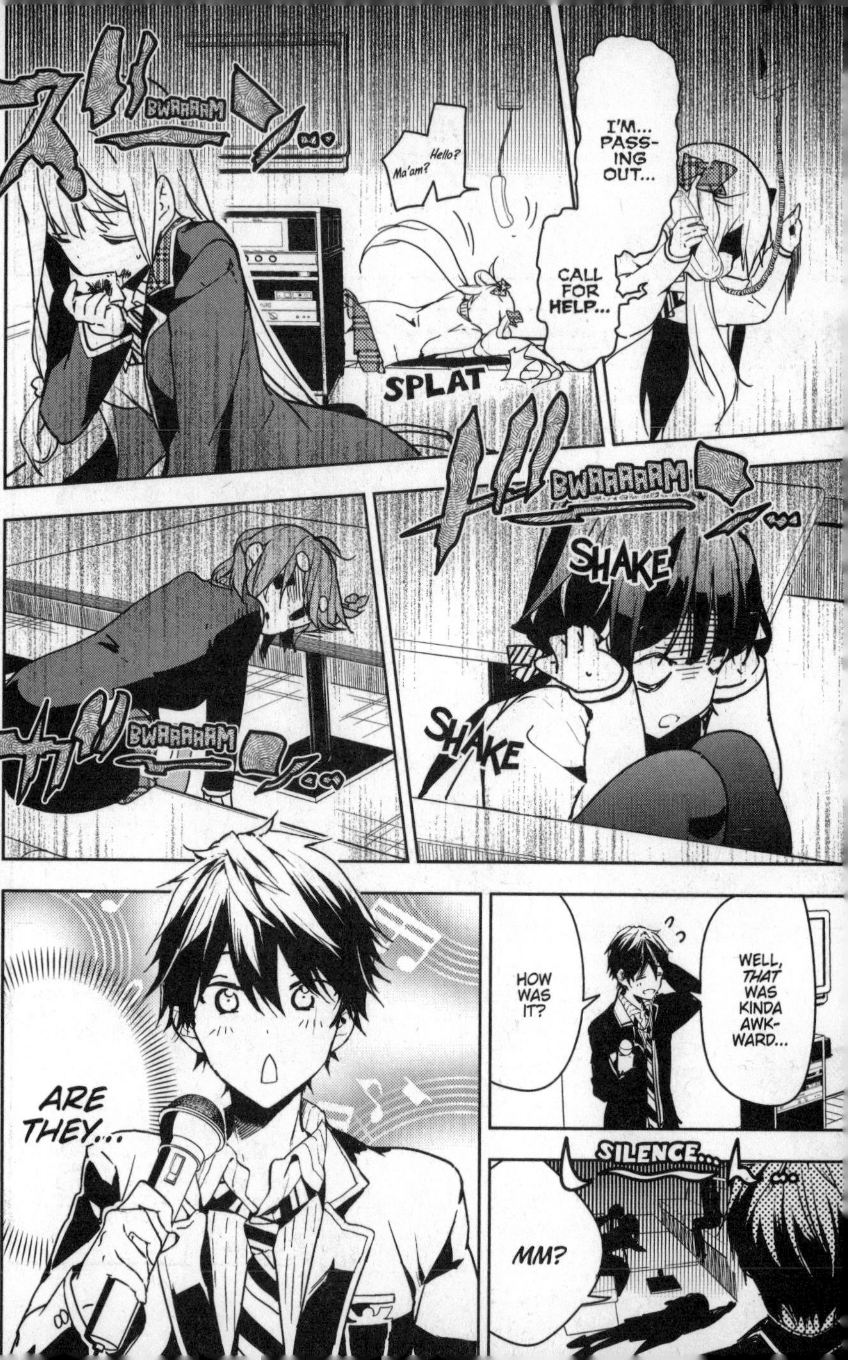
I'M... PASSING OUT...
CALL FOR HELP...
Hello? Ma'am?
SPLAT
BWAAAAM
BWAAAAAM
SHAKE
SHAKE
BWAAAAAM
WELL, THAT WAS KINDA AWK-WARD...
HOW WAS IT?
SILENCE...
MM?
ARE THEY...

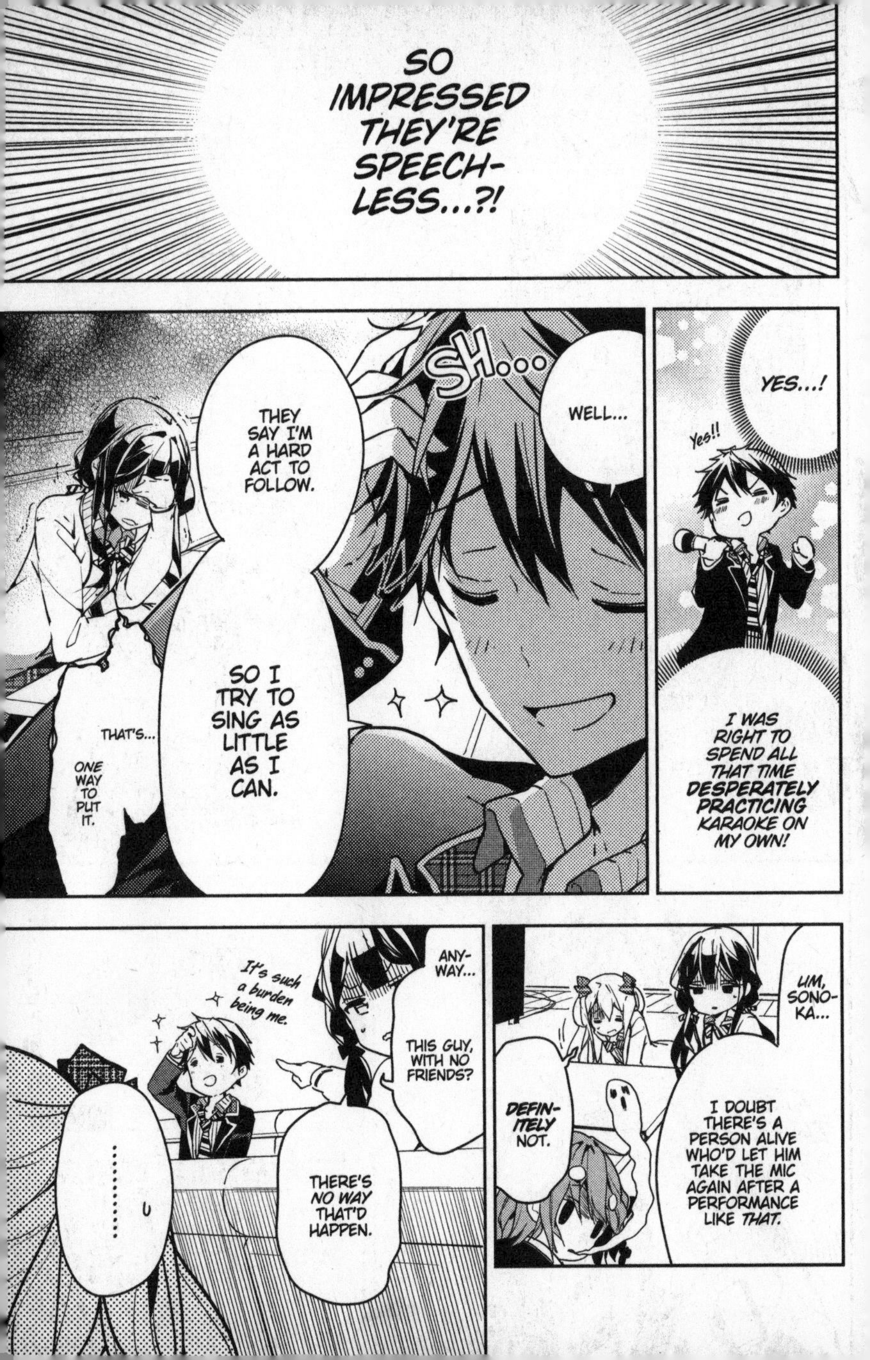
SO IMPRESSED THEY'RE SPEECHLESS...?!
YES...!
Yes!!
I WAS RIGHT TO SPEND ALL THAT TIME DESPERATELY PRACTICING KARAOKE ON MY OWN!
WELL...
SH...
THEY SAY I'M A HARD ACT TO FOLLOW.
SO I TRY TO SING AS LITTLE AS I CAN.
THAT'S...
ONE WAY TO PUT IT.
UM, SONOKA...
I DOUBT THERE'S A PERSON ALIVE WHO'D LET HIM TAKE THE MIC AGAIN AFTER A PERFORMANCE LIKE *THAT.*
DEFINITELY NOT.
ANYWAY...
THIS GUY, WITH NO FRIENDS?
It's such a burden being me.
THERE'S *NO WAY* THAT'D HAPPEN.
......

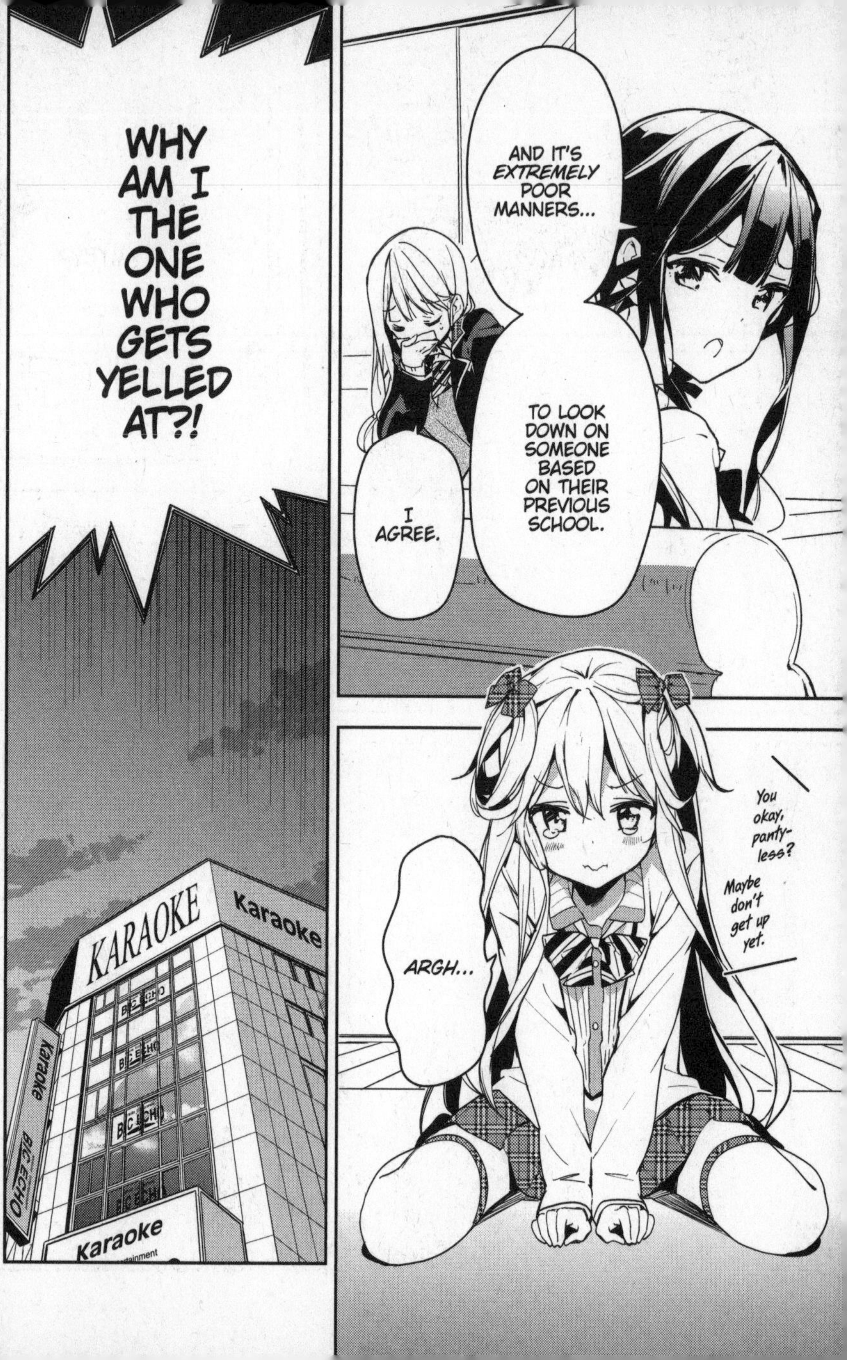
AND IT'S *EXTREMELY* POOR MANNERS...
TO LOOK DOWN ON SOMEONE BASED ON THEIR PREVIOUS SCHOOL.
I AGREE.
You okay, panty-less?
Maybe don't get up yet.
ARGH...
WHY AM I THE ONE WHO GETS YELLED AT?!
KARAOKE
Karaoke
KARAOKE
Karaoke
BIG ECHO
Karaoke

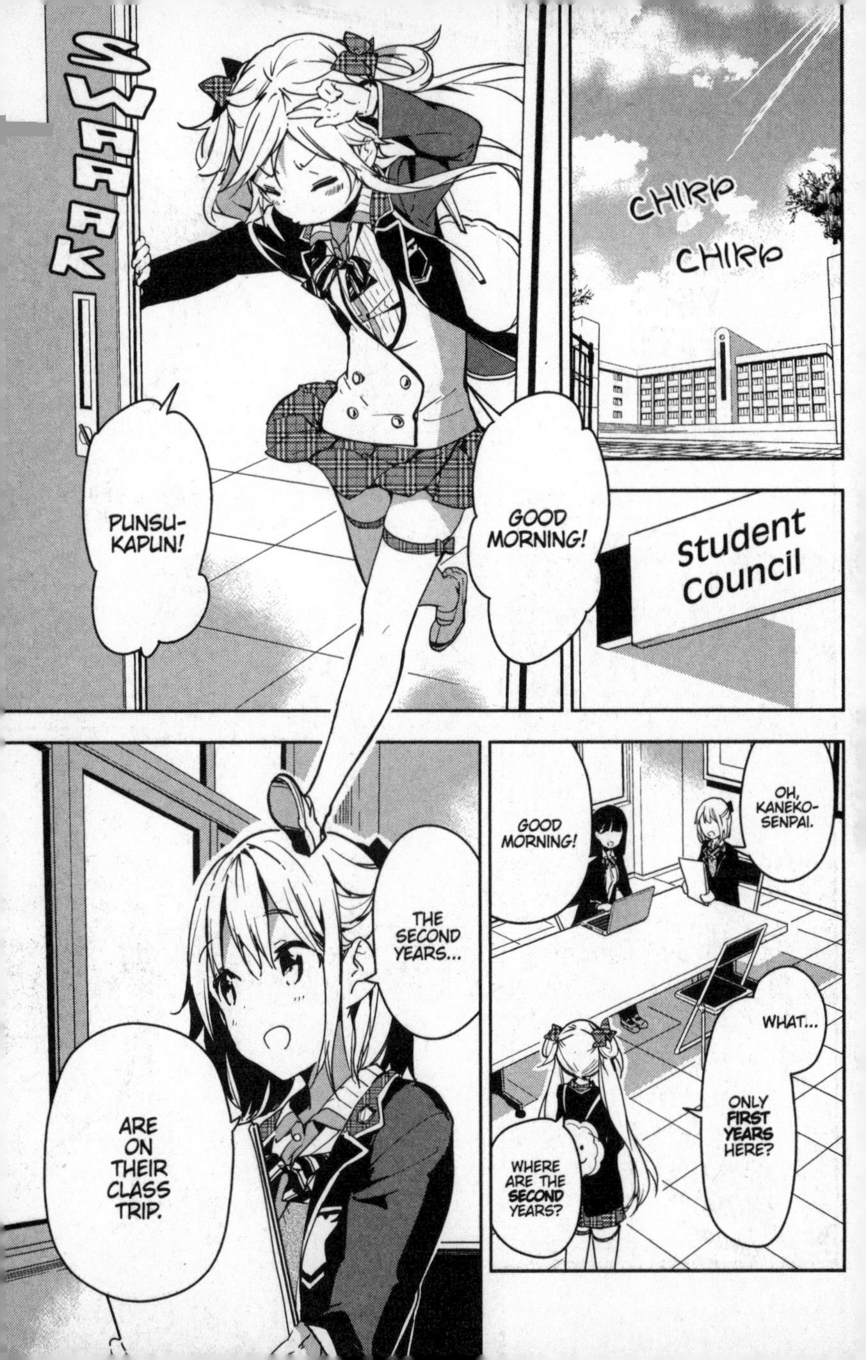
CHIRP
CHIRP
Student Council
GOOD MORNING!
SWAAAK
PUNSU-KAPUN!
OH, KANEKO-SENPAI.
GOOD MORNING!
WHAT...
ONLY FIRST YEARS HERE?
WHERE ARE THE SECOND YEARS?
THE SECOND YEARS...
ARE ON THEIR CLASS TRIP.

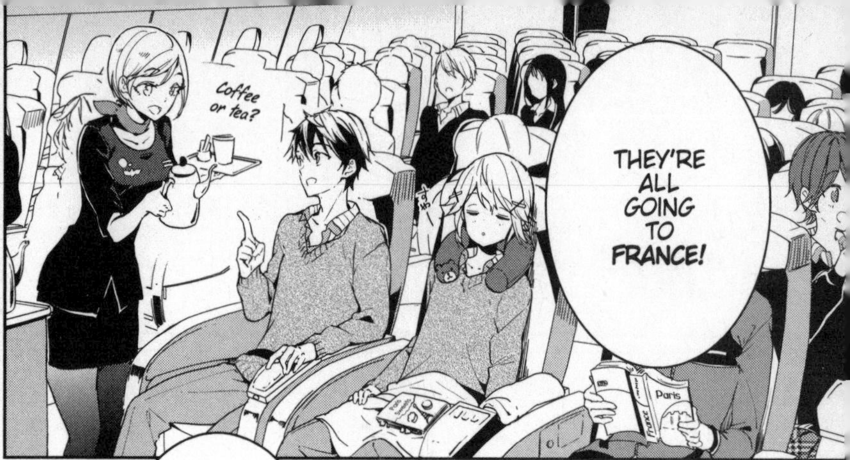
THEY'RE ALL GOING TO FRANCE!
Coffee or tea?
Paris
France

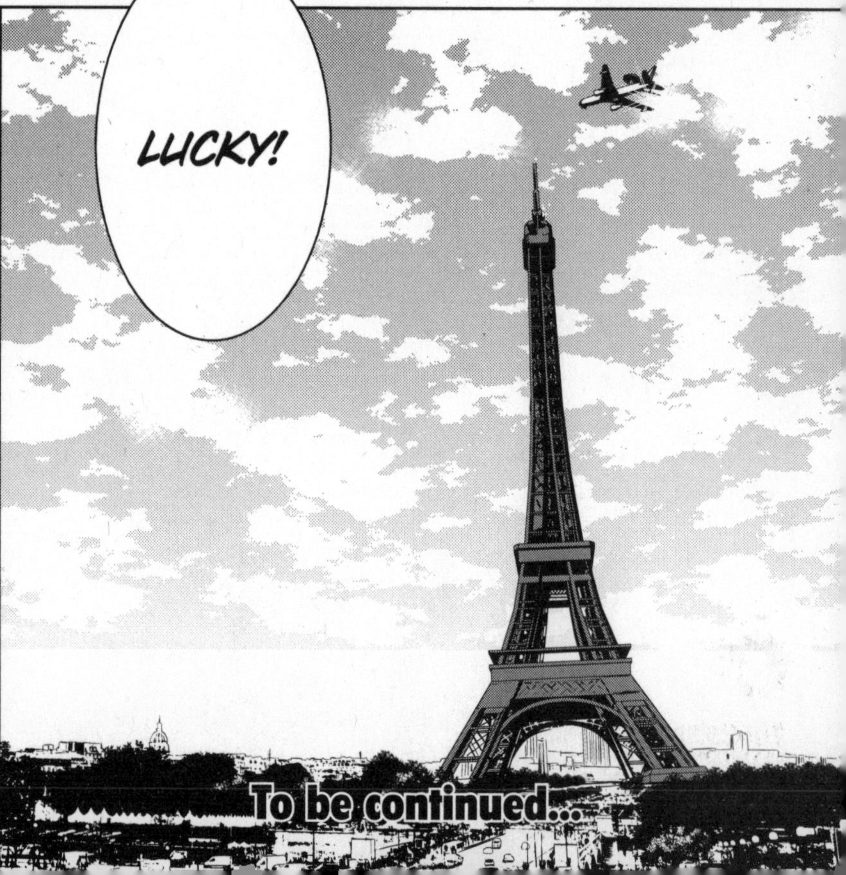
LUCKY!
To be continued...

6
Masamune-kun's
REVENGE
Presented by Hazuki Takeoka & TIV

Bonus 4-Koma 1

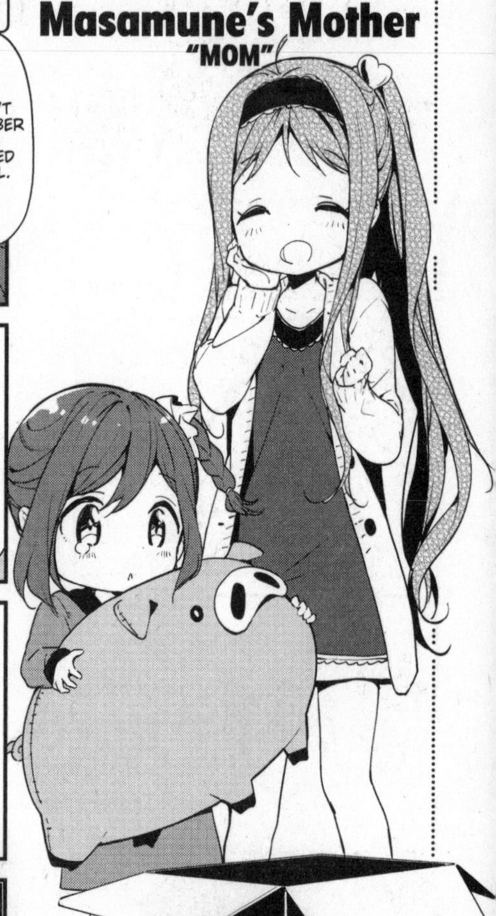
Masamune's Mother
"MOM"
Hayase Kinue (42)

Sibling Love Is 1

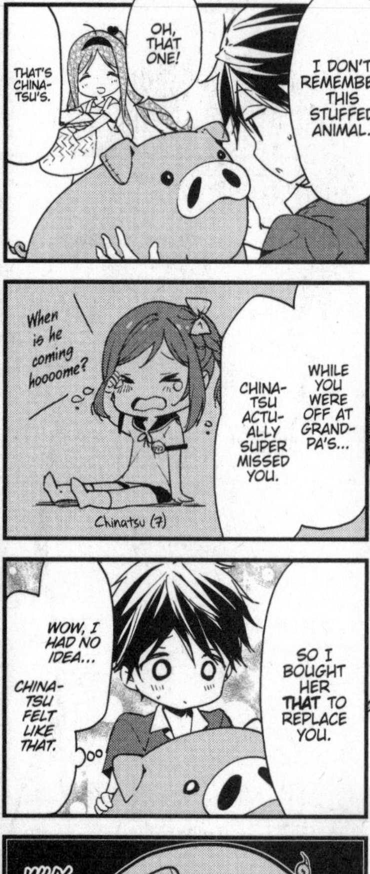
I DON'T REMEMBER THIS STUFFED ANIMAL.
OH, THAT ONE!
THAT'S CHINATSU'S.
WHILE YOU WERE OFF AT GRANDPA'S...
CHINATSU ACTUALLY SUPER MISSED YOU.
When is he coming hoooome?
Chinatsu (7)
SO I BOUGHT HER THAT TO REPLACE YOU.
WOW, I HAD NO IDEA... CHINATSU FELT LIKE THAT.
BUT...
WHY...
A PIG?

Bonus 4-Koma 2

Masamune's Sister
"SIS"

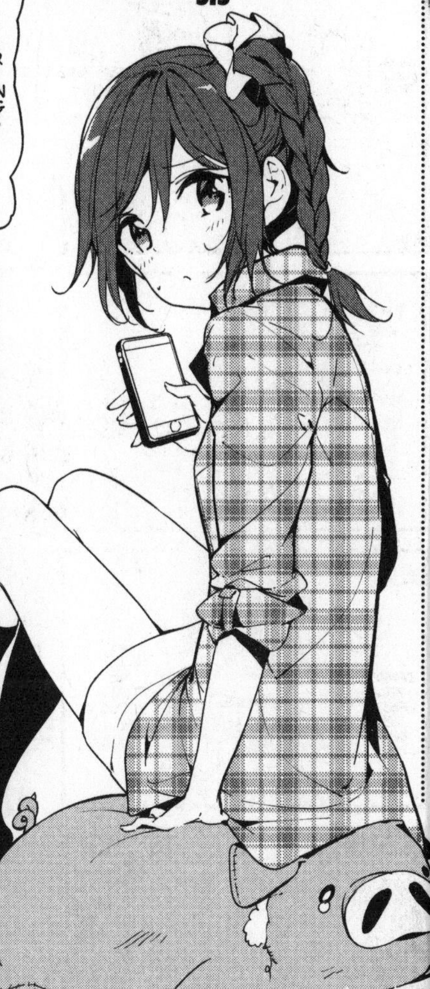

Hayase Chinatsu (14)

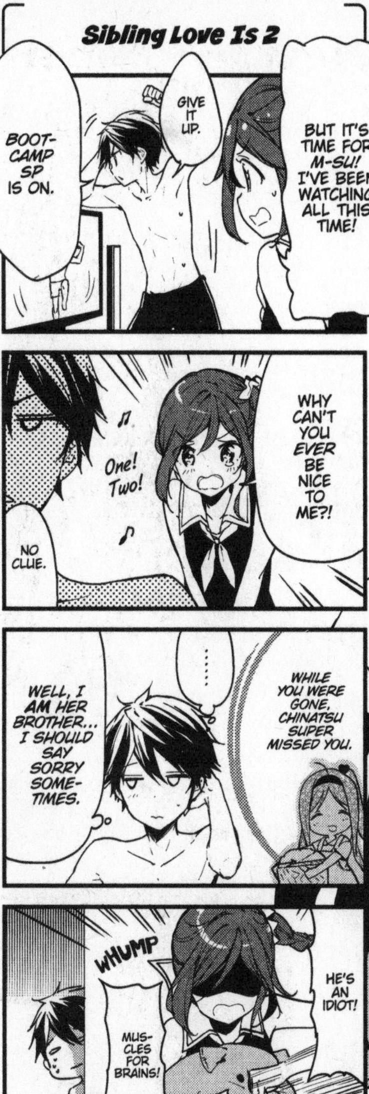
Sibling Love Is 2
BUT IT'S TIME FOR M-SU! I'VE BEEN WATCHING ALL THIS TIME!
GIVE IT UP.
BOOT-CAMP SP IS ON.
WHY CAN'T YOU EVER BE NICE TO ME?!
One! Two!
NO CLUE.
WHILE YOU WERE GONE, CHINATSU SUPER MISSED YOU.
......
WELL, I AM HER BROTHER... I SHOULD SAY SORRY SOMETIMES.
HE'S AN IDIOT!
WHUMP
MUSCLES FOR BRAINS!
WHUMP

SEVEN SEAS ENTERTAINMENT PRESENTS

Masamune-kun's REVENGE 6

story by HAZUKI TAKEOKA   art by TIV

TRANSLATION
Andrew Cunningham

ADAPTATION
Carol Fox

LETTERING AND LAYOUT
Jennifer Skarupa

LOGO DESIGN
Karis Page

COVER DESIGN
Nicky Lim

PROOFREADER
Holly Kolodziejczak

ASSISTANT EDITOR
Jenn Grunigen

PRODUCTION ASSISTANT
CK Russell

PRODUCTION MANAGER
Lissa Pattillo

EDITOR-IN-CHIEF
Adam Arnold

PUBLISHER
Jason DeAngelis

MASAMUNE-KUN'S REVENGE VOL. 6
©HAZUKI TAKEOKA · TIV 2015
First published in Japan in 2015 by ICHIJINSHA Inc., Tokyo.
English translation rights arranged with ICHIJINSHA Inc., Tokyo.

Seven Seas books may be purchased in bulk for promotional, educational, or business use. Please contact your local bookseller or the Macmillan Corporate and Premium Sales Department at 1-800-221-7945, extension 5442, or by e-mail at MacmillanSpecialMarkets@macmillan.com.

Seven Seas and the Seven Seas logo are trademarks of Seven Seas Entertainment, LLC. All rights reserved.

ISBN: 978-1-626925-61-8

Printed in Canada

First Printing: October 2017

10 9 8 7 6 5 4 3 2 1

FOLLOW US ONLINE: *www.gomanga.com*

READING DIRECTIONS

This book reads from *right to left*, Japanese style. If this is your first time reading manga, you start reading from the top right panel on each page and take it from there. If you get lost, just follow the numbered diagram here. It may seem backwards at first, but you'll get the hang of it! Have fun!!

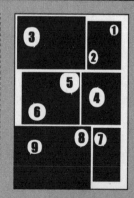